Proceedings of the Conference on Bank Credit Money and Inflation in Open Economies held in Leuven on September 15 - 16, 1974

Beihefte zu Kredit und Kapital

Heft 3

Bank Credit, Money and Inflation in Open Economies

Edited by

Michele Fratianni

Karel Tavernier

Katholieke Universiteit Leuven, Belgium

DUNCKER & HUMBLOT · BERLIN

The conference was organised by the "Centrum voor Economische Studien" of the Katholieke Universiteit Leuven, Belgium

Gedruckt 1976 bei fotokop wilhelm weihert, Darmstadt
Printed in Germany

ISBN 3 428 03765 0

CONTENTS

Part II — *The Two-Tier Exchange Market*

Part III — *Inflation in Open Economies and in the World*

INTRODUCTION

By Michele Fratianni and Karel Tavernier

The universal acceptance of Keynes' General Theory, in contrast to his earlier Treatise of Money, is now considered as a major cause of the decline and disinterest in monetary economics from the 1930's to the late 1950's. Under the potent thrust of the Chicago School, on the one hand, and independent monetarists such as Karl Brunner and Allan Meltzer, on the other hand, a strong resurgence in monetary analysis has taken place in the last decade or so. The revival in monetary economics and in a monetary interpretation of cyclical activity has been fostered, to be true, by the gradual vanishing of those conditions (i.e. a high degree of unutilized resources) which prompted Keynes to make his fundamental shift from the Treatise to the General Theory.

Several economists have challenged a few propositions held until now as part of "Accepted Wisdom". The volume, which represents the proceedings of a Conference held at the Katholieke Universiteit te Leuven on September 12-13, 1974, tries to focus on several of these challenges.

First, in the Keynesian framework money is only substitutable to fixed-income obligations. The crucial portfolio adjustment between money and real assets is obscured by the assumption that real assets are frozen in the analysis (Hicksian interpretation) or that bonds and real assets are perfect substitutes (Metzler). These two views may possibly reflect strongly different perceptions of the relative transaction costs among money, securities and real assets.

Implicit in the Hicksian analysis of Keynes are small transaction costs between money and bonds and infinite transaction costs between money and real assets; the opposite holds in Metzler. The interesting case, and indeed the one which is most relevant to "real world" situations, is that where extreme views of the relative transaction costs are relaxed. Once the market for real assets is incorporated into the analysis, the distinction between bank credit and money becomes very important. Contrary to orthodox thinking, bank credit is no longer the mirror image of money, but displays independent movements caused by forces which act differently on the two markets. The essays of Brunner, Fratianni and Heremans-Sommariva-Verheirstraeten bear crucially on this point.

The distinction between bank credit and money becomes also decisive in clarifying the extent to which monetary policy may be effective in the short run under a regime of fixed exchange rates and high degree of capital mobility. As Brunner puts it, "a fashionable trend in the literature extended the categories of trade theory to the financial markets and asserts that securities issued in different countries denominated in different currencies are usefully approximated as perfect substitutes. This analysis identified interdependence with perfect substitutes". In so doing this strand of the literature removed the role of bank credit in the analysis. And with it an important channel through which monetary authorities transmit non-vanishing impulses to the economic system even under extreme cases of capital market integration. In Brunner's framework a high substitutability between domestic and foreign securities quite naturally makes the nominal interest rates on securities incapable of "conveying monetary impulses initiated by the domestic Central Bank. But the channel operated by the asset price level remains intact and is actually enhanced by a closer substitutability between distinct national securities".

But even within the confines of offsetting capital flow theory monetary policy need not be powerless. Fratianni concludes that "empirical tests which have shown that for some countries the endogenous foreign component of the (monetary) base offsets dollar for dollar changes in the domestic and policy controlled base corroborate only one of the two conditions which must be satisfied to completely disable policy in a regime of fixed exchange rates. The other condition is that, as capital flows in and out of the home country, the foreign demand for domestic security is not affected. But once domestic securities are traded, a capital flow, "offsetting" an autonomous injection of base money, implies a reduction in the foreign holdings of domestic securities and thus a downward shift in the aggregate demand for domestic securities. The rate of interest is altered even though the total amount of base money has not".

Girton and Henderson also analyze the effectiveness of monetary policy on financial asset markets in the short run under fixed exchange rates in a world of interacting systems. In principle, "each central bank can ... use open market operations in the security denominated in its country's currency to achieve a monetary policy objective. Exactly what size open market operation is required to attain a specified objective and exactly what effects on other variables are associated with that open market operation depend both on the monetary policy response of the other central bank and on the form in which changes in international reserves are held". While it remains generally true that a given monetary impulse has a larger impact on a specified target variable under flexible exchange rates than under alternative exchange rate arrangements, it does not follow automatically that the monetary impulse has vanishing effects in the latter case. The impulse has instead a vanishing impact when the country is "small", even though domestic and foreign securities are not perfectly substitutable to each other.

The volume offers new and interesting pieces of analysis with respect to a unique experiment of segmenting the foreign exchange markets into two compartments: one compartment for current account transactions where the exchange rate or rates are pegged by policy decisions and another compartment for capital transactions where the exchange rates respond entirely to market forces. Such an experiment has been operational in Belgium since 1954 and is known as the two-tier foreign exchange market. Decaluwe and Steinherr argue on theoretical grounds that both fiscal and monetary instruments regain their independent role when a two-tier exchange market replaces completely fixed exchange rates under conditions of high capital mobility. Boll generalizes the policy implications of various two-tier exchange rate systems using the familiar IS-LM framework. The evidence on what a two-tier exchange market can or cannot do is not so clear. Up to 1971 Belgian economic operators had ample opportunity to exploit to their advantage differences between the "official" rate and the free rate of exchange. When the dollar price of the Belgian franc fell below the lower support limit an individual or a bank could buy dollars in the free market and sell them in the official market, thus reaping a capital gain. Indeed the free rate seldom if ever fell below the lower support limit long enough to be detected by monthly averages of daily data. Arbitrage also took place until 1971 on the upside of the band. Here only banks were allowed to sell foreign exchange in the free market and buy it more cheaply in the official market whenever market forces were working in the direction of a devaluation of the Belgian franc. As a matter of fact, divergences between the free rate and the official rate have only occurred in the area above the high support limit and for relatively small periods of time (with the exception of the heavy speculative movements against the Belgian franc in 1969).

Another central concern of the conference was inflation and its causes. The paper by Gray and Parkin provides test statements for discriminating among competing hypotheses of inflation in a world economy. The heuristic model proposed by the two authors incorporates some of the crucial features which have been a cause of contention between Monetarists and Keynesians. Not surprisingly, the authors conclude "that the rational expectations monetarist position is entirely untenable", leaving thus only two major schools in explaining inflation: the adaptive expectation monetarist school and the Keynesian school. Discriminating between these two turns out to be conceptually easy: "If a stable transfer function exists with weights which have equal sums in the money and price polynomials and zero in the fiscal polynomial, then the adaptive expectations "Monetarist" model cannot be rejected but the "Keynesian" model can". Barten, an econometrician of the finest Keynesian tradition, raises a battery of exceptions to the Gray-Parkin stylized representation of the two schools. "Do monetarists really consider all push factors to be completely irrelevant even in the very short run? Why are Keynesians not allowed to assume rational or adaptive expectations and to maintain that these are unbiased ... Why should a Keynesian not accept long-run homogeneity [in the excess demand for output function] ... ? " The reaction of Barten to the Gray-Parkin paper indicates that there is a wide divergence of views between what Keynesians and Monetarists regard as a Keynesian model or a Monetarist model. Any attempt to synthesize and juxtapose those two views will unavoidably elicit reactions and disclaimers: yet, the exercise remains extremely valuable because it forces, for nothing else, the opposing camps to state more precisely what their differences are.

In the conference we were reminded very forcefully by De Cecco "that there is a marked difference between Keynes himself and those who call themselves "Keynesians". Keynes of the General Theory was primarily interested in quantity changes, and not in prices. Keynes' choice was not due certainly to ignorance or neglect but motivated by a desire to emphasize an aspect of the analysis which had been ignored in the literature. It follows that if there is a transmission mechanism in Keynes this is one of quantity adjustments, except in a state of full employment.

Sweeney and Willett consider in their paper several mechanisms through which inflation is transmitted among countries. Two results stand out in their analysis. The first is that transmission mechanisms of inflation by themselves "do not seem sufficient to explain the major portion of worldwide inflation, for imported inflation could have been neutralized at least for several years by all but the smallest and most open economies". By implication this finding runs contrary to the strong results of the offsetting capital flows theory. The second result concerns the unemployment-inflation tradeoffs in fixed vs. flexible exchange rate regimes. With "sticky" prices on non-traded goods, higher foreign prices will raise the foreign demand for a given country's output. "This increase in foreign demand is, of course, the Keynesian transmission mechanism and can be neutralized by fiscal and monetary policy to hold aggregate demand constant. A reduction, say, in government expenditures is not likely to fall on exactly the goods where foreign demand has risen and hence is likely to induce some unemployment. To the extent that the reductions in government spending do not induce compensating price reductions, the increase in tradeables' prices makes a net contribution to inflation ... the Phillips Curve unemployment-inflation tradeoff has worsened". This line of inquiry seems to argue quite strongly in favor of flexible exchange rates.

But are flexible exchange rates conducive by themselves to inflation? Those who argue on the inflationary bias of flexible exchange rates point to the observation that, while inflation rises in the devaluing country, it does not fall in the revaluing country by an equivalent amount. Pattison concedes that the stylized facts of world inflation accord with such a view. But the positive correlation between world inflation and flexible rates carries no weight by itself about the direction of causality. Indeed, as Pattison points out, "theory also accents the fact that with floating exchange rates, the monetary authorities are able to follow an independent monetary policy which, in the case of excessive money creation, allows the higher average price level resulting from exchange rate changes to be financed as well as promoting inflation directly". In other words, the exchange rate, being a relative price, adjusts in such a way to reflect differences in inflation rates between countries rather than being a cause of inflation.

Behind much of the support for fixed exchange rates lies a deep mistrust for policy makers who, in the absence of a _chemise de force_ like a balance-of-payments constraint, will have no impediment in pursuing irresponsible courses of action. This is Jacques Rueff's dream of the gold standard which is _not_ comparable with our post-war experiences with fixed rates, a period during which several Houdini attempts were made to untie _la chemise de force_.

But, apart from the argument of whether fixed or flexible rates elicit different policy responses, there is another potential danger in a regime of fixed exchange rates. Namely, this regime is also very likely to be inconsistent with independent fiscal policies in all countries. This is one of the main themes of the paper by Meltzer who ingeniously assesses the contribution of the conference papers in terms of the inherited Mundellian "orthodoxy". What comes out from Meltzer's essay is much more than the routine exercise of synthesizing the highlights of the studies: it is a frontal attack to the Mundellian model of fixed exchange rates whose stability properties require the imposition of severe and, thus, unrealistic constraints on fiscal policy.

The planning and execution of a conference is seldom the effort of one or two individuals. Our Conference was no exception. The list of people and institutions to which we are indebted is too long to be fully reported here. We shall limit our acknowledgment to a selected but representative group. We received financial support from the Katholieke Universiteit Leuven, Faculteit der Economische en Toegepaste Economische Wetenschappen, Ministerie van Buitenlandse Zaken - België, Vlaamse Leergangen, Generale Bankmaatschappij, Bank van Brussel, Kredietbank, Banca d'Italia, Bank van Parijs en de Nederlanden - België, Assurantie van de Belgische Boerenbond, C.E.R.A..

The staff of the Centrum voor Economische Studiën was most gracious and understanding in helping with the many details and last-minute chores of the organization. Messrs. Heremans, Sommariva and Verheirstraeten were precious collaborators in the planning as well as in the execution of the Conference. To both those we have mentioned and those we might have forgotten goes our deepest gratitude.

THE MONEY SUPPLY PROCESS IN OPEN ECONOMIES WITH INTERDEPENDENT SECURITY MARKETS: THE CASE OF IMPERFECT SUBSTITUTABILITY*

By Karl Brunner

The role of interdependent credit markets attracted increasing attention over the past ten years. Central Banks argued that the growing interdependence impairs the usefulness of monetary policy for purposes of domestic stabilization. Some developments of international monetary analysis seem to confirm this position. A fashionable trend in the literature extended the categories of trade theory to the financial markets and asserts that securities issued in different countries denominated in different currencies are usefully approximated as perfect substitutes. This analysis identified interdependence or "tradeability" with perfect substitutability and is usually combined with a Metzlerian interpretation of the basic IS-LM framework. The procedure imposes perfect substitutability on domestic real assets and domestically

* This paper forms part of a project on monetary theory supported by a grant from the National Science Foundation. It is also closely associated with the work jointly performed over many years with Allan H. Meltzer and I am indebted for many discussions with my long time collaborator.

issued financial assets. It follows that all real assets and financial assets, irrespective of location and issuer, are perfect substitutes.

These simplifications yield elegant statements and offer useful approximations for specific purposes bearing on longer-run aspects of the balance of payments problem. Both substitutability assumptions, the one associated with the Metzlerian interpretation and the other with the standard interpretation of "tradeable securities", seem however rather inappropriate for the analysis of shorter-run, interrelated money supply processes. It appears inadvisable, to constrain examinations of the problems confronting open economies with interdependent credit markets to the case of perfectly substitutable securities. The issues are essentially empirical and should be carefully investigated. This is particularly necessary in view of the fact that the usual formulations of international monetary analysis contain a severely emasculated monetary system reduced to base money supplied by the government sector. This reduction of the monetary system removes in particular any role for bank credit in the process.

An extension of the Brunner-Meltzer money supply theory to open economies with non-perfectly substitutable securities but interdependent credit markets has already been published.[1)] The level of aggregation obscured, however, the substantial difference in information costs bearing on securities and loans. These differ-

1) "Money Supply Process and Monetary Policy in an Open Economy", International Trade and Money, London 1973, edited by Michael B. Connolly and Alexander K. Swoboda.

ences approximately determine that loans are "non-traded goods" confined within a national market whereas securities occur as "traded goods" with imperfect substitutability relative to foreign securities. The present paper disaggregates the credit markets into a loan market and a securities market, both interacting with the money market. The domestic loan market and money market interact directly with the domestic security market. They interact only indirectly with the foreign loan and money market via the interdependent securities markets. The domestic security market interacts on the other hand directly with the foreign security market. The asset markets of the distinct economic areas are thus linked via the security markets. This paper examines the effect of interdependent international security markets and interdependent loan and securities markets on the money supply process and the role of monetary policy. The nature of the problem confines the analysis to a fixed exchange rate regime and removes furthermore all feedbacks via the output market from analytic attention. The policy problems emerging from interconnected asset markets form the central issue of the paper.

I. The Money Supply Theory

The money supply process is centered on three markets: the loan market LM, the securities market SM, and the money market MM. These markets describe the behavior of banks and public in response to conditions imposed by the monetary authorities. The authorities issue base money or announce conditions at which they offer base money. They also impose constraints on the banks' allocation of assets (requirement ratios, etc.) and on the conditions governing the banks' supply of liabilities (ceiling rates, special reserve requirement affecting the cost of specific liabilities, etc.). Banks allocate their assets between loans, securities and base money, determine the proportion of borrowed base money and set the conditions governing their supply of various liabilities. The public on the other hand allocates its wealth between the liabilities offered by the monetary system. The public also demands bank loans (offers promises to pay) and holds securities. These patterns guide the formulation of the structure describing the joint determination of money stock M, the yield on securities i, the rate r charged on bank loans, the market value P of real capital (per unit), the banks' securities portfolio, the banks' loan portfolio and the distribution of securities between banks and public.

The proximate determination of r, i and P can be assigned to specific markets. The loan rate r is assigned to the loan market, i to the securities market and P to the money market. Each market will be introduced in the order mentioned. We begin with the loan market. The public's desired loan liability position is described in equation (1a). It depends on the loan rate r, the securities yield i, the output price level p, the asset price of real capital P, current output y,

(1a) $$L^{dp} = L[r, i, p, P, y, e, W_n, W_h]$$

$$L_2, L_3, L_5, L_6, L_7, L_8 > 0 > L_1, L_4$$

(1b) $$L^{db} = \alpha(r, i)\, a(r, i, P, d+h, \ldots)UB$$

$$\alpha_1 > 0 > \alpha_2;\ a_1,\ a_2 > 0 > a_3,\ a_4$$

(1c) $$L^{db} = L^{dp}$$

the anticipated real net yield e on real capital, non-human (W_n) and human (W_h) wealth. Non-human wealth is defined by the expression (2)

(2) $$W_n = PK + v(i, \tau_n) \cdot [S - \overline{IFD}] + v^{\star}(i^{\star}, \tau_n) \cdot \overline{IDF} + (1+\omega)UB$$

where ω is the banking system's net worth multiplier. Real resources invested in the banking system's operation are excluded from the public's real capital stock K. If follows that ω is positive even in a perfectly competitive banking system. The term v designates the market value of a security unit as a function of interest rate i and a tax parameter τ_n summarizing the tax schedule on income from non-human wealth. It should be noted that the interest elasticity of v is conditioned by the maturity structure of outstanding securities. A longer maturity structure pushes the elasticity nearer to minus unity. The unit value v is multiplied with the net volume of domestic securities held domestically, i.e., the total amount S available to the public minus the inherited holdings $\overline{IFD}$ of the foreign public. The last term adds the market value of the domestic public's foreign holdings $\overline{IDF}$ of securities. The terms $\overline{IDF}$ and $\overline{IFD}$ designate predetermined values at any moment of time t. They are the inherited endowment. This endowment changes over time with the distribution of securities between the domestic and foreign economy.[2)] The public's (nominal) non-human wealth consists thus of the market value of real capital K, the outstanding stock S of government securities adjusted for the public's net foreign position plus the monetary system's net worth contribution. The reader will note that this wealth equation imposes no constraint on the system. The value W_n of human wealth is determined by the asset markets and equation (2) is a definition used to specify W_n in terms of the endogenous variables P, i and UB.

Human wealth W_h depends on real income y, the anticipated wage level aw, and a tax parameter τ_h summarizing the tax schedule applicable to income from human wealth. We write thus:

(3) $$W_h = W_h[y, aw, \tau_h]; \; W_1^h, W_2^h > 0 > W_3^h$$

The reader should note that W_h is a nominal magnitude. Moreover, the systematic dependence on y is based on a postulate that income distribution between labor and capital exhibits a regular pattern.[3)]

---

2) The procedure for proper treatment of IDF and IFD was suggested by Michael Mussa. Let us define the two endowment terms as follows:

$$\overline{IDF}(t) = \lim_{t \to t-} IDF(t) \text{ and } \overline{IFD}(t) = \lim_{t \to t-} IFD(t)$$

The two terms appear thus as left sided limits of the behavior terms IDF and IFD explaining the public's desired portfolio position. The relation between the pair ($\overline{IDF}$, $\overline{IFD}$) and the pair (IDF, IFD) corresponds to the relation between initial endowment and optimal position on a contract curve within an Edgeworth box.

3) The separation of wealth into W_h and W_n is crucial for our analysis. The feedback loops initiated with changes in output y or labor market conditions operate via human wealth with a substantially different mode than via non-human wealth.

Equation (1b) describes the banks' loan portfolio. This portfolio is exhibited as a product of three factors, the "unborrowed" monetary base UB, the asset multiplier a and the asset allocation ratio α. The product $a \cdot UB$ denotes the banks' total earning assets and α describes the proportion allocated to loans. This allocation ratio is highly sensitive to interest rates and depends positively on the loan rate r and negatively on the securities yield i. The asset multiplier depends immediately on a set of allocation parameters describing the public's and the banks' behavior.[4)] These allocation parameters depend in their turn on interest rates, asset price level P, wealth and other factors. The asset multiplier depends thus indirectly on a set of arguments of which only r, i, P and the total cost of borrowing d+h are explicitly used in our analysis. The total borrowing cost is the sum of a discount rate d and a component h describing the cost of administrative harassment.[5)] It should be noted that the asset mulitplier a depends on r and i. The dependence on r is essentially mediated by

---

4) The asset multiplier a is constituted according to the following expression:

$$a = \frac{[1+t+d] \quad [1+n-(r-b)]}{(r+\ell-b) \ (1+t+d)+k}$$

where k = currency ratio, t = time deposit ratio, d = Treasury deposit ratio, n = banks' nondeposit liability ratio, r = reserve ratio, ℓ = ratio of cumulated sum of "liberated" reserves to total bank deposits, b = banks' borrowing ratio; r, ℓ, b and n are measured relative to total deposits; k and t relative to demand deposits.

5) The reader may find a more detailed discussion of the multipliers in my paper, "A Diagrammatic Exposition of the Money Supply Process", Schweizerische Zeitschrift für Volkswirtschaft und Statistik, February 1974. It also discusses the rationale for the decomposition of money stock and bank credit by means of multiplier and base.

the borrowing ratio b. The last expression 1c describes the equilibrium condition of the loan market. It will be understood to determine proximately the loan rate in terms of the remaining magnitudes.

The securities market juxtaposes the stock supply of government securities S with the demand emanating from public and banks. The public's demand involves moreover two components, the domestic investors' demand for domestic issues IDD and the foreign investors' demand for domestic issues IFD. Equations (4) describe the relevant structure of the domestic securities market:

(4a) $(1-\alpha)a\cdot UB + IDD + IFD = S$

The first term describes the banks' portfolio of securities as a function of interest rates and other variables affecting the asset multiplier (or the base UB, as we shall see). The other two terms reflect the domestic and foreign public's desired absorption of domestic securities. Total demand on the left is juxtaposed with the net stock supply listed on the right. The description of the securities market is completed with the specification of the demand components IDD and IFD.

(4b) $IDD = IDD[r, i, i^{\star}, p, P, W_n, W_h, e]$

$$IDD_1, IDD_3, IDD_8 < 0 < IDD_2, IDD_4, IDD_5, IDD_6, IDD_7.$$

We encounter here one new term, i.e., the foreign interest rate $i^{\star}$. The paper follows an established custom in designating variables referring to the foreign economy with a star. The term

IDF describing the domestic investors' absorption of foreign securities (in domestic currency values) will be required for the subsequent description of the monetary base. It depends on the same set of variables with suitably adjusted properties.

(4c) $\quad IDF = IDF[r, i, i^{\star}, p, P, W_h, W_n, e]$

$$IDF_1, IDF_2, IDF_8 < 0 < IDF_3, IDF_4, IDF_5, IDF_6, IDF_7.$$

The absorption of domestic securities by foreigners, i.e., IFD, is described by means of the foreign counterpart $IDF^{\star}$ of the domestic magnitude IDF. Equation (4d) introduces the portfolio allocation by foreign wealth owners to domestic securities stated in foreign money units

(4d) $\quad IDF^{\star} = IDF^{\star}[r^{\star}, i^{\star}, i, p^{\star}, P^{\star}, W^{\star}_h, W^{\star}_n, e^{\star}]$

The properties are similar to those stated in (4c). The term IFD is now described as the domestic currency equivalent of $IDF^{\star}$, i.e., we present

$$IFD = IDF^{\star} \cdot x$$

where x is the foreign exchange rate expressed as the ratio of domestic money per unit of foreign money.

The interaction of the securities market with the loan market is determined by the partial dependence of the banks and the domestic public's portfolio (IDD and IDF) on the loan rate, together with the loan market's dependence on the securities yield i. The interdependence of the securities market with foreign securities markets is assured by the dependence of IDD and IDF on the yield $i^\star$ on foreign security markets and the foreign investors' IFD dependence on the domestic yield i. The foreign demand component IFD depends in addition to i and $i^\star$ also on variables reflecting the foreign state of affairs.[6)]

The last market equation bears on the money market. It determines proximately the asset price level P of real capital. The left side

$$(5) \qquad m(r, i, P, d+h, \dots)UB = \lambda[r, i, p, P, W_n, W_h, e]$$

$$m_1, m_2 > 0 > m_3, m_4; \quad \lambda_1, \lambda_2, \lambda_7 < 0 < \lambda_3, \lambda_4, \lambda_5, \lambda_6$$

introduces the money stock as a product of monetary multiplier m and the unborrowed base UB. The monetary multiplier depends again on interest rates, asset price level P and borrowing costs via the allocation parameters constituting the multiplier. The dedependence differs, however, noticeably from the asset multiplier.[7)] The right side of the equation introduces money demand

---

6) The reader should note that the exchange rate is held fixed in this analysis. Floating exchange rates complicate the analysis substantially and will be examined at another occasion. The problem under examination in this paper has been typically associated with a fixed rate regime and is thus considered in this context.

7) The monetary multiplier is defined as follows:

$$m = \frac{1+k}{(r+\ell-b)\ (1+t+d)+k}$$

The component terms are listed in footnote 4.

as a function of interest rates, prices, wealth and yield on real capital. The yield on foreign securities is not incorporated. It is assumed that foreign securities are not direct substitutes for domestic money. It is also assumed that domestic equities are non-traded goods similar to loans. The foreign asset price level of real capital does not appear as an argument in the money demand function. Interdependence is completely centered on the securities markets.

The purpose of our analysis requires an additional statement describing the monetary base. It is the sum of the net domestic source component NDSC (claims against the government sector plus the

(6) UB = NDSC + IR

cumulated sum of liberated reserves) and international reserves IR. This magnitude can be replaced by means of a suitable description of the balance of payments and we obtain:

(7) UB = NDSC + CCAB + IFD - IDF

where CCAB refers to the cumulated sum of all past values of the current account balance CAB.

The occurrence of the public's net foreign position [IFD-IDF] as a source component of the base converts the unborrowed base UB into an endogenous entity jointly determined with interest rates by the credit markets and money supply process. The interdependence between national credit markets thus affects the behavior of the monetary base. The component CCAB on the other hand is certainly predetermined, it cannot be affected by current credit market processes. The net domestic source component may also be endogenously determined. This depends on the nature of the Central Bank regime. The magnitude is necessarily endogenous in regimes committed to an interest target policy. The reader should note lastly that the formulation is somewhat simplified in one respect. The banks' net foreign borrowing position is not incorporated into the analysis. Admission of this aspect requires suitable adjustments in the sources statement of the base and the composition of the multiplier.[8)]

II. A Diagrammatic Exposition

The basic diagram was introduced in a previous paper covering a closed economy with an aggregated credit market.[9)] The credit market equation is represented in an (i, P) plane by a CM-line with a negative slope, and the money market by an MM-line with a positive slope. The intersection of the two lines jointly determines i and P. A second panel describing an (i, M) plane and exhibiting the money demand and money stock relations λ and $m \cdot UB$ is used to determine the money stock. Changes in monetary policy or underlying conditions appear as shifts in the CM or MM-line producing appropriate modifications of i or P and M in the two panels.

8) The banks net foreign position was explicitly incorporated in a previously published paper listed under footnote 1.

9) "A Diagrammatic Exposition of the Money Supply Process", Schweizerische Zeitschrift für Volkswirtschaft und Statistik, February 1974.

The general form of the diagram is carried over to the present analysis without significant changes. The disaggregation with the resulting interaction between loan and security market combined with the international interdependence of security markets require, however, a reinterpretation of the diagram. The useful extension of the diagrammatic exposition involves in a first step elimination of the loan rate in the equations describing the securities market and the money market. This is accomplished by considering the loan market equation as an implicit function describing the loan rate in terms of the remaining variables occurring in the equation. Suitable elimination of r from the security and money market equations yields two expressions in terms of i and P and the remaining variables. The two equations can thus be interpreted to define (under the usual assumptions) i as an implicit function of P and other variables. It follows that each equation can be represented by a line in the plane defined by two axis associated with log i and log P. Figure 1 introduces the two lines. The SM-line corresponds to the security market equation modified by the elimination of the loan rate by means of the loan market equation. The line is constituted by all values of i and P

Figure 1

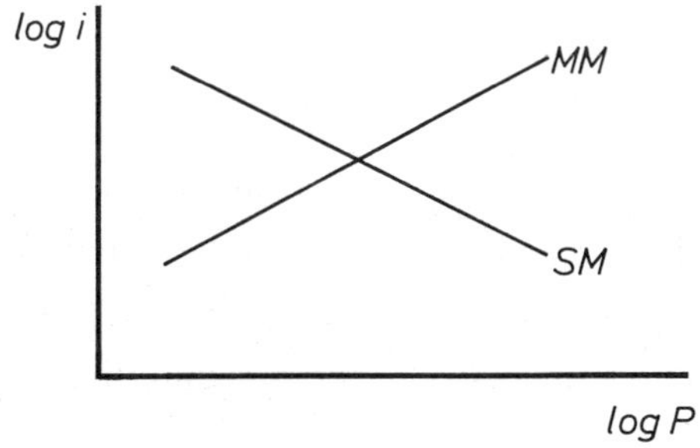

which jointly satisfy the security market and the loan market equation. The MM-line on the other hand describes all values of i and P jointly satisfying the money market and loan market, after suitable adjustment of the loan rate r to express the interaction between loan and money market. The position of both lines depends in a manner to be discussed in subsequent sections on all the variables beyond i and P occurring in the market equations. In particular, the position depends on the policy variables NDSC, and S. The position of SM also depends on the state of foreign asset markets.

The slopes of the lines in the diagram are an important building block for the subsequent analysis and thus require a closer examination. They reflect the structural properties of the markets summarized by the two lines. The previous paper demonstrated that the slopes are determined by the asset price and interest elasticities of excess demand (or supply) on the credit market and the money market. The basic interpretation still applies in the present case with an appropriate modification to reflect the interaction with the loan market. We introduce first in expression (8) the slope of SM.

$$(8) \qquad s\ell\,(SM) = -\frac{\bar{\varepsilon}(SM,\ P)}{\bar{\varepsilon}(SM,\ i)} < 0$$

Both numerators and denominators are specific elasticities of the excess demand for securities. The numerator forms the total (expressed by a bar above the ε) asset price elasticity of the security market with explicit incorporation of the feedback loop via the loan market. The expression reflects thus the interaction with the loan market mediated via adjustments to changes in the asset price P. The following series offers a complete definition of the numerator

$$(9) \qquad \bar{\varepsilon}(SM, P) = \varepsilon(SM, P) - \frac{\varepsilon(SM, r)}{\varepsilon(LM, r)} \cdot \varepsilon(LM, P) > 0$$

$$(9a) \qquad \varepsilon(SM, P) = [\varepsilon(\overset{+}{a}, P) + \varepsilon(\overset{-}{UB}, P)] \frac{(1-\alpha)aUB}{S} + \varepsilon(\overset{+}{IDD}, P) \frac{IDD}{S} > 0$$

where $\varepsilon(UB, P) = - \varepsilon(IDF, P) \frac{IDF}{UB} < 0$

$$(9b) \qquad \varepsilon(SM, r) = [-\varepsilon(\overset{+}{\alpha}, r) \frac{\alpha}{1-\alpha} + \varepsilon(\overset{+}{a}, r) + \varepsilon(\overset{+}{UB}, r)] \frac{(1-\alpha)aUB}{S} +$$

$$\varepsilon(\overset{-}{IDD}, r) \frac{IDD}{S} < 0$$

with $\varepsilon(UB, r) = - \varepsilon(IDF, r) \frac{IDF}{UB} > 0$

$$(9c) \qquad \varepsilon(LM, r) = \varepsilon(\overset{+}{\alpha}, r) + \varepsilon(\overset{+}{a}, r) + \varepsilon(\overset{+}{UB}, r) - \varepsilon(\overset{-}{L}, r) > 0$$

$$(9d) \qquad \varepsilon(LM, P) = \varepsilon(\overset{+}{a}, P) + \varepsilon(\overset{-}{UB}, P) - \varepsilon(\overset{-}{L}, P) \sim 0$$

The first term in the expression (9) constituting the total asset price elasticity of the excess demand for securities (modified for loan market interaction) describes the asset price elasticity of the security market in the absence of any loan market interaction. The elasticity $\varepsilon(SM, P)$ emerges according to (9a) as a weighted average of partial asset price elasticities of the first and second demand component in the security market. The sum of weights is less than unity whenever foreign investors absorb some of the domestic securities in their portfolios (i.e., IFD >0). The sign of

ε (SM, P) is essentially determined by the weights of $-\varepsilon$ (IDF, P) and ε (IDD, P). These responses of the domestic public are constrained to a similar order. The net result depends thus on the relative weights. The first elasticity has a weight $(1-\alpha)a.IDF \cdot S^{-1}$ and the second $IDD \cdot S^{-1}$. It is assumed that for all countries with a security market the relative absorption of foreign securities (i.e., IDF/S) is a fraction of the absorption of domestic securities (i.e., IDD/S). It follows that the sign of the last term defining ε (SM, P) prevails.

The second term in $\bar{\varepsilon}$(SM, P) describes the interaction with the loan market. This feedback via the loan market is determined by three elasticity expressions, the loan rate elasticity of the excess demand for securities ε (SM, r), the loan rate elasticitiy of the excess supply of bank loans ε(LM, r), and the asset price elasticity of the excess supply of bank loans ε (LM, P). The loan rate elasticity ε(SM, r) defined by (9b) is negative. The bracketed term is dominated by $-\varepsilon(\alpha, r)$ and is at least zero. The total expression is thus at least equal to the second term in the (generalized) average. The loan rate elasticity ε (LM, r) of the loan market introduced in (9c) is unambigously positive. It is also important to note that ε(LM, r) is a large multiple of $|\varepsilon \text{(SM, r)}|$. The bracketed expression of ε(SM, r) is smaller than the sum of the first three terms in ε (LM, r) by the amount $\varepsilon(\alpha, r) \frac{1}{1-\alpha}$. Moreover, the substantially smaller value of the bracketed expression in ε (SM, r) is multiplied with a weight less than one-third for the USA and a similarly low weight for most other countries. The second term in ε (SM, r) also falls substantially below the last term in ε (LM, r). First, the direct elasticity ε(L, r) is a multiple of the cross elasticity $\varepsilon(IDD, r)$, and secondly, the weight IDD/S remains below unity. We conclude thus that the ratio of loan rate elasticities

$$\frac{\varepsilon(SM, r)}{\varepsilon(LM, r)}$$

conditioning the feedback effect of asset price variations is probably quite small. This ratio is multiplied with the asset price elasticitiy of the excess supply of bank loans $\varepsilon(LM, P)$. The sign of this elasticity defined by (9d) depends on the relative sensitivity of the loan market to changes in P and the relative absorption of foreign securities by domestic investors. A relatively P-sensitive IDF component combined with a pronounced interconnection of national security markets yields a negative $\varepsilon(LM, P)$ and thus moderates with a negative ratio $[\varepsilon(SM, r)/\varepsilon(LM, r)]$ the positive effect of the direct and partial asset price elasticity $\varepsilon(SM, P)$. The properties noted thus flatten the slope of the SM-line. On the other hand, a comparatively P-sensitive loan market combined with a small intertwining of security markets (i.e., low IDF/UB) assures a positive $\varepsilon(LM, P)$ and thus reenforces the positive partial elasticity $\varepsilon(SM, P)$ and steepens the slope of the SM-line. It is generally expected, however, that $\varepsilon(LM, P)$ remains at a comparatively small value. It follows that the feedback loop via the loan market occurs as a product of two small terms. Our further discussion thus approximates the total elasticity $\bar{\varepsilon}(SM, P)$ with the partial elasticity $\varepsilon(SM, P)$.

The denominator of the slope expression exhibits a similar structure. It is formed by the sum of the partial (or direct)

$$(10) \qquad \bar{\varepsilon}(SM, i) = \varepsilon(SM, i) - \frac{\varepsilon(SM, r)}{\varepsilon(LM, r)} \cdot \varepsilon(LM, i)$$

interest elasticity of the excess demand for securities $\varepsilon(SM, i)$ and a term denoting the feedback via the loan market mediated by changes in interest rates on securities. The first component emerges as a weighted average of interest

$$(11) \qquad \varepsilon(SM, i) = \Big[-\overset{-}{\varepsilon(\alpha, i)} \frac{\alpha}{1-\alpha} + \overset{+}{\varepsilon(a, i)} + \overset{+}{\varepsilon(UB, i)} \Big] \frac{(1-\alpha) a \cdot UB}{S} + \overset{+}{\varepsilon(IDD, i)} \frac{IDD}{S} + \overset{+}{\varepsilon(IFD, i)} \frac{IFD}{S} > 0$$

$$\text{with} \quad \varepsilon(UB, i) = \varepsilon(IFD, i) \frac{IFD}{UB} - \varepsilon(IDF, i) \frac{IDF}{UB} > 0$$

elasticities of all demand components on the security market. The sign is positive. The ratio $\varepsilon(SM, r)/\varepsilon(LM, r)$ in the feedback has already been established to be negative and of small order. There remains the interest elasticity of the loan market $\varepsilon(LM, i)$.

$$\varepsilon(LM, i) = \overset{-}{\varepsilon(\alpha, i)} + \overset{+}{\varepsilon(a, i)} + \overset{+}{\varepsilon(UB, i)} - \overset{+}{\varepsilon(L, i)}$$

A substantial interdependence of security markets combined with moderate effects on loan demand exerted by changes in interest rates on securities assures the predominance of the third term and $\varepsilon(LM, i)$ is mildly positive. A large sensitivity of loan demand to changes in the yield on securities and a small interdependence of security markets pushes $\varepsilon(LM, i)$ into a negative range. The feedback via the loan market thus reenforces under the first set of conditions the positive partial term $\varepsilon(SM, i)$ and moderates its effect under the second set of conditions. The first set of conditions thus flattens the SM-line whereas the second set steepens the line. In summary we obtain a steeper SM-line whenever the loan market exhibits a substantial interdependence with other markets via i and P, combined with low interdependence of security markets. The opposite conditions lower on the other hand the slope of the SM-line. The set of conditions shaping the terms ε(LM, P) and ε(LM, i) in the feedback expressions suggests that the total elasticities $\bar{\varepsilon}$(SM, i) and $\bar{\varepsilon}$(SM, P) may be usefully approximated for most purposes with the partial expressions ε(SM, i) > 0 and ε(SM, P) > 0. It is also stipulated that ε(SM, P) < ε(SM, i) and the sℓ(SM) is consequently less than unity.

The MM-line exhibits an analogous structure. It defines the locus of all i and P values simultaneously satisfying the loan and the money market with proper adjustment of i and P to r. The slope is defined as the ratio of the asset price elasticity of the excess supply

$$(12) \qquad s\ell(MM) = -\frac{\bar{\varepsilon}(MM, P)}{\bar{\varepsilon}(MM, i)} > 0$$

of money to the respective interest elasticity with full account of the feedback loop via the loan market. The numerator is described by expression (13)

$$(13) \qquad \bar{\varepsilon}(MM, P) = \varepsilon(MM, P) - \frac{\varepsilon(MM, r)}{\varepsilon(LM, r)} \cdot \varepsilon(LM, P) < 0$$

$$\text{where} \quad \varepsilon(MM, P) = \overset{-}{\varepsilon(m, P)} + \overset{-}{\varepsilon(UB, P)} - \overset{+}{\varepsilon(\lambda, P)} < 0$$

$$\varepsilon(MM, r) = \overset{+}{\varepsilon(m, r)} + \overset{+}{\varepsilon(UB, r)} - \overset{-}{\varepsilon(\lambda, r)} > 0$$

The other terms defining $\bar{\varepsilon}$ (MM, P) have already been introduced. Once again the feedback via the loan market remains comparatively small. It appears again as a product of two small terms. The partial elasticity ε(MM, P) can thus be used to approximate the total elasticity $\bar{\varepsilon}$(MM, P).

The denominator is presented in equation (14)

$$(14) \quad \bar{\varepsilon}(MM, i) = \varepsilon(MM, i) - \frac{\varepsilon(MM, r)}{\varepsilon(LM, r)} \cdot \varepsilon(LM, i) > 0$$

$$(14a) \quad \varepsilon(MM, i) = \varepsilon(m, i) + \varepsilon(UB, i) - \varepsilon(\lambda, i) > 0$$

The previous discussion has already determined that the loan market feedback term is constrained to comparatively modest proportion. The first term, expressing the direct elasticity, thus dominates the total expression. The feedback term possesses in the MM-case the opposite sign of the corresponding term for the security market. It follows that the same conditions flattening the slope of SM via the operation of the loan market feedback also steepen the slope of the MM-line. We note in particular that a moderate interaction of the loan market with the other asset markets via i and P combined with a substantial interdependence of national security market yields a comparatively flat SM and a relatively steep MM-line. The reader should note, however, that the previous examination of the magnitudes involved confines the modifications of the slopes associated with the elements specified to a small range. It is not expected that such modifications significantly affect the conclusions. The approximations of the total elasticities $\bar{\varepsilon}$ (SM, x) and $\bar{\varepsilon}$ (MM, x), by the partial expressions ε (SM, x) and ε(MM, x), x = i, P, has been justified on these grounds. The following order condition is on the other hand fundamentally important for our analysis. We postulate that $-s\ell(SM) < s\ell(MM)$. The SM-line is constrained to a flatter slope than the MM-line. This constraint forms the extension of our fundamental order condition to the open economy with a disaggregate credit market. It may still be interpreted to assert that the interest elasticity on the credit market exceeds the corresponding elasticity on the money market, whereas the asset price elasticity of the money market exceeds the corresponding elasticity on the credit market.

III. A Diagrammatic Exposition of the Working of the System

The interaction of SM and MM-lines immediately determines i and P. An extension of the diagram already exploited for the closed economy can be used to describe the joint determination of i, P and the money stock (or the banks' loan or security portfolio). We require two panels for this purpose in the manner depicted in Figure 2.

Figure 2

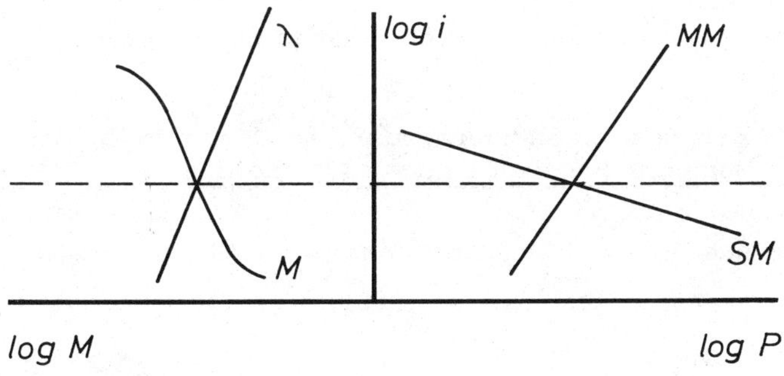

Both axes denote logs of the magnitudes listed. The graph previously introduced occurs now as the right side panel and can be used to determine interest rate i and asset price P. The left side panel determines the money stock for any given pair (i, P) determined on the right side. The λ -line describes money demand and the M-line the money stock expressed by the product $m \cdot UB$ of multiplier and base. The two lines on the left necessarily intersect on the horizontal fixed by the interest rate determined in the right side panel. It follows that actually only one of the two lines on the left is necessary to determine M once i and P are jointly determined on the right. Figure 2 can now be used to trace the responses of i, P and M to policy actions implemented by domestic and foreign authorities or to events emerging in the domestic or foreign real sectors. A similar graph may be constructed to describe the responses of the banks' loan portfolio or security portfolio. The left side panel requires suitable adjustment in each case. The λ-line must be replaced by an L-line or a line representing S-IDD-IFD, whereas the M-line is replaced by an αaUB or an $(1-\alpha)aUB$ line. The subsequent discussion examines the shifts in the SM and MM-lines associated with specific events or policy actions. Every action or event is defined by a specific combination of shifts. These shifts supplement the slopes previously introduced. Shifts and slopes jointly determine the responses of i and P in a manner to be outlined in the following sections.

1. The Response to an Increase in the Domestic Central Bank s Net Domestic Source Component of the Base.

An increase in NDSC can occur for a variety of reasons. The consequences on the monetary system are essentially the same.

An increase in NDSC raises the excess supply of loans and money and raises the excess demand for securities. We expect intuitively lower rates of return on all assets and an expansion of the money stock. The formal discussion must translate this event into appropriate effects on the SM-line and the MM-line. A vertical shift per unit (percentage) change in NDSC is thus defined for each line

$$vs(SM|NDSC) = - \frac{\bar{\varepsilon}(SM, NDSC)}{\varepsilon(SM, i)} < 0$$

$$vs(MM|NDSC) = - \frac{\bar{\varepsilon}(MM, NDSC)}{\varepsilon(MM, i)} < 0$$

We are already familiar with the denominators of both vertical shifts. The same interest elasticities of SM or MM occur as denominators of the slope expressions. We examine thus the numerators.

$$\bar{\varepsilon}(SM, NDSC) \sim \left[\frac{(1-\alpha)aUB}{S} - \frac{\varepsilon(SM, r)}{\varepsilon(LM, r)}\right] \frac{NDSC}{UB} > 0$$

$$\bar{\varepsilon}(MM, NDSC) \sim \left[1 - \frac{\varepsilon(MM, r)}{\varepsilon(LM, r)}\right] \frac{NDSC}{UB} > 0$$

Both numerators (and thus also the shift expression) are proportional to the relative importance of the source component NDSC in the base. Little importance should be attributed to this property however. A small proportion of NDSC in UB simply implies a larger relative change in NDSC and the effective shift may still be substantial. More important are the differences in order of magnitudes between the two numerators. The bracketed expression in $\bar{\varepsilon}$(MM, NDSC) is slightly below unity, whereas the corresponding expression in $\bar{\varepsilon}$(SM, NDSC) is slightly above the proportion of available securities absorbed by the banking system. This proportion is less than one-half for most monetary systems. The smaller numerator of vs(SM|NDSC) thus reenforces its larger denominator and produces the inequality $|vs(SM|NDSC)| < |vs(MM|NDSC)|$ i.e., the vertical shift of MM exceeds the vertical shift of SM. Moreover, the relative order of vs(SM|NDSC) declines with increasing interdependence of security markets and falling relative bank absorption of securities.

The impact of any given change in NDSC on i, P and M can now be traced with the aid of Figure 3.

Figure 3

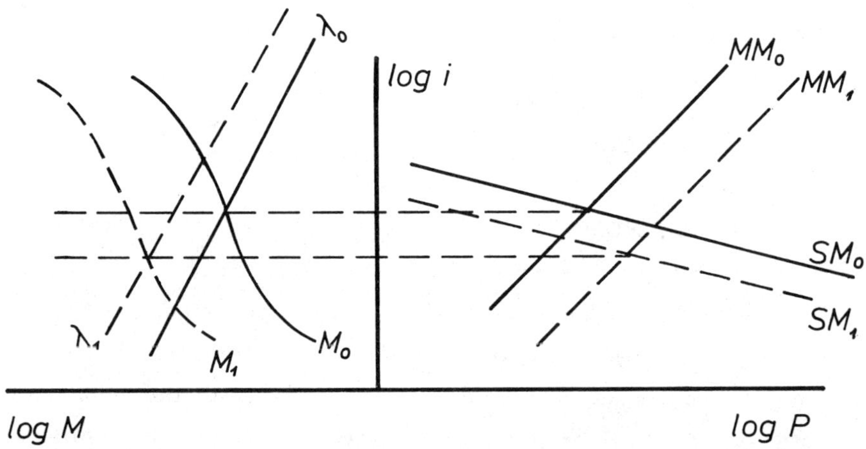

The panel on the right describes the downward shift of both lines associated with an increase in NDSC. This lowers unambiguously i. The excess of vs(MM|NDSC) over vs(SM|NDSC) assures that the new intersection point is southeast of the initial intersection and we obtain thus simultaneously a fall in i and an increase in P.

The precise description of the response in terms of an elasticity ε (i, NDSC) can be formulated by means of the geometric terms introduced above. We obtain thus:

$$(15) \qquad \varepsilon\,(P,\ NDSC) = \frac{\overset{-}{vs(MM|NDSC)} - \overset{-}{vs(SM|NDSC)}}{-\underset{+}{s\ell(MM)} + \underset{-}{s\ell(SM}} > 0$$

The sum of slope expressions in the denominator is unambiguously negative. The difference between the vertical shifts constituting the numerator is also negative as a result of the signs and order condition imposed on the two shifts. Increasing interdependence of security markets expressed by rising interest elasticities of the various demand components for securities still assures a positive response of P to NDSC.

The response of interest rate i is described by the formula (16)

$$(16) \qquad \varepsilon\,(i,\ NDSC) = \frac{\dfrac{vs(MM|NDSC)}{s\ell(MM)} - \dfrac{vs(SM|NDSC)}{s\ell(SM)}}{\dfrac{1}{s\ell(MM)} - \dfrac{1}{s\ell(SM)}} < 0$$

The sign is determined without order constraint.

The signs of the slope and vertical shift expressions determine a negative response of i to NDSC. This response is moreover conditioned by the degree of international interdependence between security markets. Increasing interdependence raises the interest-elasticities ε (SM, i) and ε.(MM, i) of excess demand for securities and the excess supply of money. The value of the denominator increases under the circumstances and the responsiveness of the interest rate to domestic monetary policy declines. The elasticity ε(i, NDSC) converges in the limit to zero. The monetary impulse emitted by a change in NDSC is still transmitted to the economic process via adjustments in P, even in the limit position. A uniform monotonic increase in interest elasticities of all security demand components induces convergences of ε(P, NDSC) to a positive value. The "non-Keynesian transmission channel" remains thus operative.

The effect of a change in NDSC on the money stock can be traced by means of the left panel of Figure 3. The response of the money stock may be described in two non-identical but logically equivalent ways. One description relies on the money demand function. The total increase in M is constituted as a sum of two components. First, we note an increase resulting from the downwards motion along the sloping λ-curve associated with a lower interest rate. Secondly, the increase in P noted in the right side panel pushes the λ-curve to the left along the horizontal interest line and adds an additional component to the monetary expansion. An alternative description relies on the money stock function M. The increase in NDSC and P moves the M-curve to the left and the reduction in interest rate induces a backward motion along the M-curve to the new interest line. The two descriptions correspond to the analytic statement (17)

$$(17) \quad 1 > 1 + [\underset{+}{\varepsilon(m, i)} + \underset{+}{\varepsilon(UB, i)}] \cdot \underset{-}{\varepsilon(i, NDSC)} + [\underset{-}{\varepsilon(m, P)} + \underset{-}{\varepsilon(UB, P)}] \cdot \underset{+}{\varepsilon(P, NDSC)} =$$

$$\underset{-}{\varepsilon(\lambda, i)} \cdot \underset{-}{\varepsilon(i, NDSC)} + \underset{+}{\varepsilon(\lambda, P)} \cdot \underset{+}{\varepsilon(P, NDSC)} > 0$$

There remains for us to consider the response of the loan rate r. The appropriate expression is stated in equation (18)

$$(18) \quad \varepsilon(r, NDSC) \sim - \frac{\frac{NDSC}{UB} + \varepsilon(LM, i) \cdot \varepsilon(i, NDSC)}{\varepsilon(LM, r)} < 0$$

Two approximations were used in this formulation. First, we used the simplification $\varepsilon(LM, P) \sim 0$ introduced previously. Moreover, the variations in L and IDF due to changes in W_n induced by NDSC via UB are of small order and are consequently neglected. These components add to the numerator an expression proportional to the comparatively small magnitude $(1+\alpha)UB/W_n$.[10] The proportionality factor is less than unity. The response of r converges with a monotonic increase of the degree of interdependence between security markets to the expression

$$- \frac{1}{\varepsilon(LM, r)} \quad \frac{NDSC}{UB}$$

This expression denotes the isolated response of the loan market without interaction with the other asset markets.

2. The Response to a Change in S

Variations in NDSC are usually associated with the government sector's budget position, and similar variations in S. The impact of the budget on the monetary system occurs via these two variables S and UB. A change in S immediately creates an excess de-

10) This wealth element was also disregarded in the description of the vertical shifts explaining the responses of i and P. They produce negligible modifications in the magnitudes without affecting the general pattern of the results.

mand (or supply) on the security market and induces changes in i disrupting the loan and money market and modifying also r and P. The increase in i associated with an increase in S induces an excess supply on the money market and an excess demand on the loan market, provided the response of the net foreign position in the monetary base does not dominate the loan market's behavior. But these adjustments to interest rates are modified somewhat by changes in wealth resulting from the increase in S. The various channels at work are clearly revealed by the relevant shifts of the two lines. These shifts are defined by expression (19).

$$\text{(19a)} \quad vs(SM|S) = \frac{1-\bar{\varepsilon}(SM, W_n)\frac{v\cdot S}{W_n}}{\bar{\varepsilon}(SM, i)} > 0$$

$$\text{(19b)} \quad vs(MM|S) = \frac{-\bar{\varepsilon}(MM, W_n)\frac{v\cdot S}{W_n}}{\bar{\varepsilon}(MM, i)} > 0$$

$$\bar{\varepsilon}(SM, W_n) = \varepsilon(SM, W_n) - \frac{\varepsilon(SM, r)}{\varepsilon(LM, r)} \cdot \varepsilon(LM, W_n) > 0$$

$$\varepsilon(SM, W_n) = [\overset{+}{\varepsilon}(a, W_n) - \overset{+}{\varepsilon}(IDF, W_n)\frac{IDF}{UB}]\ \frac{(1-\alpha)aUB}{S} + \overset{+}{\varepsilon}(IDD, W_n)\frac{IDD}{S}$$

$$\varepsilon(LM, W_n) = \overset{+}{\varepsilon}(a, W_n) - \overset{+}{\varepsilon}(IDF, W_n)\frac{IDF}{UB} - \overset{+}{\varepsilon}(L, W_n) < 0$$

$$\bar{\varepsilon}(MM, W_n) = \varepsilon(MM, W_n) - \frac{\varepsilon(MM, r)}{\varepsilon(LM, r)} \cdot \varepsilon(LM, W_n)$$

$$\varepsilon(MM, W_n) = \varepsilon(m, W_n) - \varepsilon(IDF, W_n)\frac{IDF}{UB} - \varepsilon(\lambda, W_n) < 0$$

An inspection of the resulting expressions suggests that the vertical shift of the SM-line dominates the shift of the MM-line. The latter is positive but remains quite small as a result of the factor $v \cdot S/W_n$ in the numerator. The operation of the same factor justifies a crude approximation of the shift of the SM-line by the reciprocal of $\overline{\varepsilon}$ (SM, i). A pronounced upward shift of the SM-line combined with a negligible rise in MM raises simultaneously i and P. We also note that the wealth effect moderates the effect on P and reenforces the effect on i in proportion to the relative importance of S in non-human wealth expressed by the ratio $v \cdot S/W_n$.

The adjustment of asset markets in open economies to variations in S deserves some further comments. New issues of government debt induce via rising interest rates a net import of capital. Foreign investors raise their absorption of domestic securities and domestic investors lower their foreign absorption. The domestic economy s net export of securities expressed by the public's net foreign position thus increases and the unborrowed base expands. The increase in S associated with the government's borrowing induces consequently readjustments between foreign and domestic asset markets raising also the demand for securities on the domestic security market. This interaction moderates the effect of S on interest rates. It also appears that interdependent credit markets offer excellent opportunities to moderate the effect of a persistent borrowing requirement on domestic asset markets as a result of the interaction effect. But such policies modify over the longer-run the relative marginal information costs of the domestic securities expressed by relative risk premia. This implies a corresponding change in the substitution relation between securities with distinct national designations. A policy cultivating persistent and substantial net exports of securities designed to finance the government's budget position thus lowers gradually $\bar{\varepsilon}$(SM, i) and eventually dislodges even a small country from the "small country case" to the more relevant case examined in this paper.

The responses of i and P can be expressed again in terms of slope and shift conditions:

$$\varepsilon(P, S) = \frac{vs(MM|S) - vs(SM|S)}{-s\ell(MM) + s\ell(SM)} > 0$$

$$\varepsilon(i, S) = \frac{-\frac{vs(SM|S)}{s\ell(SM)} + \frac{vs(MM|S)}{s\ell(MM)}}{\frac{1}{s\ell(SM)} + \frac{1}{s\ell(MM)}} > 0$$

Uniform convergence of interest elasticities of all demand components for securities implies convergence of ε(i, S) to zero and of ε(P, S) to a positive value. It follows that increasing interdependence of the securities markets lowers the responsiveness of the domestic asset markets with respect to variations in S, but does not remove all effects.

The response of the money stock is best assessed by means of the money stock expression $\varepsilon(M, S) = [\varepsilon(m, i) + \varepsilon(UB, i)] \cdot \varepsilon(i, S) + [\varepsilon(m, P) + \varepsilon(UB, P)] \quad \varepsilon(P, S)$. The elasticity of M with respect to S is a sum of two terms with opposing signs. It follows that the elasticity ε(M, S) remains at a very low and somewhat insignificant value.

3. Domestic and Foreign Open Market Operations

Open market operations involve an exchange between base money and outstanding securities. Purchases raise the Central Bank's portfolio of claims against the government sector and S decreases. One could argue that the reduction of S on the right side of the credit market equation is matched by an equal fall in demand on the left. This matching fall in demand is justified with an argument adducing the interdependence between the credit markets. An absorption of securities by the domestic Central Bank simply pushes domestic and foreign investors into foreign securities, IDD and IFD thus fall and IDF increases. The investors' desired portfolio balance cannot change and holdings of foreign securities replace the holdings of domestic securities. The increase in IDF expresses in this context the matching decrease in IDD. It follows that the sum IDD + IFD falls by exactly the same magnitude as S. Moreover, the unborrowed base UB remains also unchanged. The increase in NDSC (equal to minus the change in S) is completely offset by the reduction in the public's net foreign position. This argument based on the close interdependence of credit markets involves the following relations between the magnitudes:

$$-\Delta NDSC = \Delta S$$

$$\Delta IDD + \Delta IFD = \Delta S \quad \text{and} \quad \Delta IDD = -\Delta IDF$$

It follows then that $\Delta NDSC + \Delta IFD - \Delta IDF = 0$.

Open market operations of the domestic Central Bank thus simply redistribute foreign and domestic security holdings without affecting interest rates and the base. Moreover, an unchanged base combined with the absence of any change in the interest rate maintains the inherited position of the loan and money market and one concludes that open market operations in open economies with interdependent security markets fail to affect domestic price level and output.

This argument encounters a minor and a major reservation. The minor reservation bears on the omission of wealth effects. Changes in S not matched by corresponding changes in the "distributive endowment" $\overline{IDF}$ and $\overline{IFD}$ modify the public's non-human wealth W_n. This affects the domestic demand for securities, loans and money and induces a change in the loan rate, the yield of securities and the asset price P. But it should be noted that our discussion essentially disregards the induced direct wealth effects associated with changes in UB or S. The net effect remains negligible, constrained to a proportion less than the fraction of these financial assets in non-human wealth. Inclusion of the direct wealth effects thus yields some cosmetic adjustments of minor importance for the broad contours.

The second reservation is more important. The argument offers an impressionistically useful shortcut description of open market operations in open economies with <u>perfect</u> substitutability between nationally designated securities. The paper examining this case will demonstrate that the short description applies only to economies with a vanishing supply of securities relative to the world total. The analysis thus yields some precise order conditions explicating the argument. Furthermore, it does not extend to the case of interdependence with imperfect substitutability recognizing the persistent operation of information and adjustment costs. The emphasis on the redistribution of domestic and foreign securities initiated by the domestic open market operation remains however a relevant comment. Still, redistribution as such does not condemn open market operations to a hopeless endeavor. The reader is invited to consider the implications of the preceding results pertaining to open market operations.

The discussion of the two previous sections provide the elements for an examination of open market policies. Such policies are characterized by the simultaneous changes of NDSC and S in opposite directions. The response of i and P per unit percentage change of NDSC executed by means of an open market operation is described by the following two formulae:

$$\varepsilon(i,\ OMO) = \varepsilon(i,\ NDSC) - \varepsilon(i,\ S)\frac{NDSC}{S} > \varepsilon(i,\ NDSC)$$

$$\varepsilon(P,\ OMO) = \varepsilon(P,\ NDSC) - \varepsilon(P,\ S)\frac{NDSC}{S} < \varepsilon(P,\ NDSC)$$

We note thus that open market operations amplify the effect on interest rate i and moderate the effect on P. Both amplification and moderation are proportional to the ratio of the source component NDSC to the stock of available securities. This ratio is roughly one fourth in the USA. Amplification of the i-effect and moderation of the P-effect by open market operations modifies the response of the money stock by very little compared with the response to a change in the base.

It should be noted that the formulae are applicable to both domestic and foreign open market operations in the domestic asset markets. The interpretation of domestic operations is too obvious to require elaboration. Foreign operations may deserve some attention, however. Foreign Central Banks may maintain accounts at the domestic Central Bank and use occasionally some of the funds to acquire domestic securities. On other occasions a foreign Central Bank may unload domestic securities and build up its account at the domestic Central Bank. Purchases or sales of domestic securities by foreign Central Banks affect S in the same manner as domestic open market operations. Moreover, the magnitude NDSC is defined net of foreign deposits. An increase of foreign deposits lowers NDSC and operates similar to a domestic open market sale.

The reader may also assess the monetary effect of a balance of payments deficit initially raising deposits of foreign Central Banks at the domestic Central Bank with an eventual conversion of accruing funds into domestic securities. The net effect lowers S. This international imbalance thus lowers interest rate i and also lowers the market value of real capital.

4. The Effect of Foreign Influences

The discussion of changes in the base and changes in the stock of available securities revealed the similarity between the analysis of the closed economy presented in a previous paper and the analysis of the open economy with interdependent security markets. The two cases maintain a pronounced formal similarity but require substantially different interpretations of the slope and vertical shifts of the credit market and the money market line. Still, the formal similarity extends necessarily to the pattern of results pertaining to domestic influences (ceiling rates on deposits, variation in currency ratio, anticipated net yield on real capital, etc.). We simply note in passing that the detailed discussion of "reverse causation" developed in the previous paper carries over to our present case. The conclusions derived for the case of a closed economy remain valid for the open economy. This economy is exposed, on the other hand, to influences necessarily disregarded in the analysis of a closed economy. We examine thus the influence emanating from changes in foreign asset markets.

Four influences will be distinguished: variations in foreign interest rate i^*, the foreign asset price level P^*, foreign human wealth W_h^* and variations in the foreign economy's expected net yield on real capital e^*. The last three magnitudes operate via the foreign investors' demand IFD on the domestic asset market. The first magnitude operates on all demand components in the domestic security market. An increase in i^* lowers all these components and thus raises the domestic yield i. This increase, combined with a net reduction in the base UB due to a reduction in the public's net foreign position NFPP, disrupts the loan and the money market.

The diagrammatic exposition explains the pattern of domestic responses. We introduce first the vertical shift of the SM and the MM-curve associated with a change in foreign interest rates.

$$vs(SM|i^{\star}) = - \frac{\varepsilon(SM, i^{\star})}{\varepsilon(SM, i)} > 0$$

$$vs(MM|i^{\star}) = - \frac{\varepsilon(MM, i^{\star})}{\varepsilon(MM, i)} > 0$$

where

$$\varepsilon(SM, i^{\star}) = [\varepsilon(1-\alpha, i^{\star}) + \varepsilon(a, i^{\star}) + \varepsilon(UB, i^{\star})] \frac{(1-\alpha)a \cdot UB}{S} + \varepsilon(IDD, i^{\star}) \frac{IDD}{S} + \varepsilon(IFD, i^{\star}) \frac{IFD}{S} < 0$$

$$\varepsilon(MM, i^{\star}) = \varepsilon(UB, i^{\star}) < 0$$

A rising level of foreign interest rates thus shifts both curves upwards. The domestic yield i necessarily increases. The diagram can also be used to establish the limit value of the response $\varepsilon(i, i^{\star})$ with respect to increasing international interdependence. With increasingly closer substitution between foreign and domestic securities the elasticity $\varepsilon(i, i^{\star})$ converges towards unity. It is of course less than unity in the case seriously examined in this paper.

Figure 4

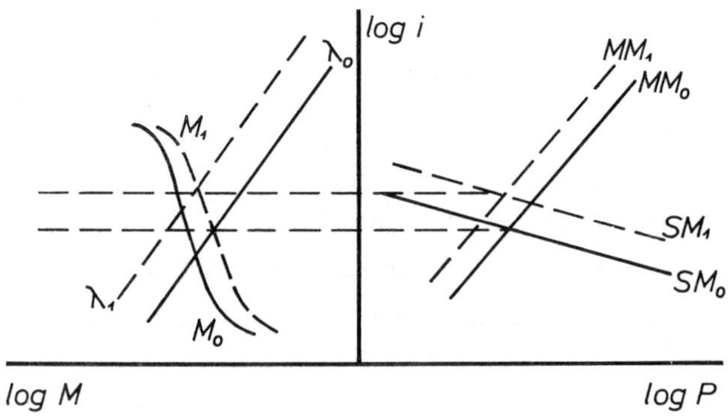

The simultaneous upward shift in both curves produces an ambiguous result for the asset price P. A comparatively large shift of the MM-line would produce a fall in P combined with a rise in i. We also notice that the limit position of an unitary elastic response of i is associated with a vanishing response in P to $i^{\star}$. The intersection point moves along the vertical line through the initial equilibrium point. It appears that in the general case relevant for our purposes the net effect on P remains comparatively small. It depends essentially on the relative magnitude of the interest elasticity of money demand and of the unborrowed base. The latter depends of course on the interest elasticities of IDF and IFD weighted with the ratios IDF/UB and IFD/UB. A small interconnection between the security markets lowers these ratios. It follows that a relatively larger interest elasticity of money demand and a small international interconnection lowers the relative shift $vs(MM|i^{\star})$ of MM and produces a positive response of P to $i^{\star}$. However, it seems useful to assume for the discussion in a subsequent section that the response of P to $i^{\star}$ is approximately zero.

$$vs(MM|i^{\star}) = -\frac{\bar{\varepsilon}(MM, i^{\star})}{\bar{\varepsilon}(MM, i)} \leq -\frac{\bar{\varepsilon}(SM, i^{\star})}{\bar{\varepsilon}(SM, i)} = vs\ (SM|i^{\star})$$

The diagram in Figure 4 was drawn to represent a fall in the money stock resulting from the increase in foreign interest rates. The two descriptions of the response of M to $i^{\star}$ yield the following expressions:

$$\begin{aligned} \varepsilon(M, i^{\star}) &= \varepsilon(UB, i^{\star}) + [\varepsilon(m, i) + \varepsilon(UB, i)] \cdot \varepsilon(i, i^{\star}) + \\ &\quad [\varepsilon(m, P) + \varepsilon(UB, P)] \cdot \varepsilon(P, i^{\star}) \\ &= \varepsilon(\lambda, i) \cdot \varepsilon(i, i^{\star}) + \varepsilon(\lambda, P) \cdot \varepsilon(P, i^{\star}). \end{aligned}$$

With $\varepsilon(P, i^{\star})$ sufficiently small the second expression based on money demand is necessarily negative. An increase in $i^{\star}$ thus lowers the domestic money stock. The first expression based on the money stock equation reveals that this result is essentially due to the relative predominance of the term $\varepsilon(UB, i^{\star})$. A small response of P to $i^{\star}$ is thus associated with a pronounced response of the unborrowed base to $i^{\star}$ attributable to induced variations in the domestic economy's net export of securities.

Consider next the effect of an increase in the foreign asset price level $P^{\star}$ on the domestic asset markets. This induces a substitution by foreign investors of securities, including domestic securities, for foreign equities. It raises thus the unborrowed base via the public's net foreign position and also raises the foreign public's demand component on the domestic security market. We would thus expect a fall in i and r. The determination of the response of P requires, however, an explicit attention to the nature of the interactions. An inspection only informs us that the fall in i and r simultaneously raises money demand and the money stock. The vertical shifts are as follows:

$$vs(SM|P^{\star}) = -\frac{\varepsilon(SM, P^{\star})}{\bar{\varepsilon}(SM, i)} < 0; \quad vs(MM|P^{\star}) = -\frac{\varepsilon(MM, P^{\star})}{\bar{\varepsilon}(MM, i)} < 0$$

$$\varepsilon(SM, P^{\star}) = \varepsilon(IFD, P^{\star}) \; [(1-\alpha)\, a+1] \; \frac{IFD}{S} > 0$$

$$\varepsilon(MM, P^{\star}) = \varepsilon(IFD, P^{\star}) \; \frac{IFD}{UB}$$

The ratio of the shift numerator yields:

$$\frac{\varepsilon(SM, P^{\star})}{\varepsilon(MM, P^{\star})} = [\,(1-\alpha)\; a+1\,] \; \frac{UB}{S} < 1$$

The relevant orders of magnitude prevailing in the USA produce a ratio less than unity. It follows, with $\varepsilon(SM, i) > \varepsilon(MM, i)$ that $0 > vs(SM|P^{\star}) > vs(MM|P^{\star})$. The fall in the interest rate determines under these conditions a rise in the domestic asset price level P. A positive elasticity $\varepsilon(P, P^{\star})$ emerges consequently as indicated in Figure 5. An increase in the foreign asset price level transmits expansionary impulses to the domestic economy.

Figure 5

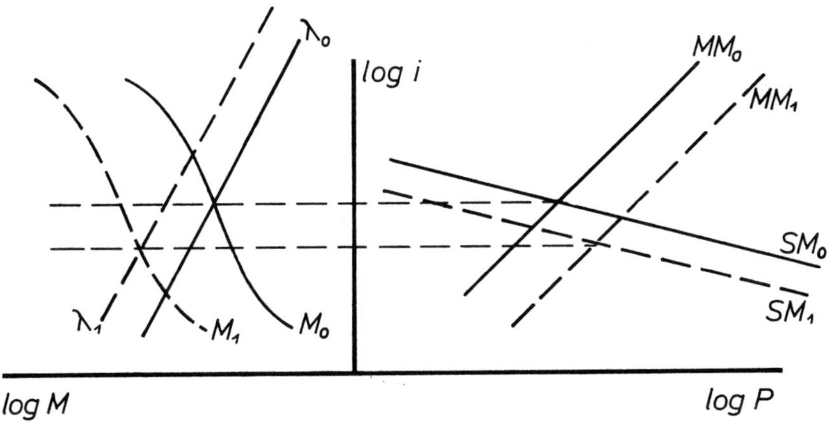

The reader will also note that the domestic money stock is raised by the foreign event. An inspection of the two descriptions of the response in M determines that this increase is due to the increase in the base UB resulting from the adjustment of the public's net foreign position to an increase in $P^{\star}$

Variations of human wealth $W_h^{\star}$ and the expected net yield of real capital $e^{\star}$ in the foreign economy also modify the position of domestic asset markets via the foreign investors' adjustments of their portfolio IFD of domestic securities. An increase in W_h^* operates similarly to an increase in P^*. Foreign investors expand their portfolio of securities, including domestic securities. Interest rates i and r fall and P rises. An increase of e^* on the other hand induces substitutions from securities, including domestic securities, to foreign equities. The foreign investors' portfolio of domestic securities declines and the effect is similar to a rise in the foreign interest rate i^*, i.e., i and r increase with comparatively small effect on P.

The patterns associated with W_h^* and e^* determine the effect of variations in foreign output y^* on the domestic asset market. An increase of y^* raises simultaneously W_h^* and e^*. Our standard postulate concerning the distribution of income implies that the channel via W_h dominates the channel via e at high rates of resource utilization. The opposite holds at low rates of utilization. An increase in foreign output at lower rates of utilization thus induces mostly deflationary impulses via the domestic asset markets. This impulse turns expansionary at high levels of utilization in the foreign economy.

5. The Operation of Loan Portfolio Controls on the Domestic Monetary System

The imposition of quantitative constraints on the banks' portfolio of loans emerged over recent years as a favorite instrument of many Central Banks. It was usually introduced without much justifying analysis. The vague rationale which may occasionally be inferred from official pronouncements and documents involves apparently the traditional confusion between money and credit. The widespread use of this instrument suggests the usefulness of a closer examination.

Imposition of a loan ceiling LC on the banks' loan portfolio substantially modifies the structure of our system. The previous description still holds for all asset market solutions satisfying the inequality $\alpha aB \leqslant LC$. If the asset markets however determine solutions violating this inequality the relevant structure becomes

$$LC = L(r, i, \ldots)$$

$$aUB - LC + IDD + IFD = S$$

$$mUB = \lambda$$

The public's loan demand encounters in this case an exogenously fixed stock supply. Imposition of a loan ceiling also affects the security market. The banks' absorption of securities is partly controlled by the loan ceiling. The banks' investment portfolio is defined by the difference $(a \cdot UB - LC)$ between total earning assets and the constrained loan portfolio.

The loan constraint changes the operation of the asset market in specific ways and also introduces an additional policy variable. The basic outline of the diagram remains, however, unchanged. Table I summarizes all the information pertaining to the slopes of SM and MM under the loan constraint. The general interpretation of the expression defining the slopes is clearly not affected by the new constraint. The two slopes still depend on the ratio of asset price elasticities of excess demand for securities (or excess supply of money) to the interest elasticity of the same excess demand (or excess supply). And as before, the elasticities constituting the slope incorporate the interaction between the securities (or money) market and the loan market. It should be noted that this interaction involves under the loan constraint only elasticities of the public's desired loan liability position L and not elasticities of the excess supply of loans on the loan market. The terms in the total asset price or interest elasticities of the excess demand for securities or excess supply of money describing the feedback via the loan market are thus modified. In particular, they all increase numerically. This modification offsets the changes of the direct elasticities of SM [i.e., $\varepsilon(SM, P)$ and $\varepsilon(SM, i)$]. The net effect of LC on the slope of $s\ell(SM)$ remains under the conditions quite small. The change in the loan market interaction also raises numerically both numerator and denominator of $s\ell(MM)$ with essentially little net effect on the slope. We conclude thus that the general form of the SM and MM-line is not seriously modified by the loan constraint.

With this interpretation at our disposal we examine the consequences of variations in the loan ceiling LC. We need for this purpose the vertical shifts induced by changing LC. These magnitudes are specified as follows:

$$vs(SM|LC) = \frac{\frac{LC}{S} - \frac{\varepsilon(SM,\ r)}{\varepsilon(L,\ r)}}{\bar{\varepsilon}(SM, i|LC)} > 0$$

$$vs(MM|LC) = \frac{1}{\bar{\varepsilon}(MM,\ i|LC)} \cdot \frac{\varepsilon(MM,\ r)}{\varepsilon(L,\ r)} > 0$$

Both shifts are positive. An increase in the loan ceiling thus raises both curves. We immediately determine that an increase in the loan ceiling raises the interest rate on security markets. This may sound somewhat surprising to those conditioned by the official rhetoric interpreting an increase on LC as an expansionary policy and a lower LC as a move to more restrictive policy. This interpretation seems impressionistically obvious. An increase in LC surely means a relaxation of a constraint and lowering LC involves tightening a constraint. But the official rhetoric obscures the adjustments imposed on asset markets with loan ceilings. An increase in the loan ceiling in the range of effective constraint (i.e., $LC < \alpha aUB$) raises indeed the stock supply of loans and tends "to ease the loan market" immediately. But it also lowers the banks' absorption (aUB-LC) of securities and disrupts the security market by creating an excess supply. A major aspect of the loan ceiling thus involves a coercive reallocation of bank assets between loan and security market. It can be and is effectively used to force a reduction in the interest rate on government securities by lowering LC at the cost of private bank borrowers. This is achieved by creating a captive market for government securities at the banks via lower LC.

We still need to examine whether this allocative and relative price effect could possibly dominate the aggregative effects of a ceiling policy. The effect of LC on P and r needs still to be considered at this stage. The response of P depends on the relative magnitude of the two vertical shifts. An inspection of the respective formulae yields an inconclusive result. The ratio of the two vertical shifts is given by:

$$\frac{vs(SM|LC)}{vs(MM|LC)} = \frac{\frac{LC}{S} - \frac{\varepsilon(SM, r)}{\varepsilon(L, r)}}{\varepsilon(MM, r)} \cdot \frac{\bar{\varepsilon}(MM, i|LC)}{\bar{\varepsilon}(SM, i|LC)} \cdot \varepsilon(L, r)$$

With a ratio exceeding unity an increase of LC raises P, and a ratio less than unity lowers P. The first factor probably exceeds unity and rises with the relative importance of the loan portfolio. The second factor is less than unity according to our fundamental order condition and the last factor barely exceeds unity. The result is somewhat inconclusive but excludes any major response of P to variations in LC.

Lastly, the net effect of LC on the loan rate is determined by

$$\varepsilon(r, LC) = \frac{1-\overset{+}{\varepsilon(L, i)} \cdot \overset{+}{\varepsilon(i, LC)} - \overset{+}{\varepsilon(L, P)} \cdot \varepsilon(P, LC)}{\varepsilon(L, r)} \sim$$

$$\frac{1-\varepsilon(L, i) \cdot \varepsilon(i, LC)}{\varepsilon(L, r)}$$

One notes that the interaction with the security market lowers the response of the loan rate to variations in LC. The response remains most probably negative. We obtain thus the following patterns: A lower loan ceiling raises the loan rate r, lowers the interest rate i on securities and nudges P in some inconclusive but very minor way. It follows that variations of a loan ceiling are essentially a device to modify the interest rate on government securities relative to the borrowing cost of the private sector. It is thus an allocative instrument effectively used by the government for the better exploitation of the private sector of the economy. This fact is obscured by a rhetoric which attributes significance to the loan ceiling for purposes of macro policy. But the aggregative effects of this policy are negligible. It essentially changes relative interest rates. It should be noted that the general pattern of the results beyond some detail is not affected by the specific formulation of the constraint. The same result emerges when the asset allocation constraint $\alpha \leqslant \bar{\alpha}$ ($\bar{\alpha}$ given) replaces the constraint $\alpha a \cdot UB \leqslant LC$. Similar results appear when the constraint applies to incremental changes beyond a given base.

6. An Extension of the Model: The Explicit Interaction Between Domestic and Foreign Asset Markets

The discussion of external influences on the domestic asset market offers an opportunity to subsume the full interaction between foreign and domestic asset markets into the analysis. The effect of feedback loops operating via the foreign asset markets are explored in this section. The system of three equations describing the domestic asset market must be supplemented for our purposes with a corresponding set of asset market equations associated with the foreign economy. The foreign asset markets need no explicit statement. They occur as mirror images of the domestic markets. The properties of the domestic asset market responses thus carry over immediately to the foreign asset markets. This can be presented somewhat more formally. The solutions of the domestic asset market equation yield the following expressions:

$$i = i(NB, S; y, y^{\star}, i^{\star}, P^{\star}, \ldots)$$

$$P = P(NB, S; y, y^{\star}; i^{\star}, P^{\star}, \ldots)$$

$$r = r(NB, S; y, y^{\star}; i^{\star}, P^{\star}, \ldots)$$

where NB is the net monetary base defined as

$$NB = UB - NFPP = NDSC + CCAB$$

the "unborrowed base" minus the public's net foreign position. The output variables y, y^*, operate via human wealth and the expected net yield on real capital. The previous sections of this paper discussed the major properties of these solution functions with references to the fundamental diagram. The foreign asset markets yield analogous solution functions

$$i^* = i^* (NB^*, S^*; y^*, y; i, P, \ldots)$$

and similarly for P^* and r^*. The properties of these solution functions need no special examination. The previous results immediately extend to this case also.

The properties discussed omitted however the interaction between the domestic and foreign asset markets. An increase in NB or S in the domestic markets was examined while holding all conditions on the foreign asset markets constant. No spillover was allowed. But changes in i and P associated with the redistribution of securities between foreign and domestic portfolios disrupt foreign asset markets. The resulting modifications of i^* and P^* impose moreover new adjustments on the domestic asset markets. This interaction is formally visible in the two sets of solution functions, where each set contains interest rate and asset price of the other area as an argument. We examine thus at this stage the mode and consequences of this interaction between asset markets and explore in particular its effect on the response of i and P to domestic policies.

Some notational changes will be useful for our purposes. The responses of the domestic asset markets without incorporation of the interaction with foreign asset markets are written as elasticities $\varepsilon(i, x|AM)$ or $\varepsilon(P, x|AM)$, x = any argument of the solution function. The conditioning term AM directs the reader's attention to the fact that these elasticities express the properties of the solution functions stated above and derived from the isolated interaction of the domestic asset markets. Similarly, we use the elasticities $\varepsilon(i^\star, x^\star|AM^\star)$ and $\varepsilon(P^\star, x^\star|AM^\star)$ to describe the properties of the solution functions associated with the foreign asset markets. We repeat here, that these elasticities have been described and derived in the previous sections. They form now our building blocks for the analysis of the interaction between foreign and domestic asset markets.

The procedure is very simple and need not detain us. We replace the occurrences of $i^\star$ and $P^\star$ in the "domestic solution functions" with their respective foreign solution functions and derive then the full responses of i and P to changes in domestic and foreign conditions. In particular, differentiation with respect to the net monetary base NB of the "domestic solution equations" after proper replacement of $i^\star$ and $P^\star$ yield the following linear system:

$$\begin{bmatrix} 1-a_{11} & a_{12} \\ a_{21} & 1-a_{22} \end{bmatrix} \begin{bmatrix} z_1 \\ z_2 \end{bmatrix} = \begin{bmatrix} \varepsilon(i, NB|AM) \\ \varepsilon(P, NB|AM) \end{bmatrix}$$

where $z_1 = \varepsilon(i, NB|AM\text{-}AM^\star)$ and $z_2 = \varepsilon(P, NB|AM\text{-}AM^\star)$ describe the full responses incorporating the feedback between foreign and domestic asset markets. This is indicated by the conditioning term $AM-AM^{\star}$. The coefficients in the matrix are defined as follows:

$$a_{11} = \varepsilon(i, i^{\star}|AM) \cdot \varepsilon(i^{\star}, i|AM^{\star}) + \varepsilon(i, P^{\star}|AM) \cdot \varepsilon(P^{\star}, i|AM^{\star}) > 0$$

$$a_{12} = -[\varepsilon(i, i^{\star}|AM) \cdot \varepsilon(i^{\star}, P|AM^{\star}) + \varepsilon(i, P^{\star}|AM) \cdot \varepsilon(P^{\star}, P|AM^{\star})] > 0$$

$$a_{21} = -[\varepsilon(P, i^{\star}|AM) \cdot \varepsilon(i^{\star}, i|AM^{\star}) + \varepsilon(P, P^{\star}|AM) \cdot \varepsilon(P^{\star}, i|AM^{\star})] \sim 0$$

$$a_{22} = \varepsilon(P, i^{\star}|AM) \cdot \varepsilon(i^{\star}, P|AM^{\star}) + \varepsilon(P, P^{\star}|AM) \cdot \varepsilon(P^{\star}, P|AM^{\star}) > 0$$

All the terms defining the coefficients a_{ij} are response patterns explicitly discussed in our previous examinations. The reader should remember here that $\varepsilon(P, i^{\star}|AM)$ is approximately zero. This result immediately extends to $\varepsilon(P^{\star}, i|AM^{\star})$, the mirror image of the domestic pattern. It follows that $a_{21} \sim 0$. Moreover, a_{11} is approximated by its first term and a_{22} by its second term. The a_{11}-term thus describes a feedback from i via $i^{\star}$, and the a_{22}-term a feedback from P via $P^{\star}$. The positive a_{12}-term describes on the other hand the feedbacks from i via $i^{\star}$ to P and from i via $P^{\star}$ to P. Lastly, for credit markets with imperfect substitutabilities we have $a_{11} < 1 > a_{22}$.

With these preparations we obtain the full response of i and P to a change in the net monetary base NB.

$$\varepsilon(i, NB|AM-AM^{\star}) = \frac{1}{1-a_{11}} \left[\varepsilon(i, NB|AM) - \frac{a_{12}}{1-a_{22}} \varepsilon(P, NB|AM)\right] < 0$$

$$\varepsilon(P, NB|AM-AM^{\star}) = \frac{1}{1-a_{22}} \cdot \varepsilon(P, NB|AM) > 0$$

The full response thus emerges in general as a linear combination of the partial responses. The coefficients of the linear combination express the interaction between the domestic and foreign asset markets. They generally increase in value with the degree of interconnection exhibited by the asset markets. A major result of the interaction becomes immediately visible upon inspection. The full response to a change in the domestic base exceeds the partial response for both interest rate i and asset price level P. The monetary impulse initiated by domestic policy is thus <u>amplified</u> by the interaction between the asset markets of two distinct economic areas. We note in the case of the asset price level P that this amplification results from the feedback via the responses of P^* in the foreign asset markets. Changes in P induced by NB affect P^* via the substitutability between securities and real assets in each economy and the substitutability between nationally designated securities, and these changes in P^* affect again P. The nature of this feedback reenforces the "direct effect" of NB on P.

The negligible dependence of P on changes in i^*, or of P^* on i, removes any contribution of feedbacks via i^* to the total effect of NB on P. We observe in the case of i however two distinct channels in the amplification of the response beyond the partial effect $\varepsilon(i, NB|AM)$. This response is first multiplied with a coefficient $(1-a_{11})^{-1}$ expressing the feedback from i via i^* to i. A fall in i spills over via the interconnected securities markets and lowers i^*. But this induced fall in i^* feeds back into a further fall of i. This feedback loop thus operates with a multiplicative coefficient exceeding unity on the partial interest response $\varepsilon(i, NB|AM)$. A second channel amplifying the response of i occurs additively. It expresses the interconnections between i and P resulting via the interdependence of the asset markets. Changes in P induce adjustments in $P^\star$ and $i^\star$ which reenforcingly affect again i. This channel is expressed by the coefficient a_{12}. It is further reenforced by the loop from P over $P^\star$ back to P expressed by a_{22}. These magnifying feedbacks on i centered on P are set in train by the initial (or partial) reaction in P to a change in NB. The magnifying coefficient $a_{12}(1-a_{22})^{-1}$ is therefore multiplied with the partial elasticity $\varepsilon(P, NB|AM)$.

A somewhat different pattern emerges for changes in the stock of government securities S. Exploitation of formal similarity immediately yields the expressions:

$$\varepsilon(i, S|AM-AM^\star) = \frac{1}{1-a_{11}} [\varepsilon(i, S|AM) - \frac{a_{12}}{1-a_{22}} \cdot \varepsilon(P, S|AM)]$$

$$\varepsilon(P,S|AM-AM^\star) = \frac{1}{1-a_{22}} \cdot \varepsilon(P, S|AM) > \varepsilon(P, S|AM) > 0$$

The interaction between the asset markets again <u>amplifies</u> unambiguously the response of P. The initial domestic response of P is reenforced by the resulting adjustments of $P^\star$ and their spillover back to P. The situation concerning i is somewhat ambiguous however. We already noted the operation of two distinct channels. The first unambiguously enlarges the total response by multiplying the partial response with $(1-a_{11})^{-1} > 1$. This amplification reflects again the loop from i to $i^\star$ back to i. But the second channel works in the opposite direction to attenuate the response of i. An increase in S also raises P and this spills over into a lower $i^\star$ as a result of the investor's portfolio adjustments between real and financial assets and the substitutability between nationally designated securities. But the lower $i^\star$ induces further adjustments. The domestic securities are relatively attractive under the circumstances and investors will substitute domestic for foreign securities. The result is a relative decline in i. The second channel initiated by the increase in P induces adjustments of the asset markets <u>moderating</u> the total response of i.

The interconnection between the asset markets exposes the domestic economy to the policy actions of the foreign area expressed by changes in $NB^\star$ and $S^\star$. The nature of foreign influences conveyed via interdependent credit markets also deserves our attention. We introduce for this purpose the "partial effect" of $NB^\star$ (or $S^\star$) on i and P defined by the expressions:

$$\varepsilon(i, NB^\star | pe) = \overset{+}{\varepsilon(i, i^\star | AM)} \cdot \overset{-}{\varepsilon(i^\star, NB^\star | AM^\star)} + \overset{-}{\varepsilon(i, P^\star | AM)} \cdot \overset{+}{\varepsilon(P^\star, NB^\star | AM)} < 0$$

$$\varepsilon(P, NB^\star | pe) \sim \overset{+}{\varepsilon(P, P^\star | AM)} \cdot \overset{+}{\varepsilon(P^\star, NB^\star | AM^\star)} > 0$$

The terms of the partial effect contain only the isolated adjustments of each area's asset markets. The direct effect of $NB^\star$ on P occurs as a product of two factors. The first factor describes the response of P to $P^\star$ omitting any interaction between the two areas, and the second denotes the response of $P^\star$ to $NB^\star$ disregarding any interaction. The expressions for $S^\star$ are obtained by suitable replacement of NB^* in the statements above. The resulting partial effects $\varepsilon(i, S^*|pe)$ and $\varepsilon(P, S^*|pe)$ are both positive. The total response including the effect of interdependent credit markets is again expressed by the formula:

$$\varepsilon(i, NB^*|AM\text{-}AM^*) = \frac{1}{1-a_{11}} [\varepsilon(i, NB^*|pe) - \frac{a_{12}}{1-a_{22}} \cdot \varepsilon(P, NB^*|pe)] < 0$$

$$\varepsilon(P, NB^*|AM\text{-}AM^*) = \frac{1}{1-a_{22}} \cdot \varepsilon(P, NB^*|pe) > 0$$

In both cases the partial effect is augmented by the interaction between the asset markets of the two areas. An expansion of the base in the foreign economy thus induces spillovers and introduces via the adjustments of the asset markets expansionary impulses into the domestic economy.

We omit the obvious extension to S^* and attend to an aspect disregarded thus far. The amplifying role of the interaction between the asset markets of the two areas depends on a more or less similar order of magnitude for the two areas. Their relative size should not be too dissimilar. The amplifying interaction vanishes in the relation between large and small areas. This is implied by the circumstance that in highly asymmetric contexts one element in the pairs of elasticities $[\varepsilon(i, i^*|AM), \varepsilon(i^*, i|AM)]$ and $[\varepsilon(P, P^*|AM), \varepsilon(P^*, P|AM^*)]$ vanishes. For a small domestic economy the elasticities $\varepsilon(i^*, i|AM^*)$ and $\varepsilon(P^*, P|AM^*)$ vanish for instance. It follows that extreme asymmetry implis $a_{11} \sim a_{22} \sim a_{12} \sim 0$. The full response of i and P to domestic or foreign events is therefore approximately equal under the circumstances to the partial effect defined by the isolated operation of domestic asset markets determined without incorporation of the interaction effect. This does not mean, however, that the response of i and P are independent of the relative size of the domestic economy. The effect of relative size on the partial responses has been explained sufficiently in the section covering changes in the base and securities. A vanishing interaction effect does not preclude the working of larger or smaller substitution relations between nationally designated securities reenforced by the weight of relative allocations expressed by IDF/S and IFD/S. These weights attached to the elasticities of the unborrowed base are much larger for the small economy than for the large economy.

TABLE I

$$s\ell(SM|LC) = -\frac{\bar{\varepsilon}(SM, P|LC)}{\bar{\varepsilon}(SM, i|LC)}\ ; \quad s\ell(MM|LC) = -\frac{\bar{\varepsilon}(MM, P|LC)}{\bar{\varepsilon}(MM, i|LC)}$$

where

$$\bar{\varepsilon}(SM, P|LC) = \varepsilon(SM, P|LC) - \frac{\varepsilon(SM, r|LC)}{\varepsilon(L, r)} \cdot \varepsilon(L, P) > 0$$

$$\bar{\varepsilon}(SM, i|LC) = \varepsilon(SM, i|LC) - \frac{\varepsilon(SM, r|LC)}{\varepsilon(L, r)} \cdot \varepsilon(L, i) > 0$$

$$\bar{\varepsilon}(MM, P|LC) = \varepsilon(MM, P) - \frac{\varepsilon(MM, r)}{\varepsilon(L, r)} \cdot \varepsilon(L, P) < 0$$

$$\bar{\varepsilon}(MM, i|LC) = \varepsilon(MM, i) - \frac{\varepsilon(MM, r)}{\varepsilon(L, r)} \cdot \varepsilon(L, i) > 0$$

with $\varepsilon(SM, P|LC) = [\varepsilon(a, P) + \varepsilon(UB, P)] \frac{a.UB}{S} + \varepsilon(IDD, P)\frac{IDD}{S}$

$$\varepsilon(SM, i|LC) = [\varepsilon(a, i) + \varepsilon(UB, i)] \frac{a \cdot UB}{S} + \varepsilon(IDD, i)\frac{IDD}{S} + \varepsilon(IFD, i)\frac{IFD}{S} > 0$$

$$\varepsilon(SM, r|LC) = [\varepsilon(a, r) + \varepsilon(UB, r)] \frac{a \cdot UB}{S} + \varepsilon(IDD, r)\frac{IDD}{S}$$

The relation between the elasticities of the excess demand of securities under the loan constraints with the corresponding elasticities without loan constraint can be exhibited as follows:

$$\varepsilon(SM, i|LC) = \varepsilon(SM, i) + [\overset{-}{\varepsilon(\alpha, i)} + \overset{+}{\varepsilon(a, i)} + \overset{+}{\varepsilon(UB, i)}] \frac{\alpha\, a \cdot UB}{S}$$

$$\varepsilon(SM, P|LC) = \varepsilon(SM, P) + [\overset{+}{\varepsilon(a, P)} + \overset{-}{\varepsilon(UB, P)}] \frac{\alpha \cdot a \cdot UB}{S} < \varepsilon(SM, P)$$

$$\varepsilon(SM, r|LC) = \varepsilon(SM, r) + [\overset{+}{\varepsilon(\alpha, r)} + \overset{+}{\varepsilon(a, r)} + \overset{+}{\varepsilon(UB, r)}] \cdot \frac{\alpha \cdot a \cdot UB}{S} > \varepsilon(SM, r)$$

IV. Concluding Remarks

The analysis of the money supply process previously developed was modified in two major respects in the current paper. The aggregated credit market was separated into a loan market and a security market. Moreover, the domestic asset markets interact with the asset markets of another economic area. This interaction between open economies was centered on the security markets. On a purely formal level it was shown that the diagrammatic exposition used for the closed economy with the associated interpretation essentially extends to the analysis of the more general case of an open economy incorporating an explicit interaction between loan and security market. On a substantive level the analysis demonstrated that open economies with interdependent credit markets do not suffer a total impotence of domestic monetary policy over the shorter run. Changes in the domestic source component of the monetary base modify interest rates and the asset price level. The degree of substitutability between nationally designated securities determines the responsiveness of domestic interest rates to domestic policies. A high substitutability removes interest rates as a channel conveying monetary impulses initiated by the domestic Central Bank. But the channel operated by the asset price level P continues to convey policy impulses. These conditions moderate on the other hand the impact of variations in the outstanding stock of government securities on the domestic asset markets.

The role of foreign influences was also examined. It emerged that changes in foreign interest rates produce a small effect on the domestic money stock. Variations in the foreign asset price level induce in contrast substantially larger repercussions for the domestic money stock. The paper examined also the patterns generated by the interaction between the asset markets of two economic areas. The interaction between areas with similar magnitude amplifies the responsiveness of interest rates and asset price level with respect to domestic policies. It reenforces thus the monetary impulse initiated by suitable Central Bank action. An explicit account of the interaction also modifies the pattern previously summarized, a pattern associated with the degree of substitutability between distinct national securities. A higher degree of substitutability raises monotonically the amplification produced by the interaction effect. The latter offsets thus the smaller responsiveness in interest rates determined by the domestic asset market in the absence of any feedbacks via foreign asset markets. It follows that an extensive substitutability between securities of two areas is not a sufficient condition to block transmission of monetary impulses via the interest rate channel. Transmission via this channel will be blocked on the other hand for a small country with extremely "substitutable" securities. The amplification of the interaction effect was shown to vanish for economies with highly dissimilar relative magnitudes.

Lastly, the paper investigated the functioning of a quantitative loan ceiling. This measure has frequently been justified as an important instrument of aggregative stabilization policy. The analysis demonstrated that variations in the loan ceiling essentially affect relative interest rates with a negligible aggregative spillover. The official rhetoric thus appears as a camouflage obscuring the crucial function of the loan ceiling designed to lower interest rates on government securities relative to the private borrowing rate. The official rhetoric is also bound to create a problem of its own. The public's attention guided by the media will be directed away from relevant anti-inflationary measures. Moreover, the official rhetoric places a burden on loan ceilings they cannot bear. It should barely affect the economy's macro-development. The official rhetoric thus fosters a pattern of apparent intractability of inflation in the face of "decisive actions", when inflation was never really exposed to any relevant financial action.

DOMESTIC BANK CREDIT, MONEY AND THE OPEN ECONOMY

By Michele Fratianni

I. Introduction and Summary of Conclusions

Central bankers have always been worried about controlling bank credit;[1] whereas economists have traditionally ignored this variable in favor of the money stock. In those papers where the distinction is made between bank credit and the money stock, it is often stated that one is the mirror image of the other. In the pioneering works of Friedman and Schwartz (1963) and Cagan (1965) relatively little effort is devoted to a careful differentiation of the two concepts. Some of the earlier writers in money and banking were aware of the distinction between bank credit and money but their efforts were directed, for the most part, to demonstrate the fallacies of the real bills doctrine [e.g. Hawtrey (1932 and

This paper was written while the author was a Visiting Professor at the Katholieke Universiteit te Leuven. I thank André Fourçans, Jacques Melitz and Johan Verstraete for their comments on earlier drafts of the paper.

1) The emphasis on bank credit rather than on the money stock is apparent in most of the official documents of the central banks and the Annual Reports of the BIS.

1950) and Mints (1945)] rather than constructing testable hypotheses. Illuminating exceptions to this trend in the literature are Tobin and Brainard (1963), Tobin (1969) and Brunner and Meltzer (1964, 1966, 1968). Although there is a formal equivalence between the Tobin-Brainard hypothesis and the Brunner-Meltzer model, the latter is much more constrained and thus yields tighter test implications. Bank credit for Brunner and Meltzer was set at center stage as the market where the bank credit rate is "proximately" determined. This view stands in sharp contrast with most models, including larger econometric models such as the FRB-MIT, which envision the money market rate as determined by the demand and supply of money [cf. Teigen (1964), Modigliani-Rasche-Cooper (1970)]. The money stock was also shown to respond to the bank credit rate and other autonomous forces in a way so substantially different from bank credit to justify a clear separation between the two concepts. The result was a rather sophisticated hypothesis and yet extremely amenable to empirical verification under various institutional settings. Developed primarily for the U.S. monetary system, the hypothesis was however incomplete in the sense that no allowance was made for the domestic bank credit and money markets to interact with their international counterparts. The European institutional setting was the ideal place for such an extension. This was done by Fratianni (1971, 1972) with regard to Italy, Willms (1971), Siebke (1972) and Neumann (1974) with respect to Germany, Korteweg (1973) for Holland, Fourçans (1974) for France and Heremans-Sommariva-Verheirstraeten (1974) for Belgium. Brunner (1973) extended the Brunner-Meltzer hypothesis to an open economy partly based on the European experience.

In this paper I intend to provide a general framework of the financial sector of an economy which interacts with an international money market under a regime of fixed or policy-controlled exchange rates. The economy I am referring to has two distinguishing characteristics: its currency is not an international medium of exchange (i.e., it is not a model applicable to the United States) and faces exogenously determined "foreign" interest rates.

The framework is set out in detail in Section II and then compressed in three equilibrium conditions in Section III. The major implications of the hypothesis are explored in Section IV. In Section V I set out some empirical tests based on Italian data. In Section VI I discuss some issues concerning the controllability of the monetary base in an open economy under fixed exchange rates and no restrictions on capital movements.

The vehicle of analysis serves a variety of purposes. First and foremost, it intends to provide a suitable econometric specification for the demand and supply schedules of the government securities market, the commercial loan market and the money market. Second, it wants to stress that monetary policy need not be impotent in a regime of fixed exchange rates. The effectiveness of monetary policy does not depend uniquely on the relative substitution between capital and securities versus capital and money as is the case in the Tobin (1969) framework. The interpretation of whether policy is expansionary or contractive is more complicated when the impact of policy is measured in terms of changes of the interest rates on securities, loan and capital. In some cases, policy is expansionary insofar as the security and loan rates are concerned, but is contractive when measured in terms of changes in the rate of return on capital. Monetary policy need not be powerless even in the face of perfectly offsetting capital flows. Empirical tests which have shown that for some countries the endogenous foreign component of the base offsets dollar for dollar changes in the domestic and policy-controlled base corroborate only one of the two conditions which must be satisfied to completely disable policy in a regime of fixed exchange rates. The other condition is that, as capital flows in and out of the home country, the foreign demand for domestic security is not affected. But once domestic securities are traded, a capital outflow, "offsetting" an autonomous injection of base money, implies a reduction in the foreign holdings of domestic securities and thus a downward shift in the aggregate demand for domestic securities. The rate of interest is altered even though the total amount of base money has not.

An increase in the Eurodollar rate has a general expansionary effect via the rate of return on capital but is deflationary via the security and the loan rates.

The impact of a devaluation depends, as we would expect, on two opposing forces. The asset readjustments induced by a devaluation have a deflationary bias, while its effects on the balance of payments may be taken to be generally expansionary.

The model is also analyzed under the assumption that loans and securities are perfect substitutes. The implications of the model so constrained are more robust, in the sense that they are more easily refutable, than the implications of the unconstrained model. The structural equations of the constrained bank credit market and of the money supply equation were estimated using Italian data over the period 1958-1972.

The notable results of the empirical research are that the monetary base is the dominating force in both the supply of bank credit and money; that the public's decisions in demanding bank credit are strongly "conditioned" by its real financial wealth and permanent income; that the real and not the nominal bank credit interest rate is the relevant price to which the public responds; that neither the Eurodollar deposit nor the ratio of the forward to the spot exchange rate has a significant impact on the bank credit market (work is now in progress to disaggregate the model so as to identify the channels through which these two variables may leave a noticeable trace); that the influence of the open economy on the demand for bank credit was found to operate via the stock of international reserves as a proxy of those foreign variables which affect the foreign demand for domestic securities; that the interest elasticity of the supply of bank credit is at least four times as large as the demand which, in turn, is quite small (-0.12).

Finally, no evidence was found that an increase in the supply of securities raises the public's demand for bank credit by an equivalent amount, suggesting that loans and securities are less than perfect substitutes.

II. The Framework of Analysis

Our economy has three domestic economic operators and the foreign public. The domestic operators are the nonbank public, the commercial banks and the central authorities. The relevant assets and liabilities considered in this paper of the nonbank public and the commercial banks are those described by equations (1) and (2) below (see Table 1 for an explanation of the symbols). Briefly, the public allocates his wealth among real capital, monetary assets and government securities. In addition, it borrows from banks. The open economy, and more importantly the existence of an international money market to which we shall refer for convenience as the Eurodollar market, significantly enlarges the range of assets and liabilities. I shall allow the domestic public to hold Eurodollar deposits and foreign (denominated in dollars) securities, as well as to borrow in the Eurodollar market. Balance sheets (1) and (2)

$$(1) \quad B^{p} + D + ED\Pi + S^{p} + S_{f}^{p}\Pi + K = L + EL\Pi + NW$$

$$(2) \quad B^{db} + L + S^{b} + (FR + FA)\Pi = D + FL\Pi + A$$

are denominated in domestic currency since all dollar-denominated assets and liabilities are multiplied by the exchange rate Π, the domestic price of the dollar. I shall further simplify the analysis by restricting the domestic public to keep dollar deposits with and obtain dollar loans from only nondomestic banks. The latter, therefore, operate in the Eurodollar market only with nonresidents. Such a simplification is here made so as to allow changes in the net foreign position of banks, $\Pi(FR + FA - FL)$, and the public, Π(ED - EL) to be fully reflected in the balance of payments. Basevi (1973) clearly brings out the divergence existing between balance-of-payments changes and changes in the foreign exchange market when the domestic public holds deposits with and borrows from domestic banks in a currency other than its own.

The stock of international reserves owned by the central bank is thus defined

$$(3) \quad Ir = Ir_{-1} + TA - (S_f^{\hat{p}}\Pi) + \hat{S}^f - \Pi(FR + \hat{FA} - FL) - \Pi(ED \hat{-} EL)$$

where the "^" sign indicates domestic currency change in the variable over a specified time interval. Equation (3) is, of course, a simplification of a "real-world" balance of payments but has the advantage of highlighting the items which are of interest in this paper. An important omission is net interest payments which would have somewhat complicated the interpretation of some of the results of the analysis. Capital, in addition, is assumed to be a non-traded asset.

By suitable summation over time (3) can be rewritten, assumming that Π has been kept unchanged, as

$$(4) \quad Ir = CTA_{-1} + TA - \Pi S_f^p + S^f - \Pi(FR + FA - FL) - \Pi(ED - EL)$$

The term CTA_{-1} represents the cumulative history up to period t-1 of the trade account. TA is the current flow of exports minus imports which depends on domestic and foreign output and prices and on the exchange rate

$$(5) \quad TA = TA(\underset{-}{y}, \underset{+}{y^{\star}}, \underset{-}{p}, \underset{+}{p^{\star}}, \underset{+}{\Pi})$$

TA is given for given values of y, $y^{\star}$, p, $p^{\star}$ and Π.

1. The Behavior of the Domestic Public

The first important point to be made is that the net worth of the public is a datum. This can be clearly seen by nothing the equilibrium condition in the output market in an open economy.

$$\text{(6)} \qquad \text{Real Saving} = \text{Real Investment} + \frac{\text{Def}}{p_a} + \frac{\text{TA}}{p_a}$$

The government finances his deficit by either issuing base money or securities:

$$\text{(6a)} \qquad \text{Def} = \hat{B}^T + \hat{S}$$

The average price level p_a is related to the price level of domestic output and foreign output prices according to the following definition

$$\text{(6b)} \qquad p_a = w_1 p + (1 - w_1) p^{\star} \Pi$$

where the weight w_1 represents the proportion of domestic absorption produced domestically. Without loss of generality, we can set initially $p = p^{\star} = \Pi = 1$; it follows that

$$\text{(7)} \qquad \text{Saving} = \hat{NW} = \hat{K} + \hat{B}^T + \hat{S} + \text{TA}$$

It follows that $\hat{NW}$ is given for given values of K, B^T, S, y, $y^{\star}$, p, $p^{\star}$ and Π.[2)] Note that, although Π is set by policy decisions,

2) The application of this model, as in most others of similar nature, is restricted to that time period during which changes in the monetary and financial variables can influence prices and output but not vice versa.

TABLE 1

Symbols Used in the Paper

Superscripts

b = domestic banks

f = foreign public

p = domestic public

★ = rest of the world

A	=	banks' borrowing from the central bank
$A^{\star}$	=	FL - FA
BC	=	domestic bank credit
B^D	=	the exogenous component of the monetary base in an open economy = B^T + CTA
B^{db}	=	domestic component of the monetary base held by banks
B^F	=	foreign component of the monetary base
B^p	=	public-held base money
B^T	=	monetary base created through the operation of the government's deficit and open market operations
b_F	=	$A^{\star}/D$
b_H	=	A/D
CK	=	net foreign liabilities of the government and non-bank public
CTA	=	cumulative trade account balance
D	=	domestic deposits
Def	=	government budget deficit
ED	=	Eurodollar deposits
EL	=	Eurodollar loans
FA	=	foreign assets (denominated in dollars) of banks
FL	=	foreign liabilities (denominated in dollars) of banks

TABLE 1
(Continued)

FR	=	foreign reserves of banks
Ir	=	stock of international reserves owned by the central bank
i_D	=	rate of return on domestic deposits
i_{ED}	=	rate of return on Eurodollar deposits
i_{EL}	=	Eurodollar loan rate
i_f	=	rate of return on foreign government securities
i_K	=	rate of return on capital
i_L	=	domestic loan rate
i_S	=	rate of return on domestic government securities
K	=	capital stock
k	=	B^p/D
L	=	domestic loans
M	=	money stock
NW	=	net worth
p	=	domestic output price level
p_a	=	average price level
r	=	B^b/D
r_E	=	excess reserve ratio
r_R	=	required reserve ratio on domestic deposits
S	=	stock of domestic government securities
S_f	=	stock of foreign (denominated in dollars) government securities
TA	=	the current trade account balance
y	=	real activity variable of the home country
Π	=	spot exchange rate (domestic-currency price of the dollar)
Π^F	=	forward exchange rate
ρ	=	discount rate
χ	=	index of international trade

it need not remain constant over time; as a matter of fact it can change as often as desired but in a manner which is independent of the market forces described in this model.

The behavior of the public follows the well-known principles of the theory of portfolio choice [cf. Tobin (1969)]. Assets are postulated to be gross substitutes. An increase in the "own" yield raises the demand for the asset. An increase in the "cross" yields produces a substitution as well as an income effect. The latter will tend to raise the demand for all the assets combined, while the former induces a substitution in favor of the asset whose yield has risen. It is generally assumed that the substitution effect prevails over the income effect. All assets have a pecuniary yield except base money holdings. Money is demanded because it allows a higher per capita output by lowering the amount of resources absorbed by the exchange of goods and services [see Brunner and Meltzer (1971)].

The dollar is the international medium of exchange. It has a comparative advantage over other currencies expressed in the form of transaction and information costs. Domestic residents hold both domestic and dollar money, the latter as deposits with banks outside the United States. Both types of money are substitutes but not perfect. First, the returns are different on the two types of money. Second, domestic money is not accepted for international transactions; dollars are not legal tender at home. Therefore, the public must bear transaction costs as well as exchange rate risks in converting one type of money into the other. One manner for the public to insure against the risk of a currency depreciation is to enter the forward market. Thus, the net rate of return on a dollar-denominated asset is equal to the promised yield minus the cost of the cover which is equal to

$$1 - \frac{\Pi^F}{\Pi}$$

One unit of domestic currency today will bring Π^F / Π units in the future.[3] As $\Pi^F \gtrless \Pi$, the costs of the cover is negative, zero or positive. Expectations of a dollar devaluation imply $\Pi^F < \Pi$.

A second way to obtain protection against the effects of a devaluation is to keep a zero net foreign asset position. It follows that as the cost of the cover rises the public is induced to raise its dollar indebtedness vis-a-vis the banks.

In addition to interest rates, the asset demand functions are positively related to the average price level p_a and the net worth NW. The influence of loan rates on asset demands has been ignored except on the demand for capital because they are considered important to the second degree.[4]

In a similar vein, the public's demand for loans is inversely related to its "own" price and positively to its "cross" prices,

---

3) One unit of domestic currency can buy $1/\Pi$ dollars. Covering the foreign exchange position requires to sell dollars forward at a rate Π^F per dollar of investment. Given the original dollar investment of $1/\Pi$, $\Pi^F[\frac{1}{\Pi}]$ is the number of units of domestic currency obtained by the forward operation.
4) An increase in the rate paid on L provokes a substitution in favor of EL as well as a decline in L + EL, consequently lowering the public's demand for all assets combined.

while the effect of asset yields on borrowing demand functions has been ignored. The rate paid on a Eurodollar loan must be adjusted for exchange-rate risk. The cost of the forward cover in this case is $1 - \Pi / \Pi^F$. 5)

The functional specification of the public's behavior is summarized in Table 2. Notice that for a given NW one of the demand functions is implicitly determined by the balance sheet constraint (1). The demand for capital will be dropped in the remainder of the analysis. Portfolio-choice theory also requires that the global effect of a change in any of the arguments affecting the public's behavior on the demand for $B^p + D + ED + S^p + S_f^p + K - L - EL$ has to add up to zero, with the exception of NW of course. The same exception holds for p_a and the trade variable χ which directly alter NW via the trade account.

2. The Behavior of the Foreign Public

The foreign public demands domestic government securities

$$(16) \quad S^f = S^f(\underset{+}{i_S}, \underset{-}{i_f}, \underset{-}{\Pi^F / \Pi}, \underset{+}{p^\star}, \underset{+}{y^\star}, \ldots)$$

Only the arguments which have a direct bearing on the hypothesis

---

5) One dollar today can be exchanged for units of domestic currency. The borrower enters into a forward purchase of dollars to coincide with the repayment of his dollar loan. One unit of domestic currency can purchase $1/\Pi^F$ dollars forward or Π/Π^F per dollar of loan.

TABLE 2 - Behavior of the Domestic Public

Signs of the Partial Derivatives

	i_k	i_S	i_f	i_D	i_{ED}	i_L	i_{EL}	Π^F/Π	p_a	NW	χ
(8) B^p	-	-	-	-	-			-	+	+	
(9) D	-	-	-	+	-			-	+	+	
(10) ED	-	-	-	-	+			+	+	+	+
(11) S^p	-	+	-	-	-			-	+	+	
(12) S_f^p	-	-	+	-	-			+	+	+	
(13) K	+	-	-	-	-	-	-	-	+	+	
(14) L						-	+	+	+	+	
(15) EL						+	-	-	+	+	+

have been explicitly considered in (16): the yield on domestic securities, i_S, the yield on foreign securities, i_f, the ratio Π^F/Π as well as foreign prices and real income. No substitution exists between foreign holdings of domestic securities and domestic capital on the grounds that the latter is a non-traded asset.

3. The Domestic Banks and the Central Bank

In a regime of fixed exchange rates and negligible transaction costs banks will look upon domestic and foreign reserves as almost perfect subsitutes. As banks shift from domestic to dollar reserves an excess demand for dollars develops in the foreign exchange market. With a commitment to a fixed exchange rate, the central bank will have to supply dollars in exchange for domestic reserves, B^{db}. If the equilibrium condition in the monetary base market is traditionally stated as

$$(17) \qquad B^T + A + Ir = B^p + B^{db}$$

a switch between domestic and foreign currency as described above implies a destruction of monetary base. The banks, however, do not "feel" to have lost any reserves, since they have simply altered the composition of such reserves. The domestic public also has not lost any of its monetary base. Yet, according to (17) the amount of total monetary base in the system has fallen. The problem with (17) is the failure to appropriately treat banks' foreign reserves. This shortcoming can be corrected by adding FR as a source and use of the monetary base

$$(17a)\quad B^T + A + Ir + FR = B^p + B^b$$

where now

$$(17b)\quad B^b = B^{db} + FR$$

Under flexible exchange rates, however, (17) and not (17a) is the relevant equation because domestic and foreign currency are not exchanged at a fixed price. A third case is also of some interest. A central bank may impose a convertibility constraint as was done in Italy in the 1960s. The relevant base-money market equilibrium condition in this case becomes

$$(17c)\quad B^T + A + Ir + sFR = B^p + B^b$$

where

$$(17d)\quad B^b = B^{db} + sFR$$

and s is the proportion of foreign reserves which can be freely exchanged into domestic reserves at rate Π [cf. Fratianni (1972, Section 2b and 2c)] .

Banks demand monetary base to meet reserve requirements on domestic deposits and the uncertainty of net cash withdrawals by the two types of depositors. The concrete case of reserve requirements on dollar deposits is here ignored for it would yield little, if any, to the analysis.

$$(18)\quad B^b = rD$$

$$(18a)\quad r = r_R + r_E$$

(18b) $r_E = r_E(\underset{-}{i_S}, \underset{-}{i_L}, \underset{-}{i_{EL}}, \underset{-}{\Pi^F/\Pi}, \underset{+}{\rho})$

r_R = reserve requirement ratio on domestic deposits

r_E = excess reserve ratio

Banks borrow funds from the central bank and the rest of the world. These two activities are assumed to be highly substitutable. The net cost of borrowing from the central banks is ρ; from the Eurodollar market is i_{ED} in case of an uncovered transaction and $i_{ED} + \Pi^F/\Pi - 1$ in case of a covered transaction. The rate i_{EL} is the yield on the banks' foreign assets.

(19) $A = A(\underset{+}{i_S}, \underset{+}{i_L}, \underset{+}{i_{EL}}, \underset{+}{i_{ED}}, \underset{+}{\Pi^F/\Pi}, \underset{-}{\rho})$

(20) $A^\star = FL - FA = A^\star(\underset{+}{i_S}, \underset{+}{i_L}, \underset{-}{i_{EL}}, \underset{-}{i_{ED}}, \underset{-}{\Pi^F/\Pi}, \underset{+}{\rho})$

The two functions (19) and (20) differ by the opposite impact that i_{EL}, i_{ED}, Π^F/Π and ρ exert on them.

Domestic deposits are supplied according to the proposition that interest rates on deposits adjust to the rates charged by banks on their earning assets. The Eurodollar deposit rate i_{ED} is given on the assumption that our country is a price taker and cannot influence by its own actions the Eurodollar rate. The Eurodollar loan rate, likewise, is given and is assumed to be equal to i_{ED} plus a mark-up. The size of the mark-up reflects the degree of competition in the Eurodollar market.

4. The Supply of Domestic Bank Credit

Given the balance sheet constraints (2) and (17a) and equation (18), the banks' demand for total domestic earning or supply of bank credit is derived as follows

$$(21) \quad L + S^b \equiv BC = [\frac{1-r}{r}] B^b + A + A^{\star}$$

$$= [\frac{1-r}{r}][B^T + A + B^F - B^p] + A + A^{\star}$$

where B^F is the foreign source component of the monetary base, Ir + FR. Using (4), (21) can be rewritten

$$(21a) \quad BC = [\frac{1-r}{r}][B^D + CK - B^p] + (A + A^{\star})\frac{1}{r} \quad .$$

B^D is the exogenous component of the monetary base in an open economy and is equal to B^T + CTA. CK is defined as $S^f - S^p_f$ + EL - ED and thus represents the net foreign liabilities of the government and nonbank public.

The next step is to express (21a) in functional form. Consider first the relationship between CK and the various arguments of the elements which define it

$$(22) \quad CK = CK(\underset{+}{i_K}, \underset{+}{i_S}, \underset{+}{i_L}, \underset{-}{i_f}, \underset{-}{i_{ED}}, \underset{-}{\pi^F/\pi}, \pi)$$

The impact of the yield on foreign securities on CK is negative when the substitution between these securities and domestic money and capital is relatively weak. When this substitution at the limit is nonexistent $\frac{\partial CK}{\partial i_K}$ turns out to be equal to $\frac{\partial S^f}{\partial i_f} + \frac{\partial S^p}{\partial i_f}$. 6) The partial derivative of CK with respect to i_{ED} is negative because the "own" price effect must be numerically larger than the "cross" price effect [i.e., $\frac{\partial ED}{\partial i_{ED}} > |\frac{\partial S_f^p}{\partial i_{ED}}|$]

A devaluation of the domestic currency has been associated with an improvement of the balance of payments provided the famous Marshall-Lerner conditions are satisfied. It is not readily apparent that this is so in the presence of internationally traded assets. In fact, <u>ceteris paribus</u>, a devaluation raises the net foreign liabilities of the government and the nonbank public if

(23) $$EL + (1 - w_1) \frac{\partial EL}{\partial p_a} > ED + S_f^p + (1 - w_1) [\frac{\partial S_f^p}{\partial p_a} + \frac{\partial ED}{\partial p_a}]$$

The condition is not likely to be met for a large number of countries. It appears that if devaluation has to improve the home country's balance of payments the effect of a devaluation on the trade account must be potent enough to make the l.h.s. of (23) plus $\frac{\partial TA}{\partial \Pi}$ larger than the r.h.s. of (23). At this point the only conclusion one can derive from the analysis is that the relative substitution of the domestic and foreign output markets versus the substitution of traded assets is crucial for an assessment of the influence of Π on B^F, keeping all other variables unchanged.

---

6) This result stems directly from $\frac{\partial S_f^p}{\partial i_f} + \frac{\partial ED}{\partial i_f} + \frac{\partial S^p}{\partial i_f} = 0$ when $\frac{\partial K}{\partial i_f} = \frac{\partial B^p}{\partial i_f} = \frac{\partial D}{\partial i_f} = 0$

The contribution of the demand for base money by the public in the bank credit function works to reinforce the interest-rates effects operating via CK, with the exception of i_f and i_{ED}. However, I shall assume the substitution between B^p and foreign securities, on the one hand, and Eurodollar deposits, on the other hand, to be so negligible that the total effect of i_f and i_{ED} on BC will remain negative.

Finally, one must assess the role of the two borrowing functions $A(\cdot)$ and $A^{\star}(\cdot)$ in (21a). We recall from our discussion above that i_{ED} (or i_{EL}), Π^F/Π and ρ affect $A(\cdot)$ and $A^{\star}(\cdot)$ in opposite directions. The general proposition that a market has a comparative advantage in influencing its "own" rate suggests the following order constraints:

$$\left|\frac{\partial A^{\star}}{\partial i_{ED}}\right| > \frac{\partial A}{\partial i_{ED}} \quad \text{and similarly for } \Pi^F/\Pi \;; \left|\frac{\partial A}{\partial \rho}\right| > \frac{\partial A^{\star}}{\partial \rho}$$

Consolidating the above mentioned relationships one can rewrite (21a) in the following general functional from

$$(24) \qquad BC = h^1(\underset{+}{i_S}, \underset{+}{i_L}, \underset{+}{i_K}; \underset{+}{B^D}, \underset{-}{r_R}, \underset{-}{i_f}, \underset{-}{i_{ED}}, \Pi^F/\Pi, \Pi, \ldots)$$

where the ";" separates, as usual, endogenous from exogenous variables.

5. The Supply of Money

The domestic supply of money is obtained implicitly in the system. It is the result of the interation between domestic public, domestic banks, the central bank and the foreign public. All of the terms appearing in the supply-of-money function have already been explained by the hypothesis. A useful way to present a derivation of the supply-of-money function is to begin by defining[7)]

(25) $$M = [\frac{M}{BC}]\ BC$$

Noting that $M = B^p + D$ and $BC = D + A + A^{\star} - B^b$ and multiplying both numerator and denominator of the ratio in parenthesis by $1/D$, (25) can be rewritten as

(25a) $$M = R \cdot h^1(\cdot)$$

(25b) $$R = \frac{1 + k}{1 - r + b_H + b_F}$$

(25c) $$k = B^p/D$$

(25d) $$r = B^b/D$$

(25e) $$b_H = A/D$$

(25f) $$b_F = A^{\star}/D$$

As Brunner and Meltzer have so forcefully emphasized (1964, 1966, 1968) money and bank credit are not the mirror image of each other. They differ in this context by the factor R. Let us

7) This procedure is implicit in the works of Brunner and Meltzer, Melitz (1973) and Fourçans (1974).

consider in more detail these differences, with the intention to clear some possible misunderstanding concerning those allocative forces which influence uniquely the behavior of the money stock relative to bank credit. Consider as a first example an autonomous increase in the public's demand for base money. Ceteris paribus, a unit increase in B^p implies a fall in BC of $1/r - 1$. It also implies a fall in the money stock. The decrease of M relative to BC is, however, determined by the way the public allocates its holding of money between base money and deposits. If B^p were to increase less than deposits at the initial point of disturbance, the money stock would fall proportionately more than bank credit. As a second example, take an increase in the required reserve ratio. The rise in r_R will depress both BC and M, but the hypothesis, however, implies a larger fall in the former than in the latter. As a third and final example, a rise in A and $A^{\star}$ will push up both BC and M; whether BC would rise proportionately more or less than M depends on the relative behavior of A and $A^{\star}$ versus deposits. If the ratios A/D and $A^{\star}/D$ were to rise, then the ratio M/BC would fall or bank credit would rise proportionately more than the money stock.

The ratios k, r, b_H and b_F, in turn, respond systematically to the variables which affect both the numerator and denominator defining the individual ratio. Consider the particularly discriminating case of an increase in the yield on capital. This will tend to lower the global demand for money and for domestic securities, but it will raise the demand for loans as firms find raising funds in the equity market more costly. It is clear that the public will find advantageous to supply more earning assets to the banking system (notice the difference between bank credit and money from the viewpoint of the public). But the important question here is the extent to which M/BC will be affected by a change in i_K. The discussion above has recognized that the h^1 function responds positively to i_K via B^p and the net foreign liability position of the government and the public, CK. The increase in i_K lowers also the demand for deposits and this effect should largely dominate the influence of i_K on B^p. In other words, the k-ratio is postulated to be an upsloping function of i_K as well as of i_S, i_L and i_{ED}. Likewise, a rise in i_K should lead to an increase in r, b_H and b_F. The global impact of i_K on R of equation (25b) depends on the opposing pull exerted by k and r, on the one hand, and b_H and b_F, on the other. The former works to augment R; the latter to lower it. I shall assume that $\frac{\partial R}{\partial i_K} > 0$.

The other rates of interest will affect R in a direction opposite to i_K. These results are assured for relatively moderate values of $\frac{\partial k}{\partial i_S}$ and $\frac{\partial k}{\partial i_{ED}}$. In compact functional form,

$$(26) \qquad R = R(\underset{-}{i_S}, \underset{-}{i_L}, \underset{+}{i_K}; \underset{-}{i_{ED}}, \ldots)$$

Compared to bank credit, the role of R tends to lower the sensitivity of M with respect to i_S, i_L and i_{ED} but to heighten it instead with respect to i_K. In principle, one cannot rule out that the slopes $\frac{\partial M}{\partial i_S}$ and $\frac{\partial M}{\partial i_L}$ may be negative. In the remainder of the paper I shall, however, assure that $0 < \frac{\partial M}{\partial i_S} < \frac{\partial BC}{\partial i_S}$ and similarly for i_L. The supply of money function is thus expressed

$$(27) \qquad M = Rh^1 = h^{11}(\underset{+}{i_S}, \underset{+}{i_L}, \underset{+}{i_K}; \underset{+}{B^D}, \underset{-}{r_R}, \underset{-}{i_{ED}}, \underset{-}{i_f}, \Pi^F/\Pi, \underset{-}{\Pi})$$

with $\frac{\partial h^{11}}{\partial i_S} < \frac{\partial h^1}{\partial i_S}$; $\frac{\partial h^{11}}{\partial i_L} < \frac{\partial h^1}{\partial i_L}$; $\frac{\partial h^{11}}{\partial i_K} > \frac{\partial h^1}{\partial i_K}$;

$\frac{\partial h^{11}}{\partial B^D} > \frac{\partial h^1}{\partial B^D}$; $\frac{\partial h^{11}}{\partial r_R} < \frac{\partial h^1}{\partial r_R}$; $\frac{\partial h^{11}}{\partial i_{ED}} < \frac{\partial h^1}{\partial i_{ED}}$

III. Three Equilibrium Conditions and a Comparison with the Brunner-Meltzer Hypothesis

We are now able to compress the total system into three markets; domestic government securities, domestic loans and domestic money.

(28) $S^p(i_S, i_L, i_K) + S^f(i_S, \ldots) + \alpha(i_S, i_L)h^1(i_S, i_L, i_K, \ldots) = S$

(29) $[(1 - \alpha(i_S, i_L)] h^1(\cdot) = L^d(i_L, \ldots)$

(30) $h^{11}(i_S, i_L, i_K, \ldots) = M^d(i_S, i_L, i_K, \ldots)$

where $\alpha(\cdot)$ represents the proportion of total domestic bank credit demanded in the form of securities and where $\frac{\partial \alpha}{\partial i_S} > 0$ and $\frac{\partial \alpha}{\partial i_L} < 0$. It follows that $[1 - \alpha(\cdot)]h^1$ is the banks' supply of domestic loans. The three equilibrium conditions solve uniquely for i_S, i_L and i_K.

It may be useful from a methodological viewpoint to discuss some variants of this basic model. First, if one were to ignore the demand for real assets and thus consider i_K exogenous in the system, the demand for money would be implicitly determined by equations (10)-(12), (14)-(15), the definition of money stock and the balance-sheet constraint (1). Equation (30) above would be used to determine the money stock. This was essentially the interpretation that Brunner and Meltzer (1964, 1966, 1968) have given to their model of bank credit and money supply process. They further assumed that securities and loans were highly substitutable, thus collapsing (28)-(30) in

$$(31) \qquad \sigma(i_{SL}; i_K, \ldots) = h^1(i_{SL}; i_K, \ldots)$$

$$(32) \qquad M = h^{11}(i_{SL}; i_K, \ldots)$$

where i_{SL} is the interest rate on bank credit and $\sigma = L^d(\cdot) - S^p(\cdot) + S$ in a closed economy, $\sigma = L^d(\cdot) - S^p(\cdot) - S^f(\cdot) + S$ in an open economy.

The bank credit market (31) is used to determine i_{SL}; (32) the money stock. More recently, Brunner and Meltzer (1972) and Brunner (1973) have advanced a model where the bank credit market, as understood by (31), is paired with the "Walrasian money market", as understood by (30). The introduction of the money demand permits to solve for the asset price level of real capital which is inversely related to i_K. This interpretation of the system will be discussed in more detail in Section IV 4 below.

IV. Implications of the Hypothesis

The model developed in Section III can be used effectively to answer some important questions. I shall limit my discussion to the impact of (1) monetary policy changes, (2) Eurodollar rate change and an autonomous shift from domestic to dollar-denominated assets, and (3) the devaluation of the domestic currency on the three rates i_S, i_L and i_K. Most of the same issues will be explored again when loans and securities are assumed to be perfect substitutes. As a general indicator, a rise in all interest rates will be taken as depressing economic activity, while a decline as stimulating economic activity. If some of the interest rates move in one direction, while others in an opposite direction no clear general assessment will be made about the ultimate impact on output and prices.

The results presented below are obtained directly from the Appendix where I have solved the system (28)-(30) in terms of differential changes in i_S, i_L and i_K.

1. Monetary Policy and Its Effectiveness

I begin by letting the exogenous component of the base change as a result of an increase in government expenditures financed neither by taxes nor by securities. The impact of the increase in government expenditures on the rates of interest is, of course, ignored. The higher value of B^D raises the supply of domestic bank credit and the supply of money in the system. The consequent fall in i_S, i_L and i_K provokes a net outflow of capital, thus lowering the endogenous foreign component of the base, CK.[8] The decrease in CK can be smaller than, equal to or bigger than

8) Notice that also A and A^* fall.

the increase in B^D, depending on the interest sensitivity of capital flows. Ignoring for the moment A and $A^\star$, it has been argued [cf. Kouri and Porter (1972, 1974) and Kouri (1973)] that when $dB^D + dCK = 0$ monetary policy is ineffective, for perfectly offsetting capital flows prevent monetary policy to alter the supply of money and thus "the" rate of interest. The argument is correct in asserting that the supply of money and domestic bank credit cannot be affected when $dB^D + dCK = 0$ (again ignoring A and $A^\star$); but it is incorrect in jumping to the conclusion that policy has no power. The reason is quite simple. A fall in CK implies, by definition, either a fall in S^f and EL and/or an increase in S_f^p and ED. But a decrease in S^f lowers the aggregate demand for domestic securities according to equilibrium condition (28) and consequently must lower the rate of interest i_S.[9)] In other words, the condition $dB^D + dCK = 0$ is not inconsistent with a change in interest rates and therefore with an effective policy. Essentially, this is the argument advanced by Brunner (1973, pp. 150-1) who concludes that even perfect capital mobility will not eliminate the short-run efficacy of monetary policy. More will be said below.

9) There are, however, secondary effects which soften the final impact on the rates of interest of a falling foreign demand for domestic securities. Following the initial fall in i_S, banks would be induced to substitute securities for loans. The loan rate would thus also fall. The rate of return on capital i_K, on the other hand, would tend to rise as the falling i_S and i_L increase the demand for money relative to its supply. Subsequent round effects would include feedback impulses from i_K on to the loan and securities markets. These feedback impulses exert an upward push on i_L and i_S. It is here assumed that the first-round effect is larger numerically than subsequent-round effects.

With reference to my framework, the impact of B^D on the three rates of interest is

$$(33a) \quad \frac{di_S}{dB^D} = \frac{1}{|A|} [\overset{+}{a}_{1B}\overset{+}{A}_1 + \overset{+}{a}_{2B}\overset{+}{A}_2 + \overset{+}{a}_{3B}A_3]$$

$$(33b) \quad \frac{di_L}{dB^D} = \frac{1}{|A|} [a_{1B}\overset{+}{A}_4 + a_{2B}\overset{+}{A}_5 + a_{3B}\overset{-}{A}_6]$$

$$(33c) \quad \frac{di_K}{dB^D} = \frac{1}{|A|} [a_{1B}\overset{-}{A}_7 + a_{2B}\overset{-}{A}_8 + a_{3B}\overset{+}{A}_9]$$

where all the terms are explained in the Appendix. To simplify the interpretation of the results I have indicated whether the terms in the expressions are positive or negative. The sign of the determinant of the coefficient matrix of (28)-(30), $|A|$, is negative. The sign pattern of the cofactors A's was obtained by virtue of the explicit properties assigned to the model and by applying the general principle that the "own" price effect is numerically larger than the "cross" price effect in any given market. With the capital market in the background and money holdings having no explicit price of their own, additional constraints had to be placed on the response of the three markets to changes in the rate of return on capital. Quite generally, the substitution between money--and not necessarily the monetary base component of the money stock--and capital was taken to be more pronounced than either money and domestic securities or loans and capital. The latter substitution, in turn, was assumed to be higher than the substitution between money and securities. With the help of the above mentioned order contraints, A_1 and A_5 acquire unambiguously a positive value and A_6 a negative value. Finally, A_3 is negative if the degree of substitution between capital and securities is small relative to capital and base money held by the public; otherwise it should be positive.

Returning to equation (33), an increase in B^D lowers definitively i_S when A_3 is positive, but its effect on i_L and i_K remains *a priori* unclear (i.e., it requires more detailed empirical knowledge). In a different vein, one can restate the implication by saying that in the Keynesian world of money and bonds, an increase in B^D has an expansionary impact on economic activity. However, when the world enlarges to money, bonds and capital and money is not identified with bank credit, the interpretation of policy becomes more complicated.[10)]

A deficit financed by new issues of government securities raises i_S and i_L but lowers i_K, suggesting that a securities-financed deficit need not be deflationary in an open economy. Notice that this result is not crucially dependent on the relative substitution between capital and securities and money and capital as is true in Tobin-type models.[11)]

---

10) The rate i_K can fall for hypersensitive values of the securities and loan markets to changes in i_S and i_L, respectively. In fact

$$\operatorname{sgn} \frac{di_K}{dB^D} = -\operatorname{sgn} [a_{1S}(a_{2L} - a_{3L}) + a_{2S}(a_{3L} - a_{1L}) + a_{3S}(a_{1L} - a_{2L})]$$

which is positive if a_{1S} and a_{2L} are strongly dominant.

11) See Branson (1972 and 1974), for example.

A purchase of securities in the open market by the monetary authorities lowers i_S by a larger amount than a base-money financed deficit. To the extent that securities and loans are highly substitutable it will also lower i_L. On the other hand, an expansionary open market operation raises the algebraic value of

$$\left.\frac{di_K}{dB^D}\right|_{dB^D = -dS}.$$ [12]

2. The Impulses from the Eurodollar Market

The Eurodollar market can influence the domestic economy in a variety of ways but here I shall only consider two cases. First, let us assume an autonomous increase in the Eurodollar rate i_{ED}, and consequently of the Eurodollar loan rate. The domestic public reacts to such an event by switching out of domestic securities, capital and money and into Eurodollar deposits. It will also lower its dollar liabilities relative to its domestic loans. The domestic banks will likewise increase their net dollar asset position. These portfolio adjustments provoke a net flow of capital out of the home country which is only partly compensated by the inflow of capital produced by the domestic public decreasing its stock of foreign securities.[13] The ultimate impact of an in-

---

12) Formally, $\left.\frac{di_K}{dB^D}\right|_{dB^D = -dS} = \frac{1}{|A|}\left[\overset{-}{A_7}(1 + \overset{+}{a_{1B}}) + \overset{+}{a_{2B}}\overset{-}{A_8} + \overset{+}{a_{3B}}\overset{+}{A_9}\right]$

13) Recall that $\frac{\partial ED}{\partial i_{ED}} > \left|\frac{\partial S_f^p}{\partial i_{ED}}\right|$ according to the principle that a market responds more pronouncedly to its "own" than its "cross" price.

crease in i_{ED} on the domestic rates of interest is given by

$$(34a)\quad \frac{di_S}{di_{ED}} = \frac{1}{|A|}[\overset{-}{a}_{1ED}\overset{+}{A}_1 + \overset{-}{a}_{2ED}\overset{+}{A}_2 + \overset{+}{a}_{3ED}A_3]$$

$$(34b)\quad \frac{di_L}{di_{ED}} = \frac{1}{|A|}[a_{1ED}\overset{+}{A}_4 + a_{2ED}\overset{+}{A}_5 + a_{3ED}\overset{-}{A}_6] > 0$$

$$(34c)\quad \frac{di_K}{di_{ED}} = \frac{1}{|A|}[a_{1ED}\overset{-}{A}_7 + a_{2ED}\overset{-}{A}_8 + a_{3ED}\overset{+}{A}_9] < 0$$

The increase in i_{ED} has a contractive impact on economic activity through i_L and most likely through i_S, given the presumed substitution between securities and loans; but it is expansionary through i_K. There is now considerable evidence that the behavior of interest rates in the Eurodollar market is closely influenced by U.S. interest rates and, ultimately, by the course of U.S. monetary policy. The existence of a well organized and efficient market such as the Eurodollar market magnifies the influence of U.S. policy actions on the financial markets of other countries.

The second channel of influence of the Eurodollar market is the relative ease the domestic public enjoys in altering the composition of its assets. Assume an autonomous shift from domestic to dollar-denominated assets, prompted by an (expected) devaluation of the domestic currency. Let λ denote such a shift; the comparative-static results are given by

$$(35a)\quad \frac{di_S}{d\lambda} = \frac{1}{|A|}[\overset{-}{a}_{1\lambda}\overset{+}{A}_1 + \overset{-}{a}_{2\lambda}\overset{+}{A}_2 + a_{3\lambda}A_3]$$

$$\text{(35b)} \quad \frac{di_L}{d\lambda} = \frac{1}{|A|} [a_{1\lambda} \overset{+}{A_4} + a_{2\lambda} \overset{+}{A_5} + a_{3\lambda} \overset{-}{A_6}]$$

$$\text{(35c)} \quad \frac{di_K}{d\lambda} = \frac{1}{|A|} [a_{1\lambda} \overset{-}{A_7} + a_{2\lambda} \overset{-}{A_8} + a_{3\lambda} \overset{+}{A_9}]$$

The term $a_{3\lambda}$ has not been assigned a sign because it responds to two opposing forces. The movement out of money tends to make it positive; the action of the public in reallocating its portfolio in favor of dollar assets and the effect that this reallocation has on the balance of payments and, hence, on the supply of money tends to make it negative. If the former force prevails $\frac{di_L}{d\lambda} > 0$ and $\frac{di_K}{d\lambda} < 0$. Given the above noted substitution between securities and loans, we can safely conclude that a reallocation from domestic to dollar assets by the domestic public produces the same qualitative impact of an increase in the Eurodollar rate. If instead $a_{3\lambda} < 0$, $\frac{di_S}{d\lambda} > 0$ (for $A_3 > 0$) and thus also $\frac{di_L}{d\lambda} > 0$, but $\frac{di_K}{d\lambda} \gtreqless 0$.

3. Devaluation of the Domestic Currency

Three effects of the devaluation must be distinguished. First, an increase in Π implies an increase, at least initially, of p_a. All assets and liability demands increase accordingly: the effect is to depress economic activity for, <u>ceteris paribus</u>, the total demand for government securities, the loan demand and the money demand increase, thus raising i_S, i_L and i_K. Second, the devaluation improves the current trade account (provided the Marshall-Lerner condition holds) and consequently increases the supplies of bank credit and money through an increase in the foreign component of the base. The effect is expansionary on economic activity because interest rates fall. Finally, the adjustment in the domestic public's portfolio due to a higher p_a implies a change in the capital account of the balance of payments. As was analyzed in Section II2 above, it is not possible a priori to ascertain whether a devaluation brings a net outflow or a net inflow of capital. It follows that when the three channels of influence of a devaluation are combined, the final outcome depends on the relative forces interacting in the process. What is important to remark is that a devaluation need not be expansionary, at least not through its influence on interest rates.[14)]

4. Perfect Substitution Between Loans and Securities

Passing references have been made to the high degree of substitution between commercial loans and domestic securities. I shall now explore the case of perfect substitution. For convenience, I shall rewrite the relevant two equilibrium conditions

$$(36) \quad \sigma(\underset{-}{i_{SL}}, \underset{+}{i_K}; \underset{+}{i_{ED}}, \Pi, S_1, \ldots) = h^1(\underset{+}{i_{SL}}, \underset{+}{i_K}; \underset{+}{B^D}, \underset{-}{i_{ED}}, \Pi, \ldots)$$

$$(37) \quad M^d(\underset{-}{i_{SL}}, \underset{-}{i_K}; \underset{-}{i_{ED}}, \underset{+}{\Pi}, \ldots) = h^{11}(\underset{+}{i_{SL}}, \underset{+}{i_K}, \underset{+}{B^D}, \underset{-}{i_{ED}}, \Pi, \ldots)$$

It should be readily apparent that (36)-(37) is the general struc-

---

14) Longer run effects of the devaluation include a change in output, domestic prices and in w_1. All such effects are excluded from my analysis.

Figure 1a: Determination of the equilibrium values of i_{SL} and i_K

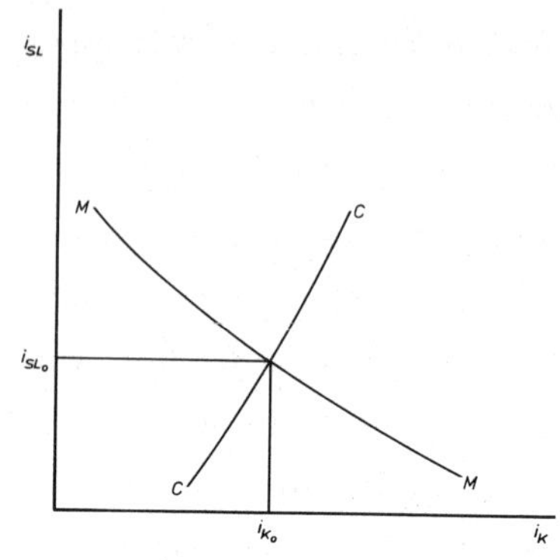

Figure 1b: Increase in B^D

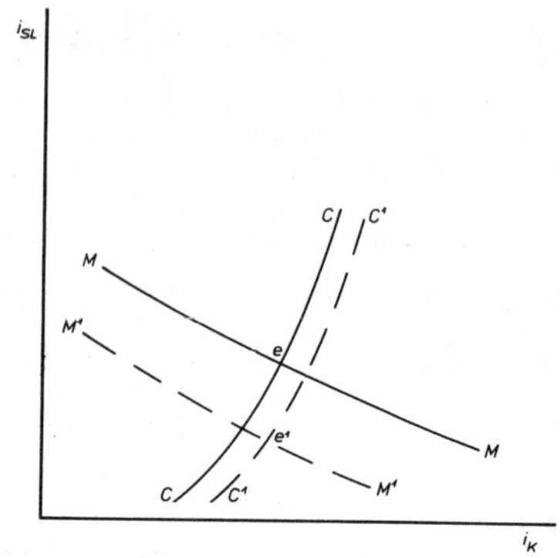

Figure 1c: Increase in S

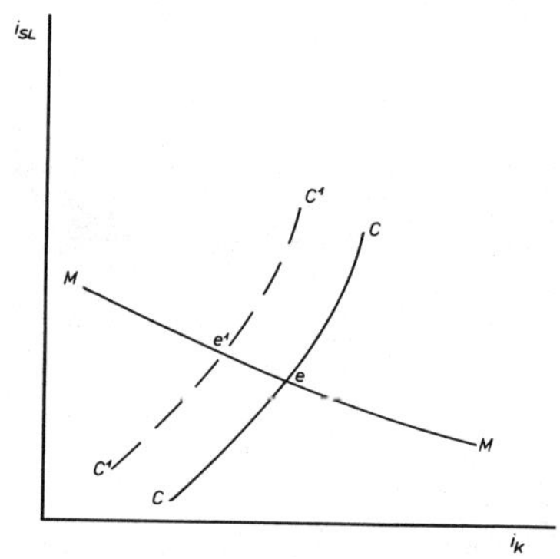

Figure 1d: Increase in i_{ED} with constraint $\left|\frac{\delta M^d}{\delta i_{ED}}\right| > \left|\frac{\delta h^{11}}{\delta i_{ED}}\right|$

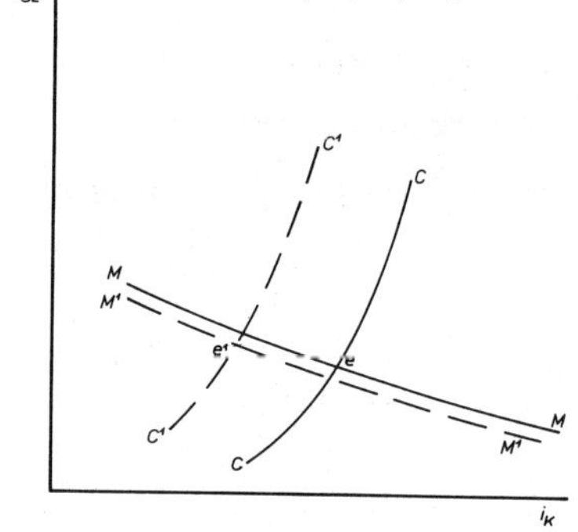

ture of the Brunner and Meltzer world. There are two differences, however, which are worth mentioning. One is that neither h^1 nor h^{11} is homogeneous of degree one with respect to the exogenous base B^D. The second difference is that in the Brunner and Meltzer model the partial derivative $\frac{\partial h^1}{\partial i_K}$ is stated to be negative, whereas it was found in this paper that h^1 responds positively to i_K.[15)]

The determination of the equilibrium value of i_{SL} and i_K is graphically shown in Figure 1a where the CC-line corresponds to the equilibrium condition in the bank credit market and the MM-line to the equilibrium condition in the money market. The CC-line can either be upsloping or downsloping, depending on whether $\frac{\partial \sigma}{\partial i_K} \gtrless \frac{h^1}{i_K}$.[16)] In the unlikely case of a negatively inclined CC-curve, stability conditions require that the MM-line be flatter than the CC-line.

The properties of the system are best perceived by repeating some of the exercises of Sections IV1 - IV3. Consider first a base-money financed deficit. Both the CC and MM schedules will fall at the new equilibrium point (Figure 1b). Clearly, i_{SL} must seek a new lower value; the effect on i_K, on the other hand, is not clear from the graph and an examination of the analytical solution (38) is required.

---

15) Brunner and Meltzer do not explicitly refer to i_K, but to the asset price of real assets which is inversely related to i_K.

16) In Brunner and Meltzer the CC-line would be unambiguously upsloping.

$$(38) \quad \frac{di_K}{dB^D} = \frac{\beta_{CS} h^{11}_B - \beta_{MS} h^{1}_B}{\Delta}$$

$$\Delta = \beta_{CS} \beta_{MK} - \beta_{MS} \beta_{CK} > 0$$

The β terms are defined as the slopes of the excess demand function of the bank credit market (subscript C) and money market (subscript M) with respect to i_{SL} (subscript S) and i_K (subscript K). All the β's are negative except for β_{CK} which can be either positive or negative, but in Figure 1 was assumed to be positive. While the denominator of (38) is unambiguously positive, the numerator is defined as the difference of two positive elements. However, the hypothesis implies that $h^{11}_B > h^{1}_B$ and $|\beta_{CS}| > |\beta_{MS}|$ and thus $\frac{di_K}{dB^D}$ is negative, as shown in Figure 1b.

An increase in the stock of government securities shifts the CC-curve to the left, thus causing i_{SL} to rise while lowering i_K (see Figure 1c). These results confirm the conclusions obtained in Section IV1 above.

An increase in the Eurodollar deposit raises the CC-line; its effect on the MM-line is instead unclear. It raises the schedule if the substitution between domestic money holdings and Eurodollar deposits is small relative to the influence of i_{ED} on the supply of money; it lowers the schedule otherwise. In the latter case i_K falls (cf. Figure 1d); in the former case i_K can rise if and only if

$$(39) \quad -\beta_{CS} \beta_{ME} > -\beta_{CE} \beta_{MS}$$

where β_{ME} and β_{CE} are the slopes of the excess demand for money and bank credit with respect to i_{ED}, respectively. Condition (39) would be satisfied if $\beta_{ME} > \beta_{CE}$, but we have little empirical knowledge on these two magnitudes. The important point to keep in mind is that rising Eurodollar rates need not depress economic activity.

Finally, a devaluation of the domestic currency imparts a vertical shift equal to $-\beta_{C\Pi}/\beta_{CS}$ to the CC-line, and $-\beta_{M\Pi}/\beta_{MS}$ to the MM-line. Appealing to the homogeneity properties $\varepsilon(L^d, p_a) = \varepsilon(S^p, p_a) = \varepsilon(M^d, p_a) = 1$, $\beta_{C\Pi}$ and $\beta_{M\Pi}$ can be written as

$$\beta_{C\Pi} = (L - S^p)[1 - w_1 - \varepsilon(h^1, \Pi)] - \varepsilon(h^1, \Pi)OA$$

$$\text{where } OA = NW + EL - ED - S_f^p - K$$

$$\beta_{M\Pi} = M[1 - w_1 - \varepsilon(h^{11}, \Pi)]$$

The issue at stake is whether a devaluation provokes excess demands or excess supplies in the asset markets. Let us take it for granted that $\varepsilon(h^1, \Pi)$ and $\varepsilon(h^{11}, \Pi)$ are positive. The more closed the economy, where closedness is measured by the value of w_1 (for a completely closed economy $w_1 = 1$), the more likely that $\beta_{C\Pi}$ and $\beta_{M\Pi}$ are negative. Or stated in a slightly different way, the smaller the proportion of foreign output in domestic absorption, the more probable that a devaluation of the domestic currency will create excess supply conditions in the asset markets. Under such circumstances the CC and MM schedules shift downward, causing i_{SL} to fall but leaving the outcome for

i_K uncertain. In countries which are relatively open and which have not experienced substantial reversals in their balance of payments following a devaluation, a devaluation can well act as a depressant on economic activity. The above discussion has remained within the confines of a model where the output market is taken as exogenous. A more complete analysis of the effects of a devaluation would have to consider the interaction of asset and output markets after an increase in Π (cf. Dornbush (1974)).

To conclude, many of the results of this section corroborate the findings of the unconstrained model. The obvious advantage of the constrained version of the model is that its implications can be narrowed down considerably and thus enhance the power of the empirical tests.

V. Some Empirical Tests

No attempt will be made here to test extensively the hypothesis presented in the paper. I shall concentrate instead on some empirical tests and issues concerning the bank credit market and the money supply equation. Certain issues will be given a preferential status to others because either they bear directly on the bank credit market and money supply equation or because they have received attention in the literature.

Let me begin with a test of the initial Brunner and Meltzer model given by the equation system (31)-(32) of Section III. The results of the test are summarized in Table 3 where the structural equations σ, h^{1} and h^{11}, or more precisely a simplified form thereof, are estimated using TSLS with autoregressive residuals adjusted according to the Fair (1970) procedure. The country study is Italy and the sample period starts with the first quarter of 1959 and ends with the third quarter of 1972. It would be inappropriate in this context to explicate the essential institutional background which would be demanded of a study entirely dedicated to the Italian bank credit and money markets; it has been covered in other works (Fratianni, 1971 and 1972) and the reader is referred to them.

As we would expect, not all of the variables appearing in (31)-(32) have been included in the estimation. In the decision of what variables to include and what others to exclude, the following criteria were applied. Let me start with the σ function. Variables such as real permanent income measured by the trend value of Italy's index of industrial production, real financial wealth,[17)] the average price level and the bank credit rate of interest were considered the core of the theory and thus were included in all experiments. The impact of the open economy on the model was restricted to the Eurodollar deposit rate, the ratio Π^{F}/Π and the exogenous variables affecting the foreign demand for domestic security, S^{f}. At the time the tests were made no suitable series for foreign output and price level was available; in their place I used the stock of international reserves owned by the central bank, Ir. The ratio Π^{F}/Π was dropped al-

17) The capital stock was excluded from the wealth variable for obvious problems of measurement.

together after a few unsuccessful attempts. The Eurodollar deposit rate was on the whole largely insignificant except in one set of regressions (3a and 3b) where it appears with the wrong signs. Two surrogates of the bank credit rate were used: the yield on a widely traded long-term bond (i_S) and a weighted average of the same yield and the "prime" loan rate charged by the industrial bank Istituto Mobiliare Italiano, where the weights are given by S^b/BC and L/BC, respectively. In all cases, the latter performed much worse than the former and consequently was abandoned.

Concerning the supply of bank credit, the selection of variables was restricted to the exogenous domestic source component of the base B^T, the reserve requirement r_R, and the ratio $k = B^P/D$ summarizing the behavior of the public.[18] Similar arguments were employed for the money supply equation h^{11}.

Several observations are pertinent about Table 3. First, the regressions of the structural equations confirm the importance of the monetary base (in this case B^T) in h^1 and h^{11}. Second, the influence of real non-human financial wealth and permanent real income seems to corroborate the a priori constraint that $\frac{\partial L^d}{\partial y_p} > \frac{\partial S^p}{\partial y_p}$ and $\frac{\partial L^d}{\partial NW} > \frac{\partial S^p}{\partial NW}$. Third, the homogeneity-of-degree-one postulate with respect to the price level p_a is not satisfied for either L^d or S^p; the evidence instead suggests a hypersensitive response of the public in demanding loans relative to its demand

18) The exogenous component of the base in an open economy B^D was not used because quarterly data on CK are not available.

for securities to changes in the general price level. Fourth, the impact of external forces on the demand for bank credit was found to be limited to Ir which, we recall, is a surrogate for the exogenous arguments in S^f. Other "open-economy" variables such as i_{ED} and Π^F/Π left no visible trace on σ and h^1. It is planned to test the model at a more disaggregated level so as to pinpoint the channels through which i_{ED} and Π^F/Π are most influential. Fifth, an implication of the perfect substitution between domestic loans and securities is that a unit increase in the supply of securities has to raise the public's demand for bank credit also by one unit. Our tests failed to show such a relationship due in part to the high collinearity between our measure of financial net worth and S. Finally, the regressions of Table 3 do not show the coefficients of i_S to be significant at acceptable levels.

The theoretical model developed in this paper assumed implicitly no inflationary expectations. Italy's average price inflation over the sample period was, however, about 3.5 percent per annum. Expected price changes induce the domestic public to raise its demand for loans, while lowering its demand for securities. In different terms, the impact of an expected price change, $\hat{p}^e$, raises σ or alternatively lowers the real price, $i_S - \hat{p}^e$, of bank credit. Table 4 tests this proposition where $\hat{p}^e$ is defined

$$\hat{p}^e = \sum_{i=1}^{6} w_i(\hat{p}_a)_{t-i} \qquad \begin{aligned} w_1 &= 6/21 \\ w_2 &= 5/21 \\ &\vdots \\ w_6 &= 1/21 \\ \Sigma\, w_i &= 1 \end{aligned}$$

TABLE 3

TSLS Estimates of Bank Credit and Money in Italy : 1959 : I - 1972 : III

Billions of Italian Lire

Regr. #	Dep. Var.	i_S	i_{ED}	W	y_p	p_a	Ir	r_R	K.1000
1a	o	-386.872		124.284	158.139	195.892	-1.248		
	(t values)	(-.902)		(5.194)	(1.723)	(2.061)	(-2.61)		
1b	h^1	552.182						-39712.74	-15.261
	(t values)	(1.393)						(-1.540)	(-3.994)
1c	h^{11}	217.214						-41541.83	-18.231
	(t values)	(.494)						(-1.940)	(-4.299)
2a	σ	-481.662		116.236	186.205	185.828	-1.26		
		(-1.041)		(4.584)	(1.89)	(1.883)	(-2.553)		
2b	h^1	621.365							-16.766
		(1.536)							(-4.475)
3a	σ	-381.543	-120.272	122.397	186.539	165.935	-1.265		
		(-.857)	(-1.224)	(5.127)	(2.022)	(1.712)	(-2.638)		
3b	h^1	296.344	249.405						-16.349
		(.792)	(1.558)						(-4.102)

TABLE 3

(Continued)

Regr. #	B^T	Const.	D_1	D_2	D_3	$\bar{R}^2$	SE	DW	u
1a		-4578.296	-588.48	-253.297	-384.577	.948	477.123	2.118	.85
		(-7.397)	(-2.865)	(-1.379)	(-2.378)				
1b	1.632	9074.808				.963	902.35	2.178	.60
	(8.885)	(3.395)							
1c	2.498	12918.949				.976	1001.58	2.387	.60
	(12.250)	(4.354)							
2a		-400.205	-630.861	-287.993	-421.899	.934	483.321	2.195	.87
		(-7.031)	(-2.961)	(-1.532)	(-2.531)				
2b	1.678	7338.72				.962	917.007	2.129	.60
	(9.112)	(2.944)							
3a		-4424.05	-640.195	-276.753	-377.575	.948	473.63	2.136	.85
		(-7.129)	(-3.114)	(-1.514)	(-2.327)				
3b	1.708	9226.404				.974	925.593	1.947	.50
	(9.084)	(2.834)							

Notes to Table 3

σ, h^1 : bank credit. Source (1)

h^{11}: money stock M^2 (currency plus postal deposits plus demand and time deposits owned by the public). Source (1)

i_S = yield on bonds issued by Istituti di Credito Mobiliari. Source (1)

i_{ED} = rate on 3-month Eurodollar deposit. Source (3)

W = (B + S)/CPI. Source (1)

y_p = long-run trend of industrial output obtained by regressing index of industrial output on a + bt, where t = time. Source (2)

p_a = Consumer price index (CPI). Source (2)

Ir = stock of international reserves owned by the Banca d'Italia. Source (1)

r_R = required reserve ratio computed as $B_R^b/(D + T)$ where T = time deposits. Source (1)

k = B^p/D. Source (1)

B^T = exogenous domestic component of the monetary base. Source (1)

D_1, D_2, D_3 = seasonal dummy variables

$\bar{R}^2$ is the coefficient of determination corrected for degrees of freedom

SE is the standard error of estimate of the regression

DW is the Durbin-Watson test statistic

u is the coefficient of the lagged disturbance term in a first-order autoregressive scheme. For estimation procedure see Fair (1970)

Numbers in parenthesis express t values. With 60 degrees of freedom, t = 1.30 is significant at the 90 percent level of the two-tailed test, whereas t = 1.66 is significant at the 95 percent level.

Notes to Table 3 (Continued)

Sources

(1): Banca d'Italia, Bollettino or Research Department

(2): OECD, Main Economic Indicators

(3): Morgan Guaranty Trust Company, World Financial Markets

TABLE 4

TSLS Estimates of Bank Credit in Italy : 1958 : I - 1972 : IV

Billions of Italian Lire

Dep. Var.	$i_S - \hat{p}^e$	i_S	W	y_p	p_a	Ir	r_R	DS
σ	-371.198		197.403	93.323	115.146	-1.9311		
(t-value)	(4.106)		(22.239)	(2.7598)	(2.116)	(6.937)		
h^1		1340.38					-13806.015	717.52
(t-value)		(2.10)					(.896)	(1.352)

Dep. Var.	B	Const.	D_1	D_2	D_3	$\bar{R}^2$	SE	DW	u
σ		-24561.4	-464.63	-88.67	-190.39	.998	455.28	1.754	.397
(t-value)		(9.8566)	(3.064)	(.532)	(1.329)				
h^1	1.8565	-10038.06				.997	713.99	1.796	.827
(t-value)	(16.34)	(2.0952)							

Interest elasticities implied by the structural estimates

$\varepsilon(i_S, B) = -1.84$ $\varepsilon(i_S, y_p) = .912$

$\varepsilon(i_S, Ir) = -.564$ $\varepsilon(i_S, W) = 2.643$

$\varepsilon(i_S, \hat{p}^e) = .1124$ $\varepsilon(i_S, p) = 1.098$

Notes to Table 4: See Table 3 for meaning of symbols;

DS = stabilization dummy . . . $\begin{cases} = 1 & 1966{:}II - 1969{:}I \\ = 0 & \text{otherwise} \end{cases}$

with weights declining arithmetically over a period of 6 quarters. Other forms of price expectations were tried but the Fisher-inspired weights performed better than any other (see Fratianni and Sommariva, 1974). Table 4 differs from Table 3 also in the specification of h^1, the banks' supply of bank credit. To begin with, various concepts of monetary base were used: B^T, $B^T + B^F$, $B^T + A$, and the total base B. The most robust results were obtained with the total base B, despite its collinearity with i_S. Second, the k ratio was omitted because it never formally appeared in the theoretical formulation of h^1. Third, I wanted to test the proposition that the interest rate pegging policy of the Banca d'Italia from the second quarter of 1966 to the first quarter of 1969 might have had an expansionary bias on bank credit (a dummy variable was set equal to one for the 12 quarters of the stabilization program and equal to zero for the remainder of the period).

The results of Table 4 are a substantial improvement over those of Table 3, especially concerning the interest rate i_S. In particular, it was found σ to be very inelastic with respect to i_S $[\varepsilon(\sigma, i_S) \approx -0.12]$. The interest elasticity of the supply of bank credit is at least four times as large as $\varepsilon(\sigma, i_S)$. Indeed, this is a minimum estimate because the total base, in turn, responds to the rate of interest via A, A^* and CK. The main channel of influence of an open economy on the demand for bank credit remains Ir as a surrogate of the variables which affect the foreign demand for domestic securities. The elasticity of σ with respect to real financial wealth W is 1.4 and is three times as large as the permanent income elasticity. The coefficients of the required reserve ratio is highly insignificant. The result is not surprising because this instrument of policy has been used only in a couple of instances and in those occasions the changes were not dramatic.

Similarly, the coefficient of the stabilization dummy variable has too large a variance for accepting the null hypothesis that the pegging program has contributed in itself to an additional supply of bank credit. The finding is consistent with the claim made by some officials of the Banca d'Italia who have denied that pegging the rate of interest was an elegant way to expand bank credit faster than through a direct control on the monetary base, or at least a portion thereof. Fazio and Savona (1971) argue that a peg need not have an expansionary bias on the supply of bank credit, although countries which have experimented with such a policy have traditionally set a "low" peg relative to the market equilibrium rate.

> In 1966 the monetary authorities faced the problem of a huge increase of the supply of bonds (which at the end of the pegging period doubled in terms of net issues) due to various needs, the most important of which was the financing of new large programs of public works. The dilemma was either to have a remarkable increase on bond yields or to flood the economy with money to permit the placement of these issues without an increase in interest rates.
>
> The first solution was readily discarded due to the prevailing slack in demand present at that time in the economy. The second one raised some fears on the possibility of controlling inflationary pressures which could develop later on.

> The experiment of the pegging proved to be very effective in reducing the quantity of money and increasing the demand for bonds by the private sector. The level of the rate that was chosen to be pegged was at that time clearly a sustainable one; only the exceptional increase of the rates on international markets together with some relevant changes in our economy— which brought up a disequilibrium on the current account section of the Italian balance of payments without a domestic expansion – enforced the Italian authorities to abandon the pegging in the autumn of 1969. (p. 3)

The theoretical underpinning of the Italian pegging policy rests on the proposition that the bond holder is willing to trade a lower current yield on securities for a smaller future variance of the bond prices. At the limit, when this variance becomes zero, the liquidity of a bond is not different from the liquidity of a bank deposit. Thus, the introduction of a stabilization program produces a portfolio reallocation from money to bond holdings. The ensuing excess demand for securities and excess supply of money tend to lower both i_S and i_K. The policy is definitely expansionary. If the authorities do not want a drastic fall in i_K they can withdraw some money out of the system. The effective constraint on policy makers in setting the peg in an open economy under fixed exchange rates is the level of interest rates abroad. Internal rates cannot be much lower than the level of international rates.

Returning to the results of Table 4, the interest rate elasticities implied by the estimates of the structural equations suggests the dominance of the monetary base, real financial wealth and permanent income in the determination of the bank credit rate. The low value of $\varepsilon(i_S, \hat{p}^e)$ implies some kind of price-expectations illusion on the part of the public. Part of the problem resides in the relatively modest trend rate of inflation over the sample period. The two-digit inflation rates of 1973 and 1974 have raised dramatically the cost of ignoring or misforecasting future price increases in the stipulation of any fixed-price contract. The available data suggest that economic operators are quickly learning to differentiate nominal from real rates and thus are making the appropriate portfolio adjustments in response to high expected inflation rates. Another problem with the $\hat{p}^e$ estimate stems from having constrained the σ function to have numerically identical slopes with respect to both i_S and $\hat{p}^e$. When $\hat{p}^e$ is entered separately in the regression, the reliability of its coefficient vanishes as well as the reliability of the coefficient of p_a to which it is highly collinear. Finally, we must keep in mind that the concept of monetary base used in Table 4 is all-inclusive. To the extent that $B^e = A + A^{\star} + CK$ responds positively to i_S, the numerical value of all the interest elasticities in Table 4 will have to be lower in a system where B^D, and not B, is the policy variable and A, $A^{\star}$ and CK appear with their structural equations. This extension of the empirical model is now in progress.

So far I have said very little about the empirical relationship of the money stock in relation to bank credit. Comparing regressions 1b and 1c of Table 3 we notice that the money stock and bank credit supply functions differ empirically primarily because of the differential impact exerted on them by the monetary base and the currency-demand deposits ratio. In the theoretical discussion, however, it was emphasized that the different behavior of $h'(\cdot)$ and $h''(\cdot)$ could be attributed to the factor $R(\cdot)$. We recall [cf. equation (26)] that changes in i_s and i_L tend to lower the money stock relative to bank credit, while the opposite is true for the rate of return on capital. Again, ignoring i_K and using i_s as the bank credit rate the above proposition was tested by the following regression[19)]

$$(40) \qquad M = \underset{(3.15)}{15950.78} + \underset{(7.79)}{1.38}\,\bar{BC} - \underset{(-2.02)}{.038}\,\bar{i}_s\,\bar{BC}$$

$$\bar{R}^2 = .999 \;,\; SE = 531.86 \;,\; DW = 1.48 \;,\; u = .98$$

where $\bar{BC}$ and $\bar{i}_s$ are the estimated values of i_s and BC of Table 4. Note that an increase of one lira in the equilibrium value of bank credit raises the money stock M2 by $1.38 - 0.38\,\bar{i}_s$. If the equilibrium value of i_s is 10 per cent, the money stock and bank credit increase by a similar amount. Since the mean value of the rate of interest i_s during the sample period is 6.73, an expansion of bank credit has historically been accompanied by a somewhat larger expansion of the money stock. An increase in the equilibrium value of i_s lowers M by $-.038\,\bar{BC}$. Since the mean value of EA during the sample period is 21158 billion lire, an increase of 100 basis points in the equilibrium value of i_s has on the average lowered M by 804 billion lire.

It is also informative to compare the different effect of a change in the monetary base, the principal instrument of policy, on both bank credit and the money stock. For convenience this impact will be measured in elasticity. The elasticity of BC with respect

---

19) The test was suggested to me by Jacques Melitz.

to B is given by

$$\varepsilon\,(BC,\ B) = \bar{\varepsilon}(h^1,\ B) + \varepsilon(h^1,\ i_s)\ \varepsilon(i_s,\ B)$$

where $\bar{\varepsilon}(h^1,\ B)$ measures the lateral displacement, in percentage terms, of the supply of bank credit function and $\varepsilon(i_s,\ B)$ the impact of B on the equilibrium value of the rate of interest. Using the information provided by Table 4 we obtain that

$$\varepsilon\,(h^1,\ B) = 1.16$$

$$\varepsilon\,(h^1,\ i_s) = .426$$

$$\varepsilon\,(i_s,\ B) = -1.84$$

and hence that $\varepsilon(BC,\ B) = .38$

The elasticity of M with respect to B is measured by

$$\varepsilon\,(M,\ B) = \varepsilon\,(h^{11},\ BC)\ \varepsilon(BC,\ B) + \varepsilon\,(h^{11},\ i_s)\ \varepsilon\,(i_s,\ B)$$

The information in (40) yields that

$\varepsilon(h^{11},\ BC) = .75$ for $\bar{i}_s = 6.73$

$\varepsilon(h^{11},\ i\ ) = -.17$ for $\overline{BC} = 21158$

and hence that $\varepsilon(M,\ B) = .60$ which is 58 per cent higher than the corresponding bank credit elasticity. The relative hypersensitive response of M to changes in B can be explained by two fundamental forces: (a) the depressing impact an increase in i_s has on M relative to BC and (b) the hypersensitivity of i_s to changes in B as a result of an extremely inelastic demand for bank credit.

VI. Offsetting Capital Flows and Controllability of the Monetary Base

The control of the monetary base and its implication for an independent monetary policy has generated renewed interest in the literature. Under a regime of fixed exchange rates the ability of the central bank to achieve target levels or growth rates of B depends crucially on how interdependent are national credit and money markets.

The nature of the problem can be seen by assuming that the authorities raise B^D through an open market purchase. The ensuing fall in interest rates provokes a net outflow of capital from the home country: CK falls. Similarly, A and A^* will decline. The net result is that a unit increase in the policy determined B^D sets in motion forces which tend to lower $B^e = A + A^* + CK$. The degree with which B^e offsets autonomous changes in B^D has important implications about the central bank's ability to alter the supply of bank credit and money. However, the argument of whether the monetary base can or cannot be controlled should not be automatically associated with the effectiveness or ineffectiveness of policy. It is a necessary but not a sufficient condition. As I have noted, this is what Kouri and Porter (1972, 1974) instead do. A careful examination of their model is now in order. Kouri and Porter propose a three-market model to test capital-flow equations. Using the notation developed in this paper, and ignoring exchange-rate expectations, the model consists of:

(41) $Ir + B^T = L(\underset{+}{Y}, \underset{+}{W}, \underset{+}{i_s}, \underset{-}{i_f})$ base money market

(42) $S = S^p(Y, \underset{+}{W}, \underset{+}{i_s}, \underset{-}{i_f}) + S^f(Y^{\star}, \underset{-}{W^{\star}}, \underset{+}{i_s}, \underset{-}{i_f})$

the market for domestic securities

(43) $S_f^p = S_f^p(Y, \underset{+}{W}, \underset{-}{i_s}, \underset{+}{i_f})$ domestic demand for foreign securities

(44) $W = L(\cdot) + S^p(.) + S_f^p(\cdot)$ Definition of financial wealth

(45) $\Delta Ir - TA + \Delta CK$ Definition of balance of payments

(46) $\Delta CK = \Delta S^f(\cdot) - \Delta S_f^p(\cdot)$ Definition of capital flows

where Y and $Y^{\star}$ are domestic and foreign nominal income, respectively, and Δ is the first difference operator. The system (41)-(46) can be collapsed into the following two equations in unknowns i_s and ΔCK

(47) $\Delta L(Y, W, i_s, i_f) = \Delta B^T + TA + \Delta CK$

(48) $\Delta CK = \Delta S^f(Y^{\star}, W^{\star}, i_s, i_f) - \Delta S_f^p(Y, W, i_s, i_f)$

whose reduced-form equations are

(49) $$\Delta i_s = \frac{-1}{\frac{\partial S^p}{\partial i_s} + \frac{\partial S^f}{\partial i_s}} \left[\left(\frac{\partial S^p}{\partial i_f} + \frac{\partial S^f}{\partial i_f} \right) \Delta i_f + TA + \Delta B^T + \ldots \right]$$

(50) $$\Delta CK = \frac{-1}{\frac{\partial S^p}{\partial i_s} + \frac{\partial S^f}{\partial i_s}} \left[\left(\frac{\partial S^f}{\partial i_s} - \frac{\partial S^p_f}{\partial i_s} \right) (\Delta B^T + TA) + \ldots \right]$$

Only the terms which are germane to the discussion have been reported in (49) and (50). The so-called offset coefficient, c, is defined as

(51) $$\left. \frac{\Delta CK}{\Delta B^T} \right|_{\substack{\text{ceteris} \\ \text{paribus}}} = - \frac{\frac{\partial S^f}{\partial i_s} - \frac{\partial S^p_f}{\partial i_s}}{\frac{\partial S^p}{\partial i_s} + \frac{\partial S^f}{\partial i_s}}$$

When $c = 0$, the economy is not "leaking" and the authorities have complete control over the base. When, at the opposite extreme, $c = -1$ policy-induced changes in the base are completely offset by equivalent and opposite changes in CK. The reason for this result is that national capital markets are perfectly integrated. Indeed, it is true that if all national securities are perfect substitutes $i_s = i_f$ and $c = -1$ as $\frac{\partial S^p_f}{\partial i_s} \rightarrow -\infty$. However, there are finite values of $\frac{\partial S^p_f}{\partial i_s}$, $\frac{\partial S^f}{\partial i_s}$ and $\frac{\partial S^p}{\partial i_s}$ which can also make $c = -1$: take for example the case of $\frac{\partial S^p_f}{\partial i_s} = -1$, $\frac{\partial S^f}{\partial i_s} = 2$ and $\frac{\partial S^p}{\partial i_s} = 1$. But these particular values also imply that $\left. \frac{\Delta i_s}{\Delta B^T} \right|_{\substack{\text{ceteris} \\ \text{paribus}}} = -1/3$ with the consequent implication that $c = -1$ is a necessary but not a sufficient condition for an ineffective monetary policy. Another implication is that regressions based solely on

(50) cannot adequately capture the degree of capital integration in the world.

The empirical findings of Kouri and Porter suggest that there is room for an independent monetary policy even in the short run. The estimates of the offset coefficients are somewhat sensitive, as we would expect, to the selection of the sample period and minor modifications in the structure. The conspicuous findings of the 1972 paper were in the words of the authors

> "We find that the "offset" coefficient approximates 100 percent for Germany and Australia and 50 percent for Italy and the Netherlands and conclude that under fixed exchange rates an independent monetary policy will only be effective in these latter countries." (p. 2)

In the 1974 paper the offset coefficients were found to be generally lower: -0.77 for Germany, -0.59 for the Netherlands, -0.47 for Australia and -0.43 for Italy.

Another group of researchers have instead interpreted the inverse relationship between B^D (or B^T) and B^e from the perspective of whether central authorities can compensate changes in B^e which are not directly under their control with appropriate changes in B^D or B^T. It is within this spirit that Korteweg (1973), in reviewing the Dutch data, concludes that the central bank "tries to compensate money inflows from abroad, but does not fully neutralize them on the average over the longer run." (p. 16)

Neumann (1974) regresses the equivalent of ΔB^T on ΔB^e + TA and finds a coefficient of -.773. His conclusions are that

> "Measured over the total period 1959-1972 the Bundesbank has been able to compensate on average 77 percent of the summed changes in source components of the base not under its direct control. This points to a relative degree of controllability." (p. 56)

The difficulty in reconciling the offsetting capital movement theory with the "compensation" approach is that a high inverse relationship between B^T and B^e is taken to be as a manifestation of weak policy in the offsetting capital movement theory, whereas it is interpreted as a symptom of tight control over the total base in the "compensation" approach.

Opposite movements between the exogenous and endogenous components of the monetary base are not restricted to the open-economy case, although they have received more attention in the literature. The issue persists in a close economy and is particularly important in countries such as France whose borrowed component of the monetary base represents a large fraction of the total base (relative to countries such as the United States) and whose banks have an unrestricted access to the discount window of the central bank. The French banks "borrow" from the monetary authorities by actually selling to them so-called eligible papers. More than a borrowing transaction in the U.S. sense where a bank obtains funds from the Fed without collateralizing at times its loan, the French form of lending to banks is in effect an open market purchase [cf. Melitz (1973) and Fourçans

(1974)] . The Banque de France sets at more or less frequent intervals the rate at which she is willing to buy from banks an unlimited amount of so-called eligible paper. The data suggest that French banks have virtually offset franc for franc changes in the unborrowed base with opposite movements in the borrowed base.[20] However, this evidence does not suggest that the French monetary authorities cannot control the total base, but instead that they have not properly altered the intervention rate so as to achieve target levels of borrowed base.[21]

---

20) This evidence is presented in Fourçans (1974, Tables 17a and b, pp. 219-22). With a more simplified reasoning let $B = UB + A + B^P$ where UB is the unborrowed component of the base and let $A = A(\underset{+}{i_S}, \underset{-}{\rho}, \underset{-}{UB})$. The percentage change in A due to a percentage change in UB is given by $\varepsilon(A, i_S)\bar{\varepsilon}(i_S, UB) + \varepsilon(A, UB)$ where $\bar{\varepsilon}(i_S, UB)$ is the elasticity of i_S with respect to UB obtained as a reduced-form equation of the complete system. Fourçans' system consists in this case of the markets for bank loans, base money, demand and time deposits. With $\varepsilon(A, i_S) \approx 0.23$, $\bar{\varepsilon}(i_S, UB) \approx -.28$ and $\varepsilon(A, UB) \approx -.80$, a percentage increase in UB provokes .87 percent decrease in A.

(21) Hawtrey back in 1932 was quite aware of the problem. "The central bank can vary its assets directly by buying or selling securities in the open market, but, so long as it accepts the functions of the lender of last resort, it may find that these operations are offset by equal decreases or increases of rediscounts. Provided it is given sufficient scope in regard to the classes of securities it may purchase, the central bank can rely on increasing its securities to any desired extent, for it can go on buying them after its rediscounts have been reduced to nothing. But it cannot necessarily reduce its securities, for it may find, as in 1839, that the demand for rediscounts more than replaces the securities sold. To effect a contraction of credit, the sales of securities must be supported by a high Bank rate as a deterrent upon rediscounting." (pp. 150-51)

APPENDIX TO SECTION IV

Equations (28)-(30) of the text totally differentiated can be written in matrix form

$$
\text{(A1)}\quad
\begin{bmatrix}
a_{1S} & a_{1L} & a_{1K} \\
a_{2S} & a_{2L} & a_{2K} \\
a_{3S} & a_{3L} & a_{3K}
\end{bmatrix}
\begin{bmatrix}
di_s \\
di_L \\
di_K
\end{bmatrix}
=
\begin{bmatrix}
dS - a_{1B}dB^D - a_{1ED}di_{ED} - a_{1\Pi}\, d\Pi - a_{1\lambda}\, d\lambda \\
- a_{2B}dB^D - a_{2ED}di_{ED} - a_{2\Pi}d\Pi - a_{2\lambda}\, d\lambda \\
- a_{3B}dB^D - a_{3ED}di_{ED} - a_{3\Pi}d\Pi - a_{\lambda}\, d\lambda
\end{bmatrix}
$$

$$a_{1S} = \frac{\partial S^p}{\partial i_S} + \frac{\partial S^f}{\partial i_S} + \alpha\frac{\partial h^1}{\partial i_S} + h^1\frac{\partial \alpha}{\partial i_S} > 0$$

$$a_{1L} = \frac{\partial S^p}{\partial i_L} + \alpha\frac{\partial h^1}{\partial i_L} + h^1\frac{\partial \alpha}{\partial i_L} < 0 \text{ on the assumption that } \left|h^1\frac{\partial \alpha}{\partial i_L} + \frac{\partial S^p}{\partial i_L}\right| > \alpha\frac{\partial h^1}{\partial i_L}$$

$$a_{1K} = \frac{\partial S^p}{\partial i_K} + \alpha\frac{\partial h^1}{\partial i_K} < 0 \text{ for high K-S substitutability}$$

$$> 0 \text{ for high K-M substitutability}$$

$$a_{2S} = (1-\alpha)\frac{\partial h^1}{\partial i_S} - h^1\frac{\partial \alpha}{\partial i_S} < 0 \text{ on the assumption that } h^1\frac{\partial \alpha}{\partial i_S} > (1-\alpha)\frac{\partial h^1}{\partial i_S}$$

$$a_{2L} = (1-\alpha)\frac{\partial h^1}{\partial i_L} - h^1\frac{\partial \alpha}{\partial i_L} - \frac{\partial L^d}{\partial i_L} > 0$$

$$a_{2K} = (1-\alpha)\frac{\partial h^1}{\partial i_K} > 0$$

$$a_{3S} = \frac{\partial h^{11}}{\partial i_S} - \frac{\partial M^d}{\partial i_S} > 0$$

$$a_{3L} = \frac{\partial h^{11}}{\partial i_L} - \frac{\partial M^d}{\partial i_L} > 0$$

$$a_{1B} = \frac{\partial S^p}{\partial NW} \frac{\partial NW}{\partial B^D} + \alpha \frac{\partial h^1}{\partial B^D} > 0$$

$$a_{2B} = (1-\alpha)\frac{\partial h^1}{\partial B^D} - \frac{\partial L^d}{\partial NW} \frac{\partial NW}{\partial B^D} > 0$$

on the empirical grounds that $(1-\alpha)\frac{\partial h^1}{\partial B^D} > 1$,

$\frac{\partial L^d}{\partial NW} < 1$ and $\frac{\partial NW}{\partial B^D} = 1$

$$a_{3B} = \frac{\partial h^{11}}{\partial B^D} - \frac{\partial M^d}{\partial NW} \frac{\partial NW}{\partial B^D} > 0$$

on the empirical grounds that $\frac{\partial h11}{\partial B^D} > 1$,

$\frac{\partial M^d}{\partial NW} < 1$ and $\frac{\partial NW}{\partial B^D} = 1$

$$a_{1ED} = \frac{\partial S^p}{\partial i_{ED}} + \alpha \frac{\partial h^1}{\partial i_{ED}} < 0$$

$$a_{2ED} = (1-\alpha)\frac{\partial h^1}{\partial i_{ED}} - \frac{\partial L^d}{\partial i_{ED}} < 0$$

$$a_{3ED} = \frac{\partial h^{11}}{\partial i_{ED}} - \frac{\partial M^d}{\partial i_{ED}} > 0$$ for a small value of $\frac{\partial h^{11}}{\partial i_{ED}}$

Holding Π^F/Π constant,

$$a_{1\Pi} = (1-w_1)\, p^{\star} \frac{\partial S^p}{\partial P_a} - \alpha \frac{\partial h^1}{\partial \Pi} > 0 \qquad \text{for } \frac{\partial h^1}{\partial \Pi} \to 0$$

$$a_{2\Pi} = (1-\alpha)\frac{\partial h^1}{\partial \Pi} - (1-w_1)p^{\star} \frac{\partial L^d}{\partial P_a} < 0 \qquad \text{for } \frac{\partial h^1}{\partial \Pi} \to 0$$

$$a_{3\Pi} = \frac{\partial h^{11}}{\partial \Pi} - (1-w_1)p^{\star} \frac{\partial M^d}{\partial P_a} < 0 \qquad \text{for } \frac{\partial h^{11}}{\partial \Pi} \to 0$$

Let λ be a shift parameter indicating the desire of the public to move from domestic to dollar denominated assets. In other words, let

$$\underset{+}{\frac{\partial ED}{\partial \lambda}} + \underset{+}{\frac{\partial S^p_f}{\partial \lambda}} + \underset{-}{\frac{\partial M}{\partial \lambda}} + \underset{-}{\frac{\partial S^p}{\partial \lambda}} + \underset{-}{\frac{\partial K}{\partial \lambda}} = 0$$

then

$$a_{1\lambda} = \frac{\partial S^p}{\partial \lambda} + \alpha \frac{\partial h^1}{\partial \lambda} < 0$$

$$a_{2\lambda} = (1-\alpha)\frac{\partial h^1}{\partial \lambda} < 0$$

$$a_{3\lambda} = \frac{\partial h^{11}}{\partial \lambda} - \frac{\partial M^d}{\partial \lambda} \gtrless 0$$

Multiplying both sides of (A1) by (-1), and imposing the constraint $a_{1K} > 0$, the coefficient matrix has the following sign pattern:

	-	+	-
(A2)	+	-	-
	-	-	-

A set of sufficient conditions for stability requires that (A2) have a dominant negative diagional; i.e.,

$$|-a_{1S}| > |-a_{2S} - a_{3S}|$$

$$|-a_{2L}| > |-a_{1L} - a_{3L}|$$

$$|-a_{3K}| > |-a_{1K} - a_{2K}|$$

The first two inequalities are satisfied; the third one is not unless we further restrict the problem. A set of necessary conditions for stability requires that the tracc of (A2) be negative, which is the case, or that the determinant of (A2) be also negative.

The comparative statics of (A1) can be solved from the following equation system.

$$\text{(A3)} \quad \begin{bmatrix} di_S \\ di_L \\ di_K \end{bmatrix} = \frac{1}{|A|} \begin{bmatrix} A_1 & A_2 & A_3 \\ A_4 & A_5 & A_6 \\ A_7 & A_8 & A_9 \end{bmatrix} \begin{bmatrix} -1 & a_{1B} & a_{1ED} & a_{1\Pi} & a_{1\lambda} \\ 0 & a_{2B} & a_{2ED} & a_{2\Pi} & a_{2\lambda} \\ 0 & a_{3B} & a_{3ED} & a_{3\Pi} & a_{3\lambda} \end{bmatrix} \begin{bmatrix} dS_D \\ dB \\ di_{ED} \\ d\Pi \\ d\lambda \end{bmatrix}$$

The matrix with the A's is the adjoint of A and has the following sign pattern,

$$a_{1S} > a_{2S}$$

$$a_{1S} > a_{3S}$$

$$a_{2L} > a_{3L}$$

$$a_{2L} > a_{3L}$$

$$a_{2L} > |a_{1L}|$$

$$a_{3K} > a_{2K}$$

$$a_{3K} > a_{1K}$$

$$\begin{bmatrix} + & + & \{\mp \\ + & + & - \\ - & - & + \end{bmatrix}$$

REFERENCES

Basevi, Girogio, "Balances of Payments and Exchange Markets; A Lost Correspondence", European Economic Review, Dec. 1973, pp. 309-328.

Branson, William H., "Macroeconomic Equilibrium with Portfolio Balance in an Open Economy", University of Stockholm, Institute for International Economic Studies Seminar, Paper Number 22, dated November 1972.

Branson, William H., Portfolio Equilibrium and Monetary Policy with Foreign and Non-traded Assets", Paper presented at the Third Paris-Dauphine Conference on Money and International Monetary Problems, March 28-30, 1974.

Brunner, Karl, and Meltzer, Allan H., "Some Further Investigations of Demand and Supply Function for Money, Journal of Finance, May 1964, pp. 240-283.

Brunner, Karl, and Meltzer, Allan H., "A Credit Market Theory of the Money Supply and an Explanation of Two Puzzles in U.S. Monetary Policy", Rivista internazionale scienze economiche e commerciali, May 1966, pp. 151-176.

Brunner, Karl, and Meltzer, Allan H., "Liquidity Traps for Money, Bank Credit, and Interest Rates", Journal of Political Economy, Jan./Feb. 1968, pp 1-37.

Brunner, Karl, and Meltzer, Allan H., "The Uses of Money: Money in the Theory of an Exchange Economy", American Economic Review, Dec. 1973, pp. 784-805.

Brunner, Karl, and Meltzer, Allan H., "A Monetarist Framework for Aggregative Analysis", in Proceedings of the First Konstanzer Seminar on Monetary Theory and Monetary Policy, Karl Brunner (ed.), Supplement to Kredit and Kapital, Heft 1, 1972, pp. 31-88.

Brunner, Karl, "Money Supply Process and Monetary Policy in an Open Economy", in International Trade and Money, Michael B. Connolly and Alexander K. Swoboda (eds.), London, George Allen & Unwin Ltd., 1973, pp. 127-166.

Cagan, Phillip, The Determinants and Effects of Changes in the Stock of Money, 1875-1960. New York, Columbia University Press, 1965.

Dornbush, Rudiger, "Currency Depreciation, Hoardings, and Relative Prices", Journal of Political Economy, July/August 1973, pp. 893-915.

Fair, Ray C., "The Estimation of Simultaneous Equation Models with Lagged Endogenous Variables and First Order Serially Correlated Errors", Econometrica, May 1970, pp. 507-516.

Fazio, Antonio, and Savona, Paolo, "Pegging of Long-term Rate, Inflation and the Control of Credit Supply in an Open Economy", draft dated June 1971.

Fratianni, Michele, Bank Credit Formation, Money Supply Processes, and Monetary and Fiscal Policies in an Open Economy: the Italian Experience, 1958-1969. Unpublished Ph. D. dissertation, Ohio State Univeristy, 1971.

Fratianni, Michele, "Bank Credit and Money Supply Processes in an Open Economy: A Model Applicable to Italy", Metroeconomica, April, 1972, pp. 24-69.

Fratianni, Michele, and Sommariva, Andrea, "Money and Price Expectations in the Italian Experience", 1974.

Fourçans, André G., Money Stock Bank Credit, and Interest Rate Formations in an Open Economy: the French Case. Unpublished D.B.A. dissertation, Indiana University, 1974.

Friedman, Milton, and Schwartz, Anna J., A Monetary History of the United States 1867-1960. Princeton, National Bureau of Economic Research, 1963.

Hawtrey, R. G., The Art of Central Banking. London, Frank Cass & Co., Ltd., First Edition 1932, Second Edition 1962.

Hawtrey, R. G., Currency and Credit. London, Longmans, Green and Co., Fourth Edition, 1950.

Heremans, Dirk, Sommariva, Andrea, and Verheirstraeten, Albert, "Money and Bank Credit in Belgium", 1974.

Korteweg, Pieter, "The Supply and Controllability of Money in an Open Economy: The Dutch Experience 1953-1971", draft dated June 1973.

Kouri, Pentti, "The Hypothesis of Offsetting Capital Flows: A Case Study of Germany", draft dated June 1973.

Kouri, Pentti, and Porter, Michael, "International Capital Flows and Portfolio Equilibrium", draft dated June, 1972; revised version published in Journal of Political Economy, May/June, 1974, pp. 443-67.

Melitz, Jacques, "Project de modèle intégré du système monetaire francais", draft dated 1973.

Mints, Lloyd W., A History of Banking Theory in Great Britain and the United States. Chicago, University of Chicago Press, 1945.

Modigliani, Franco, Rasche, Robert, Cooper, P., "Central Bank Policy, the Money Supply, and the Short-term Rate of Interest", Journal of Money, Credit and Banking, May 1970, pp. 166-218.

Neumann, Manfred J. M., "A Theoretical and Empirical Analysis of the German Money Supply Process, 1958-1972", draft dated May 1974.

Siebke, Jürgen, "An Analysis of the German Money Supply Process: The Multiplier Approach", in Proceedings of the First Konstanzer Seminar on Monetary Theory and Monetary Policy, Karl Brunner (ed.), Supplement to Kredit und Kapital, Heft 1, 1972, pp. 243-272.

Teigen, Ronald, "Demand and Supply Functions for Money in the United States", Econometrica, October 1964, pp. 476-509.

Tobin, James, and Brainard, William C., "Financial Intermediaries and the Effectiveness of Monetary Control American Economic Review, May 1963, pp. 383-400.

Tobin, James, "A General Equilibrium Approach to Monetary Theory", Journal of Money, Credit and Banking, February 1969, pp. 15-29.

Willms, Manfred "Controlling Money in an Open Economy: The German Case", Federal Reserve Bank of St. Louis Review, April 1971, pp. 10-27.

Comments on the Fratianni's Paper

By

Jacques Melitz

One of the most important problems in monetary economics today is the determination of the money stock in an open economy whose money is not an international reserve asset. We know that domestic factors influence the supply of money in such an economy under floating exchange rates. The question is to what extent such factors also influence the supply of money under fixed exchange rates. In order to treat this problem, Fratianni admits the possibility that domestic and foreign securities are imperfect substitutes. Consequently, even in the event that the yield on foreign securities in terms of domestic money is set externally, domestic factors possibly can affect the yield on domestic securities. Likewise, Fratianni admits the possibility that domestic and foreign loans are imperfect substitutes and that both are imperfect substitutes for securities. Given these elements, he considers the determination of the stock of money. This involves, as is characteristic of models that are inspired by Brunner and Meltzer, the joint determination of money and of the stock of bank credit.

Some basic acquaintance with Brunner's recent work on the money stock in the closed and the open economy is required in order to read this essay (see especially [1] , [2]). It may be noted, in addition, that Fratianni is particularly close in spirit to Brunner and Meltzer's early article, "A Credit Market Theory of the Money Supply" [3]. This 1966 work, which appeared simultaneously in a relatively obscure Italian journal and a book of essays that is often difficult to locate, is, in my opinion, a more satisfactory source of some of Brunner and Meltzer's basic ideas than is the 1968 article in the Journal of Political Economy with which these same ideas are usually associated [4]. Fratianni's kinship to this earlier piece is especially evident in his emphasis on the distinction between bank loans and securities and in his use of the ratio of money to bank credit to move from the credit market to the money market.

The most important reservation about Fratianni's work is his failure to tell us much about the extent of foreign influence on the domestic stock of money. His statistical analysis, concerning Italian data for 1959 I - 1972 III inclusive, is lacking in this respect mainly because of several discrepancies between this statistical analysis and his theoretical discussion.

One such discrepancy which I shall mention mainly in order to make the discussion more complete, is his test of an abbreviated form of his basic model. In his theoretical sections, Fratianni develops a six-equation model, consisting of a demand and supply of bank loans, demand and supply of government securities, and demand and supply of money. He also subsequently admits a four-equation system, in which the distinction between securities and bank loans is removed, and we have simply a demand and supply of bank credit and a demand and supply of money. In his statistical analysis, however, Fratianni's most ambitious effort concerns a three-equation model consisting of the preceding four-equation model minus the demand for money.

We can easily understand Fratianni's omission of the demand for money in his statistical work, since he follows Brunner and Meltzer's view that the market for money determines (proximately) the yield on real capital. Lacking an Italian series for this yield, he finds it convenient to remove the demand for money from his estimation system, thereby ridding himself of the problem of determining the yield on real capital. The seriousness of this omission, moreover, is much mitigated by the fact that he estimates the demand for credit, and thus treats a major channel of private non-bank influence on the stock of money. Though we habitually fail to accommodate the point in our theoretical writing, the impact of the demand for credit on the stock of money may be much stronger than the impact of the demand for money on this stock, depending on the general monetary setting and the reaction function of the monetary authorities.

Other lapses from theory in this work, which really bring us to our main point, are several discrepancies between the estimated and the theoretical forms of the basic equations. In his theoretical analysis, Fratianni maintains that the foreign source component of the unborrowed monetary base is largely endogenous. He identifies this endogenous element with the cumulative value of the surpluses in the national balance of payments on capital account.

Accordingly, he views the cumulative value of the surpluses on current account as exogenous. But in his tests, Fratianni never follows this distinction. Either he excludes the entire foreign source component from the exogenous base or else he includes all of it. More specifically, he excludes all of it in his tests where he ignores anticipated inflation in the demand for credit, and he includes all of it in those tests where he admits anticipated inflation in the demand for credit. From a theoretical standpoint this makes no sense. We can only infer, it seems to me, that Fratianni's attempts to use anticipated inflation in the demand for credit led him into statistical difficulties which he could only resolve by embracing a very wide measure of the exogenous base.

Another deviation from theory in Fratianni's statistical analysis concerns the use of the foreign source component of the base as an explanatory variable in the demand for credit. Fratianni defends this practice by interpreting foreign reserves in the demand for credit as a proxy for foreign output and the foreign price level. But whatever the general basis may be for such an interpretation — about which there are doubts — Fratianni cannot properly treat foreign reserves as a priori information in his demand equation. For according to his own analysis, a substantial portion of this proxy is endogenous.[1)]

---

1) The presence of foreign reserves in Fratianni's demand for credit also may largely explain his finding that the Eurodollar deposit rate and the ratio of the forward to the spot exchange rate are statistically insignificant in this demand equation. These two variables may notably affect the level of foreign reserves. Therefore the coefficient of foreign reserves in the equation could incorporate the influence of these two factors.

Last but not least, in the estimated forms of his supply equations, Fratianni omits a number of critical theoretical variables pertaining to the extent of foreign influences on the quantity of money, including the foreign interest rate, the exchange rate, and the ratio of the forward to the spot exchange rate. Of course, problems of multi collinearity may have interfered with earlier efforts to include these variables. In particular, the foreign interest rate (as measured by the Eurodollar deposit rate) may well be highly collinear with the domestic interest rate (as measured by the yield on long term government bonds). Still, the fact remains that, as Fratianni's essay now stands, we have not the faintest idea of the degree to which his estimated coefficients of the domestic interest rate reflect domestic as opposed to foreign factors. It would be better, I think, if he provided, for example, some estimate of the coefficient of the foreign interest rate in the reduced-form equation for the domestic interest rate.

I turn next to the two departures from Brunner that Fratianni stresses especially: namely, his insistence on a separate parameter estimate of the coefficient of the exogenous base in the supply equations; and his assignment of a positive sign to the yield on capital in the supply of credit. On the first point, I strongly concur with Fratianni.

Brunner's method, which requires some elucidation on this point, is to break up bank credit into exogenous reserves and the ratio of bank credit to exogenous reserves (or a credit multiplier). Similarly, he breaks up money into exogenous reserves and the ratio of money to exogenous reserves (or a money multiplier).[2)]

Brunner then omits exogenous reserves as an argument in his functional equations regarding the two ratios or multipliers. It follows then that no parameter estimate of the coefficient of exogenous reserves is required in his supply of credit and supply of money equations. The impression thus arises (see for example Fratianni, p. 33) that the two supplies are linear homogeneous of degree one with respect to the exogenous base. In fact, the impression is not entirely correct since Brunner admits the impact of exogenous reserves on various of the arguments in the two multiplier functions. The effect of a change in the exogenous base on bank credit, $\frac{dC}{dB_e}$, in his model is thus

$$\frac{\partial C}{\partial B_e} + \sum_{i=1}^{i=k} \left(\frac{\partial C}{\partial X_i} \cdot \frac{\partial X_i}{\partial B_e} \right)$$

where the X_i terms are individual arguments in the credit multiplier function that are conditioned by B_e. Similar analysis applies to $\frac{dM}{dB_e}$. Therefore, in logarithmic terms, even though $\frac{\partial C}{\partial B_e}$ necessarily equals one, $\frac{dC}{dB_e}$ may be less than one, and its value is not theoretically predetermined.

However, even within the strict confines of Brunner's framework,

---

2) In his theoretical analysis, Brunner typically refers to unborrowed reserves instead of exogenous reserves. But he clearly has in mind exogenous reserves, and supposes that all unborrowed reserves are exogenous. This point emerges best when he examines price-pegging by the monetary authorities. Then he clearly recognizes that the unborrowed base, being endogenous, can no longer serve as an independent argument in determining the stock of bank credit and money. See especially [1, pp. 516-21] .

B_e should properly be included as a separate argument in the two multiplier functions. For a rise in B_e lowers the implicit yield on bank reserves, thereby reducing this yield relative to the other yields in the two multiplier functions even if all of these other yields stay the same. It then follows that banks will wish to lower their borrowed reserves relatively to their deposits. This in turn will lower both of the multipliers. Thus, the impact of the rise in the exogenous base on the total quantity of bank credit and money will be lower than Brunner implies. Moreover, in the absence of a proxy for the implicit yield on bank reserves, there is no way of taking the previous factor into account except to introduce the unborrowed base, as such, as an argument in the credit and money multiplier functions.

The importance of the previous element of substitution between borrowed and unborrowed reserves generally tends to be recognized under conditions where borrowed reserves are large. There are repeated references to this substitution in the pre-World War II literature dealing with the U.S. in the 1920's. The same factor also receives frequent mention in France today, where recent statistical estimates show that banks reduce their borrowing by more than 50 centimes for every additional franc of unborrowed reserves.[3), 4)]

---

3) These estimates concern responses within the same quarter; but the degree of substitution may be smaller over a year. The French estimate that Fratianni cites (from André Fourçans) concerning the impact of the unborrowed base on the borrowed one [6] is the highest one on record. J. H. David [5] and Melitz [7], especially the former, obtain lower estimates. So I understand does Fourçans in more recent work.

As regards the theoretical effect of the yield on real capital on the supply of credit, Fratianni, I believe, fails to meet Brunner's argument for assigning an opposite, or a negative, sign to this relation. Brunner argues that a rise in the yield on real capital, by inducing a substitution of savings deposits in favor of equities, will raise the ratio of demand to total deposits, and thereby increase the average legal reserve requirement, thus lowering the supply of credit. Fratianni, on his side, abstracts from the difference between savings and demand deposits, thereby ignoring the difference in legal reserve requirements between the two. His argument therefore cannot be decisive, though it may show that Brunner's is not either.

Another interesting deviation from Brunner in Fratianni is his use of a M_2 rather than a M_1 definition of money. Fratianni does not explain his preference for M_2 or the incorporation of all savings deposits at commercial banks (but not at other financial institutions) in the definition of money. M_2 definitions, however,

---

4) It is noteworthy that Fratianni, however, unwittingly allows himself little room for estimating the coefficient of the exogenous base since he consistently omits B_e (B^D in his notation) from the arguments in his behavioral equations underlying his supply of credit. B_e is absent in his equations for the demand for borrowed reserves, the difference between banks' foreign assets and their foreign liabilities, and the endogenous part of the foreign source component of the base (see equations (19), (20), and (22)). According to his equation (21a), this constrains the value of the coefficient of B_e to $\frac{1-r}{r}$ in his supply of credit, where r is the ratio of bank reserves to bank deposits. Since B_e is also absent from his behavioral equation concerning r_e (equation (18b)), dealing with the excess legal reserve ratio, Fratianni has no clear basis for estimating the coefficient of B_e. The error is easily remediable and allowances can be made for it.

have some important drawbacks in continental Western European countries. Term deposits at commercial banks in these countries often involve a high opportunity cost of conversion prior to a maturity date which can be as much as five years away. In addition, the moneyness of various classes of deposits at commercial banks is notably inferior to the moneyness of certain classes of deposits at savings banks.

I close with a couple of points that do not fit conveniently in the earlier discussion. The first concerns the sign of the influences of the yield on commercial banks' earning assets on the quantity of money. Fratianni believes this sign to be ambiguous because the yield on banks' earning assets, though affecting bank credit positively, affects the ratio of money to credit negatively. Fratianni thus presents the positive sign of this yield in the supply of money as mere assumption (p. 22). I believe, though, that the sign is theoretically justified.

Assume a M_2 definition of money in order to simplify the exposition. M_2 equals currency plus checking accounts plus total commercial bank savings deposits, thus equals (approximately) the unborrowed base plus commercial bank credit. If bank credit rises, M_2 can only fall when unborrowed reserves fall even more than the rise in bank credit. But there is no reason why a rise in the yield on bank credit should necessitate any reduction in the unborrowed base. Such a rise in yield would raise the ratio of bank credit to the unborrowed base by stimulating banks to hold lower excess legal reserves, increase their borrowed reserves, and offer more services and interest to their depositors (who would then in turn perhaps convert more currency into deposits and increase the ratio of their savings to their demand deposits). Clearly none of these influences, however, will cause the unborrowed base to fall. Thus, even though bank credit may rise relative to money, money certainly will go up.

My last comment concerns an issue of estimation. Fratianni adduces a theoretical framework in which the supply of money is a product of (1) the supply of credit and (2) a function determing the ratio of money to credit, M/C. He then engages in a simultaneous-equation estimate of the first of these two functions together with, not the second, but the supply of money (and as a third equation, the demand for credit).

A properly specified money supply function in Fratianni's work, however, would take a rather complicated form, full of cross-product terms, since the function should be stated as

$$M = \frac{M}{C} (.) \; . \; C (.).$$

Fratianni neglects this point, but simply formulates this function in a linear manner without any cross-product terms. Yet in any simultaneous-equation estimate of a linearized version of $\frac{M}{C}$ (.) . C (.), on the one hand, and C (.), on the other, in theory the estimate of the former is really a means of estimating $\frac{M}{C}$ (.), whereas in practice, such an estimate clearly will partly reflect the function C (.) instead of $\frac{M}{C}$ (.). In fact, a well specified and stable function C (.) may even lead to a good estimate of a linear approximation to $\frac{M}{C}$ (.) . C (.) even though $\frac{M}{C}$ (.) is poorly specified and unstable. Logic therefore points to a simultaneous-equation estimate of C (.) and $\frac{M}{C}$ (.) rather than C (.) and $\frac{M}{C}$ (.) · C (.).

REFERENCES

1. Brunner, Karl, "A Diagrammatic Exposition of the Money Supply Process", Schweizerische Zeitschrift für Volkswirtschaft und Statistik, 109 (Dec. 1973), pp. 481-533.

2. Brunner, Karl, "Money Supply Process and Monetary Policy in an Open Economy", in Michael B. Connolly and Alexander K. Swoboda, International Trade and Money (London: George Allen & Unwin, 1973), pp. 127-66.

3. Brunner, Karl and Meltzer, Allan H., "A Credit Market Theory of the Money Supply and an Explanation of Two Puzzles in U.S. Monetary Policy", Rivista Internazionale di Scienze Economiche e Commerciali, 13 (May 1966), pp. 405-32; also in Essays in Honor of Marco Fanno (Padova, 1966).

4. Brunner, Karl and Meltzer, Allan H., "Liquidity Traps for Money, Bank Credit, and Interest Rates", Journal of Political Economy, 76 (Jan.-Feb. 1968) pp. 1-37.

5. David, Jacques-Henri, "Le comportement bancaire et l'évolution de la masse monétaire", Banque de France, Bulletin Timestriel, No. 1 (Nov. 1971), pp. 43-56.

6. Fourçans, André, Money Stock, Bank Credit, and Interest Rate Formation in an Open Economy: the French Case. Unpublished D.B.A. dissertation, Indiana University, 1974.

7. Melitz, Jacques, "Une tentative d'explication de l'offre de monnaie en France", Revue Economique, 24 (Sept. 1973), pp. 761-800.

A MONEY AND BANK CREDIT MODEL FOR AN OPEN ECONOMY

THE BELGIAN EXPERIENCE 1960-1973

By D. Heremans

A. Sommariva

A. Verheirstraeten*

Introduction

Recently, a substantial body of literature has emerged on the money supply process and bank credit formation. Most analyses, however, have been restricted to the closed economy case.[1] For the open economy, the discussion has mostly proceeded at a higher level of abstraction with little empirical work. It consists mainly of elaborations of Mundell's pathbreaking contribution. These elaborations rely upon a linear money supply hypothesis and a Keynesian income-expenditure model, and emphasize the ineffectiveness of monetary policy with respect to the domestic economic activity in an open economy.[2]

---

* The authors are indebted to A. Fourçans and S. Plasschaert for critical comments on an earlier draft of this paper, and to M. Fratianni for having revised at length the final draft.

1) Among others K. Brunner and A. H. Meltzer (1966 and 1972), K. Brunner (1973, 1), A. E. Burger (1972), A. Fourçans (1974)

2) For a survey, see M. von Neumann-Whitman (1970).

In the last few years, the need to extend the new approaches of the process of money supply and bank credit formation to the open economy has been recognized.[3)] These approaches rely upon a non-linear money and bank credit supply hypothesis and a generalized transmission mechanism. As a basic framework, our analysis will use the Brunner-Meltzer (BM) model because of the following attractive features. First, in this model both the government budget and the balance of payments act as a constraint on the money supply process. Second, in BM securities and real capital assets are not considered as perfect substitutes, as in the Keynesian view of the transmission mechanism, but are instead recognized as separate assets. As an implication, the credit market is explicitly taken into consideration in the analysis and the price for real capital is introduced into the transmission process. Hence, even if monetary policy cannot affect interest rates due to perfect offsetting capital movements, it may have an effect on domestic economic activity through changes in the price for real capital. Third, in this approach the bank credit market may be further disaggregated into a loan and government securities market. We believe such a disaggregation to be especially appropriate for the Belgian situation since (i) the portfolio of the Belgian banks contains a large amount of government debt and (ii) specific policy measures have been taken in Belgium to directly affect either the loan portfolio of the banks - such as loan ceilings - or their portfolio of government securities - such as required government financing ratios. By disaggregating the bank credit market, it is possible to examine whether such measures

---

3) M. Fratianni (1972), K. Brunner (1973, 2).

have had an aggregative impact on the total volume of bank credit or an allocative impact on the distribution of the bank credit.

The strategy of our research is to first develop a disaggregated model of the bank credit market essentially following BM (1966). Furthermore, in line with the recent developments of the BM approach, e.g. Brunner (1973, 1), the demand for money is introduced into this model which permits the determination of the rate of return on real capital. We then extend the model to take into account the features of the open economy, as in Fratianni (1976) (included elsewhere in this volume). Our contribution in this development should be viewed as more empirical than theoretical, within the broader objective of giving an initial impulse to monetary analysis in Belgium where, in fact, there has been little empirical work in the monetary field.[4)]

The paper is organized as follows. In Section I we sketch a money base framework for Belgium and discuss the different sources of money base supply. In Section II we cover the theory of the model. It contains an explanation of the functioning of the loan market, the government securities market, and the money market, based on an analysis of the portfolio behavior of the banks and the nonbank public. In Section III we try to estimate the outlined model and give the empirical evidence on the theoretically specified equation. The main results and particularly relevant policy implications for Belgium are discussed in detail in Section IV.

---

4) Notable exceptions are however J. Vuchelen (1971) and P. Reding (1974).

I. Money Base Supply in an Open Economy

We start the analysis by presenting a non-linear money supply hypothesis based on the dominant role played by the supply of money base within the context of Belgium as an open economy. This framework allows to examine a large number of propositions of significant interest. In particular, it enables us to distinguish the actions of the monetary authorities from the portfolio behavior of the banking system and the public, and to properly introduce the influence of the balance of payments on domestic monetary processes. This framework also permits the incorporation in the analysis of the major institutional elements of the Belgian monetary system. The latter also promises to yield valuable policy recommendations concerning the usefulness of existing institutional arrangements in terms of the objective of money supply control.

1. The Money Base in Belgium

The money base is broadly defined as money created by the monetary authorities, namely net monetary liabilities of the government to the commercial banks and the nonbank public. The emphasis in defining the money base is on its function to serve as a reserve aggregate for bank money creation by the commercial banks. Therefore, the money base is also defined as those financial claims banks must hold if they are to produce their own bank money.

One distinguishing characteristic of these financial claims is their monetary nature, implying that these claims should directly possess medium of exchange properties or that they can be transformed into such with zero or negligible transaction costs. The other characteristic is that these claims are net monetary liabilities of the government, or better of all monetary authorities.[5)] These authorities are usually identified in theoretical works with the central bank. In Belgium, however, numerous government agencies intervene in the money supply process. Some of these agencies are only control organisms, like the Banking Commission and the Belgium Luxemburg Foreign Exchange Institute. Others refinance themselves at the central bank, like the Institute for Rediscount and Guarantee and the Government Securities Stabilization Fund (D. Heremans, A. Sommariva, A. Verheirstraeten, 1974, 2).

By inspecting the relevant balance sheets involved, one can readily appreciate that in Belgium, both the central bank and the Treasury issue monetary liabilities that have money base properties. Money base includes: (i) currency issued by the National Bank and held by the public, C^P_{NB}, and the banks, C^B_{NB}; (ii) central bank deposit liabilities to the banks, DB^B_{NB}; (iii) currency of small denominations issued by the Treasury through the Mint to the public, C^P_{TR}, and to the banks, C^B_{TR}; (iv) postal deposit

5) For the open economy this could eventually lead to a larger interpretation. How to qualify foreign exchange held by the commercial banks and the public? In a system of fixed exchange rates these are monetary liabilities of foreign governments, whose prices, however, are to be pegged.

liabilities through the Postal Deposit Office, also to the public, PD^P, and the banks, PD^B.

More succinctly, the money base can be derived by consolidating the balance sheets of the National Bank and the Treasury. From the liabilities side we obtain the uses of base money,

$$(1) \qquad B = C_{NB}^{P} + C_{NB}^{B} + DB_{NB}^{B} + C_{TR}^{P} + C_{TR}^{B} + PD^{P} + PD^{B}$$

with base money in the hands of the public being equal to

$$(2) \qquad B^{P} = C_{NB}^{P} + C_{TR}^{P} + PD^{P}$$

and money base held by the banks (their cash reserve holding), being equal to

$$(3) \qquad R = C_{NB}^{B} + C_{TR}^{B} + DB_{NB}^{B} + PD^{B}$$

or more simply

$$(1a) \qquad B = B^{P} + R$$

The sources of money base are obtained from the assets side of the consolidated balance.

$$(4) \qquad B = AD + GF^{NB} + GF^{TR} + IR$$

where AD = domestic refinancing of the banks at the central bank,

GF^{NB} = government financing by the central bank, i.e. the government debt portfolio of the National Bank,

GF^{TR} = government financing through base money creation by the Treasury itself, i.e. via the issuance of small denomination currency and the creation of postal deposits, and

IR = international reserves of the monetary authorities.

It is useful at this point to add some comments on two other government agencies which intervene in the money base market from the supply side, although they themselves do not issue monetary liabilities. The first agency is the Government Securities Stabilization Fund (Fonds des Rentes) which buys and sells government securities with the explicit objective of smoothing out the daily fluctuations in the government bonds market. The Fund finances these operations not by creating monetary liabilities, but by issuing its own securities, by borrowing on the call money market, and by using its credit line with the National Bank. Only the last operation leads to money base creation which, however, during our sample period, was in principle constrained to a ceiling of BF 4 billion.

The other agency is the Institute for Rediscount and Guarantee (Institut de Réescompte et de Garantie) which carries out rediscount operations on domestic trade bills and export bankers' acceptances for the commercial banks.[6] These operations are financed through borrowing in the call money market, by replacing trade bills on the discount market (mainly with non-bank financial intermediaries), and by rediscounting trade bills with the National Bank. Among these various ways of financing, only the discount operations between the National Bank and the Institute for

6) Export bankers' acceptances can be considered as equivalent to domestic trade bills. At the time they are transacted on the discount market, no transaction on the foreign exchange market has yet been involved.

Rediscount and Guarantee affect the money base supply.[7)]

2. Source Components of the Money Base

To analyze the process of money base creation in an open economy, it is important to distinguish between external sources, determined by the evolution of the balance of payments, and internal sources, determined by the evolution of the government budget and banks' borrowing from the monetary authorities.

The internal source components of the money base are government debt and private debt absorbed in the portfolio of the monetary authorities. In turn, the government debt includes: (i) the portfolio of government bonds with the National Bank, i.e., a consolidated debt of BF 34 billion; (ii) advances by the National Bank against treasury bills, advances which have been subject until 1974 to a ceiling of BF 16 billion; (iii) the financing of the Government Securities Funds; and (iv) the monetary financing of the Treasury via the emission of small coins and postal deposit liabilities. The former facility is legally restricted to a small amount; the latter depends instead upon the demand of the banks and the public for postal deposits.

7) The refinancing on the call money market and on the discount market is merely a channel to redistribute base money between the banks and the nonbank public, but is not a source of additional base money creation. See D. Heremans, A. Sommariva, A. Verheirstraeten (1974, 2).

Given the small use of open market operations in Belgium, changes in the government debt component largely originate from government budget deficits and surpluses. Therefore, the latter have acted as a constraint upon the monetary authorities.

Government expenditures, G, are financed by taxes, T, by increases in government debt with the monetary authorities, GF^{NB} and GF^{TR}, and by placing government securities either abroad, S^F, or with the banks and the public, S^B and S^P.

It follows that the cumulative government budget deficit is equal to the outstanding stock of government debt, S,

$$(5) \qquad \int_{-\infty}^{T_o} (G-T)\,dt = S = GF^{NB} + GF^{TR} + S^F + S^B + S^P$$

The private debt which appears in the portfolio of the monetary authorities, AD, originates from the domestic refinancing operations of the commercial banks. In Belgium, as in other European countries, the discount window plays an important role. It mainly encompasses domestic trade bills and export bankers' acceptances rediscounted by the banks either directly with the National Bank or indirectly with the Institute for Rediscount and Guarantee. Since the monetary authorities set the discount rate, but the commercial banks decide the amount they want to rediscount, the quantity AD is not controlled by the authorities once the rediscount rate is set. Domestic bank borrowing thus is endogenously determined by the behavior of the banks. The monetary authorities may regain control over this money base source by imposing discount ceilings, affecting the refinancing at the

National Bank as well as at the Institute for Rediscount and Guarantee, on the condition, however, that these discount ceilings effectively curtail the actual amount of AD below the level desired by the banks.

Changes in the foreign source component of the monetary base originate from balance of payments disequilibria. In a system of fixed exchange rates, the balance of payments acts as a constraint on the money base supply since the monetary authorities peg the foreign exchange rate by buying or selling international reserves in the foreign exchange market:

$$(6) \qquad IR = \int_{-\infty}^{T_o} CAB \, dt + S^F + (FL - FA)^P + (FL - FA)^B$$

CAB	=	current account balance,
S^F	=	net foreign government debt, resulting from net capital imports,
$(FL - FA)^P$	=	net foreign position of the public (liabilities minus assets),
$(FL - FA)^B$	=	net foreign position of the banks.

For short run analysis, the current account balance may be considered exogenous; not so for the capital movements of the public and the banks which are determined endogenously in the model. Among others, they are affected by the prevailing regulations of the Belgian double exchange market (cfr. Decaluwe and Steinherr (1975) elsewhere in this volume).[8] Net government capital imports constitute a direct link between the government budget and the balance of payments. A substantial amount of government debt in Belgium is issued in foreign currency which is for the largest part absorbed by domestic banks and in a small part placed directly abroad. While the direct placement abroad of government securities implies a capital inflow, and thus, provokes an equivalent increase in the money base, the same need not be true when foreign denominated government debt is placed with domestic banks. In fact, banks purchase the securities by drawing down their foreign reserves which by itself creates no change in money base but simply a substitution of foreign reserves from banks to central bank. A change in international reserves might occur only subsequently as banks readjust their foreign-currency portfolio as a reaction to the initial purchase of securities.[9)]

---

8) The economic and monetary union between Belgium and Luxemburg leads to certain complications in the analysis. In particular, the international reserves of the National Bank do not change by trade and capital movements between Belgium and Luxemburg. For trade however,the relevant magnitudes for Luxemburg are very small compared to the Belgian magnitudes. Further, both economies are highly integrated, are subject to the same monetary policies, and reflect a similar evolution. Therefore, the foreign source component unadjusted for Luxemburg may, in most respects, give a good approximation for the Belgian situation. However, the importance of capital transactions between Belgium and Luxemburg requires some caution. In fact, the total foreign position of the Belgian banks should be distinguished in the position versus Luxemburg and versus third countries. Only the latter affects the quantity of base money in Belgium. Changes in the former must be considered as equivalent to a redistribution of base money between the banks and the non-bank public.

9) The Belgian banks can, for example, refinance the purchase of government securities in foreign currency in the Eurocurrency market. This thus causing a capital inflow.

The operational content of both constraints (5) and (6) can be appreciated by considering the implications of a government deficit in a small open economy as Belgium, for which interest rates are largely determined abroad. In a closed economy, such a budget deficit need not be financed by money and, in that sense, it is not a direct constraint on the behavior of the monetary authorities. However, the open economy assumption will eventually force the deficit to be monetized regardless of whether it was initially financed by money or not. In fact, if the deficit is financed by issuing securities to the public, there results a pressure on domestic interest rates to rise relative to the world interest rate, inducing an inflow of capital and, thus, an increase of money base.

The importance of the external sources for the supply of money base in a small open economy like Belgium can be seen in Table 1 of Appendix II. The share of external sources in the total sources increases from 48 pct. in 1960 to 59 pct. in 1973. In recent years its evolution was clearly dominated by the trade balance. The government component was growing slowly, while the domestic bank borrowing components have shown marked fluctuations.[10)]

---

10) For a further analysis, see D. Heremans, A. Sommariva, A. Verheirstraeten (1974, 1 and 2).

II. Theoretical Specification of a Money and Bank Credit Model

1. A Portfolio Model

Following the BM hypothesis, money in our model has a generalized substitutability over real as well as financial assets. The general equilibrium system includes five markets: money, loan, government securities, real capital, and output. In the present stage of our research, the analysis is restricted to a short run financial model in which the output market is considered as exogenously given. Three prices are determined: the loan interest rate, the government securities interest rate, and the rate on real capital. According to Walras law, one market may be left out; in our model, it is the market for real capital.

The portfolio behavior of the banks and the nonbank public explains the formation of bank credit, the money stock, and the various interest rates in these markets. The range of assets and liabilities held by the public is summarized by the following balance sheet:

$$B^P + DD + TD + S^P + K + NW^B + FA^P = L + FL^P + NW^P \tag{7}$$

with DD = demand deposits,

TD = time deposits,

S^P = government securities in hands of the public,

K = the stock of physical capital,

NW^B = the net worth of the banking system,

L = loans to the public ,

NW^P = net worth of the public.

The consolidated balance sheet of the banking system is given by:

(8) $$R + L + S^B + FA^B = DD + TD + AD + FL^B + NW^B$$

After substituting for the net worth of the banking system, the net wealth of the public is equal to:[11)]

(9) $$NW^P = B^{ex} + S + K$$

where B^{ex} denotes the exogenous base, which is defined as:

(10) $$B^{ex} = B + (FA - FL)^P + (FA - FL)^B - AD.$$

Contrary to Tobin-inspired models where wealth acts as a constraint on the public's behavior, we allow here wealth to respond to changes in two endogenous variables of the model; that is,

(9a) $$NW^P = B^{ex} + \nu(i_s, m)S + P_K.K$$

with P_K being the price of real capital and $\nu(i_s, m)$ the valuation function of outstanding government securities which depends on the interest rate and the maturity of these securities. Since in Belgium there exists no reliable time series on the stock of physical capital, hereafter a more restricted concept of financial wealth, W_f, will be used; namely, the sum of the exogenous base and the market value of the outstanding stock of government securities.

(9b) $$W_f = B^{ex} + \nu(i_s, m)S$$

11) It is known that in a non-fully competitive banking system, part of the bank deposits should also be counted as wealth.

It must be noted that the above wealth concept refers only to non-human wealth. Total wealth should also include human wealth, which in the empirical work will be approximated by a measure of permanent income, Y_p.[12)]

2. The Bank Credit Market

Total domestic bank credit equals the sum of bank credit to the private sector, L, and bank credit to the government sector, S^B. We will analyze each of them in turn.

a) The Loan Market

The volume of bank loans, L, and the interest rate on loans, i_L, are proximately determined by the interaction of the demand for bank loans by the nonbank public and the supply of these loans by the banks, which are specified respectively in equation (11) and (12).

$$(11) \quad L/P = \alpha(i_L - \dot{p}_e, i_s - \dot{p}_e, i_K, i_E, \dot{p}_e, W_f/P, Y_p/P)$$

$$\alpha_1 < 0; \alpha_2, \alpha_3, \alpha_4, \alpha_5, \alpha_6, \alpha_7 > 0$$

---

12) Human wealth is approximated by permanent human income. But since in Belgium the share of labour income in GNP remains roughly constant over time, total income can be used as a proxy for human income.

$$(12) \quad L = \beta(i_L, i_s, i_E, B, B^P/DD, \rho, \Pi_R, \Pi_D, \Pi_F, \Pi_L, \Pi_G)$$

$$\beta_1, \beta_4 > 0; \beta_2, \beta_3, \beta_5, \beta_6, \beta_7, \beta_8, \beta_9, \beta_{10}, \beta_{11} < 0$$

The demand for bank loans is specified in real terms as in BM. This demand function is derived, as stated in Melitz and Pardue (1973) and Melitz (1975), from the Fisherian framework in which the demand for bank credit for an individual results from the maximization of an utility function based on the preferences between present and future consumption. The wealth variable, W_f, and the permanent income variable, Y_p, constrain the demand for bank loans. The relevant interest rates are real interest rates, $i_L - p_e$, $i_S - p_e$, and i_K. In addition to the domestic rates we introduce i_E which is defined as the Eurodollar rate adjusted for the premium or discount in the forward foreign exchange market. The sign of i_E is unambiguously positive. As a price of a substitute for domestic loans, the foreign interest rate will have a positive influence on the demand for bank loans. As a rate of return on investment in the Eurodollar market, again a positive relation is implied.

The supply of loans by the banks is specified in equation (12).[13)] It is a positive function of the own rate i_L, and a negative func-

---

13) Following the nonlinear money and bank credit supply hypothesis, bank credit derives from the product of the money base and the bank asset multiplier. In this model, the analysis is, however, simplified by using semi-reduced form relations in which the supply of bank credit is a direct function of the money base and of ultimate determining variables.

tion of the rate on the substitutable government securities, i_S. The Eurodollar rate, i_E, influences the supply of domestic loans in two ways, both having a negative impact: as an asset rate on a substitute for domestic credit, and as a rate on bank borrowing in the international market. The loan supply of the banks responds positively to the money base, B, and is also influenced by the distribution of the base between the public and the banks, approximated by the ratio B^P/DD. Its expected sign is negative. In Belgium, the strong declining trend in the currency to deposit ratio (from about 2 in 1960 to about 1 in 1973) has been an important source of bank credit and money creation. Finally, we have included policy variables such as the discount rate, ρ, required reserve coefficients, Π_R, ceilings on rediscounts at the central bank, Π_D, ceilings on the net foreign liability position of the banks, Π_F, quantitative loan ceilings, Π_L, and the requirement for the banks to invest part of their deposits in government securities, Π_G.

It must be further noted that the total amount of loans supplied by commercial banks is the sum of the net loan assets they hold in their portfolio, LA, and the loan assets they have rediscounted at the central bank, AD. Those loan assets which are rediscounted by nonbank financial intermediaries are netted out from the total amount of bank loans supplied to the nonbank public.[14)] In addition to the supply of bank loans, L, we have to specify a

14) On the domestic bank refinancing possibilities outside the National Bank in Belgium, more research remains to be done. As previously mentioned, such transactions lead to a redistribution of base money between the nonbank public and the banks.

function for the domestic refinancing of the commercial banks at the central bank. Equation (13) reflects a peculiar treatment of the loan market which is discussed in detail in Melitz (1973) and Fourçans (1974).

(13) $L = LA + AD$

(14) $AD = \gamma(\rho, i_L, i_S, i_E, BU, \Pi_R, \Pi_D, \Pi_F)$

with $BU = B - AD$.

$\gamma_1, \gamma_5, \gamma_7 < 0; \quad \gamma_2, \gamma_3, \gamma_4, \gamma_6, \gamma_8 > 0$

Banks resort to the discount window of the National Bank when they are in short supply of money base to finance their credits. We postulate the domestic bank borrowing at the National Bank to be inversely related to the other sources of money base, in this case the unborrowed base, BU. Furthermore, domestic bank borrowing responds positively to the level of interest rates on loans, i_L, and on government securities, i_S, and negatively to the discount rate, ρ, and to the rediscount ceiling, Π_D. The sign for the Eurodollar rate is positive since it represents, on the one hand, an alternative borrowing rate, and on the other hand, a rate on an alternative (foreign) asset. Reserve requirements, Π_R, positively influence the demand for domestic refinancing. The same applies for restrictions on the foreign debt positions of the banks, Π_F.

b) The Government Securities Market

The interest rate on government securities is proximately determined in the government securities market.[15] As we have explained, the total supply of government debt, S, is absorbed: by the monetary authorities, $GF^{NB} + GF^{TR}$, which leads to base money creation by the banks, S^B, by the non-bank public, S^P, and by domestic banks and the rest of the world in case of securities denominated in foreign exchange, S^F. Only the stocks of government securities held by the banks and the public are endogenous in the model. In Belgium, 27 percent of the outstanding government debt, as of the end of 1973, was held by the commercial banks, and the banks' share is increasing over time (see Table 2, Appendix II).

In the banks' demand for government securities (equation 15), the loan ceiling and the required government financing ratio appear with a positive sign in contrast to the bank loan supply function. The demand for government securities by the non-bank public (equation 16) is specified in real terms. These holdings include not only the households and the business sector, but also the saving institutions and all other non-bank financial intermediaries. This observation is relevant for the specification of (16) insofar as the Belgian government extended in 1972 to the non-bank financial intermediaries the required government financing ratio. We introduce, therefore, Π_G in (16) to capture the effect of the new regulation.

$$(15) \qquad S^B = \omega\,(i_S, i_L, i_E, B, B^P/DD, \Pi_R, \Pi_D, \Pi_F, \Pi_G, \Pi_L)$$

$$\omega_1, \omega_4, \omega_9, \omega_{10} > 0; \quad \omega_2, \omega_3, \omega_5, \omega_6, \omega_7, \omega_8 < 0$$

15) Government securities stand for total government debt, as no distinction is made between the particular forms of debt financing.

(16) $S^P/P = \phi(i_S, i_L, i_E, W_f/P, Y_p/P, \Pi_G)$

$$\phi_1, \phi_4, \phi_5 > 0; \ \phi_2, \phi_3 < 0$$

The reader should be aware that Π_G has an indeterminate sign in (16). Since in this model the supply of government securities is given, it should be expected that the effects of Π_G across (15) and (16) sum to zero. There could be several errors of specification, however, which could account for the constraint not to be satisfied empirically. First, S^P includes both the stock of government securities held by the nonbank financial intermediaries and the nonbank public. It is obvious that Π_G can have a direct effect only on the demand for bonds by nonbank financial intermediaries. Second, in a fully specified market we would have had to endogenize the demand for domestic bonds by the rest of the world. With four separate demand schedules, the constraint that Π_G must have a zero effect across the bond market, for a given supply curve, would be more likely satisfied than in the present specification. Finally, there is no reason to rule out the interesting case that governments use these regulations to create captive markets for their bonds. If this were true, then the overall effect of Π_G would be to expand the total stock of government bonds.

In spite of these shortcomings, we did opt for the simpler specification largely on the ground that the data relevant to carry out empirically the more appropriate approach were unavailable.

The equilibrium condition in the government securities market is directly derived from the government budget constraint,

$$\text{(5a)} \quad S - (GF^{NB} + GF^{TR} + S^{F}) = S^{B} + S^{P}$$

3. The Money Market

Equilibrium in the money market proximately determines the rate of return on real capital, i_K. Demand and supply schedules in this market pertain to the broad money stock concept, M_2, as defined in equation (17). Data of the Belgian money stock are reported in Table 3, Appendix II.

$$\text{(17)} \quad M_2 = B^{P} + DD + TD$$

The demand of the public for each of the three money stock components is specified in (18)-(20),

$$\text{(18)} \quad B^{P}/P = \lambda(i_K, i_S - \dot{p}_e, i_T - \dot{p}_e, W_f/P, Y_p/P, \dot{p}_e, \Pi_A)$$

$$\lambda_1, \lambda_2, \lambda_3, \lambda_6, \lambda_7 < 0; \lambda_4, \lambda_5 > 0$$

$$\text{(19)} \quad DD/P = \tau(i_K, i_S - \dot{p}_e, i_T - \dot{p}_e, W_f/P, Y_p/P, \dot{p}_e, \Pi_A)$$

$$\tau_1, \tau_2, \tau_3, \tau_6 < 0; \tau_4, \tau_5, \tau_7 > 0$$

$$\text{(20)} \quad TD/P = \xi(i_K, i_S - \dot{p}_e, i_T - \dot{p}_e, W_f/P, Y_p/P, \dot{p}_e)$$

$$\xi_1, \xi_2, \xi_6 < 0; \xi_3, \xi_4, \xi_5, \xi_6 > 0$$

The interest rate on time deposits, i_T, is included in the demand functions for base money, B^P, demand deposits, DD, and time deposits, TD. During our sample period i_T has been fixed by a cartel agreement among commercial banks. The cartel has received the imprimatur of the National Bank, with the single exception, made for interest payments on large deposits (BF 5 billion minimum).[16)]

In the demand functions of the public for base money and for demand deposits, an additional explanatory variable, Π_A, is included to capture the influence of institutional changes, especially the legal stipulation, operative since November 1967, requiring all firms to open a postal or bank account. Since public's money base is mainly held in the form of currency, and since the postal deposits to demand deposits ratio has been decreasing, Π_A should have a negative influence on the demand function for B^P, and a positive influence on the demand for DD.

Finally, once the money base demand of the public is specified, equation (1a) implies that the amount of money base absorbed by the commercial banks in the form of reserves, R, is also determined.

The supply of money is implicitly determined in our model.[17)]

---

16) The interest rate in time deposits could be derived as the result of a price setting function for the banks taking into account discount rate, the external rate, and the internal market rates.
17) Since the deposit component of the money supply is not independent of the relations which have been specified for the bank credit market, it is not a proper procedure, in this model, to specify an independent global money supply function. The authors thank A. Fourçans for having made this point.

The amount of demand and time deposits banks are willing to supply can be derived from the balance sheet of the commercial banking system given in equation (8). By adding B^P to both sides of this equation, we obtain the money stock in terms of bank loans, bank credit to the government, and the money base net of the domestic and foreign borrowing of the banks.

$$M = DD + TD + B^P = L + S^B + B - AD - (FL - FA)^B$$

The money supply thus is shown to be the outcome, together with total bank credit, of a fully specified general equilibrium system.

Additional equations have to be specified because three sources of money base are endogenous: the net domestic refinancing of the commercial banks, AD, the net foreign liability position of the banks, $(FL - FA)^B$, and the net foreign liability position of the public, $(FL - FA)^P$. We have already explained domestic bank borrowing; the other two behavioural relations are given by equations(21) and (22).

(21) $(FL - FA)^B = \mu(i_E, i_L, i_S, \rho, BA, FE, \Pi_R, \Pi_D, \Pi_F)$

with $BA = B - (FL - FA)^B$

$\mu_1, \mu_5, \mu_9 < o; \mu_2, \mu_3, \mu_4, \mu_6, \mu_7, \mu_8 > o$

(22) $(FA - FL)^P = \kappa(i_E, i_S, W_f, FE, \Pi_F)$

$\kappa_1, \kappa_3, \kappa_5 > o; \kappa_2, \kappa_4 < o$

Refinancing in the international financial markets is, for the Belgian banks, an important alternative to domestic refinancing at the central bank. Therefore, the same set of explanatory variables enters in both equations (14) and (21). In the equation for the net foreign liability position of the banks, the relevant money base is the total money base adjusted for foreign bank borrowing. The influence of the Eurodollar rate on this equation is unequivocally negative. Also, the foreign exchange rate on the Belgian free market, FE, (the value of the dollar in terms of BF) enters in the equation to capture speculative capital movements. In contrast to banks, the public in Belgium always has an excess of foreign assets over foreign liabilities, which is a justification for expressing (22) as a net capital outflow.

III. Empirical Estimation of the Model

The equations of the model are estimated on quarterly data for the period 1960-I/1973-IV. We use end of quarter seasonally unadjusted data. Dummy variables are introduced to take account of seasonal influences. The equations of the model are estimated simultaneously using a two stage least squares procedure as described in Fair (1970).

It must be remarked that there is no one-to-one correspondence between the theoretical relationships and the equations which have been estimated, primarily because of problems of multicollinearity. Multicollinearity, in fact, is particular troublesome with the simultaneous use of policy variables and interest rates. We adopted a strategy of dropping those instruments of policy which, being highly collinear, made impossible to disentangle their separate effects.

1. Some principal statistical measures for Belgium

Some of the variables, which enter in the specification of the model, were not readily available. As is common in such cases we resorted to the construction of proxy variables. Hereafter a description is given of the procedures we followed.

First, no satisfactory data on bank loan rate are published in Belgium for the period under consideration. Traditionally, however, a strong link has been observed between bank loan rates and the official lending rate of the National Bank of Belgium. We used, therefore, the later as a proxy for the bank loan rate.

Second, policy variables such as loan ceilings (dummy the 1965-1966 and 1969-1971 period), impositions of required reserves holding by the commercial banks (since the second half of 1972), the requirement of minimum government financing ratios by the banks, and the regulations of the net foreign position of the banks are captured in the empirical estimates by dummy variables. Although this procedure is the least satisfactory, it was adopted because of the lack of information on exact quantitative measures. Research is currently being undertaken to improve this aspect of the analysis.

Third, permanent income is computed according to the following formula[18)]

$$Y_p = \left[\sum_{i=1}^{19} \left(\frac{0.9}{1+g}\right) \right]^{-1} \left[\sum_{i=1}^{19} (0.9)^i \; Y_{t-1} \right]$$

where g is the observed growth rate of real income during the period under investigation.

Fourth, lacking data on physical capital and its rate of return in Belgium, the real rate of return on capital was computed as follows. Using the approach of Gordon (1962), we define r, the rate of return required by stockholders, as the rate which equates the present value of expected future dividends, D_t with its current market price, P_o,

$$P_o = \int_o^\infty D_t e^{-rt} dt$$

where

$$D_t = D_o e^{gt}$$

$$g = \text{expected growth rate of dividends}$$

we can transform the above formulation into

$$P_o = D_o \int_o^\infty e^{-t(r-g)} dt$$

18) The same formula is applied as in J. Melitz (1972, 2), yielding weights approximating Friedman's permanent income weights.

and carrying out the integration, we obtain

$$P_o = \frac{D_o}{r-g} \quad \text{or} \quad r = \frac{D_o}{P_o} + g$$

The real rate, i_k, is finally obtained by

$$i_k = \frac{D_o/P}{P_o} + g$$

where

g = expected real rate of growth of dividends.

From this expression, it follows that the expected real rate of return on shares is equal to the sum of the current real dividend yield and the expected real growth rate of dividends. The expected rate is derived from the observed real growth rate of dividends in previous periods. A logistic lag structure is applied extending over nine years.

Fifth, different measures for the price expectations variable are utilized in the empirical estimates. The first measure is calculated on the basis of a Fisherian weighting scheme with an arithmetic progression extending over six quarters and summing to one. The second measure is based on quantification of qualitative results from business surveys.[19)] Data are taken from a business survey conducted by the E.E.C. among a large group of business

19) "Enquete mensuelle harmonisé auprès des chefs des entreprises de la C.E.E.," General Directorate of Economic and Financial Affairs -- E.E.C. Commission, Brussels.

firms. The two price expectations measures are tested alternatively in the empirical estimates.

Finally, stock data on the foreign liabilities and assets of the Belgian public are not available. However, an attempt was made to construct a statistical series for the foreign position of the public in the following way. Stock data, for an initial period, were derived from the national income accounts by discounting net interest payments paid to the outside world at a representative Belgian interest rate, namely, an index of yields on treasury bills and other government securities. The same procedure was applied to obtain the foreign assets. In this case, the discount rate is an index of interest rates on Eurodollars, Eurobonds, and Moody's composite yield for the New York Stock Exchange. Finally, the net foreign position of the public was obtained by subtracting the net foreign position of the government and of the banking system from the above computation. Starting with this initial figure, the net foreign position of the public for each quarter was calculated by adding the flows from the balance of payment statistics.

2. Analysis of empirical results

The model contains eleven behavioral functions, whose empirical estimates are shown in Table 1. Mean elasticities of the different variables are given in Appendix IV. Most results are consistent with the implications of the theory, thus confirming the relevance of the theoretical model in explaining monetary phenomena in Belgium.

The estimates for the supply of bank loans to the public and credit to the government clearly point to the importance of the money base in explaining the formation of bank credit and money supply in Belgium. Mean elasticities of B in the bank credit supply to the government and to the public have a value of about unity. When these functions are estimated for different subperiods, the elasticities remain stable.

The coefficient of the unborrowed base in the AD equation highlights the "offsetting" behavior of banks, through discount borrowing facilities, with respect to autonomous changes in the unborrowed base. A similar "offsetting" behavior can be noted in the foreign borrowing function, $(FL - FA)^B$. Here banks respond to an autonomous change in the adjusted money base, BA, by raising or lowering their net foreign indebtedness.

Remark, however, that these coefficients are partial rather than total derivatives. An increase in AD, brought about by an autonomous decrease in the unborrowed base, influences interest rates and thus induces a change in BU. Similarly, a change in $(FL - FA)^B$, caused by an autonomous change in BA, influences interest rate and induces a change in BA. To compute the total offsetting behavior of the banks, we should take into account the responsiveness of domestic rates, BU, and BA to a change in the exogenous components of the money base. Namely,

$$\frac{dAD}{dB^{ex}} = \frac{\partial AD}{\partial BU} \cdot \frac{dBU}{dB^{ex}} + \frac{\partial AD}{\partial i_s} \cdot \frac{di_s}{dB^{ex}}$$

TABLE 1

Empirical estimates of the model: 1960-I - 1973-IV[a)]

$$(11)\quad L/P = \underset{(1.68)}{-8.81}(i_L-\dot{p}_e) + \underset{(1.18)}{7.99}(i_S-\dot{p}_e) + \underset{(0.59)}{1.09}\, i_E + \underset{(5.19)}{0.63}\, W_f/P + \underset{(1.48)}{3.17}\, Y_p/P + \underset{(1.03)}{0.79}\, Y_T + \underset{(1.22)}{57.30}\, \dot{p}_e$$

$$\underset{(1.04)}{-3.64}\, D_1 + \underset{(0.40)}{2.08}\, D_2 + \underset{(0.39)}{1.54}\, D_3 - \underset{(5.46)}{1060.50}$$

$R^2 = 0.986 \quad D.W. = 1.66 \quad S.E. = 10.58$

$$(12)\quad L = \underset{(1.26)}{2.53}\, i_L - \underset{(0.83)}{3.38}\, i_S - \underset{(1.22)}{0.56}\, i_E + \underset{(4.18)}{1.53}\, B - \underset{(1.98)}{61.83}\, KR - \underset{(2.19)}{8.77}\, \Pi_L + \underset{(1.01)}{11.85}\, \Pi_D - \underset{(0.19)}{51.93}$$

$R^2 = 0.990 \quad D.W. = 2.07 \quad S.E. = 10.57$

$$(13)\quad AD = \underset{(1.49)}{3.55}\, i_S + \underset{(1.50)}{0.81}\, i_E + \underset{(0.10)}{3.25}\, \rho - \underset{(4.34)}{0.39}\, BU + \underset{(2.23)}{11.81}\, \Pi_R - \underset{(3.86)}{4.39}\, D_2 + \underset{(1.70)}{2.03}\, D_3 - \underset{(3.47)}{3.75}\, D_4 + \underset{(3.21)}{125.16}$$

$R^2 = 0.824 \quad D.W. = 2.24 \quad S.E. = 4.09$

$$(15)\quad S^B = \underset{(1.56)}{9.98}\, i_S - \underset{(0.60)}{2.41}\, i_L - \underset{(0.13)}{0.10}\, i_E - \underset{(3.45)}{51.20}\, KR + \underset{(6.35)}{1.00}\, B + \underset{(1.87)}{4.62}\, \Pi_G - \underset{(0.87)}{5.23}\, \Pi_D - \underset{(1.25)}{2.35}\, D_1$$

$$\underset{(3.15)}{+6.33}\, D_2 - \underset{(3.91)}{8.42}\, D_3 - \underset{(0.73)}{70.63}$$

$R^2 = 0.993 \quad D.W. = 2.30 \quad S.E. = 4.90$

TABLE 1 - Continued

(16) $$S^P = \underset{(4.06)}{30.99}\, i_S - \underset{(1.81)}{3.47}\, i_E + \underset{(21.62)}{0.91}\, W_f + \underset{(3.10)}{15.07}\, \Pi_G - 514.28$$

$R^2 = 0.984$ D.W. = 2.16 S.E. = 12.02

(18) $$B^P/P = \underset{(8.56)}{-2.99}\, i_K - \underset{(2.97)}{8.18}\, i_S - \underset{(0.55)}{0.62}\, i_T + \underset{(4.15)}{0.06}\, W_f/P + \underset{(15.68)}{1.19}\, Y_p/P - \underset{(5.44)}{0.53}\, \Pi_A + \underset{(5.53)}{73.47}$$

$R^2 = 0.909$ D.W. = 1.80 S.E. = 4.62

(19) $$DD/P = \underset{(1.30)}{-0.95}\, i_K + \underset{(6.07)}{8.84}(i_T - \dot{p}_e) - \underset{(2.78)}{2.69}\, i_E + \underset{(16.74)}{0.33}\, W_f/P + \underset{(1.42)}{0.26}\, Y_p/P - \underset{(0.33)}{0.06}\, Y_T - \underset{(2.80)}{8.95}\, \dot{p}_e + \underset{(3.62)}{7.98}\, \Pi_A$$
$$+ \underset{(0.42)}{1.26}\, D_1 - \underset{(1.66)}{0.74}\, D_2 + \underset{(0.82)}{2.92}\, D_3 - \underset{(5.42)}{180.6}$$

$R^2 = 0.991$ D.W. = 2.06 S.E. = 3.65

(20) $$TD/P = \underset{(0.66)}{-1.08}\, i_K + \underset{(7.48)}{17.13}\, i_T - \underset{(0.14)}{0.16}\, i_E + \underset{(19.34)}{0.65}\, W_f/P - \underset{(1.85)}{2.76}\, \dot{p}_e - \underset{(20.90)}{456.16}$$

$R^2 = 0.981$ D.W. = 2.01 S.E. = 8.53

(21) $$(FL-FA)^B = \underset{(1.68)}{6.92}(i_S - \rho) - \underset{(1.14)}{0.55}\, i_E + \underset{(0.23)}{0.60}\, \rho - \underset{(2.21)}{0.12}\, BA + \underset{(3.37)}{6.15}\, \Pi_F + \underset{(2.26)}{10.39}\, \Pi_R + \underset{(2.42)}{10.05}\, \Pi_D + \underset{(2.80)}{103.04}$$

$R^2 = 0.977$ D.W. = 1.63 S.E. = 3.70

TABLE 1 - Continued

$$(22)\quad (FA-FL)^{P} = \underset{(1.98)}{-2.80\, i_S} + \underset{(2.02)}{2.72\, i_E} - \underset{(6.54)}{2.70\, FE} + \underset{(6.80)}{0.20\, W_f} - \underset{(9.54)}{2.02P} + \underset{(9.54)}{299.21}$$

$R^2 = 0.909$ D.W. = 2.07 S.E. = 4.78

$$(10b)\quad 100\, \nu(m, i_s) = \underset{(15.30)}{-5.48\, i_S} + \underset{(2.19)}{0.61\, m} + \underset{(31.29)}{125.63}$$

$R^2 = 0.972$ D.W. = 1.75 S.E. = 5.75

a) Figures between brackets are t values.

$$\frac{d(FL-FA)^B}{dB^{ex}} = \frac{\partial(FL-FA)^B}{\partial BA} \cdot \frac{dBA}{dB^{ex}} + \frac{\partial(FL-FA)^B}{\partial i_s} \cdot \frac{di_s}{dB^{ex}}$$

Solution of the model gives the following total effects of a change in B^{ex} on AD and $(FL-FA)^B$; $\frac{dAD}{dB^{ex}} = -.28$ and $\frac{d(FL-FA)^B}{dB^{ex}} = -.23$. Thus, an increase in the exogenous money base of 1 BF lowers the banks' borrowing by 28 centimes and the net foreign borrowing by 23 centimes. The combined effect is to reduce the money base by 51 centimes, thus suggesting that monetary policy may produce effective results. We will see later, however, that net foreign indebtedness of the public responds negatively to a change in the exogenous money base, with the net results that the endogenous and exogenous component of B offsets each other by -0.78.

The coefficients of the different interest rates, although having the right sign, are not always statistically significant because of the high degree of covariance among them. We have noticed that when the foreign interest rate i_E is excluded from the relations, the significance of the estimated coefficients of the domestic interest rates increases. In effect, the total impact of a change in the foreign interest rate i_E on the loan rate i_L is positive and equal to 0.52. This result, in conjunction with the less than perfect offsetting movement between the exogenous and endogenous money base, shows that Belgian capital market is highly, but not perfectly, integrated with the world capital market.

The response of the domestic rates to a change in B^{ex} further confirms the fact that monetary authorities enjoy a certain degree of independence in controlling monetary developments in

Belgium. From the estimates of Table 1 we obtain that the total impact of a change in B^{ex} on i_L and i_S is equal to -.025 and -.026, respectively. The full implication of the leverage monetary policy retains even in a highly open economy can be appreciated by considering that an increase of BF 1 billion in B^{ex} (0.5 percent of the mean value of B^{ex}) lowers i_S by 3 basis points.

In all the demand functions of the public the wealth elasticities are about unity. Also, permanent income, which is introduced in our model as a proxy for human wealth, is mostly significant and has the expected sign. Only in the demand function for time deposits it was found insignificant and, therefore, excluded.

The measure of price expectations based on business survey data turned out to be highly collinear with our measure of permanent income. Since it was not possible to disentangle this price effect from an output effect, we resorted to the alternative measure of price expectations computed according to a Fisherian weighting scheme. This variable is denoted by p^e in Table 1.

Price expectations exert an important effect on the demand functions for the different components of money, and on the demand for bank loans by the public. Generally, however, the value of the elasticities are small, a result which is not so surprising in the light of our sample period which excludes the high inflation years.

The remaining policy measures are captured by dummy variables. Problems of collinearity arise when these are all introduced together, in turn reflecting to the fact that most policy measures were taken concurrently and worked in the same direction. This is especially true for the application of loan ceilings and the required government financing ratios. The positive and significant coefficients of Π_G in (15) and (16) suggest the importance of breaking down S^P into the components nonbank financial intermediaries and nonbank public, and/or to endogenize the supply of government securities as a positive function of Π_G.

Finally, we present some empirical evidence on financial wealth, the value of which is endogenously determined in the system. We recall that W_f is equal to the sum of the exogenous money base and the market value of government securities. The underlying government bond valuation function is explained by a linear relation of the long-term bond yield and the average maturity of the outstanding debt. We find the relation between interest rate and the price of government securities to be unambiguously negative. The sign of the coefficient of the average term to maturity can go either way. Maturity lengthening will amplify price changes, with the direction determined by the profile of the term structure of interest rates during the sample period.

In our model we allowed the stock of reserves held by banks to be determined as a residual, whereas the money base held by the public is explicitly formulated. We could have followed, alternatively, another procedure: namely, to formulate an explicit relationship for bank reserves, and thus allowing public-held money base to be determined implicitly by the model. In Appendix V we present evidence bearing on this second alternative, which should throw valuable information on the reserve behavior of the banking system.

Bank reserves may be distinguished in required and excess reserves. In Belgium, the regulation on reserve requirements is unduly complicated. These have been successively imposed on demand and time deposits, on foreign deposits in Belgian francs, on foreign liabilities of the Belgian banks in foreign currency (but only applicable to the official exchange market), and finally, on changes in loans to the private sector.[20] Reserve requirements have been intensively used as policy instruments since July 1972. Total bank reserves, R, are specified as a function of reserve requirements, π_R, the size of deposits, D, the composition of these deposits, TDR, and interest rates.[21]

A dummy variable is introduced in the total reserve function to capture the effect of π_R, which shows to have a significant influence. We should expect banks to hold a lower amount of reserves the higher the ratio of time to demand deposits, for a given level of total deposits. In addition, reserve requirement regulation discriminates in favor of time deposits relative to demand deposits. On the ground of both the behavior of banks in holding an

---

20) Required reserves applied not only to the volume, but also to changes in foreign deposits in Belgian francs, restricted, however, to those that were channeled through the official foreign exchange market.

21) The reserve behavior equation is quite stable when, aside from the deposits in BF of residents, the foreign deposits in BF are also included.

optimum amount of reserves and the existing reserve legislation we expect the coefficient of TDR on R to be negative, which is the case.

IV. Policy Implications of the Model

The empirical evidence presented in the previous section suggests several policy implications. We must caution the reader, however, that the use of dummy variables, as well as the simultaneous occurence of policy measures, working in the same direction, creates estimation problems, and therefore makes it difficult to quantitatively distinguish the separate effects of different policy instruments.

The importance of the money base in the bank credit and money supply process has already been pointed out. As a result, we may assert that, by appropriately manipulating the money base, the monetary authorities could substantially influence bank credit and money supply. The question remains, however, to what extent can the monetary authorities in Belgium control the money base, and how can they achieve that control. The issue is particularly relevant for a country where movements in monetary aggregates do not seem to be dominated by conscious acts of monetary policy, but by developments in the balance of payments, the financing needs of the government, and the behavior of the commercial banking system. In fact, as a very open economy, Belgium is heavily exposed to changes in external sources of money base. We have already pointed out the offsetting behavior of banks. The endogenous money base is also affected, however, by changes in the foreign indebtedness of the public. The total effect of a change in B^{ex} on $(FL-FA)^P$ can be computed as

$$\frac{d(FL-FA)^P}{dB^{ex}} = \frac{\partial (FL-FA)^P}{\partial i_s} \cdot \frac{di_s}{dB^{ex}} + \frac{\partial (FL-FA)^P}{\partial W_f} \cdot \frac{dW_f}{dB^{ex}}$$

which is equal to -.27. Recalling that $B = B^{en} + B^{ex}$ and the definition of B^{en}, we can assess the total offsetting behaviour between B^{en} and B^{ex} as the sum of the total derivatives $\frac{d(FL-FA)^P}{dB^{ex}}$, $\frac{d(FL-FA)^P}{dB^{ex}}$ and $\frac{dAD}{dB^{ex}}$, or -0.78.

The control of the money base in Belgium is not only hampered by discount window and capital flows, but also by other institutional features. For example, the bulk of the domestic component of the money base is "imposed" on the central bank by the financing requirement of the government. In a country with an active market for government securities the central bank could in principle sell "unwanted" government bonds in the open market, thus achieving desirable growth rates of the domestic money base. This has not happened in Belgium, where central authorities have done little to encourage the development of secondary money market.

Monetary authorities in Belgium have not even been interested in controlling monetary aggregates like the money base. They have interpreted monetary processes with a credit policy view based upon theories of borrowing cost and credit availability. They have also placed the burden of restrictive actions on the application of loan ceilings to the private sector. In general, the emphasis has been on the following policy instruments: the discount rate, discount ceilings, ceilings on loans to the private sector, required ratios for government financing imposed on the banks, and, more recently, required reserves and regulations of the foreign positions of the banks. Our empirical evidence casts doubts on the effectiveness of several of these instruments.

For the discount rate, we did not find at this stage a significant relationship with domestic refinancing of the banks. The positive relationship with the net foreign position of the banks at the other hand gives the impression that, in Belgium, discount rate policy has also been guided by external considerations.

Discount ceilings were found to have no traceable impact on bank credit. In the supply of loans to the public, discount ceilings have the wrong sign. Our results are consistent with the observation that the "disposable margin" of banks applicable to their discount ceilings became very small only at the end of 1973. As a result, these ceilings have not been biting during most of the period under consideration.

Concerning the regulations of the net foreign position of the banks, we found significant results only in the foreign borrowing function. Questions as to whether or not such a policy measure induces an offsetting behavior by banks in their domestic refinancing could not be answered.

The coefficients of required reserves provide ample evidence of offsetting movements in both domestic and foreign refinancing of commercial banks. To the extent that these offset opportunities are not brought under control, serious doubts arise as to the effectiveness of these reserve requirements in Belgium.

Other instruments, such as loan ceilings and a required government financing ratio, may be expected to have mainly allocative rather than aggregative effects. Loan ceilings, rather than restricting the total credit creation potential of the banking system, may induce more lending to the government and lower interest rates on the government securities market. The government financing ratio consists of imposing on banks the maintenance of a specific amount of government securities as a proportion of total deposits. In 1972, banks were required, in addition, to invest 50 percent of the growth of their deposits in government securities. Such a measure raised the total demand for government securities and consequently reduced the yield on these securities. Empirically, distinguishing between the effect of loan ceiling and required government financing turned out to be very difficult. Both measures were mostly imposed concurrently and working the same direction. Loan ceilings were important in lowering the loan supply. Required government financing has had a positive effect on the demand for government securities. These results do not unambiguously confirm the allocative effect of these policy measures. No further conclusions seem to be warranted at this stage of the research because of the quality of the data on these policy measures.

To summarize, we find that the instruments actually used by the Belgian central bank are not optimally designed to achieve an effective monetary policy. The approach and the evidence presented in this paper propose an alternative to the currently held view of the monetary process in Belgium. It emphasizes that monetary policy, defined strictu sensu as the control over money base, is a feasible outcome even in a highly open economy. This approach also brings to the foreground the interplay of market forces, a knowledge of which appears compelling to central authorities, if their actions are to redirect money markets (without impeding or distorting their functioning) in terms of ultimate objectives.

APPENDIX I - List of Variables

Endogenous variables

AD	=	domestic borrowing of the banks
B	=	money base
B^P	=	money base in the hands of the public
BA	=	$B - (FL - FA)^B$ = adjusted money base
BU	=	$B - AD$ = unborrowed money base
DD	=	demand deposits
$(FL-FA)^B$	=	foreign borrowing of the banks
$(FA-FL)^P$	=	net foreign asset position of the public
i_K	=	rate of return on real capital
i_L	=	interest rate on loans
i_S	=	interest rate on government securities
IR	=	international reserves
L	=	bank loans
LA	=	loan assets in the portfolio of the banks
M_2	=	money stock, broadly defined
R	=	bank reserves
S^B	=	government securities in the portfolio of the banks
S^P	=	government securities in the hands of the public
TD	=	time deposits
W_f	=	financial wealth

Exogenous variables

BX	= B - AD - $(FL - FA)^B$ - $(FL - FA)^B$ = exogenous money base
FE	= foreign exchange rate on the free market
GF^{NB}	= government financing by the National Bank of Belgium
GF^{TR}	= government financing by the Treasury
i_E	= interest rate on interbank Eurodollar deposits, covered
i_T	= interest rate on time deposits
K	= physical capital
m	= average maturity of the outstanding government debt
NW^B	= net worth of the banks
NW^P	= net worth of the public
P	= price of domestic output (consumer price index)
$\dot{p}_e$	= price expectations
P_K	= price of real capital goods
Π_D	= discount ceiling
Π_F	= regulation of the net foreign position of the banks
Π_G	= minimum requirements of government financing by the banks
Π_L	= loan ceiling
Π_R	= reserve requirements
ρ	= discount rate
S	= total outstanding government debt
S^F	= government debt held by foreigners
Y_P	= permanent income
Y_T	= transitory income

APPENDIX II - Some Statistical Information on the Money Base, the Bank Credit Market and the Money Market in Belgium

TABLE 1

The Sources of Money Base in Belgium

End of period	Money base b. of BF	External Sources b. of BF	(pct.)	Governm. Comp.(a) b. of BF	(pct.)	Dom. Bank Borrowing b. of BF	(pct.)
1960	160	77	(48)	76	(48)	7	(4)
1965	221	114	(52)	95	(43)	12	(5)
1970	251	140	(56)	104	(41)	7	(3)
1973	345	202	(59)	100	(29)	42	(12)
Index 1960 = 100	208	262	-	154	-	600	-

(a) Decreased with the residual item "others" on the balance sheet of monetary authorities.

TABLE 2

Government debt financing and bank loans in Belgium (b. of BF)

End of period	Credit to the Government (a)					Bank Loans	Total Domestic Bank Credit
	By Monetary Authorities (b)	In Foreign Currency		By the Non-bank Public	By the Banks		
		By Belgian Banks	Other				
1960	78	6	40	248	62	56	118
1965	97	14	33	285	99	127	227
1970	112	35	17	386	149	276	424
1973	117	6	1	538	246	423	669
Index 1960 = 100	150	100	25	217	397	755	567

(a) Central + local government

(b) Including the postal deposits.

TABLE 3

The Money Stock Components in Belgium (b. of BF)

End of period	Currency	Postal Deposits	Demand Deposits at Banks	Time Deposits at Banks	Money Stock M_2	Ratio M_2 to GNP
1960	127	27	57	35	247	4.3
1965	173	38	95	77	384	4.5
1970	191	50	152	166	558	4.3
1973	241	61	227	298	827	4.6
Index 1960 = 100	190	300	398	851	435	-

APPENDIX III - Summary of the Theoretical Model

1. The Money base system

(1) $B = B^P + R$

(4) $B = AD + GF^{NB} + GF^{TR} + IR$

(6) $IR = \int_{-\infty}^{T_o} CAB\, dt + S^F + (FL - FA)^B - (FA - FL)^P$

(18) $B^P/P = \lambda (i_K, i_S - \dot{p}_e, i_T - \dot{p}_e, W_f/P, Y_p/P, \dot{p}_e, \Pi_A)$

(14) $AD = \gamma (\rho, i_L, i_S, i_E, BU, \Pi_R, \Pi_D, \Pi_F)$

(21) $(FL-FA)^B = \mu(i_E, i_L, i_S, \rho, BA, FE, \Pi_R, \Pi_D, \Pi_F)$

(22) $(FA-FL)^P = \kappa (i_E, i_S, W_f, FE, \Pi_F)$

2. The Bank loan market

(12) $L = \beta (i_L, i_S, i_E, B, B^P/DD, \rho, \Pi_R, \Pi_D, \Pi_F, \Pi_L, \Pi_G)$

(11) $L/P = \alpha (i_L - \dot{p}_e, i_S - \dot{p}_e, i_K, i_E, \dot{p}_e, W_f/P, Y_p/P)$

3. The government securities market

(15) $S^B = \omega (i_S, i_L, i_E, B, B^P/DD, \Pi_R, \Pi_D, \Pi_F, \Pi_G, \Pi_L)$

(16) $S^P/P = \phi(i_S, i_E, W_f/P, Y_p/P, \Pi_G)$

(5) $S - (GF^{NB} + GF^{TR} + S^F) = S^B + S^P$

4. The money market

(17) $M_2 = B^P + DD + TD$

(19) $DD/P = \tau(i_K, i_S - \dot{p}_e, i_T - \dot{p}_e, W_f/P, Y_p/P, \dot{p}_e, \Pi_A)$

(20) $TD/P = \xi(i_K, i_S - \dot{p}_e, i_T - \dot{p}_e, W_f/P, Y_p/P, \dot{p}_e)$

(9) $DD + TD = L + S^B + R - AD - (FL - FA)^B - NW^B$

5. Financial wealth

(10) $W_f = B^{ex} + \nu(i_s, m)S$

APPENDIX IV

The following elasticities, being mean elasticities, expressed as $\frac{\bar{X}}{\bar{Y}} \cdot \frac{\partial Y}{\partial X}$, can be derived:

Equation (11): demand for bank loans by the public

$\varepsilon(L/P,\ i_L - \dot{p}_e) = -.16$

$\varepsilon(L/P,\ i_S - \dot{p}_e) = .10$

$\varepsilon(L/P,\ \dot{p}_e) = 1.09$

$\varepsilon(L/P,\ W_f/P) = 1.52$

$\varepsilon(L/P,\ Y_p/P) = 1.80$

$\varepsilon(L/P,\ i_E) = -0.03$

Equation (12): supply of bank loans

$\varepsilon(L,\ i_L) = 0.10$

$\varepsilon(L,\ i_B) = -.09$

$\varepsilon(L,\ KR) = -0.67$

$\varepsilon(L,\ B) = 1.22$

$\varepsilon(L,\ i_E) = 0.01$

Equation (13): domestic borrowing by the banks

$\varepsilon(AD,\ i_S - \rho) = 0.36$

$\varepsilon(AD,\ UBB) = -7.42$

$\varepsilon(AD,\ i_E) = 0.39$

$\varepsilon(AD,\ \rho) = 0.05$

Equation (15): demand for government securities by the banks

$\varepsilon(S^B,\ i_S) = 0.52$

$\varepsilon(S^B,\ B) = 1.06$

$\varepsilon(S^B, i_L) = -0.15$

$\varepsilon(S^B, KR) = -0.96$

$\varepsilon(S^B, i_E) = -0.01$

Equation (16): demand for government securities by the public

$\varepsilon(S^P, i_S) = 0.44$

$\varepsilon(S^P, i_E) = -0.05$

$\varepsilon(S^P, W_f) = 1.92$

Equation (18): demand for base money by the public

$\varepsilon(B^P/P, i_K) = -0.07$

$\varepsilon(B^P/P, W_f/P) = 0.98$

$\varepsilon(B^P/P, i_S) = -0.19$

$\varepsilon(B^P/P, Y_p/P) = 0.80$

$\varepsilon(B^P/P, i_T) = -0.01$

Equation (19): demand for demand deposits by the public

$\varepsilon(DD/P, i_K) = -0.04$

$\varepsilon(DD/P, Y_p/P) = 0.20$

$\varepsilon(DD/P, W_f/P) = 1.81$

$\varepsilon(DD/P, i_T - \dot{p}_e) = 0.02$

$\varepsilon(DD/P, \dot{p}_e) = -0.26$

$\varepsilon(DD/P, i_E) = -0.12$

Equation (20): demand for time deposits by the public

$\varepsilon(TD/P, i_K) = -0.05$

$\varepsilon(TD/P, i_T) = 0.51$

$\varepsilon(TD/P, W_f/P) = 1.24$

$\varepsilon(TD/P, i_E) = -0.01$

$\varepsilon(TD/P, \dot{p}_e) = -0.10$

Equation (21): foreign borrowing of the banks

$\varepsilon((FL - FA)^B, i_S - \rho) = 0.31$ $\varepsilon((FL - FA)^B, i_E) = -0.11$

$\varepsilon((FL - FA)^B, BA) = -0.88$ $\varepsilon((FL - FA)^B, \rho) = -0.11$

Equation (22): net foreign position of the public

$\varepsilon((FA - FL)^P, i_S) = -0.08$ $\varepsilon((FA - FL)^P, FE) = -1.39$

$\varepsilon((FA - FL)^P, i_E) = 0.15$ $\varepsilon((FA - FL)^P, W_f) = 1.70$

$\varepsilon((FA - FL)^P, P) = -1.99$

APPENDIX V - The Reserve Behavior of the Banks

(Billions of BF), 1960-1973

$$R = -1.60\,(i_D - \rho) + 0.03\,D - 9.51\,TDR + 9.74\,\Pi_R - 2.73\,D_1$$

t-values (1.88) (3.85) (1.83) (6.80) (6.09)

$$- 2.83\,D_2 + 1.41\,D_3 + 10.68$$

(6.22) (3.50) (2.69)

$R^2 = 0.954$ D.W. $= 2.18$ S.E. $= 1.37$

with

R	=	total reserves of the bank
i_D	=	$(i_L + i_S)/2$
i_L	=	interest rate on loans
i_S	=	interest rate on government securities
ρ	=	discount rate
D	=	total bank deposits
TDR	=	time to demand deposits ratio
Π_R	=	required reserves dummy
D_1, D_2, D_3	=	seasonal dummies

Mean elasticities

$\varepsilon(R, i_L)$	$= -1,10$
$\varepsilon(R, i_S)$	$= -1,28$
$\varepsilon(R, \rho)$	$= +0,97$
$\varepsilon(R, D)$	$= +1,00$
$\varepsilon(R, TDR)$	$= -1,08$

REFERENCES

Brunner, K., "A Diagrammatic Exposition of the Money Supply Process", Schweizerische Zeitschrift für Volkswirtschaft und Statistik, December 1973, pp. 481-533.

Brunner, K., "Money Supply Process and Monetary Policy in an Open Economy", in M. B. Conolly and A. K. Swoboda, International Trade and Money, Allen and Unwin, London, 1973, pp. 127-167.

Brunner, K., Meltzer, A. H., "A Credit Market Theory of the Money Supply and an Explanation of Two Puzzles in U.S. Monetary Policy", Rivista Internazionale di Scienze Economische é Commerciali, May 1966, pp. 405-431.

Brunner, K., Meltzer, A. H., "Money, Debt and Economic Activity", Journal of Political Economy, September-October 1972, pp. 951-977.

Burger, A. E., The Money Supply Process, Wadsworth, Belmont California, 1972.

Fair, R. C., "The Estimation of Simultaneous Equations Models with Lagged Endogenous Variables and First Order Serially Correlated Errors", Econometrica, May 1970, pp. 507-516.

Gordon, P. H., Investment, Financing and Valuation of the Corporation, Homewood, R. D. Irwin, 1962, p. 256.

Hendershott, P. H., Van Horne, J. C., "Expected Inflation Implied by Capital Market Rates", The Journal of Finance, May 1973, pp. 301-314.

Heremans, D., Theories of Offsetting International Capital Movements and Controllability of the Money Stock in a Small Open Economy, Ph. D. Dissertation, University of California, Los Angeles, 1976, p. 150 (forthcoming).

Heremans, D., Sommariva, A., Verheirstraeten, A., "The Determinants of the Growth of the Money Supply in Belgium", Revue de la Banque, 1974, nr. 5, pp. 528-548.

Heremans, D., Sommariva, A., Verheirstraeten A., "A Money Base Framework for Belgium", Tijdschrift voor Economie, nr. 2, 1974, pp. 187-208.

Fourçans, A., "The Bank Credit Market in France: A Theoretical and Empirical Analysis", 1974, p. 46 (mimeographed).

Fratianni, M., "Bank Credit and Money Supply Processes in an Open Economy: A Model Applicable to Italy" Metroeconomica, Gennaio-Aprile 1972, pp. 24-69.

Melitz, J., "Projet de modèle intégré du système monétaire français", October 1973, p. 48 (mimeographed).

Melitz, J., "La demande de monnaie en France: tentative d' explication", Statistiques et études financières, 1973, nr. 11, pp. 22-48.

Melitz, J., Pardue, M., "The Demand and Supply of Commercial Bank Loans", Journal of Money, Credit and Banking, May 1973, pp. 669-692.

Melitz, J., "Une étude économétrique de la demande de crédit bancaire en France, Revue d'économie politique, 1975, nr. 1, pp. 84-116.

von Neumann-Whitman, M., Policies for Internal Balance, Special Papers in International Economies, nr. 9, Princeton University, December 1970.

Reding, P., "Offre de monnaie et politiquie monétaire en Belgique 1960-1973. Une approche par l'analyse base-multiplicateur", Recherches économiques de Louvain, 1974, nr. 2, pp. 155-179.

Vuchelen, J., Een ekonometrisch monetair model voor België, V.U.B., Brussel 1971, p. 231 (mimeographed).

Wilms, M., "Controlling Money in an Open Economy: the German Case", Federal Reserve Bank of St. Louis Review, April 1971, pp. 10-27.

OBJECTIVES AND TOOLS OF MONETARY POLICY IN BELGIUM

By

R. Vandeputte

It is the intention of this paper to give an appreciation of the objectives and tools of monetary policy as they were viewed in Belgium in 1973-1974. In this period Belgium, as most other countries, still enjoyed a booming economic activity with low unemployment but with disturbing inflation rates. Under these conditions the prevailing concern for monetary policy certainly was to contribute within its scope to the government's objective of a drastic reduction of the inflation rate. How should such a situation be tackled and what level of effectiveness could be expected?

On the domestic front, it was thought that saving should be promoted so as to reduce demand. High interest rates were therefore an essential encouragement. The National Bank of Belgium had for many months repeatedly stated that it advocated such a policy. Its discount rate was 8.75 % and the advance rate 9.50 %; in comparison with rates in other industrialised countries, Belgian rates were in the middle range. Of course, some central banks practised higher rates, but this was not the case everywhere. Since the Treasury frequently makes loan issues - either directly, or through other public bodies - the rates of the National Bank of Belgium must always take account of the conditions under which the Government feels that it can approach the market.

Whenever it had an opportunity to do so, the National Bank favored an increase in interest rates. In July 1974 the Bank restricted considerably the amounts up to which financial intermediaries obtained their support at the above-mentioned official rates. As soon as severely fixed quotas were exhausted, rediscount could no longer be made directly at the National Bank, but at the Rediscount and Guarantee Institute, a public organization partly financed by the National Bank itself. On this last refinancing, banks had to pay fairly high rates because the Rediscount and Guarantee Institute charges a rate substantially above the official discount rate of the central bank on discount transactions in excess of the quotas. For advances against public securities, the National Bank only applied the rate of 9.50 % within very narrow limits. Any additional support was given at a rate approaching those existing in the Euro-currency market. The term of such lending, moreover, remained very short.

It was sometimes argued that high rates might encourage inflation, since companies that only could obtain bank loans at high rates would in times of high economic activity increase their selling prices accordingly. This reasoning overlooked the fact that a sufficiently restrictive interest rate policy should weaken excess demand pressure enough to make it more difficult to transfer the increase of financing costs to selling prices.

In 1973, the expansion of credits to enterprises and households was the main source of money creation. These credits showed again a marked increase in the first months of 1974. Thus, if a restrictive demand management policy was to be pursued, it was necessary to check the granting of credits. This policy was all the more important, since credits often serve to build up abnormally high inventories to offset future rises in prices or to take advantage of monetary depreciation, the borrower repaying in real value a lower sum than he received.

The Belgian government in this period clearly recommended a restrictive policy for private credits and entrusted this task to the National Bank. The criterion being applied was the following: increases in outstanding credits were not allowed to exceed increases in the Gross National Product at current prices.

Financial institutions which ignored these rules were penalized. More specifically, the sanctions included the requirement of monetary reserves to the central bank, without renumeration and following a schedule of progressive rates based on the importance of the credit expansion in excess of the allowed increase.

The application of a restrictive monetary policy can be seriously frustrated by the course of public finances. The Council of Ministers of the EEC has stated that the increase in government expenditures should not exceed - allowance being made for special conditions - the rate of growth of nominal GNP. In Belgium, the budget was not able to comply with this norm. To restrict the volume of credits granted by financial intermediaries and to help the Government meet its borrowing requirements over and above the proceeds of its public loan issues, the monetary authorities compelled these intermediaries to invest in government securities a large percentage of the increase in their resources. Banks were forced to lend the Government 43 % of the increase in their liabilities in Belgian francs. It is obvious that credits designed to cover the current budget deficit, and financed through funds obtained on a short-term basis by financial intermediaries, had an effect opposite to that prescribed by a sound monetary policy.

In order to check the evolution of the money supply and bring it down to acceptable figures many countries have followed, over the last few years, a more restrictive attitude with regard to monetary reserves. In Belgium too this tool has been used, but moderately. The Government always fears that it will have difficulty in floating its loans if a large proportion of liquid funds is taken out of the market. In this field, too, a compromise must be made between what seems clearly desirable as an anti-inflationary strategy and the requirements of budget financing.

A weak link in carrying out an effective monetary policy in Belgium is the nonexistence of a well organised market for short-term securities. According to Ralph A. Young who, under the sponsorship of the International Monetary Fund, published a book in 1973 on the operation of the Federal Reserve System, "The United States is one of three countries in which open market operations have developed into a major instrument of central banking monetary policy". Ralph Young feels that in Britain and Canada the open market policy works well. Other countries, like France and West Germany, have also been trying to expand liquidity by the purchase of Treasury or commercial bills and to restrict liquidity by sales. In Belgium, the application of an open market policy has been contemplated for years. The "Conseil Supérieur des Finances" in 1973 unanimously favoured such a development. In practice, for the major part of the floating debt, the Government negotiates, on a bilateral basis, the offering of its securities. The primary market is thus not well developed and there is no secondary market for these securities.

After having briefly covered some of the now classic tools available to monetary authorities in a close economy, let us now examine what monetary authorities are able to achieve in the field of foreign exchange and in their relations with foreign countries. The system of floating exchange rates, which has characterized international monetary relations since the non-convertibility of the dollar, has thoroughly changed the situation. Earlier, central banks merely had to maintain their currencies within the limits of parity, in accordance with international commitments; this is no longer the case. By willingly selling foreign exchange, the central banks increase the value of their currency on the markets, reduce the money supply, since they receive in their own currency the counterpart of the foreign exchange sold, and contribute to some decrease in the price of imported products. In buying foreign exchange, they achieve the opposite effect: they increase the money supply and induce some depreciation of their currency.

Belgium enjoys only partial freedom of operation in this field. Under the agreements made with countries whose currencies remain in the snake, now called "petit serpent" (small snake), the allowed maximum spot difference is 2.25 % between quotations of the Belgian franc and the currencies of the other members. In support of this system, Belgium must, when necessary, if its currency is weak, intervene in the markets at the lower margin of fluctuation, by borrowing and selling the currency of the country that is at the upper limit of 2.25 %. If the Belgian currency is strong, the contrary happens : Belgium will lend its currency to the country whose exchange rate against the Belgian franc is at the lower limit and this country will sell on its market the borrowed Belgian francs.

Theoretically, it is advisable that the "petit serpent" countries could have an overall common policy with regard to currencies other than their own. They could, in particular, group together to weaken or strenghten the dollar. In practice, this has not been done.

With a system of floating rates, capital movements from one country to another are in principle governed by market forces. If large amounts of funds are transferred from one currency to another, the price of one currency will rise until the owners of such funds give up these transfer operations because of the premium they have to pay. One can imagine however that a central bank does not wish to remain passive, but rather influence, by its action, the inflow and outflow of capital. In order to attract capital, the bank will increase its discount rate or its advance rate, but that will induce an increase in the money supply. In order to discourage capital inflow, it would have to lower its lending rates, but such a measure would conflict with the domestic policy of high interest rates that is needed to fight against inflation. As a deterrent to capital inflow, a central bank can prohibit the payment of interest on foreign capital invested in its own currency. It can even impose the payment of a periodic fee on this capital. In 1973, several countries, including Belgium, used this method.

Can the import or export of capital be prevented by direct intervention? In other words, are exchange regulations really effective in this field? In the light of experience gained in recent years, the answer appears to be "no". We should remember, however, that the Common Market authorities have requested the implementation of measures designed to control capital transfers. These authorities thus appear to have a certain amount of confidence in these measures. The Belgian experience shows also that the fixing of ceilings for the net assets or the net liabilities of banks in foreign funds is, to a certain extent, effective in coping with the problem that concerns us. Belgium is the only country in the world to have established and maintained a dual exchange market system for many years. Does this system allow us to control capital transactions by channelling them through one of the markets and, thus, forcing those who make such transactions to find an alternative to the central bank? Let us not claim too much. Let us simply say that the dual exchange market may have contributed to a slowing down of capital transfers during periods of violent international monetary disturbances.

After this rather lenghty enumeration of the instruments of monetary policy on both the domestic and international levels, we should then ask how successful they have been. Among the methods that can be devised to fight inflation many governments favor monetary measures. Is it because they consider them particularly useful? Is it not partly because, politically, such measures run into less opposition and can be implemented more easily? Generally speaking, international authorities, under the influence of their technical advisers, recommend the adoption of monetary measures designed to abolish or reduce the harmful effects of excessive economic expansion : these authorities too have a certain degree of confidence in such measures. They certainly do not propose just to let things go.

We are in a field where an accurate assessment of the results obtained from such policies is difficult. Monetary science is not an exact science, far from it. Approximate judgements have to be accepted and one has to be satisfied with an estimate of the likely results of the decisions which have been taken. Again, it is sometimes necessary to restrict oneself to a formulation of objectives which the recommended measures may help to achieve. When asked to comment on this matter by the review "Banking", some years ago, the present Vice-President of the Federal Reserve System, George MITCHELL, stated : "The science of central banking is not yet up to predicting precisely how and when the financial and business community will react to any particular monetary dosage".[1)]

Everyone recognizes that the German government and the Bundesbank have on several occasions applied a restrictive monetary policy with determination and discipline, and that this strategy has yielded results. A restrictive, and sometimes very restrictive, credit policy is essential to check the inflationary pressures arising from an over-heated economy. This principle is not challenged, but its application can run into difficulties, as experience has shown. It must indeed be realized that quantitative credit restrictions impose a thankless task on financial intermediaries in turning away customers. The "Conseil National du Crédit de France" states, in its latest report, that by accounting subterfuges, various large banks, even nationalized ones, have evaded the provisions of credit policy. At present, some managers of these banks are being threatened with personal sanctions if they do not achieve the objectives laid down. Big companies can be led to seek abroad credits which have been refused in their own country; such behavior directly disturbs the credit policy. Germany has tried to put and end to such proceedings by compelling borrowers to deposit, interest-free, with the Bundesbank, a

1) M.W. Holtrop, "On the Effectiveness of Monetary Policy", Journal of Money, Credit and Banking, 1972, p. 283.

large proportion of the loans obtained from foreign creditors. This sanction, it appears, has had only limited effects.

To discourage borrowers, central banks use the weapon of high rates, as we have seen. Is it an effective weapon? It does not do much to deter the borrower in times of strong inflation, if he sees the prospect of repaying, in terms of purchasing power, a much lower sum than that which he has borrowed in the first place, or if he has the opportunity to use the product of his loan to finance highly lucrative industrial or commercial business.

The quantity theory enjoys at the moment quite an extraordinary revival, mainly through the works of Milton Friedman and his adepts of the Chicago School. On a practical level, no country is unconcerned - far from it - about the evolution of the money supply, and the sometimes very large monetary reserves imposed on financial intermediaries are evidence of that concern. Shall we infer from this that the country that brings the increase of money supply down to reasonable proportions can escape inflation? Unfortunately not! The French are entitled to feel fairly satisfied at present with the development of the money supply, and yet the rate of inflation is still very high. The increase in the speed of circulation of money may completely offset the benefit of a slowing down in the growth rate of the money supply.

It has been rightly said that the struggle against inflation must be conducted on several fronts. If inflation depends essentially on a single cause, it is obviously this cause which must be eliminated. But, generally, factors of both national and international character contribute to the excessive rise in prices. The causes of inflation often escape the measure imposed by the authorities of one country, because they originate abroad and there is not much which can be done to shield the domestic economy from such effects. At a national level, the anti-inflationary policy must normally be applied in several directions. The role of monetary authorities is to make a contribution whose effectiveness cannot be accurately estimated. But it can be stated without hesitation that it would be ludicrous to deny the usefulness of monetary policy in the fight against inflation; and that the effects of such a policy will be all the more appreciable if it is carried out with flexibility, determination and discipline.

Comments on the Paper

of D. Heremans, A. Sommariva and A. Verheirstraeten

By

By André Fourçans

The model built by the authors is an interesting contribution to the understanding of monetary process in an open economy, especially insofar as it clarifies monetary mechanisms within an European institutional framework. The framework incorporates the behavior of the monetary authorities, the banking system, the public, and, to a certain extent, the foreign sector. The authorities play a crucial role insofar as they issue base money and can rely on other policy instruments in order to affect the behavior of the banks and the public. The authors have succeeded in conveying the idea that economic variables are formed through a market process, and therefore are the result of supply and demand conditions in different markets. Furthermore, the supply and demand functions, derived from a price theoretical approach, can be explained with a few key variables and can thus have an empirical content which permits the drawing of implications as to economic policy. This is not to deny the influence of institutional constraints. On the contrary, they are incorporated in the model and their efficiency, or lack of it, can be empirically analysed.

Needless to say, this methodological approach is of great value to derive a scientific knowledge of economic processes rather than to contend oneself with ad-hoc explanations of these mechanisms.

Having made these remarks, I would like to raise several points about the model the authors propose.

My first point relates to the loan market, and more specifically to the supply-of-loans function. Supply and demand for loans interact so as to (proximately) determine the yield on bank loans. The demand for loans is homogeneous of degree one in the price level (i.e., expressed in real terms) whereas the supply-of-loans is the sum of two elements: banks' demand for earning assets (net loan assets LA) and commercial banks' demand for refinancing at the central bank (AD). Yet, the authors do not specify a functional form for each of these components of the supply function. They only establish a <u>total</u> supply-of-loans function (the β function) and a refinancing functional form (the γ function). The model is then not sufficiently constrained. Indeed, in spite of what the authors say (equation 12), the marginal influence of the base (B) upon the <u>total</u> supply of loans (L) becomes ambiguous, at least at the theoretical level. If banks' demand for net loan assets (LA) is positively affected by B, equation (14) tells us that, through the unborrowed base BU, the demand for refinancing (AD) is <u>negatively</u> affected by the monetary base. Hence, it is <u>a priori</u> impossible to say whether the base B should have a positive or a negative influence upon the total supply-of-loans function (i.e. β_4 of equation (12) may be positive or negative), since L is the sum of LA and AD (equation 13).

The same remark can be made about the influence of B^P/DD on L in equation (12) once it is recognized that the unborrowed base BU should, in my opinion, be defined as $BU = B - AD - B^P$ instead of $BU = B - AD$. Indeed, BU represents the amount of base money that banks obtain without having recourse to the rediscount window, in other words $BU = R - AD = B - AD - B^P$.

This formulation of BU is economically more satisfactory insofar as it considers that banks would adjust their refinancing behavior also in function of the amount of base money that they lose, or gain, whenever the public transforms its bank deposits into base money, or conversely (i.e., whenever B^P/DD increases or decreases). In such a case, the base-deposit ratio B^P/DD would affect banks' demand for earning assets (LA) and for refinancing (AD) in opposite direction. The influence of this ratio upon the total supply-of-loans function becomes therefore ambiguous (β_5 in equation (12) may be positive or negative).

To avoid these ambiguous effects, it seems to me that instead of a <u>total</u> supply-of-loans function the authors should have established, and tested, a demand for earning assets and a demand for refinancing by the banking system. The total supply of loans would then have been obtained as the sum of these two components. Empirically, it comes out that the monetary base has a positive effect upon the total loan supply function, a result which may suggest that the positive effect of B on banks demand for earning assets is stronger than the negative effect upon their demand for refinancing. However, since the authors have dropped, in the empirical part, the variable B^P/DD from the L function, it is impossible to find out whether the net effect of this ratio on the total loan supply function is positive or negative. From the test of equation (13) one can also notice that the coefficient of BU is rather small compared to what one could expect from the presumed high substitutability between borrowed and unborrowed reserves. In all likelihood the incomplete definition of BU explains this result[1].

The discount rate has also been dropped from the econometric tests of equation (12) and (13). The authors justify this exclusion from the refinancing equation on the grounds that the variable was not statistically significant, but have nothing to say about the supply-of-loans equation. The finding is disturbing insofar as one would expect that in a monetary system where banks' borrowing from the authorities is very important, the cost of this borrowing should significantly affect the behavior of commercial banks. From price theory it is hard to believe that banks are insensitive to the price they have to pay whenever they obtain funds from the central bank. It is also doubtful that this outcome can be attributed to the small variance of the discount rate. If, as the authors suggest, the discount rate policy has been mostly guided by ex-

1) In France banks appear to offset about 80 % of their unborrowed base movements through their behavior at the discount window (cf André Fourçans, "The Impact of Monetary and Fiscal Policies Upon Interest Rates, Bank Credit, and Money in France: A Simultaneous Equation Approach", ESSEC, working paper (1975)and La Politique de la Monnaie, Editions Economica, Paris, 1976; Jacques Melitz, "Une Tentative d'Explication de l'Offre de Monnaie en France", Revue Economique, septembre 1973).

ternal considerations, it should have moved accordingly, especially from 1969 to 1973.

I would like to raise another point with respect to the net foreign liability position of the banking system $(FL-FA)^B$. The authors take this position as resulting from an autonomous behavior of the banking system. When this position is constrained by the authorities, as it is true in Belgium, banks have very few means of influencing it by their autonomous behavior. They rather behave as price takers in the Eurocurrency markets (especially in a small country like Belgium). Their net foreign position is then the result of the public's behavior, be it resident or non-resident. If that is the case, the μ functional form (equation 21) should be expressed differently. It should be derived from the hypothesis that the public would desire these assets and liabilities for transaction, wealth, and speculative motives.

To conclude, I would like to say that the role of a discussant is generally more to criticize a paper than to praise it. Having discharged my duty, I would like to be on record in praising Heremans, Sommariva and Verheirstraeten for having produced a valuable contribution to the understanding of Belgian, and, more generally, European monetary processes. Their model supports the general hypothesis that economic theory, and a scientific approach to economic problems can be of a great help in understanding economic mechanisms. More specifically, the model showed that price theoretical approaches can go a long way in explaining monetary processes even in the presence of several institutional constraints.

As a final word, I would like to draw attention to the great similarity existing between the Belgian and the French monetary system. Which country "copied" the other I do not know! But, even if both systems do not appear to be optimally set up to control monetary processes in the least costly manner, the similarity has a very positive aspect: it should greatly facilitate the establishment of a European monetary policy.

Comments on the Paper

of D. Heremans, A. Sommariva and A. Verheirstraeten

By

Sylvain R. F. Plasschaert

My comments mainly consist in raising a few queries which will hopefully stir some debate. I am not an active practitioner of econometrics; therefore, I will confine myself to the authors' interpretation about selected aspects of the Belgian financial system.

At the outset I would like to express my genuine appreciation to Heremans, Sommariva and Verheirstraeten, for their efforts in raising the quality of and interest in monetary analysis in Belgium.

Nonetheless, I have a few questions and comments on their paper. First, I have some qualms regarding the inclusion of postal deposits on the uses side of the monetary base. Admittedly, the National Bank of Belgium treats the Postal Office as a money-creating institution and views postal deposits as a way to finance the budget deficit. Also, postal deposits are money, and represent readily usable purchasing power to their holders. However, one may wonder whether they really represent assets "created" by the monetary authorites. As a matter of fact, the initiative in bringing about postal deposits lies mainly with the holders of the accounts, through conversion of other financial assets, mainly currency, into postal account deposits, although the government tends to direct its own payments largely through the postal checking system, thus feeding the amount of postal deposits within a fairly closed circuit. Anyhow, the government would not have the postal deposits at its disposal if the holders were unwilling to maintain such deposits.

Since the outstanding amounts of postal deposits is rather stable and since the risk of massive withdrawal is minimal, the postal checking system provides the government with very cheap credit extended by the public and the banks. Postal deposits suggest a closer analogy with float money (i.e. a temporary credit arising from lags in payments procedures) than with base money. Furthermore, the rather obvious similarity, if not identity, of postal deposits with demand deposits at commercial banks also would seem to disqualify postal deposits as part of money base.

Secondly, one institutional feature of the Belgian financial system should have been brought out more explicitly. Namely, the important role which Treasury-financing needs have played until recently in the borrowing activities by the Belgian banking system on the Eurodollar market. The Treasury has almost permanently issued short-term Treasury certificates to Belgian banks -- in essence, to fifteen or so major Belgian banks -- which the latter have financed through borrowings on the Eurocurrency markets. This observation does not invalidate the authors' specification of the supply function of bank loans. On the contrary, it strengthens their contention that restrictive measures on the cost and availability of loans to the private sector do not seem to have had major aggregative effects, but did primarily affect the allocation of credits largely to the benefit of the government sector.

Finally, a comment on the challenging and pessimistic conclusions about the efficacy of monetary policy in Belgium. Unless these conclusions are reversed or substantially qualified by subsequent research, the outlook is not comforting at all. The monetary instruments that have been traditionally used appear to be dull. Discount rate changes, traditionally the main instrument in the tool-kit, are said to be largely ineffective, not only because anti-inflationary discount rate hikes tend to induce unwanted capital inflows, but also because the banks and the non-bank end-users have access to credit markets. In fact, the authors could in fact also have argued that the high interest rates do not discourage the demand for loans, since a high inflation rate greatly reduces the real cost of borrowing (the tax deductibility feature further reduces the interest cost by about half). The authors equally contend that the direct quantitative ceilings on rediscount facilities, that have been introduced in recent years, could also be circumvened by recourse to the international market, thus thrusting Belgian monetary policy in the primary role of compensating the external impact on the monetary base. This pessimistic evaluation about the efficiency of monetary instruments, as used until now in Belgium, is linked to the notoriously weak role of fiscal policy in Belgium.

I do not have any convincing evidence to disclaim the above conclusions. And after all, the authors, like magicians, have pulled out awesome econometric coefficients from their model. But I would like to venture the pedestrian observation that, in the period under consideration, the Belgian economy has not performed too badly in terms of growth and in terms of internal and external equilibrium (until most recently). So, perhaps, has monetary policy been more inspired and effective than the authors are led to believe on the basis of their research. Were perhaps "real" (i.e., non-monetary) factors to allow a fair sailing of our economy, in spite of the somewhat inadequate impulses generated by monetary policy? Or, did perhaps the highly selective allocation of credits, which is typical of Belgium -- and which, for example, Prof. Donald Hodgman found quite pronounced when compared with other countries in Western Europe (see his paper on "Credit Allocation Techniques and Monetary Policy" in the Conference series n. 11 of the Federal Reserve Bank of Boston, 1974) -- have less harmful effect than most experts favoring the free play of market forces are inclined to believe? Finally, one may ask whether the authors' findings, which encompass the 1960-72 period, should not be differentiated or at least qualified as between two subperiods, namely the one with modest inflationary pressures until 1969 and the period since 1969 characterized by accelerating inflation which later evolved into untractable stagflation?

CRITICAL DETERMINANTS OF THE EFFECTIVENESS OF MONETARY POLICY IN THE OPEN ECONOMY

By Lance Girton
Dale W. Henderson*

During the 1960's, rapid movements of large amounts of liquid financial capital increasingly frustrated attempts by the authorities in individual countries to conduct monetary policies that diverged to any great extent from those being followed in the world at large. The unwillingness of monetary authorities to reconcile themselves to limited opportunities for pursuing domestic objectives within the constraints imposed by the par value system led to the breakdown of that system and its replacement by a system of managed floating. It is important to identify the features of the

---

*) Economists at the Board of Governors of the Federal Reserve System. The authors would like to express their appreciation to their colleagues in the International Finance Division for helpful comments and suggestions. No one but the authors is responsible for the paper's remaining shortcomings. The analysis and conclusions of this paper should not be interpreted as representing the views of the Board of Governors of the Federal Reserve System or anyone else on its staff.

monetary policy-making environment which contributed to these developments.

In this paper a short-run, two-country model of financial markets is used to isolate some of the factors which influence the effectiveness of monetary policy in national economies which are part of a highly integrated world economy. The authorities in any single economy are constrained in pursuing domestic objectives with monetary policy by the monetary policies pursued abroad, by the practical implications of a reserve currency system, by the extent to which they are committed to an exchange rate target, by the degree to which financial assets issued in their country are regarded by private wealth holders as substitutes for financial assets issued abroad, and by the relative economic size of their country.

After the basic model is described, each of these determinants of the effectiveness of monetary policy is discussed in turn.

I. The Model

The model developed here is designed to analyze the effects of monetary policy on financial asset markets in the short run. Monetary policy actions cause instantaneous adjustments in interest rates, the financial asset holdings of both wealth holders and central banks, and, under flexible exchange rates, the exchange rate. However, monetary policy actions are assumed to affect home currency price levels, incomes, and employment levels with a lag, and these variables are regarded as predetermined. In accordance with the short-run nature of the model, the effects of savings on wealth and the effects of investment on the capital stock are ignored.

The model contains two countries, the United States (U.S.) and the United Kingdom (U.K.). The U.S. currency is the dollar; the U.K. currency is the pound. The behavior of four groups is analyzed: wealth holders in the U.S., wealth holders in the U.K., the U.S. central bank (the Federal Reserve, or FR), and the U.K. central bank (the Bank of England, or BOE).

It is assumed that there are only four types of assets: dollar deposits (U.S. money), pound deposits (U.K. money), dollar denominated securities (U.S. securities), and pound denominated securities (U.K. securities).[1)] All deposits are liabilities of one of the two central banks,[2)] and each central bank accepts only deposits denominated in its country's currency.[3)] The nominal interest rate on deposits is fixed at zero. Securities are fixed in nominal value in the currency of the country in which the issuer resides and have variable nominal interest rates.

---

1) Forward contracts are added to the model in Girton and Henderson (1976 forthcoming). See footnote 5.

2) The implications of adding a fractional reserve banking system for each country to the model are explored in Girton and Henderson (1976).

3) The model can be modified to allow both central banks to accept deposits denominated in both currencies so long as some assumptions are made which determine the desired liability composition for each central bank.

The exchange rate, S, defined as the dollar price of pounds, may be fixed by the central banks or may be flexible. The expected percentage change in the exchange rate, s, is the same for all wealth holders.[4)] s is assumed to be a given number, usually zero, under fixed rates and is taken to be a decreasing function of the gap between the current exchange rate and its "normal" level, $\bar{S}$, under flexible rates:

$$s = s(S-\bar{S}), \quad s_{S-\bar{S}} < 0.$$

This formulation implies that expectations are stabilizing, and it is retained through most of the analysis though occassionally reference is made to the case of destabilizing expectations ($s_{S-\bar{S}} > 0$).

Wealth holders in each country hold domestic money and both types of securities. They regard the three assets they hold as imperfect substitutes.[5)] Wealth holders in the U.S. base their nominal demands in terms of dollars for U.S. securities, B^d, for U.K. securities, SF^d, and for U.S. money, M^d, on their existing dollar denominated nominal wealth, W. It is assumed that the fraction of their nominal wealth which they wish to hold in each of these three assets depends on the interest rate on U.S. securities, r, and the interest rate on U.K. securities adjusted for the expected rate of depreciation of the dollar, $r' + s$, but not on

4) The assumption that all wealth holders expect the same percentage change in the exchange rate makes possible considerable simplification in the exposition of the model, but this assumption can be dropped without affecting any of the conclusions.

5) See next page.

their current savings[6] so that

(1) $B^d = b(r, r' + s)W$

(2) $SF^d = f(r, r' + s)W$

(3) $M^d = m(r, r' + s)W$

Similarly, U.K. wealth holders base their pound denominated nominal demands for U.S. securities, $\frac{1}{S}B^{d'}$, for U.K. securities,

---

5) Wealth holders in each country might regard the two securities as imperfect substitutes for two sets of reasons. First, the two securities are issued in different countries and wealth holders might believe that the returns on the two securities are uncertain and that these returns are not perfectly correlated either because they perceive that fluctuations in economic activity are not perfectly correlated across countries, or because they view governments as having different degrees of "responsibility"; that is, business and political risks might be different in the two countries. Second, the two securities are denominated in different currencies so actual or potential exchange rate movements or exchange controls add exchange risk to the other risks associated with holding "foreign" assets. Either set of reasons is sufficient to insure that wealth holders in both countries would, in general, want to hold well defined amounts of both securities.
Adding forward contracts to the model so that a security denominated in one currency can be converted into a security denominated in the other currency does not change this conclusion. In Girton and Henderson (1975) it is shown that if securities denominated in different currencies are regarded as imperfect substitutes only because of exchange risk and if capital markets are perfect, forward contracts are redundant assets. Black (1973) imposes somewhat less stringent assumptions on a model which includes forward contracts.

6) The demand functions used in the text can be arrived at from more general demand functions by ignoring interest payments, assuming first degree homogeneity in wealth, and subsuming variables held constant into the functional form.

$F^{d'}$, and for U.K. money, $N^{d'}$, on their existing pound denominated nominal wealth, W', so that

(4) $$\frac{1}{S}B^{d'} = b'(r-s,\ r')W'$$

(5) $$F^{d'} = f'(r-s,\ r')W'$$

(6) $$N^{d'} = n'(r-s,\ r')W'$$

W and W' are given by

$$W = M^A + B^A + SF^{A'}$$

$$W' = N^{A'} + \frac{1}{S}B^{A'} + F^{A'}$$

where the superscript $(^A)$ denotes actual holdings of a given asset.

The balance sheet constraint for U.S. wealth holders requires that the sum of their nominal demands for all assets must be equal to their wealth which is defined to be the sum of the nominal values of the securities and money they currently hold. This constraint implies that b, f, and m must sum to one and that the sum of the partial effects on the three asset demands of a change in either of the two interest rates must be zero.[7] U.K. wealth holders face a similar balance sheet constraint. Thus, two of the three asset demand functions are independent in each country. The two securities and home country money are assumed to be strict gross substitutes in the portfolios of wealth holders in each of the two countries. This assumption means that if the interest rate on a given security rises, desired holdings of that se-

7) See next page.

curity increase while the desired holdings of the other security and money decline.

The liabilities of the FR are the stock of U.S. money held by the U.S. public, M^{s}, and the stock of dollars held by the BOE, $M^{c'}$; its assets are its holdings of U.S. securities, B^{c}, and the dollar value of its outside reserve assets, σ R.[8] R is the FR holding of outside reserve assets, and σ is the dollar price of outside reserve assets. The FR balance sheet is

$$(7) \qquad M^{s} = B^{c} + \sigma R - M^{c'} + A$$

where A is a balancing item which changes to offset changes in σ.[9] For the BOE we have

$$(8) \qquad N^{s'} = F^{c'} + \sigma' R' + \frac{1}{S} (B^{c'} + M^{c'}) + A'$$

where $N^{s'}$ is the stock of U.K. money held by the U.K. public, $F^{c'}$ is the BOE holdings of U.K. securities, σ' is the pound price

---

7) See Tobin (1969). The U.S. balance sheet constraint is

$$W = B^{A} + SF^{A} + M^{A} \equiv B^{d} + SF^{d} + M^{d}$$

where B^{A}, F^{A}, and M^{A} are predetermined actual holdings. This identity and equations (1) through (3) imply

$$M^{d} = m(r, r' + s) \equiv [1-b(r, r' + s) - f(r, r' + s)] W$$

so $b_{r} + f_{r} + m_{r} \equiv b_{r'+s} + f_{r'+s} + m_{r'+s} \equiv 0$

where b_{r} is the partial derivative of $b(r, r'+ s)$ with respect to r, etc. Similar relationships hold for the U.K.

8) We assume that the FR does not hold U.K. securities or U.K. money.

9) See next page.

of outside reserve assets, R' is the BOE holdings of outside reserve assets, S is the dollar price of pounds, $B^{c'}$ is the dollar value of BOE holdings of U.S. securities, $M^{c'}$ is the dollar value of BOE holdings of U.S. money, and A' is a balancing item which changes to offset changes in σ' and S. The total world supply of outside reserve assets $(\bar{R})$ is fixed, that is,

(9) $$\bar{R} = R + R'.$$

Equilibrium in the world market for U.S. securities requires that the supply of U.S. securities available to the public, B^s,

---

9) A change in the exchange rate may be reflected in a change in σ, the dollar price of outside reserve assets; in σ', the pound price of outside reserve assets; or in both. Of course, at least one currency price of reserve assets must change. The relationship between dS, $d\sigma$, and $d\sigma'$ is given by

$$dS = \frac{1}{\sigma'} d\sigma - \frac{\sigma}{\sigma'^2} d\sigma'.$$

Changes in S, σ, and σ' alter the domestic currency value of initial reserve holdings of at least one central bank. However, these changes themselves have no effect on the money supply of either country. We assume that in order to balance their balance sheets, the two central banks simply change A and A' so as to offset the effects of changes in σ, σ', and S on the domestic currency value of their assets,

$$dA = R\, d\sigma$$

$$dA' = (\bar{R} - R)d\sigma' - \frac{1}{S^2}(B^{c'} + M^{c'})dS.$$

given by the total supply of U.S. securities, $\bar{B}$,[10] minus the holdings of the FR and the BOE, equal the demand for these securities by wealth holders in the two countries:

$$(10) \quad B^S = \bar{B} - B^c - B^{c'} = b(r, r' + s)W + Sb'(r-s, r')W'.$$

Similarly, the supply of U.K. securities available to the public, F^S, given by the total supply of U.K. securities, $\bar{F}$, minus the holdings of the BOE, must equal the demand for these securities by wealth holders so that, in dollar terms,

$$(11) \quad SF^S = S(\bar{F}-F^{c'}) = f(r, r' + s)W + Sf'(r-s, r')W'.$$

Using the central bank balance sheet identities and the fact that the total supply of outside reserve assets is fixed, the money market equilibrium conditions for the two countries can be written as follows:

---

10) The total supply of U.S. securities ($\bar{B}$) is equal to the sum of cumulated U.S. government deficits and the value of net claims to the income of the capital stock of the U.S. non-financial corporate sector. $\bar{B}$ might also include consumer debt, but we assume that obligations of ultimate wealth holders to one another are netted out. $\bar{F}$ has a similar interpretation.
Instead of including in $\bar{B}$ and $\bar{F}$ all securities issued in the two countries, it may be useful to restrict attention to some subset of securities. A significant part of short-run financial capital movements seems to be made up of changes in holdings of short-term (liquid) assets. If people quickly balance money and short-term security holdings according to rates of return independently of their holdings of long-term (illiquid) securities, then, for some purposes, defining W and W′ to include only short-run securities and money may be useful. The treatment here is theoretical, and no attempt is made to prejudge the question of what is the best empirical definition of allocatable wealth in any particular application.

(12) $M^{s} = B^{c} + \sigma R - M^{c'} + A = m(r, r' + s)W$

(13) $SN^{s} = S[F^{c'} + \sigma'(\overline{R}-R)] + B^{c'} + M^{c'} + SA' = Sn'(r-s, r')W'.$

Three of the four market equilibrium conditions are independent, so three endogenous variables can be determined.[11)] Different sets of three variables are taken to be endogenous at different stages in the study depending upon the situation which is being analyzed. In one important case under fixed rates, for example, the two interest rates, r and r′, and the stock of reserves held by the FR, R, are regarded as being endogenously determined, and all the other variables are considered to be given exogenously.

The policy tools of the monetary authorities in the two countries are asset exchanges which alter the composition of the balance sheets of the authorities and the public, while in the first instance at least, leaving the size of these balance sheets unchanged. The two central banks, taken together, have three independent policy tools with which they can attain three objectives subject to the proviso that the two central banks cannot achieve conflicting values of a single variable such as R or S. Perhaps the easiest way to understand the opportunities open to the authorities is to

---

11) Adding the left-hand sides of (10), (11), (12) and (13) yields the total dollar value of all assets available to wealth holders, which can be expressed as $\overline{B} + S\overline{F} + \sigma\overline{R}$ since $S = \sigma/\sigma'$. Adding the right-hand sides of (10), (11), (12), and (13), taking account of the fact that $b + f + m \equiv b' + f' + n' \equiv 1$, yields world wealth in dollar terms, $W + SW'$. $\overline{B} + S\overline{F} + \sigma\overline{R}$ is identically equal to $W + SW'$, so only three of the four market equilibrium conditions are independent.

consider the set of independent equations (10) - (12) and to note that the U.K. central bank can use a different asset exchange to shift each of the three equations while leaving the other two unaffected. All of the other possible asset exchanges available to the two central banks can be shown to be linear combinations of these three exchanges. This observation makes quite clear what it means for the monetary authorities to agree to support a preestablished par value under a fixed exchange rate regime or adopt an exchange rate target under a regime of managed floating. In either case, one policy tool is committed to attaining an exchange rate objective and is not, therefore, available for any other purpose. Whatever the supposed benefits from pegging the exchange rate, they must be weighed against the costs imposed by the loss of a degree of policy making freedom.

In Figure 1, four schedules are plotted which show the pairs of r and r′ which are compatible with equilibrium in each of the four financial asset markets. The curve labeled B_0B_0 gives the combinations of r and r′ for which the private demand for securities issued in the U.S. is equal to the fixed supply of securities issued in the U.S. minus the holdings of U.S. securities by the FR and the BOE. The curve slopes upward; an increase in r causes an excess demand for U.S. securities so that r′ must rise in order to cut demand back until it matches the fixed supply of U.S. securities available to wealth holders. Minus (plus) signs in a region near the schedule for a given market indicate that the rate pairs in that region imply excess supply (demand) in that market; vertical (horizontal) arrows represent the direction of pressure on r (r′) in each of the regions. The curve labeled

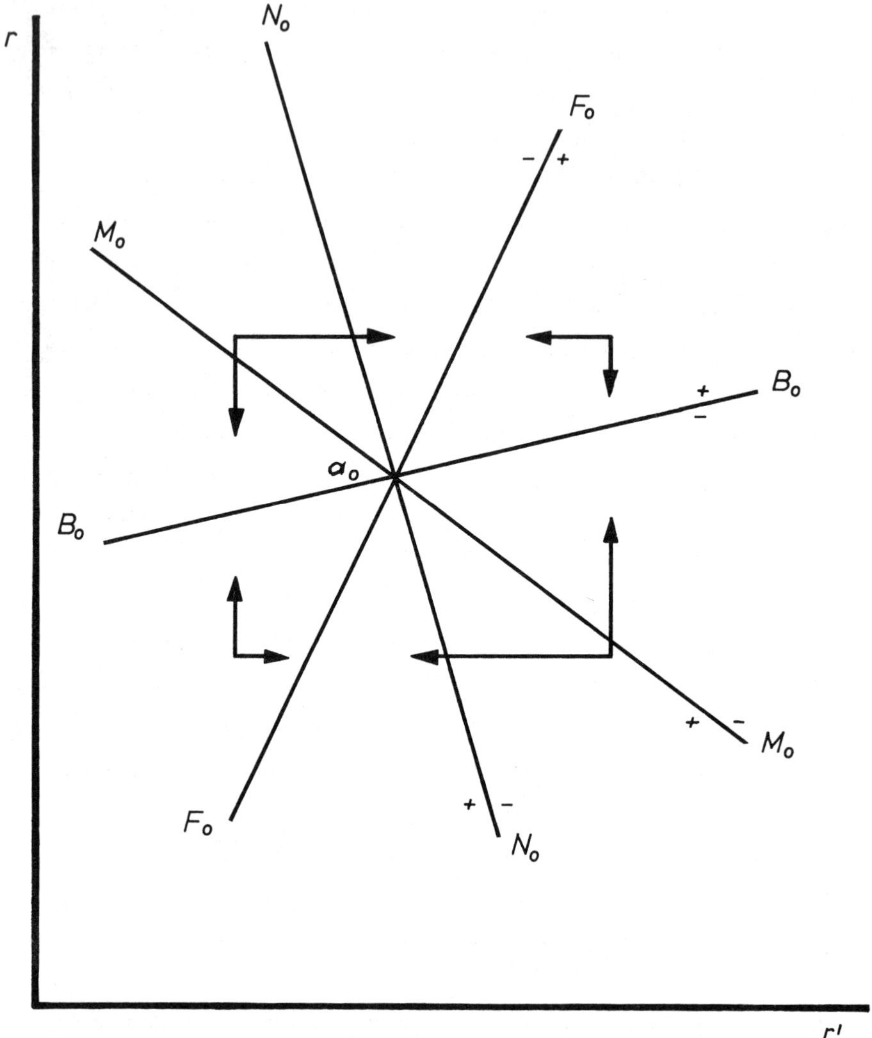

Figure 1

F_0F_0 represents the combinations of r and r′ which insure that wealth holders′ demands for securities issued in the U.K. are equal to the available supply. The F_0F_0-curve is positively sloped; an increase in r is required to offset the excess demand caused by an increase in r′ if private wealth holders are to continue to be satisfied holding the available supply of U.K. securities. Combinations of r and r′ that equate the demand for and supply of U.S. money, given a fixed U.S. money supply available for the public to hold, are plotted as the M_0M_0-curve. The M_0M_0-curve is negatively sloped since an increase in either r or r′ reduces the demand for U.S. money. Combinations of r and r′ that equate the demand for the fixed supply of U.K. money are plotted as the N_0N_0-curve. The N_0N_0-curve is negatively sloped since an increase in either r or r′ reduces the demand for U.K. money.

The assumption that the three assets held by wealth holders in each of the two countries are strict gross substitutes, insures that the slope of the F_0F_0-curve must be greater than the slope of the B_0B_0-curve. Suppose that all four markets are in equilibrium as at a_0. At every point in the quadrant northeast of a_0, there are excess supplies of the two kinds of money. The balance sheet constraints for wealth holders imply that the sum of the excess supplies for all assets must be zero, so at no point in the quadrant can there be excess supplies of both of the two securities. This possibility is ruled out only if F_0F_0 is steeper than B_0B_0.

It is assumed that wealth holders in each country regard their currency as a better substitute for the security denominated in that currency than for the security denominated in the other currency. This plausible assumption is sufficient to insure that the N_0N_0-curve has a steeper (more negative) slope than the M_0M_0-curve.

Interest rate changes alone are not sufficient to insure that three independent schedules will have a common intersection point. A third variable not shown explicitly on the graph, for example, the stock of reserves held by the FR, must be free to vary in order to insure that a common intersection exists. If three of the four schedules intersect at a common point, the fourth schedule must also pass through that point. It is useful to retain all four schedules even though in a given situation three schedules are sufficient to determine the equilibrium values of the endogenous variables.

II. The Effectiveness of Monetary Policy Under Fixed Exchange Rates and Alternative Reserve Regimes

The discussion of instruments and targets above makes it clear that, even when central banks have agreed to keep the exchange rate fixed, the two central banks, taken together, still have available two policy instruments. Each central bank can, in general, use open market operations in the security denominated in its country's currency to achieve a monetary policy objective. Exactly what size open market operation is required to attain a specified objective and exactly what effects on other variables are associated with that open market operation depend both on the monetary policy response of the other central bank and on the form in which changes in international reserves are held. If the

FR untertakes an open market operation, the BOE may respond by remaining passive, stabilizing the U.K. interest rate, or stabilizing the U.K. money supply. Institutional arrangements and BOE preferences may make it possible and desirable for the BOE to take all of its reserve changes in the form of outside reserve assets such as gold or SDR's. Proposals for full asset settlement considered by the Committee of Twenty envisioned such an "outside reserve regime". Alternatively, the BOE may desire or consider itself constrained to hold changes in its reserves in the form of claims denominated in the "key currency", U.S. dollars.

In Figure 2 we trace the implications of an expansionary open market operation by the FR for a variety of BOE policy responses under the assumption that all reserve changes are held in the form of outside reserves. The initial equilibrium position is given by the intersection of the curves with the ($_0$) subscript. If the U.S. authorities increase their holdings of U.S. securities by a given amount and then allow no further change in these holdings, the BB-curve shifts down, say from B_0B_0 to B_1B_1 since, for a given value of r', the public will hold a reduced supply of U.S. securities only if r is lower. The new equilibrium must be on the new BB-curve.

Consider the case in which the BOE remains passive, neither buying nor selling U.K. securities. In order to increase its holdings of U.S. securities by a given amount, the FR offers to supply dollar deposits in exchange for U.S. securities. At the initial interest rate pair there is excess demand for U.S. securities and an excess supply of U.S. money. FR bidding for U.S. secu-

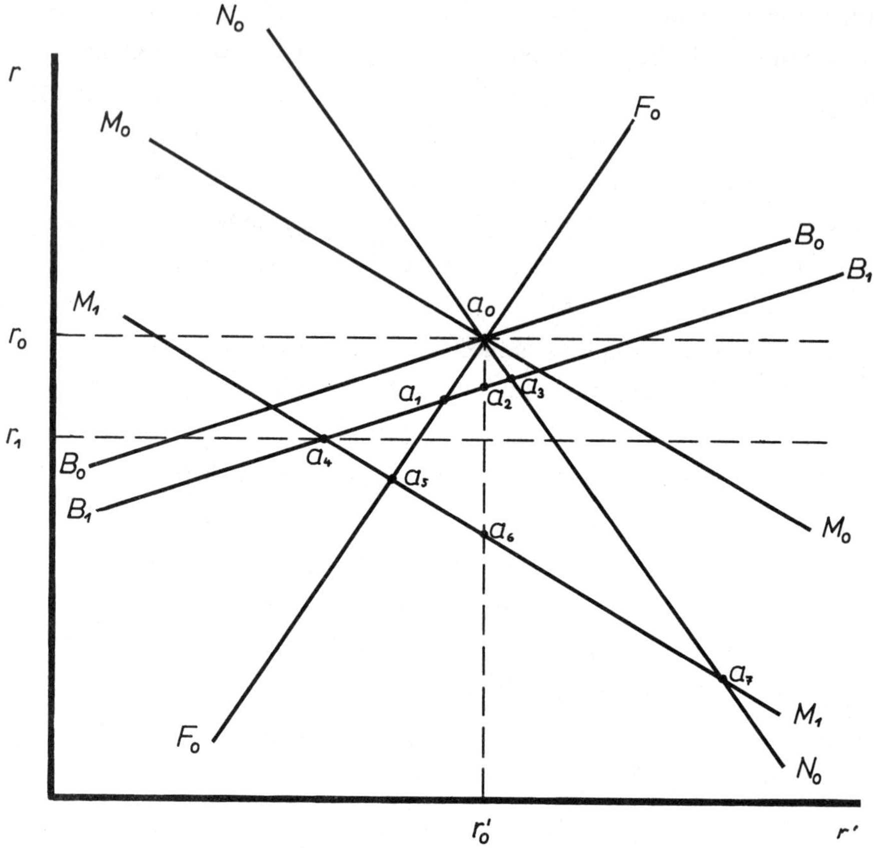

Figure 2

rities leads to a downward movement in r, an increase in private demand in the U.S. and U.K. for U.K. securities, and a downward movement in r′. As interest rates are bid down, an excess demand for U.K. money appears; this development coupled with the remaining excess supply of U.S. money results in upward pressure on S. In order to keep S from rising, the BOE must buy dollars for pounds, an action which reduces the U.S. money supply and raises the U.K. money supply by equal amounts measured in dollars. Thus, the initial excess supply of money in the U.S. is removed partly by increases in the U.S. demand for money and partly by decreases in the U.S. money supply matched by increases in the supply of and demand for U.K. money. Money demands increase, and U.S. security demands fall in both countries because of interest rate declines. The FR loses reserves because the BOE converts the proceeds of its exchange rate stabilization operations into reserve assets.

The size of the FR reserve loss can be represented graphically. If the U.S. public increased its money holdings by an amount exactly equal to the quantity of securities the FR purchases, the MM-curve would be shifted from M_0M_0 to M_1M_1 which must lie below the intersection of B_1B_1 and F_0F_0. However, the U.S. public actually increases its money holdings by an amount corresponding to the distance between M_0M_0 and the MM-curve (not shown) which passes through a_1. The part of the initial excess supply of money which is removed by a decline in the U.S. money supply and a matching loss of reserves by the FR is represented by the distance between M_1M_1 and the MM-curve which passes through a_1.

If the BOE stabilizes r′, the new equilibrium is at a_2, and if it stabilizes the U.K. money stock, the new equilibrium is at a_3. Successively larger sales of U.K. securities which shift FF until it passes through a_2 or a_3 are required by these two responses. Successively less of the initial excess supply of U.S. money is removed by interest rate declines which raise the U.S. demand for money, and successively more of the initial excess supply is removed by decreases in the U.S. money supply matched by losses of reserves by the U.S. The reserve losses can be represented by the distances between M_1M_1 and MM-curves which pass through a_2 and a_3 respectively. The actions of the BOE when it sterilizes present a sharp contrast to its actions when it is passive. Instead of being content to trade U.K. money for U.S. money, the BOE takes measures which are tantamount to replacing that part of the U.S. money stock which it receives through the exchange market with U.K. securities.

The BOE can pursue a fourth kind of policy response; it can stabilize its stock of international reserves. In order to keep from gaining reserves, the BOE must see to it that interest rates move so as to make U.S. residents content with an increase in their money holdings exactly equal to the amount of securities the FR wants to buy. To achieve its desired result, the BOE must buy enough securities to shift FF from F_0F_0 until it passes through the intersection of B_1B_1 and M_1M_1 at point a_4. Since the supplies of both securities are reduced, both interest rates must end up lower than in the original position. At these lower rates, U.K. residents are content to increase their money holdings by an amount equal to the open market purchases of the BOE.

The discussion above of FR open market operations provides all the information necessary for analyzing FR actions designed to increase the U.S. money supply (say from the level represented by M_0M_0 to that represented by M_1M_1), or to lower the U.S. interest rate (say from r_0 to r_1), given various BOE policy responses under the outside reserve regime. In order to obtain either of these two objectives, larger and larger open market operations must be undertaken and larger and larger reserve losses incurred as the BOE policy response moves from passiveness, to interest rate stabilization, to money stock stabilization. The effectiveness of FR monetary policy in terms of "bang per buck" and the costs associated with using it depend upon the reactions of the BOE.

It is interesting to ask how the policymaking environment for the FR is changed if the BOE takes changes in its international reserves in the form of assets denominated in dollars since the international monetary system conformed more and more closely to this "key currency reserve regime" during the final decade of the Bretton Woods system.[12)] The first point to note is that if

12) International economists have focused considerable attention on some aspects of the key currency reserve regime. It has been argued that the pressure to take corrective measures in the face of persistent payments imbalances and the burden of adjustment when it takes place are distributed asymmetrically under such a regime. In a two country, flexible price version of the income-expenditure model, Don Roper (1973) has shown that if adjustment is actually to take place, the adjustment burden will usually be distributed asymmetrically in favor of the key currency country. Although securities and, therefore, the sterilization process are not given explicit treatment in Roper's model, he has emphasized that the key currency country is relieved of the task of sterilization since the non-center countries sterilize for the center country.

the BOE holds its reserve changes in the form of U.S. money, no change is required in the preceding analysis, since whether or not the BOE converts the proceeds of its support operation into outside reserves has no effect on the position of the four schedules. However, virtually all changes in international reserves are taken in the form of interest bearing assets, so the most interesting case arises when the BOE takes its reserve changes in the form of U.S. securities. In this case, an open market operation by the FR, which shifts the BB-curve from B_0B_0 to B_1B_1 in Figure 2, raises the U.S. money supply from the level associated with M_0M_0 to the level associated with M_1M_1 no matter what the monetary policy response of the BOE. Suppose, for example, that the BOE follows a passive monetary policy. The FR offer to supply dollar deposits in exchange for U.S. securities creates downward pressure on r and r′ and upward pressure on S. There is a tendency for the U.S. money stock to decline as the FR makes net purchases of securities from U.K. residents. However, the dollars acquired by the BOE in its support operation are neither held as deposits nor converted into outside reserves, but rather are used to purchase U.S. securities in the market, so the U.S. money supply remains constant.[13)] When the non key currency country holds changes in reserves in the form of key currency securities, they, in effect, sterilize the key currency country′s money supply. The reserve accumulations by the BOE cause BB to shift from B_1B_1 until it passes through a_5 and cause further downward movements in r and r′, movements which are required for equilibrium to be attained given that the U.S. money stock is kept constant.

13) See next page.

While the effect of an open market operation by the FR on the U.S. money supply is independent of the monetary policy response of the BOE under the key currency reserve regime, the effect on the U.S. interest rate is not. If the BOE stabilizes r' instead of remaining passive, the equilibrium is at a_6, and if the BOE stabilizes N^S, the equilibrium is at a_7. Thus, in contrast to the result obtained under the outside reserve regime, the effectiveness of an open market operation by the FR in lowering r is greater the smaller the change which the BOE permits in its money supply. This result arises because sales of U.K. securities by the BOE reduce (increase) the downward (upward) pressure on r' so

---

13) From time to time, some of the increases in dollar denominated, interest bearing assets acquired by foreign official institutions with the dollars accumulated in their support operations have been in the form of special non-marketable securities issued by the U.S. Treasury. When reserve changes are taken in this form, there is no reduction in the supply of U.S. securities available to the public. The decrease in U.S. money in the hands of the public is matched by an increase in U.S. money held by the Treasury.
If the Treasury decides to get rid of its new cash balances immediately, it retires debt, and the money supply in the hands of the public is restored to its previous level. However, if the Treasury does not run down its new cash balances, then the Federal Reserve must actively pursue open market operations if it wants to keep the U.S. money supply in the hands of the public constant.
It is unlikely that the Treasury will want to add to its cash balances just because foreign central banks have accumulated dollar balances. It will generally run down its cash balances over a relatively short period by reducing its offerings of new debt below the gap between its expenditures and its tax receipts. However, when a significant portion of large and rapid dollar accumulations abroad are converted into so called "specials", as was the case in the spring of 1973, the Federal Reserve may have to deal with a non negligible, but temporary, disturbance when attempting to achieve money supply management goals.

that r must fall farther to make U.S. residents willing to hold the U.S. money stock corresponding to M_1M_1.

Two conclusions can be drawn regarding U.S. reserve losses (increases in U.S. liabilities to the BOE) associated with an expansionary open market operation by the FR under the key currency reserve regime. First, just as in the case of the outside reserve regime, U.S. reserve losses become greater as the BOE policy response progresses from passiveness, to interest rate stabilization, to money stock stabilization. To see this, compare the shifts in BB which are required to move it from B_1B_1 to a_5, a_6, and a_7 respectively. Second, for any specified policy response by the BOE, the FR loses more reserves as a result of an open market operation of a given size under the key currency regime than under the outside reserve regime. For a passive response by the BOE, reserve gains are reflected in the NN-schedule which must shift farther to reach a_5 than to reach a_1; for a money stock stabilization response by the BOE, reserve gains are reflected in the FF-schedule which must shift farther to reach a_7 than to reach a_3. Both of these conclusions and the conclusions regarding reserve changes under the outside reserve regime are special cases of a more general result. This result, which is proved elsewhere, is that for any given shock to portfolio equilibrium, the less reserve changes are allowed to affect money supplies, the larger the total reserve change required to reestablish equilibrium.[14)]

---

14) This result is proved in Girton and Henderson (1976).

Up to this point, the effectiveness of monetary policy has been measured in terms of the change in a specified target variable associated with an open market operation of a given size. Using this criterion, FR monetary policy is more effective under the key currency reserve regime. However, it has higher costs in terms of reserve losses. An alternative way of measuring the effectiveness of monetary policy is in terms of the change in a specified target variable associated with a change in reserve holdings of a given size. Using this criterion, FR monetary policy is equally effective under both reserve regimes. To see this, simply observe that in order for the FR to achieve a specified objective, such as the money supply represented by M_1M_1 or the interest rate r_1 in Figure 2, with a given monetary policy response by the BOE it must experience the same reserve loss under both reserve regimes.

It is important to remember, however, that the FR may face a less binding reserve constraint under the key currency reserve regime. An open market purchase involves a loss of outside reserves under the outside reserve regime and an increase in U.S. liabilities to foreign official holders under the key currency regime, and the FR may feel or actually may be more constrained from undertaking an expansionary open market operation by the former than by the latter.

For the U.K., the situation is somewhat different. Figure 3 shows the effect of an expansionary open market operation by the BOE which shifts FF from F_0F_0 to F_1F_1. With passive behavior by the FR, the new equilibrium is at a_3 under the key cur-

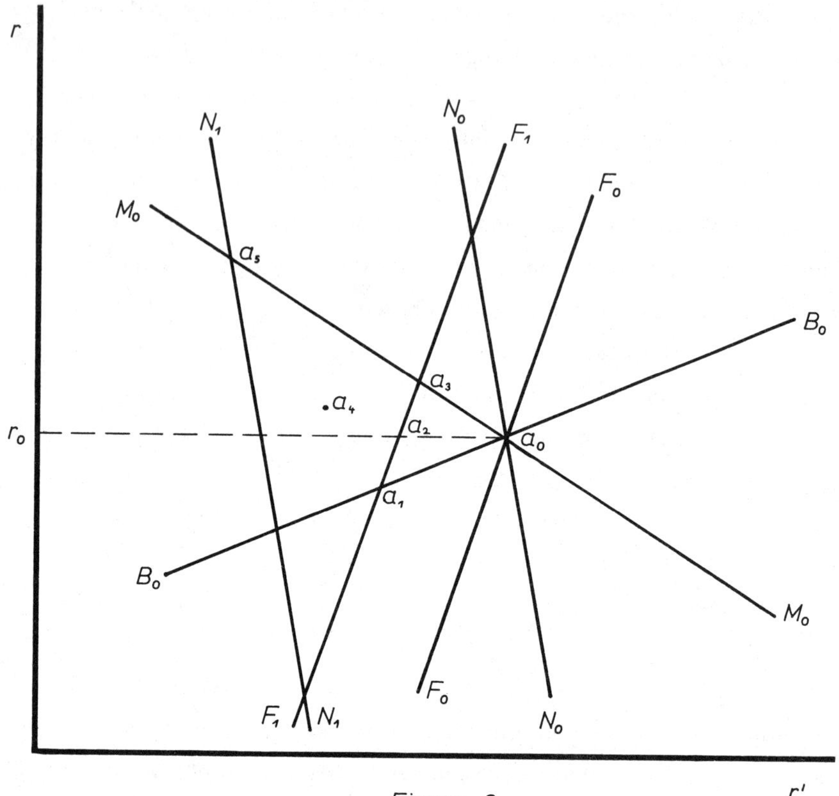

Figure 3

rency reserve regime, while under the outside reserve regime it is at a_1. The open market operation leads to smaller changes in N^S and r′ and involves larger reserve losses under the key currency reserve regime, so U.K. monetary policy is less effective in terms of both of the measures considered above. Of course, if the FR stabilizes r, a_2 is reached under both regimes, and, if the FR stabilizes M^S under the outside reserve regime, a_3 is attained under both regimes. The monetary policy environment for the BOE is at best left unchanged if a key currency reserve regime is substituted for full asset settlement, and it may be made more unfavorable.

III. The Effectiveness of Monetary Policy and Intervention Policy

Under the current regime of managed floating, central banks need not intervene to support predetermined par values. If exchange rates are allowed to vary, given sized monetary policy actions have larger impacts on target variables under many circumstances.

A first step in analyzing the impact of different types and degrees of intervention on the effectiveness of monetary policy is to consider the effect of an open market operation under freely floating exchange rates. Suppose the BOE undertakes an expansionary open market operation and the FR remains passive. The original equilibrium is given by the intersection of the schedules with the $(_0)$ subscript at a_0 in Figure 3, and the BOE open market purchase shifts FF and NN to F_1F_1 and N_1N_1 respectively. At unchanged values of r, r′, and S, there is an excess supply of U.K. money and an excess demand for U.K. securities. The excess demand for U.K. securities puts downward pressure on r′ which tends to create excess demand for U.S. securities with resulting downward pressure on r; the excess supply of U.K. money puts downward pressure on S, the dollar price of pounds. The depreciation of the pound stimulates demand for pound assets shifting N_1N_1 and F_1F_1 upward for two reasons. First, the dollar value of U.S. wealth falls, and the pound value of U.K. wealth rises.[15) But these changes accrue completely in the form of reduced values of pound holdings in the U.S. and increased pound values of dollar holdings in the U.K., so that both groups want more pound assets. Both groups also want fewer dollar assets, so M_0M_0 shifts down, and B_0B_0 shifts up. Second, given our assumption of stabilizing expectations, a decline in S causes s to rise, a movement which stimulates demand for pound assets and reduces demand for dollar assets. Even if expectations are destabilizing, the schedules will shift in the directions described above if the wealth effects are strong enough.[16)] The new equilibrium pair of r and r′ must lie within the kite-shaped area bounded by the M_0M_0, N_1N_1, B_0B_0, and F_1F_1-schedules, say at a_4. Thus, the expansionary open market purchase by the BOE with the FR passive lowers r′ and S, but the net effect on r is indeterminate. The U.S. interest rate will fall (rise) if the leftward shift in the

---

15) Throughout this paper, we assume that F^A and $B^{A'}$ are positive; that is, we assume that residents of both the U.S. and the U.K. have positive net holdings of foreign securities. If either F^A or $B^{A'}$, or both are negative, the description of how the schedules shift when the exchange rate changes must be modified Somewhat, and some of the results may be changed.
16) See next page.

M_0M_0-schedule due to a decrease in S is greater (less) than the leftward shift in the B_0B_0-schedule resulting from a decrease in S. An interesting special case of the model arises when money demands do not depend on wealth and when the expected change in the exchange rate does not depend on its level so that money demands in both countries are independent of S.[17] In this case, the equilibrium is at a_5, and r definitely rises.

---

16) That is, letting $s_{S-\bar{S}} = s' < 0$, if

$$(b_{r'}W - b'_r W')s' + bF^A + b'(N^{A'} + F^{A'}) > 0,$$

$$(f_{r'}W - f'_r W')s' - f(M^A + B^A) - f'B^{A'} < 0,$$

$$m_{r'}Ws' + mF^{A'} > 0, \qquad - n'_r W's' - n'B^{A'} < 0.$$

If these conditions are met, a necessary condition for stability under plausible adjustment assumptions is definitely satisfied. However, even if some of these conditions are not met, the same necessary condition for stability may be satisfied. Whether or not these conditions are met, necessary and sufficient conditions for stability may not be satisfied unless some restrictions are placed on the relative speeds of adjustment in the various markets. A more detailed analysis of stability conditions does not yield many additional insights.
While the model may be stable if some of the conditions above are violated, some of the comparative statics results may be changed.

17) In this case the U.S. asset demands, for example, are given by

$$M^d = \tilde{M}(r, r' + s),$$
$$B^d = \tilde{B}(r, r' + s, W),$$
$$SF^d = \tilde{F}(r, r' + s, W),$$

where s is a parameter, the signs of the interest rate effects are the same as before and

$$\tilde{B}_W + \tilde{F}_W \equiv 1.$$

Comparing the results of a U.K. open market purchase under flexible rates with the results under fixed rates, it is clear that monetary policy is more effective in most cases. As is well known, with a freely floating exchange rate an open market purchase increases the money supply by the full amount of the purchase, whereas under fixed rates, the same operation by a non key currency country which does not sterilize increases the money supply by only a fraction of the amount of the operation. Less obviously, an open market purchase must lower r′ by more with flexible rates than it would with fixed rates and a constant U.S. money supply; a_4 must lie to the left of a_3. This result is important, since when rates are fixed, it is quite likely that the FR would remain passive under a key currency regime or would sterilize under an outside reserve regime. In these situations the M_0M_0- schedule represents the opportunity set for the BOE, and, by letting the exchange rate vary, the BOE can cause this opportunity locus to shift in a favorable way.[18] An open market purchase lowers r′ by more under flexible rates than it would under either fixed rate regime given an interest rate stabilization policy by the FR; a_4 must lie to the left of a_2 on the dashed line, indicating a constant r. An open market purchase may lower r′ by more or less with flexible rates than it would with fixed rates and a passive response by the FR under an outside reserve regime. r′ is lowered by more (less) with flexible rates if the upward shift in the F_1F_1-schedule due to a decrease in S is greater (less) than the upward shift in the B_0B_0-schedule resulting from a decrease in S.

---

18) The M_0M_0-schedule is analogous to the foreign offer curve in optimum tariff analysis.

Perhaps more interesting from a policy-making point of view is the regime of managed floating under which the authorities are willing to let the exchange rate move to some extent for some purposes, but intervene to keep it from moving freely. Suppose the BOE performs an open market operation which shifts FF and NN from F_0F_0 and N_0N_0 to F_1F_1 and N_1N_1 in Figure 4, and decides to allow the exchange rate to depreciate enough to shift M_0M_0, B_0B_0, F_1F_1, and N_1N_1 to M_2M_2, B_2B_2, F_2F_2, and N_2N_2. Exactly where the new equilibrium point is located depends upon the intervention policy used by the BOE to keep S from declining further. If the BOE buys U.K. money with U.S. money, the MM and NN-curves are shifted until they pass through a_5 which lies to the left (right) of a_1 if a_4 (the equilibrium under freely floating rates) lies to the left (right) of a_1. The U.K. money supply increases by more than it would under fixed exchange rates and by less than it would under freely floating exchange rates. If the FR sterilizes the effect of the purchase of pounds for dollars by the BOE on its money supply, or if the BOE sells off dollar securities and uses the proceeds to purchase U.K. money, the NN and BB-curves are shifted until they pass through a_6 which must lie to the left of a_3. This type of intervention reduces the effectiveness of an open market purchase from what it would be under floating rates but increases the effectiveness of an open market purchase over what it would be with no exchange rate change at all, both in terms of the increase in the U.K. money supply and of the decrease in r'. It results in a smaller net increase in the U.K. money supply than intervention accomplished by an exchange of moneys with the FR passive. If the BOE sells dollar securities and uses the proceeds to buy pound securities

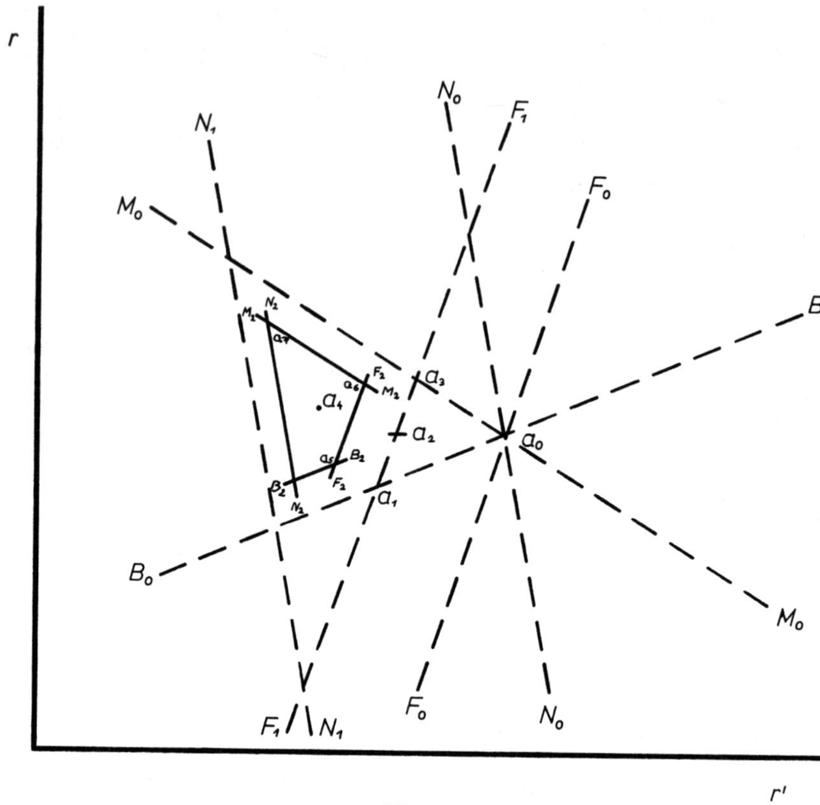
r
r'
N₀
F₁
N₁
F₀
M₀
B₀
M₂
N₂
a₇
F₂
a₆
a₃
a₄
a₂
a₀
a₅
B₂
a₁
B₀
M₀
F₁
N₁
F₀
N₀

Figure 4

additional to those purchased in the open market operation, or if they use dollar deposits to buy pound securities over the exchanges and the FR sterilizes the U.S. money supply, the BB and FF-curves are shifted until they pass through a_7 which must be to the left of a_4, the equilibrium under freely floating rates. In this case, the U.K. money supply rises by the full amount of the open market operation just as under freely floating rates, and r' is decreased even more than it would be under floating rates. The latter result arises primarily because additional U.K. securities are purchased as part of the exchange market intervention.

Leaving aside the details and qualifications of the preceding analysis, the main point is that the effects of monetary policy depend crucially on the exchange market policy being followed. Indeed, it is instructive to recognize that open market operations and exchange market intervention of various types are all simply asset exchanges and that it is the net result of all the asset exchanges which determine the ultimate equilibrium values of the exchange rate, the interest rates, and the money supplies.

IV. The Effectiveness of Monetary Policy and the Degree of Substitutability between Securities

Investigating the impact of changes in the degree of substitutability between home and foreign securities is interesting for two reasons. During the final years of the Bretton Woods system it was argued that increased capital market integration made it more difficult for monetary authorities, primarily those in non key currency countries, to achieve their objectives. One aspect of increased capital market integration is increased substitutability. Also, it has been argued that allowing exchange rates to float makes the task of the monetary authorities easier because exchange rate flexibility reduces the degree of substitutability between assets.

Other analysts have considered the effects of monetary policy in models in which wealth holders in a given country regard securities issued in that country as being either perfectly substitutable or completely non-substitutable for securities issued abroad.[19)] Often these analysts have restricted their attention to the case of a single open economy which is small in economic size when compared to the rest of the world. While familiar polar assumptions yield familiar results in our model, it can also be used to explore the effects of changes in the degree of substitutability in the intermediate range in which U.S. and U.K. securities are substitutes but not perfect substitutes for one another. In order to separate the effects of changes in the degree of asset substitutability from the effects of relative economic size, the assumption that the two countries are of roughly equal economic size is retained.

As before, the basic monetary policy action considered is an open market operation by the BOE with a passive response by the

---

19) For models in which it is assumed that wealth holders regard securities issued at home and abroad as perfect substitutes, see Mundell (1968, Chapter 18) and McKinnon and Oates (1966). For a model in which it is assumed that wealth holders regard securities issued abroad as completely non-substitutable for both securities issued at home and domestic money, see McKinnon (1969).

FR. Whenever fixed rates are assumed, full asset settlement is also assumed unless otherwise indicated.

Consider first the case in which U.S. and U.K. securities are perfect substitutes. Perfect substitutability implies that the returns on the two securities differ only by the expected rate of change in the exchange rate, no matter what the composition of the world supply of securities. A sufficient condition for the two securities to be perfect substitutes under both fixed and flexible exchange rates is that wealth holders be risk neutral, but weaker conditions may insure that the two securities are regarded as perfect substitutes, expecially under fixed exchange rates. In the case of perfect substitutes, the model can be reduced to the following three equations:

$$(14) \qquad M^{s} = B^{c} + \sigma R - M^{c'} + A = m(r)W$$

$$(15) \qquad SN^{s} = S[F^{c'} + \sigma'(\bar{R}-R)] + B^{c'} + M^{c'} + SA' = Sn'(r')W'$$

$$(16) \qquad r = r' + s(S-\bar{S})$$

where W and W′ are defined as before and where the single world securities market has been omitted because it is redundant by Walras' Law. After substitution for r′ using (16), equations (14) and (15) can be used to determine r and S.

The m_0m_0 (n_0n_0)-schedule in Figure 5 shows the pairs of r and S which clear the U.S. (U.K.) money market given that (16) holds. Consider an open market purchase by the BOE which would shift nn from n_0n_0 to n_1n_1 if the U.K. money supply expanded by the

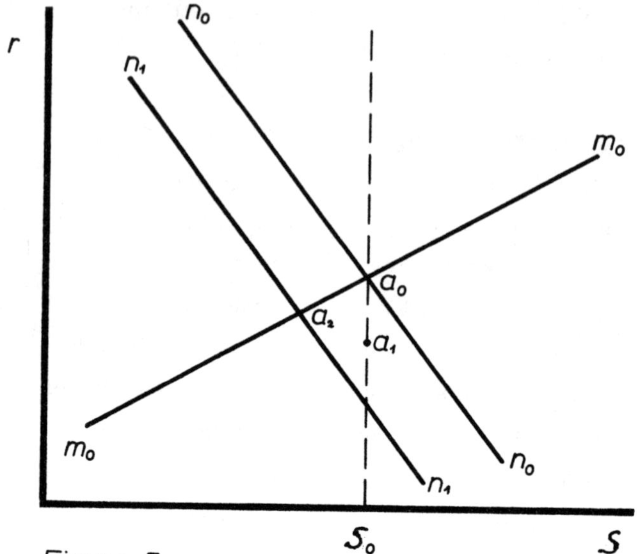

Figure 5

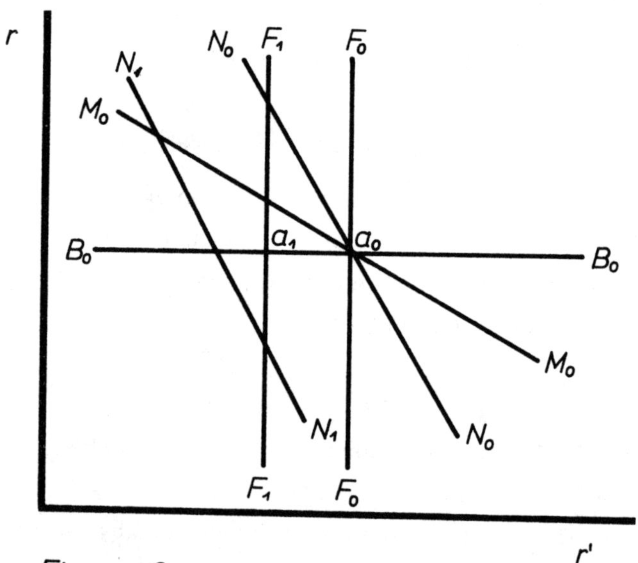

Figure 6

full amount of the purchase. Under fixed rates with full asset settlement and a passive response by the FR, the new equilibrium lies at a point such as a_1 which lies between $n_0 n_0$ and $n_1 n_1$ on the dashed line which represents a constant exchange rate. The U.S. and U.K. interest rates fall by the same amount since they are locked together in the fixed rate case. The U.K. money supply increases by less than the amount of the open market purchase, and the U.S. money supply rises. If the U.S. sterilizes, or if the U.K. sells off U.S. securities to finance its intervention, the equilibrium is at a_0 and the open market purchase achieves nothing except a reduction in U.K. reserves. In these cases, if the BOE keeps trying to lower world interest rates and raise its money supply, it continues to lose reserves and no new equilibrium is reached.

Under flexible exchange rates the new equilibrium is at a_2. The U.K. money supply rises by the full amount of the open market purchase, and r′ is lowered more than r because the pound depreciates.

In terms of the graphical framework used earlier in the paper, the slopes of the BB and FF-curves approach positive one as the degree of asset substitutability increases without limit. As the two securities become virtually identical, any increase in r′ must be offset by an almost identical increase in r in order for either of the two securities markets to remain in equilibrium. The slopes of the MM and NN-schedules approach negative one as the two securities become indistinguishable.[20)]

20) See next page.

The other limiting case in which U.S. and U.K. residents view the two types of securities as being completely nonsubstitutable for one another even though both groups of residents view both types of securities as substitutes for domestic money is portrayed in Figure 6.[21] Under fixed rates with full asset settlement and the FR passive, equilibrium following an open market purchase by the BOE is at a_1. The rate on U.K. securities falls by enough to make both U.K. and U.S. residents willing to reduce their holdings of U.K. securities and increase their holdings of money by the amount of the open market purchase. The interest differential changes by the amount of the decline in the U.K. rate, and the BOE loses reserves. Under flexible rates, the new equilibrium point lies in the kite-shaped area bounded by M_0M_0, N_1N_1, B_0B_0, and F_1F_1.

---

20) For a more detailed discussion of the effects of increases in the degree of substitutability on the four schedules of the model, see Appendix A.

21) If U.S. (U.K.) citizens do not consider U.K. (U.S.) securities to be substitutes for either U.S. (U.K.) securities or U.S. (U.K.) money so that, as far as financial asset holding is concerned, the U.S. (U.K.) is a "closed" economy, the MM and BB-schedules (NN and FF-schedules) coincide. Since, in each country, money and securities issued at home are the only assets considered suitable for wealth holding, the same value of the interest rate on securities issued at home must clear both the money market and the market for securities issued at home. In this case, an open market purchase by the BOE causes the rate on U.K. securities to fall by more than the case described in the text, since this rate must decline by enough to make U.K. residents willing to reduce their holdings of U.K. securities and increase their holdings of money by the amount of the open market purchase. Of course, the differential between the U.S. and U.K. rates changes by the full amount of the decline in the U.K. rate.

Determining the impact of increases in the degree of substitutability between securities on the effects of monetary policy when securities are neither completely nonsubstitutable nor virtually perfect substitutes is somewhat more difficult. In order to make the problem more tractable, some stronger assumptions are made. It is assumed that "own rate effects" are greater than "cross rate effects" on the demands for securities by both U.S. and U.K. wealth holders.[22] Throughout the paper it has been assumed that in each country the absolute value of the response of money demand to a one percentage point increase in the rate on securities issued abroad is less than the absolute value of the response of money demand to a one percentage point increase in the rate on securities issued at home. These assumptions imply that the BB (FF)-curve has a positive slope which is less (greater) than one and that the MM (NN)-curve has a negative slope which is less (more) negative than negative one.

If the demand functions of wealth holders in the two countries are not "too different", increases in the degree of substitutability cause the slope of the BB (FF)-schedule to increase (decrease) continuously toward positive one.[23] Since wealth holders in the U.S. (U.K.) come to view the two securities as being more and more alike, the responses of their money demand to the two interest rates become more similar and the slope of the MM (NN)-

---

22) The restrictions on the interest rate responses of the asset demand functions implied by these assumptions are spelled out in detail in Appendix A.

23) The exact conditions are discussed in more detail in Appendix A.

schedule falls (rises) continuously toward negative one as the two securities become better substitutes.

The impact of an increase in the degree of asset substitutability on the effectiveness of monetary policy can be assessed using Figure 7. The unprimed schedules refer to the original degree of substitutability while the primed schedules refer to a higher degree of substitutability. An open market operation by the BOE with the original degree of substitutability leads to equilibrium at a_1, a_2, or a_3 under fixed rates, depending upon the FR policy response. An open market operation with increased substitutability shifts FF from $F'_0F'_0$ to $F'_1F'_1$ (not shown) which intersects the horizontal dashed line somewhere between a_0 and a_2, because one of the effects of increasing the degree of substitutability is to reduce the change in r′ required to offset a given disturbance in the market for U.K. securities. It is assumed that the interest rate responses of money demands become more similar in such a way that an equal change in both interest rates in the same direction causes money demand to rise or fall by the same amount no matter what the degree of substitutability between the two securities. This assumption implies that a given movement of the NN-schedule along the dashed line with a slope of positive one is associated with the same change in money demand no matter what the slope of the NN-schedule, so N_1N_1 and $N'_1N'_1$ intersect on this line following the open market operation. Under fixed rates, with full asset convertibility, the new equilibrium must lie on $B'_0B'_0$, somewhere between a_0 and the point of intersection with a line parallel to $F'_0F'_0$ through a_2. As one would expect, an increase in substitutability implies that an open mar-

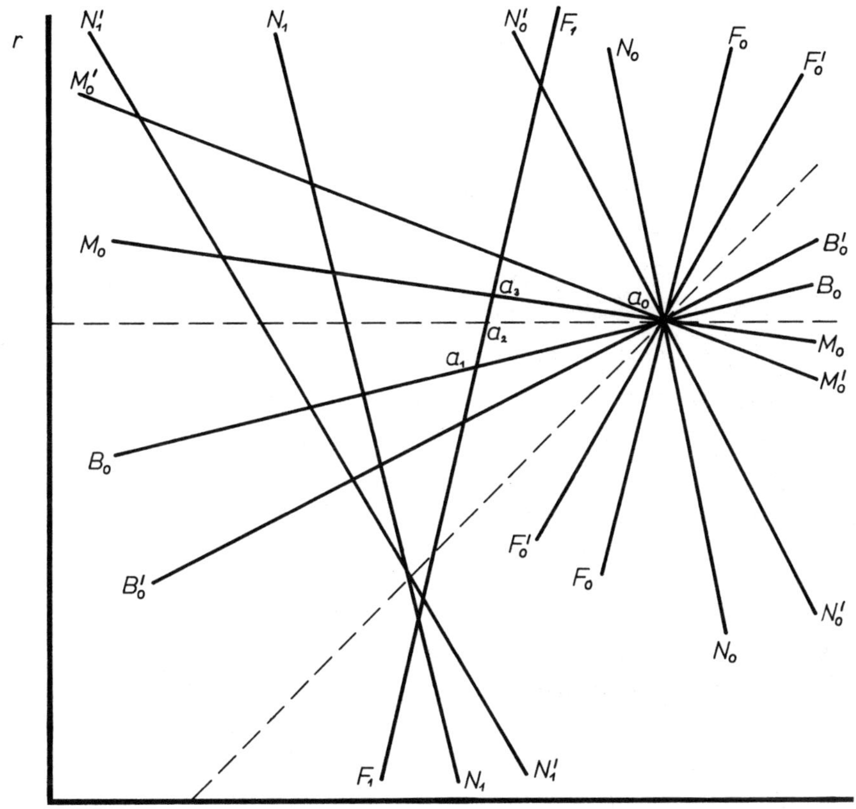

r
r'
N'₁
N₁
N'₀
F₁
N₀
F₀
F'₀
M'₀
M₀
B'₀
B₀
M₀
M'₀
a₀
a₃
a₂
a₁
B₀
B'₀
F'₀
F₀
N₀
N'₀
F₁
N₁
N'₁

Figure 7

ket purchase of a given size causes less of a change in the differential between the U.S. and U.K. rates. This result follows simply from the fact that $B'_0B'_0$ is flatter than B_0B_0. However, the impact of increased substitutability on the decline in r′ is ambiguous. The increased direct effect (reduced leftward shift in FF) of a decline in r′ on the demand for U.K. securities tends to reduce the required decrease in r′ following the open market purchase while the increased induced effect (rotation of the FF and BB-schedules) tends to raise the required decrease in r′ following the open market purchase. We have not been able to determine whether or not one of these tendencies dominates the other except in one special case.[24)] Experimentation with the graph reveals that for a given leftward shift in the FF-schedule, the smaller the amount of rotation of either the BB or FF-schedules, the more likely it is that an increase in substitutability leads to a reduction in the amount by which r′ falls after an open market purchase. Given the range of possibilities for the location of the

---

24) When the two countries are exactly identical in terms of the responses of asset demands to interest rate changes, a rise in substitutability causes dr′ to become less negative. The assumption that the responses of asset demands to interest rate changes are identical in the two countries is not compatible with our earlier assumption regarding the responses of money demands in the two countries to interest rate changes. Two restrictions required by our interpretation of what it means for countries to be identical are that $m_r = n'_r$ and $m_{r'} = n'_{r'}$. We have assumed above that $|m_r| > |m_{r'}|$, and this assumption in conjunction with our new restrictions implies $|n'_r| > |n'_{r'}|$ which violates our earlier assumptions. If we are to assume that countries are identical, in the sense described here, and to retain as much of the spirit of our earlier arguments regarding the interest rate responses of money demand functions as possible, we must also assume $m_r = m_{r'}$.

new equilibrium point, it is not possible to determine whether the U.K. reserve loss is larger or smaller with increased substitutability.

If the U.S. sterilizes with full asset convertibility, or if the U.K. takes its reserve losses in the form of U.S. securities, results are more definite. The equilibrium with increased substitutability lies on $M_0'M_0'$, between a_0 and the point of intersection with a line drawn parallel to $F_0'F_0'$ through a_2. With increased substitutability, r′ definitely falls less, the interest differential is changed by less, and the U.K. loses more reserves. The last of these results is established by noting that $N_1'N_1'$ must move farther along the dashed line with a slope of positive one to reach the new equilibrium point, than N_1N_1 must move to reach a_3.

If the introduction of flexible rates reduces the degree of asset substitutability, the primed schedules can be taken to represent the fixed rates situation and the unprimed schedules the flexible rates situation. The flexible rates equilibrium then lies in the kite-shaped area bounded by N_1N_1, F_1F_1, B_0B_0, and M_0M_0. An open market operation by the U.K. will clearly be more effective in changing the U.K. money supply and r′ when compared to the fixed rates case, either with FR sterilization or under a key currency reserve regime, but whether or not it will be more effective in moving r′ when compared to the fixed rates case with passive behavior by the FR and full asset settlement is indeterminate here as in previous cases.

V. The Effectiveness of Monetary Policy and Relative Economic Size

In this section, we explore the implications of the assumption that the U.K. is a "small country" in the sense that its economic size as measured by nominal wealth in dollar terms is negligible when compared with the economic size of the U.S. measured in the same way. First, assume that U.S. and U.K. securities are perfect substitutes. Consider an open market purchase by the BOE which would lower the nn-schedule to n_1n_1 in Figure 5 if the U.K. money supply expanded by the full amount of the purchase. When the U.K. is small relative to the U.S., the mm-schedule does not move from m_0m_0, so under fixed rates, the equilibrium point remains at a_0. In the limit, U.S. residents are willing to reduce their holdings of securities by the relatively small amount of a plausible-sized BOE open market purchase and increase their holdings of money by the same amount with a negligible decrease in the rigidly linked interest rates.[25] U.K. reserves decrease by the amount of the open market purchase.

Under flexible exchange rates, the mm-curve remains fixed at m_0m_0 if, as seems reasonable, the net pound position of U.S. residents goes to zero as W' goes to zero. The pound depreciates by enough to shift n_1n_1 until it passes through a_0, r remains unchanged, and r' is driven down by an amount equal to the increase in the expected rate of appreciation of the pound.

Now consider the case in which the U.K. is small but in which

25) This result is derived formally in Appendix B.

U.S. and U.K. securities are neither completely nonsubstitutable nor perfectly substitutable for one another in the portfolios of wealth holders. This case is shown in Figure 8. In contrast to the case in which the two countries are of roughly equal economic size, the open market operation leaves the F_0F_0-schedule unaffected when the U.K. is a small country. In the limit, it takes a negligible decrease in r′ to induce the fall in the demand for U.K. securities necessary to offset the relatively small decrease in the supply of U.K. securities resulting from a plausible-sized U.K. open market purchase unless U.K. securities are "indispensable assets" in the portfolios of U.S. wealth holders.[26] Since the FF-schedule is unaffected by the open market purchase, the equilibrium values of the two interest rates are unchanged. The U.K. money supply remains at its initial level, and the U.K. loses reserves equal to the full amount of the open market purchase. This reserve loss can be measured by the distance between N_1N_1, the position the NN-schedule would occupy if the U.K. money supply were increased by the full amount of the open market purchase, and N_0N_0. Thus, the central bank in a small country is able to affect neither the interest rate on securities issued in its country nor its country′s money supply by an open market purchase, even if its securities are not perfect substitutes for those issued in the rest of the world, provided that its securities are not regarded as indispensable assets by the world′s wealth holders.

Turning to the case of flexible rates, it is useful to consider two

---

26) This result is derived formally in Appendix B.

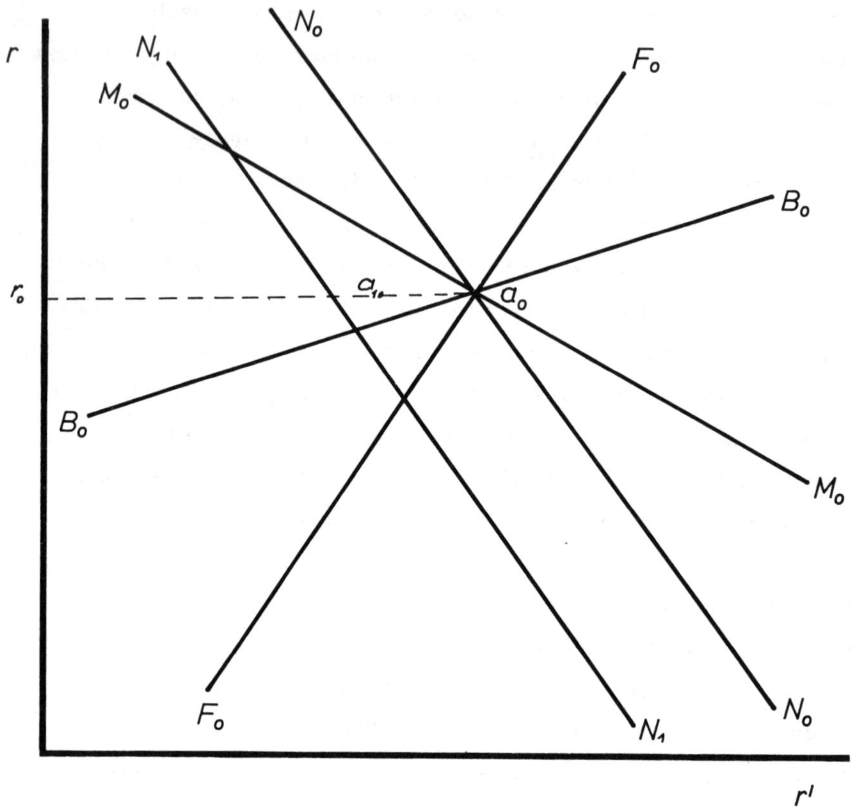

Figure 8

subcases. As before, the FF-schedule is unaffected by the open market purchase, but the NN-schedule is shifted from N_0N_0 to N_1N_1. First, assume that the expected change in the exchange rate is not sensitive to the level of the spot rate so that $s_{S-\bar{S}} = 0$. If, as seems reasonable, the net pound position of U.S. residents goes to zero as W′ goes to zero, depreciation of the pound leaves the BB, FF, and MM-curves unaffected, but the NN-curve shifts up from N_1N_1 until it passes through a_0. In this case, the only effect of the open market operation is to depreciate the pound. Second, assume again that $s_{S-\bar{S}}$ 0. If decreases in the level of the spot rate lead to increases in the expected rate of change of the spot rate, the new equilibrium is at a point like a_1 which lies between a_0 and N_1N_1 on the dashed line, indicating a constant r. Decreases in S shift the BB, FF, and MM-schedules to the left by the same distance. r and r′ + s must remain constant, but r′ can fall because s rises. Just as in the perfect substitutes case, the central bank in a small country can change its interest rate under flexible exchange rates if exchange rate expectations depend on the spot rate.

APPENDIX A

The purpose of this Appendix is to specify some conditions under which increases in the degree of substitutability between securities affect the equilibrium schedules in the way described in the text.

Let x be a variable which takes on the value zero when the two securities are completely nonsubstitutable and which rises continuously and without limit as substitutability increases. All of the demand responses to interest rate changes are functions of x and can be written as, for example, $b_r(x)$, but to conserve space, the explicit functional notation is often suppressed. It is convenient to define the following five vectors:

$$\alpha = \begin{bmatrix} b_r \\ f_{r'} \\ b'_r \\ f'_{r'} \end{bmatrix}, \quad \beta = \begin{bmatrix} f_r \\ b_{r'} \\ f'_r \\ b'_{r'} \end{bmatrix}, \quad \gamma = \begin{bmatrix} m_r \\ m_{r'} \\ n'_r \\ n'_{r'} \end{bmatrix}, \quad \delta = \begin{bmatrix} b_{r'} \\ f_r \\ b'_{r'} \\ f'_r \end{bmatrix}, \quad \mu = \begin{bmatrix} \hat{m} \\ \hat{m} \\ \hat{n}' \\ \hat{n}' \end{bmatrix},$$

where α is a vector of own rate effects; β and δ are vectors of cross rate effects; γ is a vector of money demand responses; and μ is a vector of constants, the elements of which satisfy $m_r(0) \leq \hat{m} \leq m_{r'}(0)$, and $n'_{r'}(0) \leq \hat{n}' \leq n'_r(0)$. The two balance sheet constraints imply that $\alpha(x) + \beta(x) + \gamma(x) \equiv \underline{0}$. The assumption that own rate effects are greater than cross rate effects implies that $\alpha(x) + \delta(x) > \underline{0}$ for all x. When the two securities are perfectly nonsubstitutable for one another, $\alpha(0) = -\gamma(0)$ and

$\beta(0) = \underline{0}.$

As the degree of asset substitutability increases, the asset demand responses are assumed to change as follows: (1) the values of the own rate effects rise continuously without limit and the values of the cross rate effects decrease continuously without limit,

$$\alpha_x > \underline{0}, \qquad \lim_{x \to \infty} \alpha = \underline{\infty},$$

$$\beta_x < \underline{0}, \qquad \lim_{x \to \infty} \beta = -\underline{\infty};$$

(2) own rate effects and cross rate effects on the same demand function become continuously more alike,

$$\alpha_x + \delta_x < \underline{0};$$

and (3) the responses U.S. (U.K.) money demand to the two interest rates approach one another continuously and tend toward a common value which lies between them as a limit,

$$m_{rx} \geq 0, \; m_{r'x} \leq 0, \; n'_{r'x} \geq 0, \; n'_{rx} \leq 0, \; \lim_{x \to \infty} \gamma = \mu.$$

These assumptions and the two balance sheet constraints imply

$$b_{r'x} - f_{rx} \begin{cases} < 0 \text{ if } b_{r'} - f_r > 0 \\ > 0 \text{ if } b_{r'} - f_r < 0 \end{cases}, \quad b'_{r'x} - f'_{rx} \begin{cases} < 0 \text{ if } b'_{r'} - f'_r > 0 \\ > 0 \text{ if } b'_{r'} - f'_r < 0 \end{cases},$$

$$\lim_{x \to \infty} (\beta - \delta) = 0, \qquad \lim_{x \to \infty} (\alpha + \delta) = \lim_{x \to \infty} (\alpha + \beta) = \mu.$$

The assumptions regarding the interest rate responses of money demands are sufficient to insure that the slope of the MM (NN)-curve becomes continuously more (less) negative and approaches negative one as a limit as the degree of substitutability increases. The slopes of the MM and NN-curves never actually take on the value of negative one for, if the two securities were exactly identical in every respect, a decline in r would lead residents in both countries to try to move completely out of U.S. securities into U.K. securities, but there seems to be no reason why wealth holders should want to change their money holdings. When the two securities are exactly alike, the MM and NN-schedules reduce to single points which must lie on the line with a slope of positive one which represents the BB and FF-schedules.

The analysis of what happens to the BB and FF-curves as substitutability increases is somewhat more complicated. The slope of the BB-curve is given by,

$$\left.\frac{dr}{dr'}\right|_{BB} = \omega\left(-\frac{b_{r'}}{b_r}\right) + (1-\omega)\left(-\frac{b'_{r'}}{b'_r}\right),$$

where

$$\omega = \frac{b_r W}{b_r W + b'_r W'} .$$

Since the numerators and denominators of $-\frac{b_{r'}}{b_r}$ and $-\frac{b'_{r'}}{b'_r}$ are either increasing or decreasing without limit and since the sum of the numerator and denominator of each ratio approaches a constant, both ratios approach positive one as x approaches infinity, so

$$\lim_{x \to \infty} \left[\frac{dr}{dr'}\Big|_{BB} \right] = 1.$$

Differentiating the expression for the slope of the BB-curve we have,

$$\frac{d\left[\frac{dr}{dr'}\Big|_{BB}\right]}{dx} = \omega \frac{d\left[-\frac{b_{r'}}{b_r}\right]}{dx} + (1-\omega) \frac{d\left[-\frac{b'_{r'}}{b'_r}\right]}{dx} + \left(\frac{b'_{r'}}{b'_r} - \frac{b_{r'}}{b_r}\right) \omega_x,$$

$$\omega_x = \frac{b'_r b_r WW'}{(b_r W + b'_r W')^2} \left[\frac{b_{rx}}{b_r} - \frac{b'_{rx}}{b'_r}\right].$$

The assumption that own rate effects and cross rate effects on the demand for U.S. securities become more alike in both countries is sufficient to insure that the first two terms on the right-hand side are positive; that is, with the weights held constant, the weighted average definitely rises. The weighted average rises (falls) if the weight on the larger of the two terms $-\frac{b'_{r'}}{b'_r}$ and $-\frac{b_{r'}}{b_r}$ rises (falls). ω rises (falls) if the per cent increase in b_r is greater (less) than the per cent increase in b'_r. While the sign of the third term cannot be determined, it is smaller in absolute value the more alike are the two countries either in terms of the ratios of cross effects to own effects or in terms of per cent changes in own effects and is zero if the two countries are exactly alike in either or both respects. Thus, the possibility of a "perverse" movement in the slope of the BB-curve arises because of differences in the two countries.[27] In the text we assume that the two countries are "similar enough" that the slope of the BB-curve rises continuously as x increases. It can be shown that the

27) See next page.

assumptions above are sufficient to insure that the slope of the FF-curve approaches positive one as x approaches infinity and that the slope of the FF-curve decreases continuously as x increases if the two countries are "similar" enough.

It is assumed in the text that equal changes in the two interest rates in the same direction causes the same change in money demands no matter what the degree of substitutability between the two securities,

$$m_r(x) + m_{r'}(x) \equiv 2\,\hat{m}$$

$$n'_{r'}(x) + n'_r(x) \equiv 2\,\hat{n}'.$$

This assumption is plausible and greatly facilitates the derivation of conclusions in the graphical framework, but the conclusions of the paper continue to hold under weaker assumptions.

For a further discussion of the impact of increases in the degree of substitutability on the effectiveness of monetary policy, see Girton and Henderson (1973).

---

27) A similar problem would arise in the analysis of a closed economy with two well defined groups of wealth holders with different demand schedules for two types of securities and money. In closed-economy macro economics, problems like this are said to be due to "distribution effects" which are usually assumed away. It seems somewhat less natural to assume that such distribution effects are unimportant in a two country world.

APPENDIX B

The purpose of this Appendix is to provide a formal representation of the arguments used in the text to derive results for the case in which the U.K. is small.

Let $\overline{W}$ represent the nominal value of world wealth in dollars which is assumed to remain constant, so $\overline{W} - SW'$ is equal to W, the nominal value of U.S. wealth. Assume that in both countries the ratio of central bank held securities to wealth is independent of wealth, so

$$B^c = \varepsilon W, \qquad F^{c'} = \varepsilon' W'.$$

An open market purchase by the BOE is represented by an increase in ε'.

First, it is shown that the mm-schedule used in the perfect substitutes case does not shift following an open market purchase by the U.K. Suppose the U.S. reserves rise (U.K. reserves decline) by the full amount of the U.K. open market purchase:

$$\sigma\, dR = SW' d\varepsilon'.$$

The U.S. money market equilibrium condition is

$$M^s = B^c + \sigma R - M^{c'} + A = m(r)(\overline{W} - SW').$$

Differentiating this condition, substituting in the expression above for σdR, and solving for the change in r required to offset an increase in ε' yields

$$\left.\frac{dr}{d\varepsilon'}\right|_{S=\overline{S}}^{mm} = \frac{SW'}{m_r(\overline{W}-SW')} .$$

The size of the shift in the mm-schedule resulting from an increase in U.S. reserves which is equal to the full amount of the U.K. open market purchase approaches zero continuously as W′ approaches zero.

Second, it is shown that when U.S. and U.K. securities are imperfect substitutes, the FF-schedule does not shift following an open market purchase by the U.K. The expression for the shift in the FF-schedule caused by an increase in ε' is

$$\left.\frac{dr'}{d\varepsilon'}\right|_{r=\overline{r}}^{FF} = -\frac{W'}{\frac{1}{S} f_{r'+s}(\overline{W}-SW') + f'_{r'}W'} .$$

The size of the shift in the FF-schedule caused by an open market purchase by the BOE approaches zero as W′ approaches zero unless U.K. securities are indispensable assets in the portfolios of U.S. wealth holders, that is, unless the interest sensitivity of U.S. demand for U.K. securities approaches zero as W′ approaches zero.

REFERENCES

Black, S. W., <u>International Money Markets and Flexible Exchange Rates,</u> Princeton Studies in International Finance No. 25, Princeton, N.J., 1973.

Girton, L. and Henderson, D. W., "Central Bank Operations in Foreign and Domestic Assets Under Fixed and Flexible Exchange Rates", <u>The Effects of Exchange Rate Adjustments,</u> edited by P. Clark, D. Logue, and R. Sweeney, (U.S. Government Printing Office, 1976 forthcoming).

Girton, L. and Henderson, D. W., "Financial Capital Movements and Central Bank Behavior in a Two Country, Short Run Portfolio Balance Model", <u>Journal of Monetary Economics,</u> Vol. 2 (January 1976).

Girton, L. and Henderson, D. W., "A Two Country Model of Financial Capital Movements as Stock Adjustments with Emphasis on the Effects of Central Bank Policy", Discussion Paper No. 24, Division of International Finance, Board of Governors of the Federal Reserve System (mimeo, 1973).

McKinnon, R. I. and Oates, W. E., "The Implications of International Economic Integration for Monetary Fiscal, and Exchange-Rate Policy", Princeton Studies in International Finance, No. 16 (Princeton: International Finance Section, 1966).

McKinnon, R. I., "Portfolio Balance and International Payments Adjustment", <u>Monetary Problems of the International Economy,</u> edited by R. Mundell and A. K. Swoboda (Chicago and London: The University of Chicago Press, 1969).

Mundell, R. A., <u>International Economics,</u> (New York: The MacMillan Company, 1968).

Roper, D. E., "Implications of the Gold-Exchange Standard for Balance of Payments Adjustment", <u>Economia Internazionale,</u> Vol. XXVI (August-November 1973).

Tobin, J., "A General Equilibrium Approach to Monetary Theory", <u>Journal of Money, Credit, and Banking,</u> Vol. 1 (February 1969).

THE TWO-TIER FOREIGN EXCHANGE MARKET IN BELGIUM

By B. Decaluwé
A. Steinherr

I. Introduction

During the last decade we have witnessed an increase in both the commercial and financial interdependence among the developed countries of the West. While in general desirable, this interdependence has also created, or at least amplified, some problems. Of particular concern are sudden and massive shifts of capital whithin the international financial community. In most European countries policy makers have serious difficulties in applying measures which effectively could control capital flows.

Faced with these problems it is sometimes suggested to split the foreign exchange market into one compartment for current and one for capital transactions. If the latter compartment were left on its own, movements in the capital exchange rate would eliminate all net capital movements into or out of that country.

The purpose of the present paper is to report on the experience made in Belgium with such a two-tier exchange market, and to assess its performance. To this end we describe the institutional framework of the market in Section II and interpret its performance for the period from 1960 to 1973. In Section III we then develop a model for the financial and exchange markets and test the hypothesis that a two-tier exchange market allows the Belgian policy makers to effectively control the country's level of foreign exchange reserves and thus the level of domestic liquidity. Finally, in Section IV, we summarize our main conclusions.

Before we look at a particular experience it is desirable, however, to see what can be expected from a two-tier exchange system. There is, naturally, a long list of pros and cons.

First of all, it is often argued that a split of the foreign exchange market is not feasible in practice. Past experience shows that a perfectly watertight separation is, indeed, impossible. The question, however, is whether an effective (albeit imperfect) separation is possible. This is a hypothesis which we wish to investigate in the case of Belgium.

Second, assuming that such an effective separation is possible, the other remaining question is whether this solution is more efficient than alternative ones. Granted that the use of monetary policy for controlling the capital account is undesirable[1] as well as relatively ineffective, the principal remaining alternative consists in direct controls of capital flows.

1) See T.D. Willett in [15].

In a recent paper one of the present authors has compared the efficiency of fiscal and monetary policies under various exchange rate systems.[2] It is well known that with a very high mobility of international capital monetary policy has no impact at all on the internal target under pegged exchange rates. However, with a two-tier exchange market it can be shown that both fiscal and monetary policy are efficient tools for the internal target and thus regain their independence.

Since massive international capital flows may produce internal desequilibria in lending and receiving countries, it would be interesting to examine the short-run stability properties of an economy with a two-tier exchange market. In the Appendix we show with a model where international capital flows result from stock adjustment, that

(i) official intervention in the free market is highly stabilizing;

(ii) if interest payments on foreign assets are converted at the capital rather than at the official rate, the system will have a higher degree of stability;

(iii) instability cannot be excluded a priori. Depending on the way expectations concerning future rates are formed instability may obtain as is the case in a non-divided foreign exchange market.

---

2) B. Decaluwe [7].

II. The Foreign Exchange Market in the Belgo-Luxembourg Economic Union (BLEU)

1. The Institutional Framework

Although France, Italy, Switzerland and the United Kingdom operated at times various forms of a two-tier exchange market the experience of the BLEU is unique by the length of time and the amplitude of its operation.

The free market compartment was introduced in stages between 1951 and 1952. At first, transactions were limited to those with member countries of the European Payments Union (EPU), but a rapid transition to include non-member countries was made. During this initial period the BLEU had a balance of payments surplus vis-à-vis the countries of the EPU (whose currencies were inconvertible), but a deficit vis-à-vis the dollar area, and the inconvertibility of the EPU currencies made a compensation of this geographical disequilibrium impossible. In these circumstances, the Belgo-Luxembourg Exchange Institut (BLEI) wished to limit the accumulation of exchange reserves in EPU currencies on the one hand, and to protect itself from the capital outflows into the dollar area, on the other. The double exchange rate system was implemented precisely in order to cope with these problems.

The basic rules of the BLEU dual exchange system for the period prior to May 1971 can be classified according to three criteria: the nature of the transaction, the direction of settlements and the currency denomination of the transaction.

a) The Nature of the Transaction

The BLEI classifies transactions leading to exchange market operations into four types: A, B, C and D. The type of transaction determines the exchange market (official vs. free) upon which the corresponding exchange operation will take place. All direct transactions linked to merchandise trade are of type A. Invisible transactions excluding foreign investment income are of type B, the latter being of type C. Capital transactions consisting of direct foreign investment repatriations and administration expenditures are also of type C. All other capital and non-capital transactions are of type D.

b) The Direction of Settlements

International transactions are also classified according to the direction of settlements (receipts or payments). The dual exchange rate system is said to protect against capital inflows (outflows) if receipts (payments) are to be channelled through the free market. In other words, where the two markets are thoroughly separated, that is, if currencies may not be acquired on one market to be resold on the other, the two-tier exchange market protects the home economy against both capital inflows and outflows.

Before May 1971 the direction of settlements' criterion was implemented in the following way:

- Payments (-) associated with transactions of type A, B, and C and receipts (+) associated with type C and D transactions are permitted on both the official and the free market.

- Receipts related to type A and B transactions are channelled through the official market whereas payments for transactions of type D are to be dealt with on the free market.

These rules are summarized in Table 1.

TABLE 1

Official Exchange Market			Free Exchange Market	
A^+	A^-			A^-
B^+	B^-			B^-
C^+	C^-		C^+	C^-
D^+			D^+	D^-

A "direct link" between both market segments was thus set up, since foreign exchange acquired on the free market was allowed to be sold on the official market. This link implies that the free rate cannot be sustained at a premium over the official rate. Since the opposite transaction was prohibited a discount of the free rate, on the other hand, was made possible.

As the free exchange rate is always either equal or superior to the official rate, the hypothesis of profit maximizing by operators in the exchange markets implies the following equilibrium conditions:

Official market: $A^+ + B^+ = A^- + B^- + C^-$.

Free market: $C^{+} + D^{+} = D^{-}$.

c) The Currency Denomination of the Transaction

The official exchange market is ruled by the IMF provisions for convertible currencies. Monetary authorities are required to intervene whenever the official rate tends to reach the upper or lower limit of the band. Dealing in currencies other than "convertible" currencies is restricted to the free market. The division of the exchange market entails also the division of foreign accounts with chartered banks. In the BLEU, the latter are responsible for the control of the nature of operations in either market.

d) The Reorganization of the Exchange Market of 1971

Prior to the first dollar crisis in August 1971 the Belgian franc was expected to be revalued, causing important capital inflows. Exchange regulations were then modified to improve the separation of the two exchange markets and, more specifically, to discourage capital inflows.

The direction of settlements criterion was modified in the following way:

- Financial settlements of types A, B, as well as expenditures of categories C_1 (administrative expenses) and C_2 (repatriation of returns on foreign investments) go through the official market, while transactions of type D must be settled on the free market;

- Transactions which are permitted to be settled on either market are reduced to expenditures of type C_3 (repatriation of foreign investments) and receipts of type C_1 and C_2.

The new rules are summarized in Table 2.

TABLE 2

Official Exchange Market			Free Exchange Market	
A^+	A^-			
B^+	B^-			
C_1^+	C_1^-		C_1^+	
C_2^+	C_2^-		C_2^+	
	C_3^-			C_3^-
			D^+	D^-

Suppressing the direct link between the two markets (reselling on the official market currencies acquired on the free market being henceforth prohibited) now permits discounts as well as premia of the free rate.

Summing up, the organization of the foreign exchange market in Belgium is characterized by the following four main properties:

(i) First of all, the separation of transactions is incomplete. For reasons of expedience, some commercial transactions pass through the free market while some financial transactions go through the official market.

(ii) The Belgian system allows chartered banks to carry foreign exchange balances in both markets.

(iii) The Banque Nationale may, and does, intervene in the free market.

(iv) Before May 1971 the system was set up to protect the country against capital losses. After that date the system was reorganized in order to provide protection also against excessive capital inflows.

2. Evaluation of the Performance of the BLEU Exchange System

An examination of Figure 1 shows that the divergence between the free and the official rates was relatively negligeable during the entire period 1961-66. Only for very limited periods did the differential exceed 2 % (August - October 1960 and February - June 1961). This considerable stability of the exchange rate might be explained on two different levels, one international and the other specifically related to internal conditions in Belgium. First, with the exception of the Congo crisis in the early sixties, Belgium as well as most other Western countries enjoyed relatively harmonious international trade and financial relationships. Second, in the BLEU, foreign capital transactions of the public sector had a largely compensating effect. Independently of the

Figure 1

<u>Exchange Market</u>

US-$ rates in Belgian francs
Daily averages-quarterly data
1960-1971

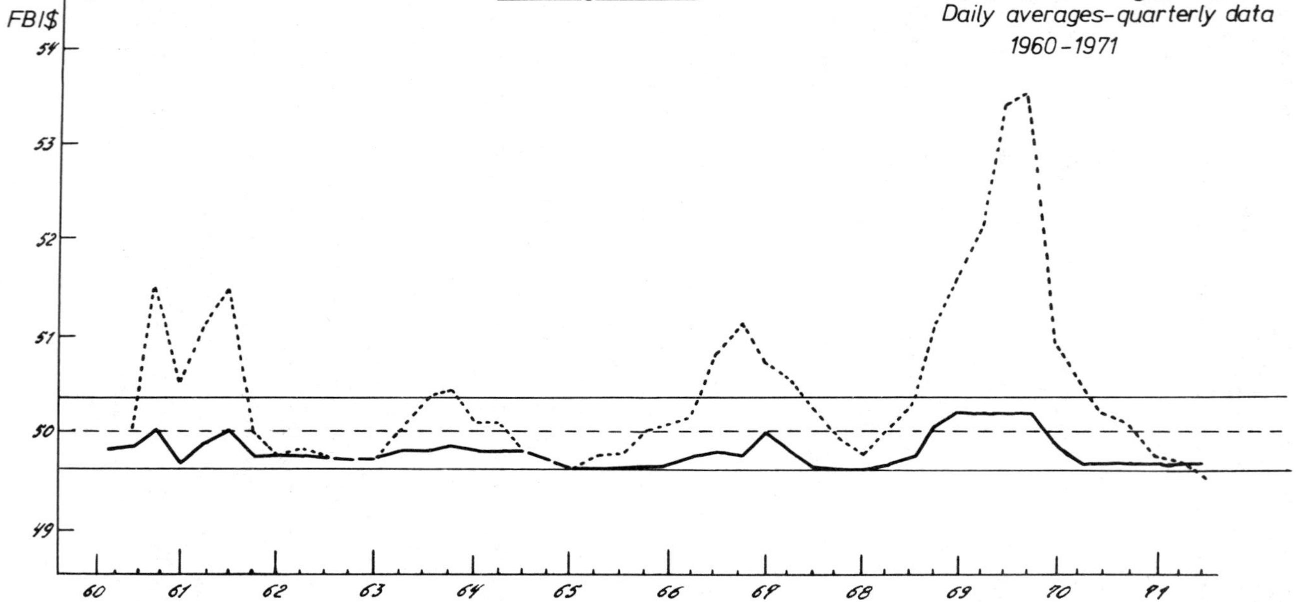

(1) Ceiling rates 50.375
(2) Parity 50.000
(3) Floor rates 49.625

—— Official Market
---- Free Market

daily interventions of the Banque Nationale the foreign capital transactions of the public sector exhibited during the period under consideration a compensating effect of oscillatory current and capital transactions of the private sector.

The following analysis is organized around four elements: official international transactions on the one hand, and the relationships between the exchange rate differential and the current account, overall reserves, and the interest rate differential, on the other.

a) Official International Borrowing and Lending

In Figure 2 we plot the accumulated foreign debt of the public sector and the differential between free and official exchange rates. Our definition of official transactions includes direct official borrowing and lending (as appearing in the balance of payments) to which we add those of public authorities, state companies, and indirect official transactions via the banking sector. As Figure II shows there has been, with a few exceptions, a strict relationship between the exchange rate differential and public foreign borrowing. Except for the period 1960 - 1961 (for which data are not available) the public sector has increased its foreign liabilities most of the time when the discount has been increasing and decreased its liabilities when the discount has been falling.

Thus, the monetary authorities in Belgium have made continuous use of foreign borrowing or lending in order to finance substantial parts of the overall balance of payments disequilibrium. In

Figure 2

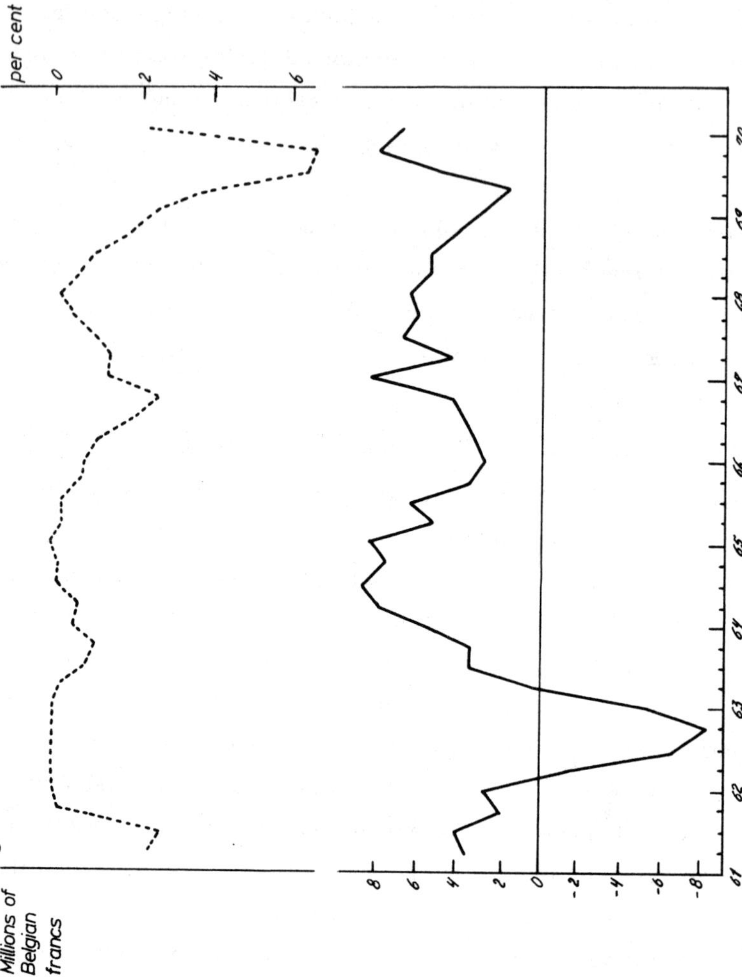

Accumulated foreign liabilities of the public sector (left-hand scale) ——
Exchange rate differential (right-hand scale) - - - - -

this way they were not only able to reduce the balance of payments impacts on domestic liquidity (since a decrease in the current account surplus always has been concomitant with a depreciation of the free exchange rate) but also to moderate the discount of the free rate in periods of capital outflows. This subtle stabilization of exchange reserves and of the capital rate has a clear advantage over direct controls. Indeed, if speculators base their expectations upon variations in the level of exchange reserves or on the exchange rate differential the interventions of the Banque Nationale tend to stabilize expectations about future rates.

b) The Current Account and the Exchange Rate Differential

The second element that we wish to analyze is the behavior of traders in the official market. Obviously, the two-tier exchange market is unable to prevent leads and lags in foreign payments. Thus, whenever a depreciation of the official franc is expected importers speed up their payments while exporters see their receipts delayed, and the current account worsens.

In Figure 3 we plot the accumulated current account balance and the exchange rate differential. It clearly appears that there has been a strict negative relationship between these two variables. To an increase of the exchange rate differential corresponds, in general, a decrease of the current account surplus.

These observations lead to the following conclusions. First, adjustments in both compartments of the exchange market are positively related with each other, an outflow of capital leading to a

Figure 3

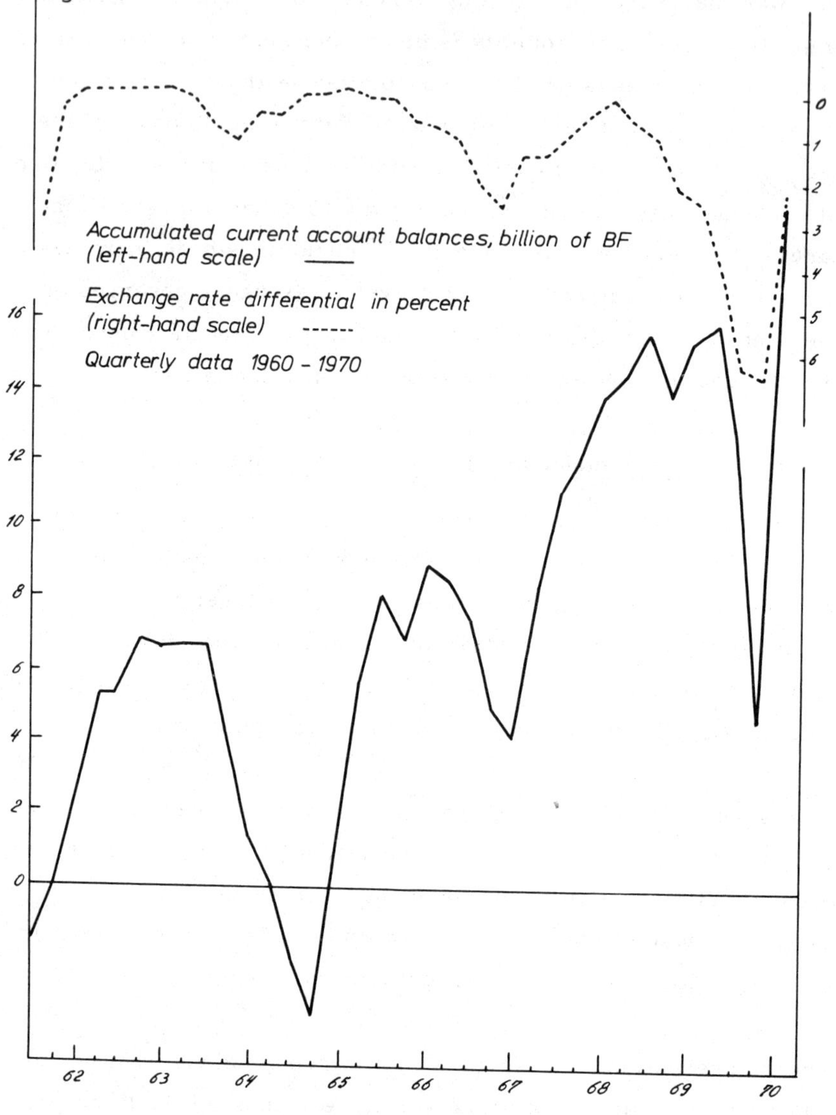

Accumulated current account balances, billion of BF
(left-hand scale)
Exchange rate differential in percent
(right-hand scale)
Quarterly data 1960 - 1970
16
14
12
10
8
6
4
2
0
0
1
2
3
4
5
6
62
63
64
65
66
67
68
69
70

deficit of the current account. Second, the short-term fluctuations of the current account balance are dominated by payment leads and lags. They, in turn, are related to the exchange rate differential.

It is thus clear that when the exchange rate differential becomes sizeable

(i) depreciation of the free market rate reduces confidence in the currency and encourages speculations in the official market;

(ii) it becomes increasingly difficult to maintain the effective split of the exchange market. It may also be inferred that some of the movements in the current account are due to illegal transactions in the official market.

c) Interest Rates and Exchange Rate Differentials

As a general rule when the free rate depreciates and interest payments are to be converted at the official rate, returns on foreign securities become less attractive. On the other hand, if interest payments are converted at the capital rate, a depreciation only leads to diminished returns on foreign currency assets if, after the acquisition, the exchange rate of the Belgian franc appreciates.

The rules of the BLEU allow conversion of interest payments on foreign currency assets at either rate. As a matter of fact, interest receipts are in general converted at the free rate (since $R_f > R_o$) while interest payments to foreigners are converted at the official rate. Thus, a depreciation of the capital rate diminishes returns on foreign assets if wealth holders expect a return of the free rate to previous levels.

The second link between interest rates and the capital exchange rate consists in the following. If interest rates on foreign assets are above domestic rates there will be a net capital outflow, leading to a depreciation of the free exchange rate. This depreciation would imply a capital loss if the free rate were appreciating again in the future. Only as long as expected capital losses fall short of the interest differential will there be a net capital outflow.

Figure 4 shows that the depreciation of the free rate compensated, at least partially, increases in net returns on foreign assets. In this way, the depreciation of the free rate tends to restrict capital outflows. This argument is further strenghtened if we believe that wealth holders consider the official rate as an indicator of the most likely future free rate. In this case they will expect that capital invested abroad has to be repatriated at an exchange rate below the one at which the capital outflow was converted.

A remaining question is whether the free rate discount was able to provide an effective protection against capital outflows when international capital holders speculated against the Belgian franc in 1966 and again in 1968 and 1969.

A reexamination of Figure 4 indicates that the depreciation of the free rate did indeed penalize capital outflows during that pe-

Figure 4

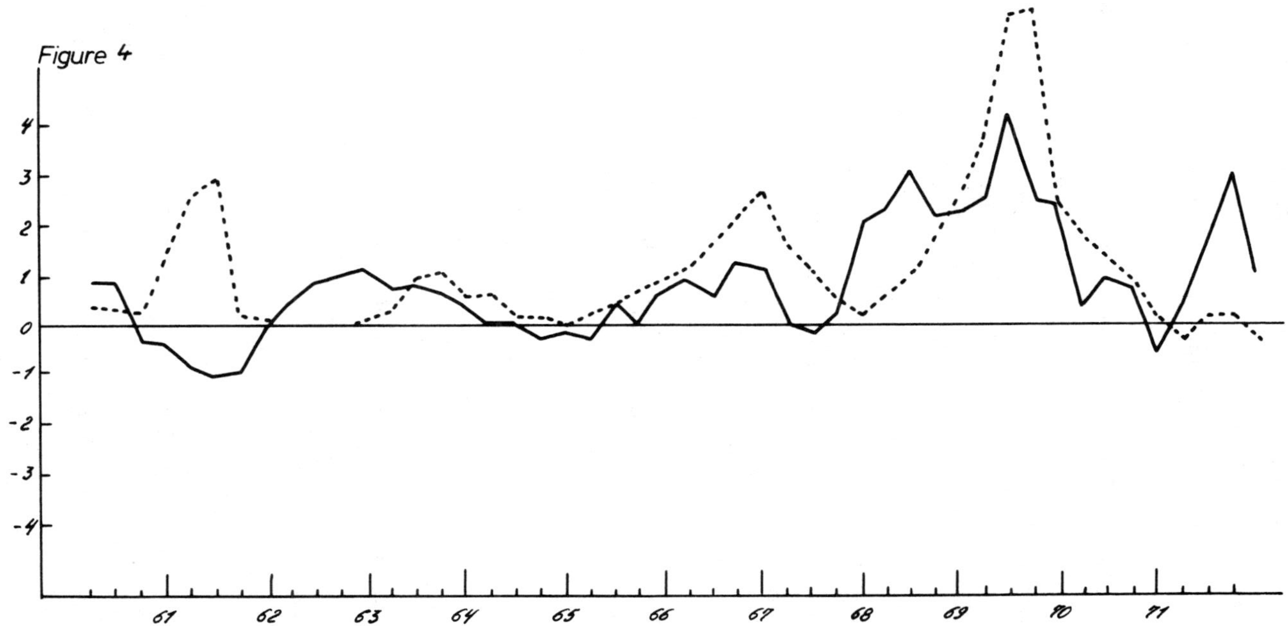

Interest Rate Differential ———
Exchange Rate Differential --------

Quarterly data 1960–1971

riod. For example, between May and September 1966 the average exchange rate differential was 2.4 % whereas the interest rate differential was only 0.9 %. Between January and September 1969 the difference was even higher, since the average exchange rate differential amounted to 5 % while only to 2.6 % for the interest rate differential. Those speculators who had to repatriate their foreign investments at a free rate close to the official rate took therefore a net loss.

The existence of a discount of the capital exchange rate during 1969 has doubtlessly contributed to limiting capital outflows motivated by higher capital gains abroad, since speculators could not reasonably expect a devaluation of the official franc superior to the exchange rate differential.

d) Official Reserves and the Exchange Rate Differential

With a two-tier exchange system the monetary authorities may intervene on the free market to regain their autonomy for domestic monetary policy. If, as has been the case in Belgium most of the time, the current account is in surplus while deficits in the capital account provoke a depreciation of the free franc, monetary authorities sell on the free market foreign exchange bought on the official market. Thereby they reduce both the free rate discount and the impact of the current account surplus on domestic liquidity.

This intervention mechanism may have contributed to restricting the exchange rate differential during the period of monetary tranquillity (before 1968 - 1969). Sales and purchases took place regularly in order to even out daily fluctuations as well as seasonal factors and exogenous shocks. These interventions combined with foreign borrowing and lending of the public sector explain the small divergence of capital and official rates during the period 1960 to 1968.

The efficiency of these interventions, unfortunately, is seriously reduced in periods of strong speculative capital movements. If speculation works against the Belgian franc, and recalling the link between both market compartments, current and capital accounts tend to be both in deficit. The Banque Nationale is now supposed to buy foreign exchange in the free market to compensate for the losses in the official market. This intervention depresses the free rate even further, a factor which should limit capital outflows. However, while theoretically optimal, it does not work well in practice. The increase of the exchange rate differential accentuates speculation in the official market and makes an effective market split more difficult. Obviously, the higher the exchange rate differential the more profitable becomes the (illegitimate) arbitrage between both markets.

An examination of the evolution of the exchange reserve position of the Banque Nationale shows that during those periods where the exchange rate differential exceeded 1 %, reserves remained constant or even decreased, indicating that the Banque Nationale supported the free rate, instead of buying in the free market. See Figure 5.

In this context we also have to discuss the behavior of the banking sector during the period of speculation against the Belgian franc 1968 to 1969. As we mentioned before the Belgian system allows chartered banks to carry working balances in both market compartments. As a consequence of the non-existence of precise stipulations concerning these balances chartered banks enjoyed a high degree of freedom in the administration of these balances. They were practically free to transfer them between the two market compartments. This freedom gave rise to substantial, and very profitable, operations in 1968 - 1969. Very low at the beginning of 1968, official foreign currency balances of chartered banks increased sharply during the year to attain a maximum of 14.3 billion Belgian franc in March 1969. During the same period the free foreign exchange balances decreased somewhat.

The phenomena we just described throw serious doubt on the efficiency of a two-tier exchange system in periods of strong speculative capital movements. Figure 5 shows a strict relationship between the evolution of the stock of exchange reserves and the exchange rate differential. This can be explained, as we did before, with increased capital operations in the official market. Hence, when the exchange rate differential rises it becomes increasingly difficult to maintain an effective market split. In the absence of additional direct controls, such as the control of foreign currency positions of the banking sector, and the control of leads and lags in payments, the two-tier exchange market cannot provide efficient protection against speculative capital flows.

Since the behavior of the banking sector explains already a large

Figure 5

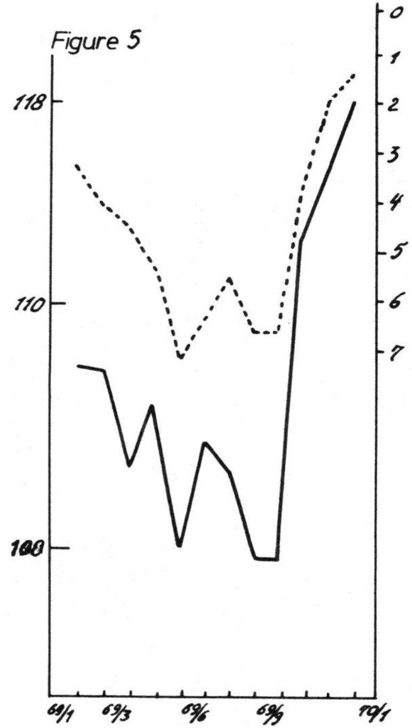

—— Exchange reserves, billion BF (left-hand scale)
----- Exchange rate differential (right-hand scale)

Figure 6

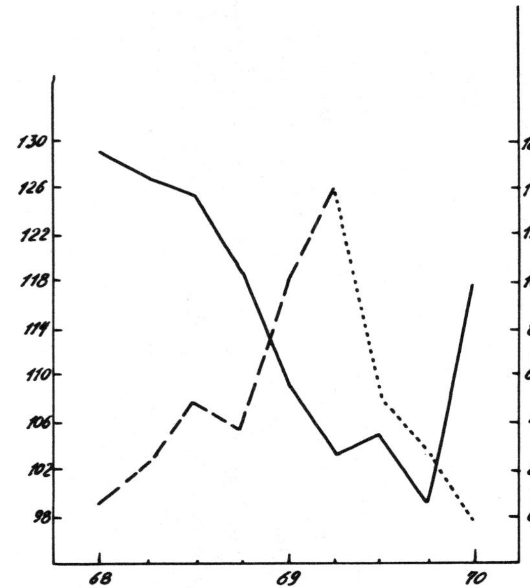

—— Exchange reserves, billion BF (left-hand scale)
----- Official exchange position of commercial banks (right-hand scale)

part of the exchange losses in 1968 - 1969 (see Figure 6) control of this sector became particularly desirable. After March 1969 the BLEI has, indeed, extended its control over bank balances and has forced chartered banks to reduce their official balances.

After May 1971 the divergences of the free rate from the official rate have become minimal partly because the monetary authorities frequently adjusted the official rate. The official rate, tied to some other European currencies inside of the snake, closely followed the shifts of speculative capital out of dollar positions and in favor of a number of European currencies among which the Belgian franc could be found.

For the years 1971 - 1973 the overall balance of payments shows very high surpluses resulting in a rapid growth of foreign exchange reserves of the Banque Nationale. Capital inflows have been excessive in spite of the revaluation of the official franc with respect to the dollar, and in spite of the reorganization of the two-tier exchange market.

In 1971 the Banque Nationale was finally led to impose quantitative controls on the net foreign positions (in Belgian francs and foreign currency) of the banking sector. These measures were only applied for a short period of time but recourse to them indicates the inadequacy of the two-tier exchange market for stopping speculative capital inflows.

Looking for reasons of this failure we might interpret the absence of any sizeable divergences between official and free rates as follows. The fact that in spite of massive capital inflows the free rate hardly ever rose to a premium could mean that speculators had no serious difficulties in using the official market. Repeated revaluations of the official rates together with steadily growing exchange reserves tend to confirm this interpretation. The observed variations of official exchange balances of chartered banks furnish further support to this interpretation. For example, in March 1972 official foreign exchange balances of banks amounted to Belgian francs 15 billion while they were only Belgian francs 4 billion in December 1971.

The BLEU then set limits to the foreign currency liabilities at the official rates of the banking sector and on convertible Belgian franc deposits by non-residents. Moreover, a special tax of 0.25 % weekly on increases in convertible Belgian franc accounts was imposed (May - July and September - December 1973).

The question, however, remains why the two-tier exchange system has functioned relatively well before 1971 but less well after that date. We recall that before 1971 the system was organized in order to prevent capital outflows while the overall balance of payments, at the same time, was in surplus. Even without a two-tier exchange market current account and capital account balances would have been partly offsetting. By contrast, after 1971, capital inflows accentuate the overall surplus. It may therefore be concluded that a two-tier exchange market is useful in regulating compensatory movements but not in counteracting one-way flows.

We may then derive the following conclusions from our analysis:

(i) It is impossible to sustain for long periods of time sizeable premia or discounts of the free rate. Unavoidably they lead to the expectation of a parity adjustment and through speculatory capital flows in both market compartments the parity change will effectively become necessary.

(ii) When the current account is in long-run equilibrium, interventions of the monetary authorities in the free market ought to be conducted in such a way as to assure an overall equilibrium of the balance of payments. The loss of this degree of freedom for policies is due to the above argument that exchange rate differentials cannot be sustained.

(iii) However, the two-tier exchange market is a useful and efficient institution in two circumstances. First, when current and capital account balances are partially compensating. Second, when it is supposed to even out exogenous shifts of short duration.

III. A Model for the Two-Tier Exchange Market in the BLEU

To investigate the performance of the two-tier exchange market more rigorously we use a small model for the financial and exchange markets in the BLEU. Although the model is very simple it accomodates the main characteristics of the institutions discussed in Section II.

Notation

List of variables

B = government bonds

C = central bank credit to the banking sector

D = domestic component of the money supply

G = central bank credit to the public sector

H = domestic demand for domestic bonds

J = domestic demand for foreign bonds

K = foreign demand for foreign bonds

L = demand for base money

M = base money

r = return on bonds

R_o = commercial (official) exchange rate

R_f = capital (free) exchange rate

R_F = forward official exchange rate

TB = trade balance

Y = national income

W = wealth of the private sector

Z = variation in total foreign exchange reserves (one period)

ZO = current account surplus

ZF = capital account surplus

Operators

d or 1 = domestic variable

f or 2 = foreign variable

e = expected value of a variable

1. The Theoretical Framework

a) Asset markets

Asset markets are specified according to the portfolio equilibrium approach. There are three types of financial assets: cash balances, domestic and foreign short-term bonds. (1) to (3) are demand functions of residents; (4) is the definition of private wealth.

$$(1) \qquad M^1 = L(Y_1, r_1, r_2, R_f, R_f^e, W^1),$$

$$(2) \qquad B_1^1 = H(Y_1, r_1, r_2, R_f, R_f^e, W^1);$$

$$(3) \qquad B_2^1 = J(Y_1, r_1, r_2, R_f, R_f^e, W^1);$$

$$(4) \qquad W^1 = L + H + J.$$

A novelty in the specification of (1) - (3) is the presence of the exchange rates, actual and expected, among the arguments of the asset demand functions. Clearly, domestic demand for foreign assets is a function of the exchange rates. Logically, due to substitution possibilities, demand for domestic assets must therefore also become functions of the exchange rate.

Invoking the wealth constraints, i.e.,

$$L_W + H_W + J_W = 1$$

$$L_i + H_i + J_i = 0 \qquad\qquad i = r_1, r_2, R_f, R_f^e, Y_1$$

we obtain the following restrictions on the partial derivatives:[3)]

$$L_{r_1},\ L_{r_2},\ H_{r_2},\ J_{r_1},\ L_{R_f^e},\ H_{R_f^e} < 0;$$

$$H_{r_1},\ J_{r_2},\ L_{R_f},\ H_{R_f},\ J_{R_f},\ J_{R_f^e} > 0.$$

A depreciation of the capital franc (increase of R_f) tends to increase the value of foreign currency assets converted in Belgian francs. This capital gain leads to an increase of demand for all assets. But a depreciation influences desired portfolios in still another way. If interest payments are converted at the official rate a depreciation of the free rate implies a higher return of foreign assets, and thus a higher desired stock of foreign assets. Due to the wealth constraint demand of at least one domestic asset has to decrease.

With regard to future exchange rates an expected depreciation of the capital franc leads to an expected capital gain on foreign currency assets. This stimulates demand for foreign assets and diminishes demand for domestic assets.

We now turn to asset supplies. The domestic monetary base is composed of a domestic component D, itself the sum of credits extended by the Banque Nationale to the public sector (G) and to the banking sector (C), and of a foreign component (Z), the non-sterilized part of variations in the stock of foreign exchange reserves.

---

3) See J. Tobin (1969) for a more extensive discussion.

In addition to cash balances the governmental authorities issue short-term bonds denominated in domestic currency but traded internationally. Foreign demand for domestic bonds is perfectly similar to domestic demand for foreign bonds, i.e.,

(5) $$B_1^2 = K(Y_2, r_1, r_2, R_f, R_f^e, W_2)$$

with $K_{Y_2}, K_{r_2}, K_{R_f}, K_{R_f^e} < 0$ and $K_{r_1}, K_{W_2} > 0$.

The conditions for equilibrium in the markets for assets can be written:

(6) $$M^{1(supply)} = D + \Sigma Z = L$$

(7) $$B^{1(supply)} = H + K$$

b) The Foreign Exchange Market

We assume that all commercial transactions pass through the official market and that the trade balance surplus (TB) is a function of domestic and foreign national income, changes in the interest rate differential (since leads and lags in international payments are influenced by variations in the returns on foreign balances), and the official exchange rates (present and expected).

(8) $$TB = TB(Y_1, Y_2, \Delta r_1, \Delta r_2, R_o, R_o^e)$$

with $TB_{Y_2}, TB_{\Delta r_1}, TB_{R_o} > 0$

$TB_{Y_1}, TB_{\Delta r_2}, TB_{R_o^e} < 0$

In the official market modifications of the exchange rate compel the authorities to intervene in support of the parity. We assume therefore that

(9) $ZO = ZO\,(R_o - \bar{R}_o)$

with $ZO_{(R_o - \bar{R}_o)} < 0$

where ZO is the variation in exchange reserves resulting from intervention in the official market.

The equilibrium condition in this market is:

(10) $TB\,(\cdot) - ZO\,(\cdot) = 0$

On the other hand, capital movements are channeled through the free market:

(11) $(\Delta K)_t = K_t - K_{t-1}$

(12) $(\Delta J)_t = J_t - J_{t-1}$

The restrictions on the partial derivatives of (11) and (12) can easily be deduced from our previous discussion, with the sole exception of changes of the capital exchange rate. We argued before that a depreciation of the franc increases wealth of residents. This leads to an increase in demand for all assets but the increase for any one asset is necessarily smaller than the total increase in wealth. Hence the actual stock of foreign assets exceeds the desired level leading to a decrease in foreign asset holdings. These considerations are further supported by our previous discussion of the effects of a depreciation on returns. We thus have

$$\Delta J_{R_f} < 0, \qquad \Delta K_{R_f} > 0$$

The interventions of the Banque Nationale in the free market, influencing the capital rate, affect both foreign indebtedness and domestic liquidity. Cet. par., official purchases of foreign exchange tend to depreciate the Belgian franc which, in turn, attracts net capital inflows. Domestically, the counterpart of these official purchases consists in an expansion of liquidity which tends to reduce domestic interest rates thus discouraging capital inflows. Assuming that changes in the overall stock of exchange reserves ($\overline{Z}$) are controlled by policy makers we have:

$$(13) \qquad \overline{Z} = ZO + ZF;$$

where ZF represents the interventions in the free market for a given period.

Free exchange market equilibrium can then be written:

$$(14) \qquad \Delta J(\cdot) - \Delta K(\cdot) + \overline{Z} - ZO(\cdot) = 0.$$

Dropping the bond market by virtue of Walras' Law the complete model can be reduced to equilibrium conditions (15) - (17):

$$(15) \qquad \Delta L(\cdot) - \Delta D - \overline{Z} = 0$$

$$(16) \qquad TB(\cdot) - ZO(\cdot) = 0$$

$$(17) \quad \Delta J(\cdot) - \Delta K(\cdot) + \overline{Z} - ZO(\cdot) = 0$$

Equations (15) - (17) determine Δr_1, R_o, and R_f. ΔD and Z are the instruments for monetary policy. Y_1, Y_2, ΔY_1, ΔY_2, Δr_2, ΔW_1, ΔW_2 are exogenous.

We assume that expectations concerning the official and free exchange rates are formed as follows:

Official exchange rate:

$$(18) \quad R_o^e = \lambda_1 [R_f - R_o] + \lambda_2 [R_o - R_{o,t-1}] + \lambda_3 [R_f - R_{f,t-1}];$$

$$\text{with } \lambda_1, \lambda_3 > 0; \quad \lambda_2 < 0.$$

Free exchange rate:

$$(19) \quad R_f^e = \delta_1 R_{f,t} + \delta_2 [R_f - R_{f,t-1}] + \delta_3 [R_f - R_{f,t-1}]_{t-1};$$

$$\text{with } \delta_1, \delta_2 < 0; \quad \delta_3 > 0.$$

A few comments on these functions are in order here. First, forward rates are absent from our formulation since forward markets are extremely thin and of little importance in the BLEU. A more appropriate indicator of confidence in the Belgian franc is the free spot rate. Second, and in relation to this point, we have assumed that the level and rate of change of the free rate influences the expected official spot rate, but not vice versa. Third, the conditions imposed on the signs of the λ's and δ's are such as to allow for oscillatory movements of exchange rates and to make them compatible with stability conditions. See the simulation results in this Section under b) and the Appendix.

2. Comparative Static Properties

To get a better grasp of the structure of the proposed model it might be useful to study its analytic comparative static properties.

After substitution (18) and (19) into (15) - (17) and upon total differentiation, we obtain the system

$$A\,Y_t = B\,X_t + C\,W_t$$

where A, B, C denote the matrices of coefficients of the endogenous, exogenous, and lagged endogenous variables, respectively, and Y_t, X_t, W_t are the corresponding vectors of variables. More precisely,

$$A = \begin{bmatrix} -L_{r_1} & 0 & -[L_{R_f} + L_{R_f^e}(\delta_1 + \delta_2)] \\ TB_{r_1} & TB_{R_o} - TB_{R_o^e}\lambda_1 - ZO_{R_o} & TB_{R_o^e}\lambda_3 \\ B_{r_1} & -ZO_{R_o} & B_{R_f} + B_{R_f^e}(\delta_1 + \delta_2) \end{bmatrix}$$

$$B = \begin{bmatrix} L_\phi & L_{Y_1} & 0 & 0 & L_{Y_2} & -1 & -1 \\ ZO_\phi - TB_\phi - ZO_{R_o}\overline{R}_o & 0 & -TB_{Y_1} & -TB_{Y_2} & TB_{Y_2} & 0 & 0 \\ ZO_\phi - B_\phi & -B_{Y_1} & 0 & 0 & B_{Y_2} & 0 & -1 \end{bmatrix}$$

$$C = \begin{bmatrix} 0 & \frac{L}{R_f^e}(\delta_3 - \delta_2) & -\frac{L}{R_f^e}\delta_3 \\ \frac{TB}{R_o^e}\lambda_2 & 0 & 0 \\ 0 & -\frac{B}{R_f^e}(\delta_3 - \delta_2) & \frac{B}{R_f^e}\delta_3 \end{bmatrix}.$$

where ϕ refers to the intercept term, and

$$Y_t' = [\Delta r_1 \quad R_o \quad \Delta R_f]$$

$$X_t' = [1 \quad \Delta Y_1 \quad \Delta Y_2 \quad Y_1 \quad Y_2 \quad \Delta D \quad Z]$$

$$W_t' = [R_{o,t-1} \quad \Delta R_{f,t-1} \quad \Delta R_{f,t-2}]$$

Resolving the system we obtain:

$$|A| \; Y_t = A^{\circ} \; B \; X_t + A^{\circ} \; C \; W_t$$

in which $|\ |$ and $^{\circ}$ represent the determinant and the adjoint of the corresponding matrix, respectively. $|A|$ is negative if the system is stable.

Table 3 summarizes the signs of the multiplier solutions of the model.

TABLE 3

Endogenous variables	Exogenous variables							Endogenous variables lagged		
	ΔY_1	ΔY_2	Y_1	Y_2	Δr_2	ΔD	Z	$R_{o,t-1}$	$\Delta R_{f,t-1}$	$\Delta R_{f,t-1}$
Δr_1	?	+	+	-	? (+)	?	?	+	?	?
R_o	-	+	+	-	+	+	+	+	+	-
ΔR_f	-	+	+	-	+	+	+	+	+	-

Some of these results depend on particular assumptions made such as the signs of the income multipliers, but other results are of greater general interest.

For example, a rise in foreign interest rates leads most likely to a rise in domestic interest rates, in spite of the two-tier exchange market. This is due to the fact that more attractive foreign interest rates and a consequently depreciating free exchange rate might generate capital outflows through the official market. The condition for $\Delta r_1 / \Delta r_2 > 0$ is therefore $|TB_{R_o^e} \lambda_3| > |B_{R_f} + B_{R_f^e} (\delta_1 + \delta_2)|$.

In general, monetary expansion leads to a reduction of the interest rate level. In the limiting case of perfectly elastic capital flows this monetary expansion would be offset under fixed exchange rates by capital outflows, such that domestic interest rates could not diverge for longer periods from foreign interest rates. In our model, however, capital outflows lead to a depreciation of the free exchange rate. This depreciation tends to offset the unfavorable interest rate differential, but, simultaneously, capital flows through the official market are made more attractive. If the Banque Nationale really controls the stock of exchange reserves it would have to repurchase on the free market the additional amount of foreign exchange sold on the official market. The free rate will therefore depreciate even more. The condition for expansionary monetary policy to reduce interest rates, at the same time as free and official exchange rates depreciate, is $|TB_{R_o^e} \lambda_3| < |B_{R_f} + B_{R_f^e} (\delta_1 + \delta_2)|$.

Changes in the stock of exchange reserves represent in our model another instrument of monetary policy. The direction of its effects are similar to those of traditional monetary policy, but not its amplitudes. An increase in exchange reserves requires net purchases on the free market by the authorities, thereby provoking a depreciation of the free rate. On the other hand, this increase in exchange reserves is translated into higher domestic liquidity and lower interest rates. An examination of the multiplier expressions reveals that if $L_{R_f} + L_{R_f^e} (\delta_1 + \delta_2)$, and $(TB_{R_o} - TB_{R_o^e} \lambda_2)$ are close to zero, i.e., that the demand for cash balances and the current account are inelastic with respect to changes in the free and official exchange rates, respectively, manipulation of the stock of exchange reserves has the same effects on domestic interest rates as variations in the domestic base of the money supply, but tends to accentuate more the depreciation of official and free exchange rates.

It follows therefore that if the authorities wish to stabilize the free exchange rate it can still pursue an independent monetary policy by simultaneously expanding the money supply and supporting the free rate through a decumulation of exchange reserves.

3. Estimation Results

The estimation of the structural form of the model is impossible for two major reasons. First, asset market and exchange market adjustments are very short-term phenomena. Quarterly data is therefore poorly suited for our purpose. Unfortunately, most balance of payments data are only available in quarterly series. In addition, the distribution of commercial and financial transactions between the two exchange markets cannot be carried out on the basis of published data by the Banque Nationale. Part of the current account operations appearing in the balance of payments correspond to transactions in the free market and some transactions reported as capital movements go through the official market.

Secondly, the monetary authorities of the BLEU have never revealed the amounts of their interventions in the free market which makes it impossible to estimate demand and supply function for foreign exchange on the part of the monetary authorities.

We are thus left with two possible approaches. The first is to estimate R_o, R_f, and M (the monetary base) from the equilibrium conditions, supposing that the interest rates and the foreign component of the monetary base are policy variables. To eliminate the simultaneous equation bias we have used the Two-Stage Least Square (TSLS) method.

The second test we perform consists in reversing the hypothesis that Z is controlled and estimate Z from the reduced form of:

(20) $\Delta L(\cdot) = \Delta D + Z$

(21) $Z = TB(\cdot) + \Delta K(\cdot) - \Delta J(\cdot).$

a) Estimation of R_o, R_f, and M

Substituting (18) in (16) and solving for R_o yields:

(22) $$R_o = \frac{ZO_\phi - TB_\phi - ZO_{R_o}\bar{R}_o}{d} - \frac{TB_{Y_1}}{d} Y_1 - \frac{TB_{Y_2}}{d} Y_2$$

$$- \frac{TB_r}{d} \Delta(r_1 - r_2) - (\lambda_1 + \lambda_3) \frac{TB_{R_o^e}}{d} R_f + \frac{TB_{R_o^e}\lambda_3}{d} R_{f,t-1}$$

$$+ \frac{TB_{R_o^e}\lambda_2}{d} R_{o,t-1}$$

where $d = TB_{R_o} - TB_{R_o^e}\lambda_1 - TB_{R_o^e}\lambda_2 - ZO_{R_o} > 0$

$$= \alpha_o + \alpha_1 Y_1 + \alpha_2 Y_2 + \alpha_3 \Delta(r_1 - r_2) + \alpha_4 R_f + \alpha_5 R_{f,t-1}$$

$$+ \alpha_6 R_{o,t-1};$$

with $\alpha_1, \alpha_4, \alpha_6 > 0$; $\alpha_2, \alpha_3, \alpha_5 < 0$.

The estimation results are listed in Table 4. We report two different results, labelled 22(a) and 22(b).

In equation 22(a) all coefficients are statistically significant and, with the exception of the increase in the interest differential, have the right sign. Since Y_1 and Y_2 are highly correlated we have reestimated equation (22) by imposing the constraint $\alpha_1 = \alpha_2 \cdot (Y_1 - Y_2)$. Moreover, among the independent variables we have not separated ΔR_f into $R_{f,t}$ and $R_{f,t-1}$ in order to eliminate possible trends in these variables. All signs of 22(b) are again correct, with exception of the coefficient of changes in the interest rate differential. However,when we regressed R_o on the difference of the level of domestic and foreign interest rates then we obtained in both equations the correct sign for interest rates, but a t-ratio which does not allow us to reject the null hypothesis.

We may, very tentatively, give the following interpretation of these results. The non-significance of the interest <u>levels</u> confirms our stock view of trade finance. The wrong sign of the significant <u>changes</u> in interest differentials, on the other hand, could be due to the fact that we have used uncovered interest differentials. In fact, that forward discounts led, in general, in Belgium to favorable interest differentials was shown in a recent thesis.[4] Since the

4) See M. Hernandez-Lopez, <u>Les déterminants des taux d'intérêts,</u> doctoral dissertation, Catholic University of Louvain, 1974.

TABLE 4 [5)]

Equations	22(a)	22(b)	23(a)	23(b)	24
dependent variable	R_o	R_o	ΔR_f	R_f	ΔM
constant	16.57 (4.76)	16.90 (4.80)	0.01 (0.30)	2.46 (0.93)	0.97 (5.99)
Y_1	0.0025 (1.96)				
Y_2	-0.0025 (-2.43)				
ΔY_1			-0.002 (-0.68)	-0.001 (-0.57)	-0.06 (-3.06)
ΔY_2			-0.004 (-1.18)	-0.005 (-1.29)	
(Y_1-Y_2)		0.002 (2.16)			
$\Delta(r_1-r_2)$	0.04 (2.36)	0.04 (2.68)	-0.17 (-2.98)	-0.19 (-3.28)	
Δr_1					1.09 (-1.31)
Δr_2					0.56 (1.16)
R_f	0.20 (5.30)	0.07 (4.19)			
$R_{f,t-1}$	-0.12 (-3.44)			0.95 (1.85)	
ΔR_f		0.12 (3.30)			1.46 (2.14)
$\Delta R_{f,t-1}$			0.42 (5.59)	0.47 (6.24)	-1.12 (-1.48)
$\Delta R_{f,t-2}$			-0.26 (3.36)	-0.30 (-3.89)	0.78 (1.07)

TABLE 4 (continued)

Equations	22(a)	22(b)	23(a)	23(b)	24
dependent variable	R_o	R_o	ΔR_f	R_f	ΔM
$R_{o,t-1}$	0.58 (6.88)	0.57 (6.72)			
$R_o - \overline{R}_o$			-0.12 (-0.69)	0.14 (0.40)	
Z			-0.06 (-6.11)	-0.05 (-4.09)	
Q_1					-7.13 (-9.90)
Q_2					4.55 (6.69)
Q_3					-3.56 (-4.84)
$\overline{R}^2$	0.93	0.93	0.54	0.95	0.72
DW	1.96	1.96	2.12	2.02	2.02
ρ	0.245	0.06		0.13	

---

5) Structural equations: monthly data 1962.1 - 1970.12. Reduced form equations: quarterly data 1960.1 - 1970.4.
Figures in parentheses = t - statistics; $\overline{R}^2$ adjusted for the degrees of freedom; DW = Durbin-Watson statistic.

Y_1 : Proxy for national income in Belgium: index of industrial production, OECD Main Economic Indicators.

Y_2 : Proxy for world income: index of industrial production of Germany, OECD Main Economic Indicators.

r_1 : Three month Treasury Certificates: Bulletin de la Banque Nationale de Belgique, Table XIX.3.

use of covered interest differentials as independent variables would have given rise to biased and inconsistent estimates[6], we have retained the uncovered differential. But to test the sign in question we have re-run equation (22) with the covered interest differential and have, indeed, obtained a nonsignificant coefficient, but with the correct sign. Substituting (19) in (17) and solving for ΔR_f leads to:

$$\text{(23)} \quad \Delta R_f = \frac{(ZO_\phi - B_\phi)}{c} - \frac{B_{Y_1}}{c}\Delta Y_1 - \frac{B_{Y_2}}{c}\Delta Y_2 - \frac{B_r}{c}\Delta(r_1 - r_2)$$

$$- \frac{Z}{c} + \frac{ZO_{R_o}}{c}[R_o - \overline{R}_o] - \frac{B_{R_f^e}(\delta_3 - \delta_2)}{c}[R_f - R_{f,t-1}]_{t-1}$$

$$+ \frac{B_{R_f^e}\,\delta_3}{c}[R_f - R_{f,t-1}]_{t-2}$$

---

r_2 : Three month Eurodollar-rate: International Financial Statistics.

Z : Variation in the net foreign position of the Banque Nationale less export bills: Bulletin de la Banque Nationale de Belgique, Table XIII. 2. a.

D : Net domestic assets of the Banque Nationale = Discount bills of the Banque Nationale plus loans to the government of Belgium by the Banque Nationale: Bulletin de la Banque Nationale de Belgique, Table XIII. 8 and Table XIII. 2. a.

R_o : Official market exchange rate of the U. S. dollar: Bulletin de la Banque Nationale de Belgique, Table X. 4.

R_f : Free market exchange rate of the U. S. dollar: Bulletin de la Banque Nationale de Belgique, Table X. 4.

R_F : Three month forward exchange rate of the U. S. dollar in the official market: Bulletin de la Banque Nationale de Belgique, Table X. 4.

6) See J. Stein, "International Short-Term Capital Movements", American Economic Review, (March, 1965).

where B = J - K, i.e., the net capital outflow, and

$$c = B_{R_f} + B_{R_f^e} (\delta_1 + \delta_2) < 0:$$

$$\Delta R_f = \beta_o + \beta_1 \Delta Y_1 + \beta_2 \Delta Y_2 + \beta_3 \Delta(r_1 - r_2)$$

$$+ \beta_4 Z + \beta_5 ZO [R_o - \overline{R}_o]$$

$$+ \beta_6 [R_f - R_{f,t-1}]_{t-1} + \beta_7 [R_f - R_{f,t-1}]_{t-2}$$

with $\beta_1, \beta_3, \beta_5, \beta_7 < 0$; $\beta_2, \beta_4, \beta_6 > 0$.

Whereas we estimate ΔR_f in equation 23(a) we have estimated the level of R_f in equation 23(b) (see Table 4). The estimated coefficients show very little variation from one estimation to the other. Moreover, in 23(b), the coefficient of $R_{f,t-1}$ is 0.95, i.e., sufficiently close to 1 to consider 23(b) an acceptable substitute for 23(a).

All coefficients have the right sign with exception of the variation in the stock of exchange reserves. The latter result suggests that our hypothesis of an effective control of Z by the Belgian monetary authorities is not adequate. On the other hand, the estimation results support our assumptions concerning the expectation functions of R_o and R_f.

After substitution of equation (19) into (15) we obtain:

$$(24)\quad M = \gamma_o + L_{Y_1} \Delta Y_1 + L_{r_1} \Delta r_1 + L_{r_2} \Delta r_2$$

$$+ (L_{R_f} + L_{R_f^e} (\delta_1 + \delta_2)) [R_f - R_{f,t-1}]$$

$$+ L_{R_f^e} (\delta_3 - \delta_2) [R_f - R_{f,t-1}]_{t-1} - L_{R_f^e} \delta_3 [R_f - R_{f,t-1}]_{t-2}$$

$$= \gamma_o + \gamma_1 \Delta Y_1 + \gamma_2 \Delta r_1 + \gamma_3 \Delta r_2 + \gamma_4 [R_f - R_{f,t-1}]$$

$$+ \gamma_5 [R_f - R_{f,t-1}]_{t-1} + \gamma_6 [R_f - R_{f,t-1}]_{t-2}$$

with $\gamma_1, \gamma_4, \gamma_6 > 0; \quad \gamma_2, \gamma_3, \gamma_5 < 0.$

To take seasonal variations in January, August, and December into account we have added three dummy variables Q_1, Q_2, and Q_3.

The regression results are rather disappointing. Some coefficients are not statistically significant, such as interest rates, while others have the wrong sign. However, this is not surprising. First, our money market model is much too simple for a determination of the monetary base. Simplicity was thought desirable since our aim is to estimate the exchange rates. Second, we pointed out already that the hypothesis of an exogenously controlled stock of exchange reserves ought to be rejected. This hypothesis influences, of course, strongly equation (24). Third, although the monetary authorities of the BLEU attempt to control interest rates they are only partially successful since they are constrained by external considerations.

b) Simulations

We performed two types of within-sample simulations with equations (22) and (23(a)) for the official and free exchange rates: dynamic and non-dynamic (static) simulations. The dynamic simulation generates the values of the lagged endogenous variables, while the non-dynamic simulation uses the actual historical values.

Endogenous variable	Static simulation	dynamic simulation
	Root mean square percentage deviation (RMSPD)	
R_o	0.2	0.3
R_f	0.4	2.1

The very small deviation of the simulated official rate from actual values is, of course, not too surprising since the parity bands allow only a variation within 1.5 percent. But, as our mean divergence represents only 1/10 of the possible official exchange rate variation, the result is rather satisfactory.

Figure 7 shows that the simulated path for R_o follows closely the actual path. It is noteworthy that after 1964-9 we catch all turning points as well as the general movements. This period includes the speculation against the Belgian franc in 1966 and 1969, and against Sterling in 1967. The simulation results are less satisfactory for the initial period up to 1964-9 which was marked by exchange market stability. Since we did not impose explicit bands for the official rate we predict an appreciation of

Figure 7 *Dynamic simulation of the official exchange rate (R₀)*

1962-8 – 1970-12 (100 periods)

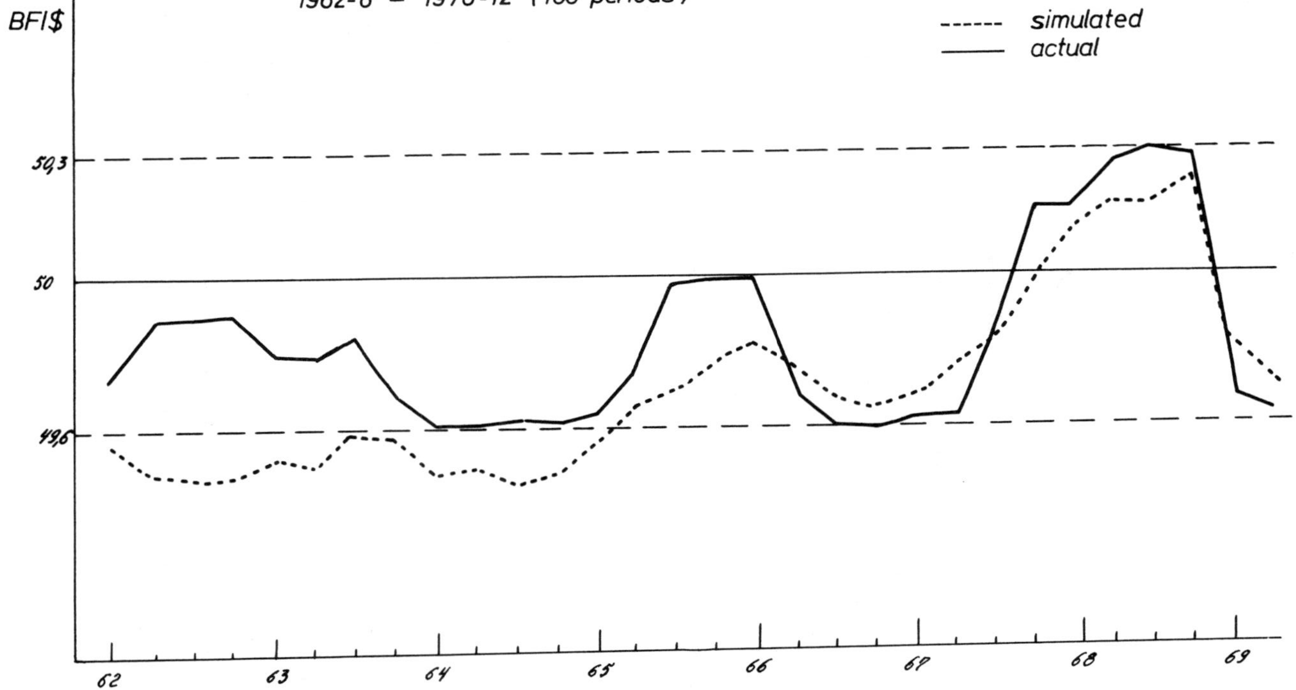

R_o while, in fact, the Banque Nationale accumulated exchange reserves. It might be useful to recall that the system was organized to protect the BLEU against exchange reserve losses.

The dynamic simulation of R_f is shown in Figure 8. Error accumulation becomes important after 1963-12. The result is nevertheless encouraging. First, turning points in 1962-8, 1964-12, 1965-10, 1966-10, and 1968-9 are all well captured. Second, the simulated path for 100 periods is stable. Third, and most importantly, the divergence between simulated and actual paths consists in a consistent overestimation of the depreciation of the free exchange rate. But our previous discussions have made sufficiently clear that due to operations transferred from the free market to the official market, such a depreciation could not have occurred. This interpretation is strongly supported by our equally persistent overestimation of the official franc appreciation.

c) Estimation of Z

The purpose of the estimation of Z is to test whether the domestic component of the monetary base is compensated by variations in the foreign component, i.e., changes in the stock of exchange reserves. The basic assumption is that the monetary authorities stabilize both exchange rates R_o and R_f and let the level of exchange reserves fluctuate.

Figure 8

Dynamic simulation of the free exchange rate (R_f)

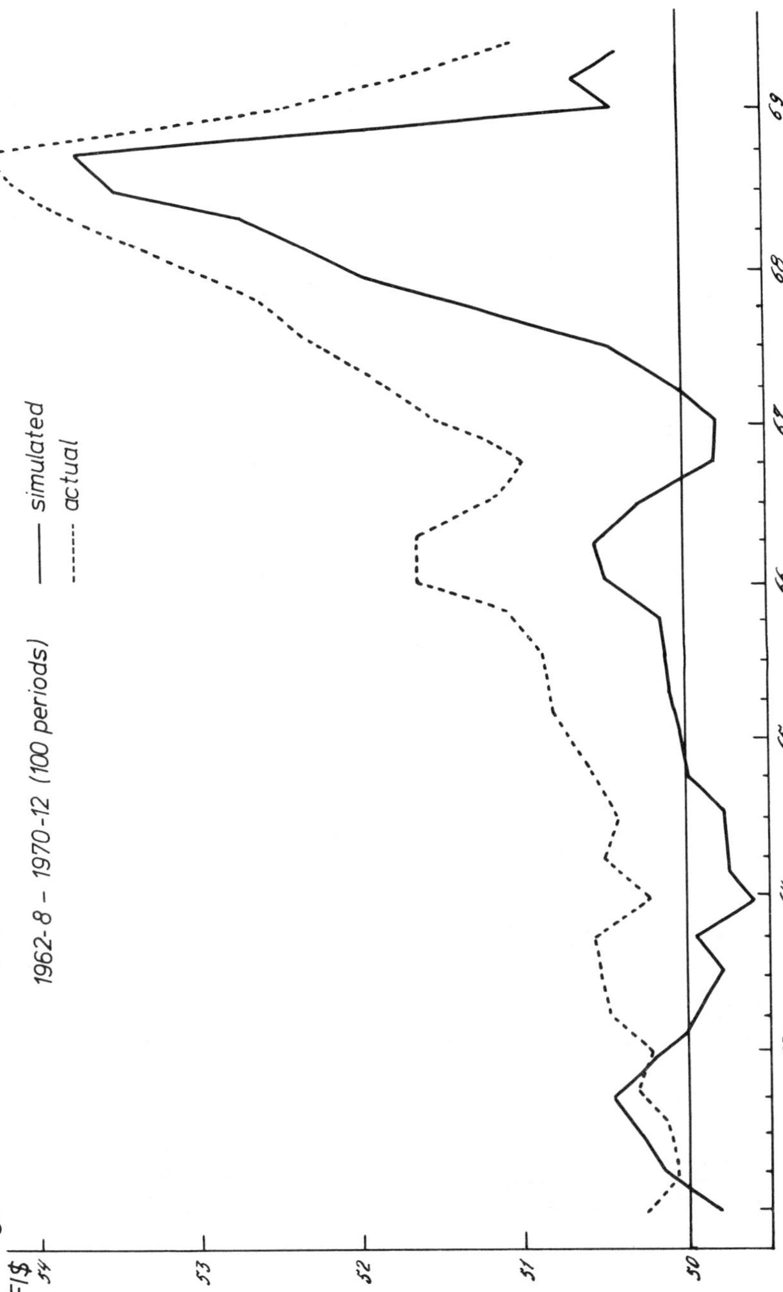

After substituting equations (18) and (19)[7], the reduced form for Z from equations (20) and (21) can be written[8]:

$$(25) \quad Z = \alpha_o + [L_{Y_1}(B_{r_1} - TB_{r_1}) - L_{r_1} - B_{Y_1}]\frac{\Delta Y_1}{g} + (L_{r_1} \cdot B_{Y_2})\frac{\Delta Y_2}{g}$$

$$+ (L_{r_1} \cdot TB_{Y_1})\frac{Y_1}{g} + (TB_{Y_2} \cdot L_{r_1})\frac{Y_2}{g}$$

$$+ [L_{r_1}(TB_{r_2} - B_{r_2}) + L_{r_2}(B_{r_1} - TB_{r_1})]\frac{\Delta r_2}{g}$$

$$+ [L_{r_1}(TB_{R_o} - TB_{R_o^e}\lambda_2]\frac{R_o}{g} - (L_{r_1} \cdot TB_{R_o^e}\lambda_2)\frac{R_{o,t-1}}{g}$$

$$+ [L_{r_1}(TB_{R_o^e}\lambda_3 - B_{R_f} - B_{R_f^e}(\delta_1 + \delta_2))$$

$$+ (L_{R_f} + L_{R_f^e}(\delta_1 + \delta_2))(B_{r_1} - TB_{r_1})]\frac{\Delta R_f}{g}$$

$$- [L_{R_f^e}(\delta_3 - \delta_2)(TB_{r_1} - B_{r_1}) - L_{r_1} \cdot B_{R_f^e}(\delta_3 - \delta_2)]\frac{\Delta R_{f,t-1}}{g}$$

$$+ [L_{r_1} \cdot B_{R_f^e}\delta_3 - L_{R_f^e}\delta_3(B_{r_1} - TB_{r_1})]\frac{\Delta R_{f,t-1}}{g}$$

$$+ (TB_{r_1} - B_{r_1})\frac{\Delta D}{g}$$

where $g = L_{r_1} + B_{r_1} - TB_{r_1} < 0$.

In preliminary estimates the lagged exchange rate variables turned out nonsignificant. We have therefore estimated:

7) We assume for analytical simplicity $\lambda_1 = 0$.
8) The other endogenous variable would be Δr_1.

$$Z = \alpha_o + \alpha_1 \Delta Y_1 + \alpha_2 \Delta Y_2 + \alpha_3 Y_1 + \alpha_4 Y_2 + \alpha_5 \Delta r_2 + \alpha_6 \Delta R_f + \alpha_7 \Delta D + \alpha_8 R_o;$$

with $\alpha_1, \alpha_4 > 0; \alpha_2, \alpha_3, \alpha_5, \alpha_7 < 0; \alpha_6, \alpha_8 \gtrless 0.$

The estimation results are listed in Table 5.

The fit of the regression [25(a)] is satisfactory. It is interesting to note that none of the income variables is significant. This confirms some of our previous results. The negative coefficient of ΔR_f could mean this: when the free exchange rate depreciates, the positive effect on capital inflows is weaker than the negative effect on the current balance via expectations of a devaluation of the official parity (since R_o^e is a positive function of R_f, and $TB_{R_o^e} < 0$). To let the free rate fall to a discount might therefore not be a sure means to improve the exchange reserve position. Furthermore, $\alpha_8 < 0$, meaning that an exogenous upward shift of R_o results in a decrease in exchange reserves, can be explained with our assumption of increased sales of foreign exchange by the authorities whenever R_o depreciates. All coefficients have the right sign with the exception of Δr_2.

The negative coefficient of ΔD indicates that about 57 % of changes in the domestic part of the money supply are offset through variations in the stock of exchange reserves. For an open economy of the size of Belgium the degree of control over the domestic money supply appears thus to be relatively high.

TABLE 5

Estimations of variations in exchange reserves (Z)

Equations	Constant	Y_1	Y_2	ΔY_1	ΔY_2	Δr_2	ΔR_f	R_o	ΔD	Q_1	Q_2	R^2	DW
25(a)	444.80	-0.24	0.21	0.39	-0.19	1.94	-3.37	-8.86	-0.57			0.75	2.65
	(2.40)	(-1.50)	(1.66)	(1.24)	(-0.70)	(2.13)	(-3.27)	(-2.38)	(-5.38)				
25(b)	518.84	-0.30	0.26	0.27	-0.12	0.36	-4.03	-10.33	-0.55	11.06	-11.15	0.83	2.08
	(3.28)	(-2.14)	(2.30)	(0.98)	(-0.50)	(0.42)	(-4.56)	(-3.26)	(-6.14)	(2.98)	(-3.06)		

To take some institutional changes into account we have reestimated equation (25) with two dummy variables: Q_1 for 1969-2 since the controls of the foreign exchange position of banks in the official market became effective for the first time in this quarter (see our discussion in Section II); and Q_2 for 1970-1 since during that quarter the exchange rate differential was extremely low in spite of a deficit in the capital account. Perhaps this indicates important interventions of the monetary authorities.

Apart from the better fit regression 25(b) is interesting from several points of view. The coefficient of the change in foreign interest rate has become insignificant, thus confirming our previous tentative explanation. Moreover, the levels of domestic and foreign incomes have become significant. These results may mean that the portfolio approach, according to which durable capital flows are functions of the changes in income and interest rate differentials, is not an entirely satisfactory theoretical framework for the analysis of the financial and exchange markets in Belgium. Finally, the coefficient of the domestic component of the money supply is stable and statistically highly significant.

We have plotted the actual and estimated (from equation (25(b)) changes in exchange reserves in Figure 9. The general movements are well captured, and in particular the turning points before and after exchange market crises (1968-4, 1969-4), as well as the fluctuations during the period 1966-68. The fit is less satisfactory for 1964-4. Since the exchange rate differential remained very close to zero during that quarter we predict rather constant exchange flows whereas they increased in fact.

Figure 9 — Plot of actual (------) and estimated (——) values of reserve flows (Z)
Quarterly data 1960 - 1971

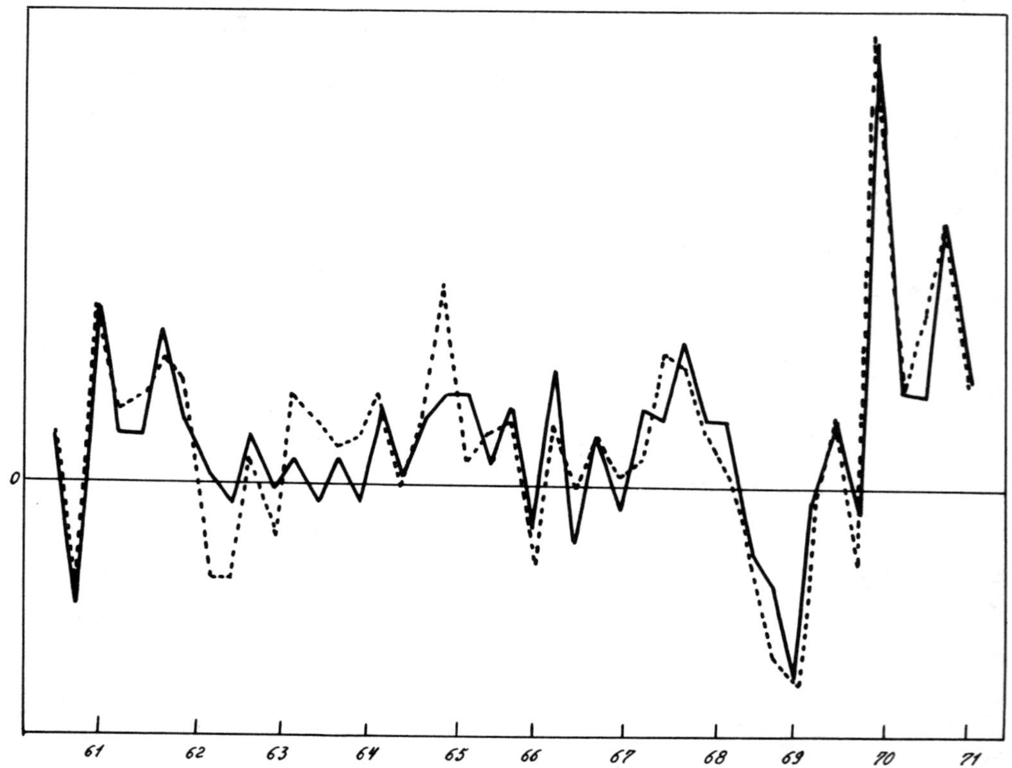

IV. Conclusion and Summary of Results

In this paper we described the general organization of the two-tier exchange market in the BLEU. We then proceeded to a general evaluation of its performance.

We were led to conclude that, in general, and up to 1971, flexibility of the capital rate reduced the magnitude of capital flows out of the BLEU since there was a tendency for the unfavorable exchange rate differential ($R_f > R_o$) to compensate for the (generally favorable) interest rate differential ($r_2 > r_1$). Monetary policy gained thereby a greater independence in the BLEU than it would have had otherwise.

Whenever the exchange rate differential became sizeable, however, speculative transactions in the official market accelerated and it became increasingly difficult to maintain an effective segmentation of the exchange market. Our econometric results allowed us to reject the hypothesis that the Banque Nationale could effectively control its exchange reserves. It had, in fact, to stabilize the free exchange rate.

The model we have developed for the foreign exchange and money markets in the BLEU was used for two purposes. First, we derived structural estimates for the official and free exchange rates assuming that the stock of foreign exchange reserves is controlled exogenously. The explanatory power of the model, in terms of both estimation and simulation results, is high. Since the assumption of exogenously controlled exchange reserves had to be rejected, we performed a second test by assuming exchange rates to be exogenously determined. This allowed us to examine the question to which extent the monetary authorities in the BLEU were able to control the domestic monetary base. The results indicate that while variations in exchange reserves offset substantially policy induced changes of the domestic component of the monetary base, for a country of the size of the BLEU the degree of monetary independence is relatively high. Thus, the two-tier exchange market has, at least, contributed to a greater independence of monetary policy.

APPENDIX: Stability

I. Consider the following model:

(A1) $\dot{Z} = T(Y) - I$

(A2) $\dot{r} = \lambda_1 [L(Y, r) - \alpha Z - M]$

(A3) $\dot{B}^f = \lambda_2 [\Theta^f(r, R, R^e(r)) W^f - \Theta^d(r, R, R^e(r)) W^d - B^f]$

(A4) $\dot{R} = -[\dot{B}^f + (1-\alpha) \dot{Z}]$

where $I = r \Theta^f W^f - r^f \Theta^d W^d$ and λ_1, λ_2 are (positive) speeds of adjustment; d and f denote domestic and foreign parameters, respectively.

Equation (A1) depicts the official exchange market. Trade in commodities (T is the trade balance) and interest payments (I) are assumed to be converted at the official rate. Equation (A4) represents the free market for capital movements. We assume that a proportion $(1 - \alpha)$ of the surplus (deficit) of the current account is used for intervention in the free market. (A2) is the money market equation with M representing the domestic source of the money supply and αZ the foreign source. (A3) implies that net foreign capital inflows $(\dot{B}^f)$ are a function of the difference between desired and actual foreign portfolios, and the speed of adjustment. Desired foreign portfolios are assumed to be fractions of total wealth (W), these fractions Θ being functions of domestic (r) and foreign rates of return (r^f), the actual (R) and the expected future free exchange rate (R^e). All foreign parameters are assumed constant, as well as the real sector of the economy and the official exchange rate.

$$\frac{\partial I}{\partial r} = I_r = \Theta^f W^f + rW^f(\Theta^f_r + \Theta^f_{R^e} R^e_f) - r^f W^d(\Theta^d_r + \Theta^d_{R^e} R^e_r) > 0$$

$$\text{assuming } \Theta^f_r > 0, \quad \Theta^d_r < 0, \quad \Theta^f_R > 0, \quad \Theta^d_R < 0,$$

$$\Theta^f_{R^e} < 0, \quad \Theta^d_{R^e} > 0, \quad R^e_r < 0;$$

$$\frac{\partial I}{\partial R} = I_R = r^f \Theta^d_R W^d - r\Theta^f_R W^f < 0;$$

$$\frac{\partial B^{fx}}{\partial R} = B^{fx}_R = \Theta^f_R W^f - \Theta_R W^d - B^f_R > 0$$

$$\text{where } B^{fx} = \Theta^f(.)W^f - \Theta^d(.)W^d - B^f$$

$$\frac{\partial B^{fx}}{\partial r} = B^{fx}_r > 0.$$

The characteristic equation of the linearized version of this system is:

$$\begin{bmatrix} -\rho & -I_r & 0 & -I_R \\ -\lambda_1\alpha & \lambda_1 L_r - \rho & 0 & 0 \\ 0 & \lambda_2 B^{fx}_r & -(\lambda_2 + \rho) & \lambda_2 B^{fx}_R \\ (1-\alpha)\rho & 0 & -\rho & -\rho \end{bmatrix}$$

$$= \rho^4 + a_1\rho^3 + a_2\rho^2 + a_3\rho = 0$$

where

$$a_1 = -\frac{1}{\lambda_2} L_r + \frac{1}{\lambda_1} + \frac{1}{\lambda_1} B_R^{fx} - (1 - \alpha) I_R > 0$$

$$a_2 = - L_r - L_r B_R^{fx} - \frac{1}{\lambda_2} \alpha I_r - (1 - \alpha) \frac{1}{\lambda_1} I_R - (1 - \alpha) \cdot \frac{1}{\lambda_2} L_r I_R \gtrless 0$$

$$a_3 = - \alpha I_r - \alpha I_r B_R^{fx} + I_R B_R^{fx} - (1 - \alpha) L_r I_R \gtrless 0.$$

The Routh-Hurwitz conditions for local stability of the equilibrium point are:

(i) $a_1 > 0, \; a_2 > 0, \; a_3 > 0.$

(ii) $a_1 a_2 - a_3 > 0$

(iii) $a_1 a_2 a_3 - a_3^2 > 0$

The possibility of instability cannot be excluded a priori. In a_2 the third and fifth terms are negative, as well as the first and second term in a_3. Two remarks are in order here.

(a) Two of the four negative terms depend on the speed of adjustment λ_2. Since λ_2 can safely be considered as very large these terms will be small relative to the positve terms.

(b) If $\alpha \to 0$ three of the four negative terms approach zero as well. Thus, governmental intervention in the free market is highly stabilizing. The stabilizing effect of official intervention can be explained as follows. In the absence of intervention a current account surplus tends to increase the domestic money supply and to exert a downward pressure on the domestic interest rate. This in turn will stimulate capital outflows and thus produce a depreciation of the free rate. If, however, part of the current account surplus is sold on the free market, the free rate will appreciate and counteract the depreciation caused by the fall in domestic interest rates.

From remarks (a) and (b) it can be concluded that stability is very likely to be obtained.

II. Suppose now that discounts or premia of the free rate with respect to the official rate lead to expectations about parity changes of the official rate:

$$R^{eo} = R^{eo}(R - \bar{R}^{o})$$

$$R^{eo}_{(R-\bar{R}^{o})} > 0.$$

As we argued in the text, this can be expected to have a negative influence on capital flows:

$$B^{f} = \lambda_2 \, [\Theta^{f}(r, R, R^{e}(r), R^{eo}(R-\bar{R}^{o}))W^{f}$$
$$- \Theta^{d}(r, R, R^{e}(r), R^{eo}(R-\bar{R}^{o})W^{d} - B^{f}]$$

The term B^{fx}_{R} changes then as below:

$$\dot{B}^{fx}_{R} = [\Theta^{f}_{R} + \Theta^{f}_{R^{eo}} R^{eo}_{(R-\bar{R}^{o})}] W^{f} - [\Theta_{R} + \Theta_{R^{eo}} R^{eo}_{(R-\bar{R}^{o})}] W^{d} - B^{f}_{R}$$

In general the first terms in parentheses should dominate the second terms so that $\dot{B}^{fx}_{R}$ remains positive. The risk of instability is thus unaffected by taking the interdependence of both rates in the formation of expectations into account.

III. When interest payments on foreign assets are also converted at the free exchange rate then the characteristic equation changes to:

$$\begin{bmatrix} -\rho & 0 & 0 & 0 \\ -\lambda_1 \alpha & \lambda_1 L_r - \rho & 0 & 0 \\ 0 & \lambda_2 B^{fx}_{r} & -(\lambda_2 + \rho) & \lambda_2 B^{fx}_{R} \\ (1-\alpha)\rho & I_r & -\rho & I_R - \rho \end{bmatrix}$$

$$= \rho^4 + a_1 \rho^3 + a_2 \rho^2 + a_3 \rho = 0$$

where

$$a_1 = \lambda_2 - I_R \overset{+}{+} \lambda_2 B^{fx}_{R} > 0$$

$$a_2 = - \lambda_2 \bar{I}_R > 0$$

$$a_3 = - \lambda_1 \bar{L}_r > 0.$$

The system is clearly stable. Furthermore, stability is completely independent of intervention in the free market.

Since national income (Y) is exogenous to our model the only influence of monetary conditions on the current account is through interest payments. Changes in the current account, in turn, influence domestic liquidity. If, however, foreign interest payments are converted at the free rate this link ceases to exist and the sole interdependence which might create instability in this model is eliminated.

IV. The same model without dual exchange markets reduces to

$$\dot{Z} = T(Y) - I + \dot{B}^f$$

$$\dot{r} = \lambda_1 [L(Y, r) - \alpha Z - M]$$

$$\dot{B}^f = \lambda_2 [\Theta^f W^f - \Theta^d W^d - B^f]$$

$$\begin{bmatrix} -\rho & -I_r & \rho \\ -\lambda_1 \alpha & \lambda_1 L_r - \rho & 0 \\ 0 & \lambda_2 B_r^{fx} & -(\lambda_2 + \rho) \end{bmatrix}$$

$$= \rho^3 + a_1 \rho^2 + a_2 \rho^1 + a_3 = 0$$

$$= \rho^3 + \rho^2 [\lambda_2 + \lambda_1 L_r] + \rho [\lambda_2 \lambda_1 L_r + \lambda_1 \alpha I_r - \lambda_1 \lambda_2 \alpha B_R^{fx}] + \lambda_1 \lambda_2 \alpha I_r = 0;$$

where

$$a_1 = \lambda_2 + \lambda_1 L_r \gtrless 0$$

$$a_2 = \lambda_2 \lambda_1 L_r + \lambda_1 \alpha I_r - \lambda_1 \lambda_2 \alpha B^{fx}_{\underset{+}{R}} < 0$$

$$a_3 = \lambda_1 \lambda_2 \alpha I_r < 0.$$

Instability if $\lambda_2 > - \lambda_1 L_r$

i.e., if international portfolio allocations occur quickly enough.

V. Suppose now that $R^e = R^e(Z)$ with $R^e_Z < 0$. Then the Θ's are also functions of R^e and $\dot{B}^f_{R^e} < 0$.

We then obtain the following linearized system:

$$\begin{bmatrix} -\rho & -I_r & \rho \\ -\lambda_1\alpha & \lambda_1 L_r - \rho & 0 \\ \lambda_2 B^{fx}_{R^e} R^e_Z & \lambda_2 B^{fx}_r & -(\lambda_2 + \rho) \end{bmatrix}$$

$$= \rho^3 + a_1\rho^2 + a_2\rho + a_3 = 0$$

with

$$a_1 = \lambda_2 + \lambda_1 L_r + B^{fx}_{R^e} R^e_Z \gtrless 0$$

$$a_2 = \lambda_2 \lambda_1 L_r + \lambda_1 \alpha I_r - \lambda_1 \lambda_2 \alpha B^{fx}_R - \lambda_1 L_r B^{fx}_{R^e} R^e_Z \gtrless 0$$

$$a_3 = \lambda_1 \lambda_2 \alpha I_r < 0.$$

Instability if

$$\lambda_2 + B^{fx}_{R^e} R^e_Z > - \lambda_1 L_r$$

or

$$\lambda_1 L_r B^{fx}_{R^e} R^e_Z > - (\lambda_2 \lambda_1 L_r + \lambda_1 \alpha I_r - \lambda_1 \lambda_2 \alpha B^{fx}_R)$$

Hence, if expectations are sufficiently strong instability will occur. This danger of instability can be better appreciated with the following example.

Suppose the free rate of the Belgian Franc (FB) is at a discount. Foreign importers will then try to acquire FB in the free market, thereby producing an excess demand for FB, thus reducing R. Furthermore, if the discount leads to expectations of a devaluation of the official rate then

(i) importers will try to reduce payment lags, thereby increasing the trade deficit; and

(ii) if interests are passed through the official market, expected returns of foreign investments in Belgium are decreased, and expected returns on Belgian investment in foreign currency are increased. This produces a net capital outflow and hence a further depreciation of the free rate. An offsetting argument might, however, be the increased competitivity of Belgian exporters due to a depreciated official exchange rate.

VI. So far we have analyzed the stability properties of a simple macroeconomic model for an economy with a two-tier exchange market. We also have made various assumptions about the organization of the exchange market, on the one hand, and the formation of exchange rate expectations, on the other.

To investigate this latter aspect in more detail, we now proceed to investigate the stability properties of the simplified exchange rate expectation functions proposed in the main text. (A5) and (A7) are simplified versions of equations (22) and (23), while (A6) and (A8) correspond to the functions (18) and (19).

$$\text{(A5)} \quad \dot{R}_o = \alpha_1 T(R_o, \ldots.) + \alpha_2 R_o^e + \alpha_3 Z;$$

$$T_1 > 0; \quad \alpha_1 < 0; \quad \alpha_2 > 0; \quad \alpha_3 < 0.$$

$$\text{(A6)} \quad R_o^e = \lambda_1 (R_f - R_o) + \lambda_2 R_o; \qquad \lambda_1 > 0; \quad \lambda_2 < 0.$$

$$\text{(A7)} \quad \dot{R}_f = \beta_1 K(R_f, R_f^e, i, \ldots.) + \beta_2 Z;$$

$$\beta_1 < 0; \quad \beta_2 > 0; \quad K_1 > 0; \quad K_2 < 0.$$

$$\text{(A8)} \quad R_f^e = d_1 R_f + d_2 \dot{R}_f; \qquad d_1 \lesseqgtr 0; \quad d_2 < 0.$$

or, alternatively,

(A8′) $R_f^e = d_1 R_f + d_2 (R_f - R_o)$; $d_1 \lessgtr 0$; $d_2 < 0$.

Assuming for the moment that official interventions are exogenously determined, the conditions for stability of (A5) and (A7), after substituting (A6) in (A5) and (A8) in (A7), are:

$$\text{(i)} \quad \overset{-}{\alpha_1} \overset{+}{T_1} + \overset{+}{\alpha_2} (\overset{-}{\lambda_2} - \overset{+}{\lambda_1}) < 0;$$

$$\text{(ii)} \quad \frac{\overset{-}{\beta_1} \overset{-}{K_2} \overset{\mp}{d_1} + \overset{-}{\beta_1} \overset{+}{K_1}}{1 - \underset{-}{\beta_1} \underset{-}{d_2} \underset{-}{K_2}} < 0.$$

If $d_1 < 0$, the system cannot become unstable. On the other hand, if $d_1 > 0$, then stability obtains if and only if $K_1 > K_2 d_1$.

In this case instability could easily occur since, especially during monetary crises, $K_2 d_1 > K_1$ is very likely.

Let us now consider hypothesis (A8′). The stability conditions change to:

$$\text{(i)} \quad \overset{-}{\alpha_1} \overset{+}{T_1} + \overset{+}{\alpha_2} (\overset{-}{\lambda_2} - \overset{+}{\lambda_1}) + \overset{-}{\beta_1} \overset{-}{K_2} (\overset{+}{d_1} + \overset{-}{d_2}) + \overset{-}{\beta_1} \overset{+}{K_1} < 0;$$

$$\text{(ii)} \quad \overset{-}{(\alpha_1 T_1 + \alpha_2 (\lambda_2 - \lambda_1))} \; \overset{-}{[\beta_1 K_2 (d_1 + d_2) + \beta_1 K_1]}$$

$$+ \overset{-}{\alpha_1} \overset{+}{\lambda_1} \overset{-}{\beta_1} \overset{-}{K_2} \overset{-}{d_2} > 0.$$

In this case the possibility of instability is reduced, but still exists, if $d_1 > 0$ and $|d_1| > |d_2|$ i.e., if the extrapolative element of (A8′) dominates the second term which is stabilizing.

If we endogenize official interventions in the foreign exchange markets by postulating

$$Z = Z\,(R_o, R_f); \qquad Z_1 > 0, \quad Z_2 < 0,$$

we obtain the following equilibrium conditions:

$$\text{(i)} \quad \alpha_1 T_1 + \alpha_2(\lambda_2 - \lambda_1) + \beta_1 K_2(d_1 + d_2) + \beta_1 K_1 + \overset{-\;+}{\alpha_3 Z_1} + \overset{+\;-}{\beta_2 Z_2} < 0;$$

$$\text{(ii)} \quad [\overset{-\;+}{\alpha_1 T_1} + \overset{+\;-}{\alpha_2(\lambda_2} - \overset{+}{\lambda_1}) + \overset{-\;+}{\alpha_3 Z_1}]\,[\overset{-\;+}{\beta_1 K_2}(\overset{+}{d_1} + \overset{-}{d_2}) + \overset{-\;+}{\beta_1 K_1} + \overset{+\;-}{\beta_2 Z_2}]$$
$$+ (\overset{-\;+}{\alpha_1 \lambda_1} + \overset{-\;-}{\alpha_3 Z_2})(\overset{-\;-\;-}{\beta_1 K_2 d_2} - \overset{+\;+}{\beta_2 Z_1}) > 0.$$

These conditions show clearly that official intervention can only increase the stability of the system.

REFERENCES

1. Abraham, J. P., and Martin, G., "Dubbele Belgische Wisselkoers en Internationale Renteverschillen 1967-1969", Economische - Statistische Berichten, October 1970.

2. Abraham, J. P., "Recente Ervaringen op de Belgische Dubbele Wisselmarkt", Cahiers du Centre d'Etudes Bancaires et Financières, January 1974.

3. Argy, V., and Porter, M., "The Forward Exchange Market and the Effect of Domestic and External Disturbances under Alternative Exchange Rate Systems", IMF Staff Papers, November 1972

4. Barattieri, V., and Ragazzi, G., "An Analysis of the Two-Tier Foreign Exchange Market", Banca Nazionale del Lavoro Quarterly Review, December 1971.

5. Boll, F., De Kock, S., and Jadoul, B., "The Dual Exchange Rate System", mimeo, Centrum voor Economie, Katholieke Universiteit Leuven, September 1973.

6. Bulletin d'Information et de Documentation, "Les mouvements conjoncturels enregistrés dans la balance des paiements de l'U.E.B.L. de 1951 à 1967", April 1969.

7. Decaluwe, B., "Two-Tier Exchange Market and Other Systems: A Comparison", Tijdschrift voor Economie, vol. 14, n 1, 1974.

8. Fleming, J. M., "Domestic Financial Policies under Floating Exchange Rates", IMF Staff Papers, November 1962.

9. Fleming, J. M., "Dual Exchange Rates for Current and Capital Transactions: A Theoretical Examination", Chap. 12 in Essays in International Economics, Cambridge 1971.

10. Kouri, P. J. K., and Porter, M. G., "International Capital Flows and Portfolio Equilibrium", Journal of Political Economy, n 82, May/June 1974.

11. Salin, P., "Un double marché des changes est-il justifié?" Revue d'Economie Politique, December 1971.

12. Swoboda, K., "The Dual Exchange Rate System and Monetary Independence", Paper presented at the Wingspread Conference on National Monetary Policies and the International Financial System, July 26-29 1972.

13. TALENT, (Groupe), "Le systême belge du double taux de change", Cahiers Economiques de Bruxelles, 2e trim. 1970.

14. Tobin, J., "A General Equilibrium Approach to Monetary Theory", Journal of Money, Credit, and Banking, February 1969.

15. Willett, T. D., Katz, S. I., and Branson, W. B., "Exchange Rate Systems, Interest Rates, and Capital Flows", Essays in International Finance, n 78, Princeton, January 1970.

POLICY IMPLICATIONS OF ALTERNATIVE TWO-TIER EXCHANGE RATE SYSTEMS

By Frank Boll *

We intend to analyse the stabilization characteristics of two prototype dual exchange rate systems. First, a dual exchange rate system without central bank interventions on the free market. A fixed rate applies to current account transactions (as under the unified fixed rate system), and a free one to capital transactions. Thus, the capital account automatically balances and the balance of payments equals the current account. Second, a dual exchange rate system with interventions. This latter system is similar to the former, but in addition there are transactions by the central bank on the free market in order to keep foreign exchange reserves constant. To put such an analysis into a more familiar context we will compare the policy implications of the two dual rate systems with those of the unified fixed and the unified floating exchange rate regimes.

In studying economic policy under each of these exchange rate systems, three targets are considered. First, internal balance or full employment output at a constant price and money wage

* I am indebted to G. Basevi, W. M. Corden, P. De Grauwe, J. S. Flemming, P. M. Oppenheimer and members of the British Money Study Group, for comments.

level. Second, external balance or no changes in international reserves. Third, optimal growth of productive capacity or optimal gross investments. There are two discretionary instruments: fiscal and monetary policy which are defined below, and one automatic instrument: unconstrained exchange rate variations in all but the unified exchange rate systems.

The central issue of our inquiry consists of the following questions: how many targets, and which ones, can be attained with either, or with a particular mix, of the two discretionary policy instruments under each of the exchange rate systems (section II. 1)? And, how do the systems compare on this account (section II. 2)? But first we will briefly outline the model, its underlying geometry, the effects of instrument manipulation and the notion of quasi-equilibrium (section I). Finally, we investigate the implications of two alternative definitions of monetary policy (section III).

I. 1. The Model and its Assumptions

Four markets are considered: the market for goods and services (or the real market), the money market, the market for bonds, and the foreign exchange market(s) or the foreign sector. In accordance with the law of Walras we choose to drop the bond market from explicit consideration. In this and other respects, our model is similar to the open IS-LM model of Fleming (1962), Mundell (1963), and Johnson (1966).

Private consumption depends positively on disposable income, and gross investments negatively on the rate of interest. The demand for money varies directly with income and inversely with the rate of interest. Current account imports depend directly on income and inversely on the exchange rate. The exchange rate is defined as the domestic price of one unit of foreign exchange. Exports of goods and services vary directly with the exchange rate. The net capital inflow is explained by the differential between the domestic and the foreign rate of interest in the unified fixed and floating rate systems. In the dual rate systems there are no net capital movements; gross capital movements are determined by the interest rate differential <u>and</u> the free rate in the dual rate system <u>without</u> interventions, and, in the case of a dual rate system <u>with</u> interventions, <u>also</u> by the changes in reserves due to current account imbalances.[1] The various exchange markets are both Walrasian and Marshallian stable. Variables are expressed in domestic prices, unless stated otherwise.

A number of crucial assumptions are either implied by all the above, or made in addition.

a) <u>Constant domestic price level.</u> There exist no single set of assumptions that will let the GNP price deflator unaffected in all four systems as a result of instrument manipulation. In all but the unified floating rate system the domestic price level is assumed to remain constant up till full employment. A sufficient condition therefore is that the foreign supply of imports and the home supply of nontradeable and exportable goods are perfectly

1) The mathematical counterpart of part of this paper is to be found in Boll (1975).

price-elastic. The same assumptions are retained in the unified floating rate system. Thus, upon a disturbance of the system, nominal GNP will not equal real GNP in the unified floating rate system.

b) Disregard of portfolio considerations. Changes in wealth do not affect private consumption or the demand for money. Money substitutes only for bonds, and not for real capital or goods.[2] International capital flows are explained by interest rate differentials and are not related to equilibrium portfolio considerations.[3]

c) Absence of foreign exchange speculation. Current account transactions are always settled on the current spot foreign exchange market when they occur, i.e. for goods when they are sold or shipped into the country, and for services when they are rendered. This assumption has two consequences. First, working balances to finance current account transactions are not held and trade credit is never granted. Hence there will be no capital movements directly connected with current account transactions. Second, forward foreign exchange markets do not exist. To exclude speculation on the spot market, we assume that the expec-

---

2) For this and other critiques of the IS-LM model see e.g. Carlson (1974), pp. 15-18. Nevertheless, unless the contrary is proven, these deficiencies can be presumed to be neutral with respect to the results of a comparison between the four systems on the basis of a same model.

3) This is of course unsatisfactory, but could be justified by the short-term nature of the model at hand: e.g. by truncating the multiplier after a few circular-flow-of-income periods. Furthermore, this assumption also excludes a monetary approach to the balance of payments.

ted future unified or current account spot rate always equals its actual counterpart.[4] By contrast, for the free exchange rate in the dual rate systems, it must be assumed that, for some actual free spot rate, expectations concerning its future equivalent become inelastic.

d) Small country assumption. This means that foreign income levels, interest rates and price levels remain fixed. Thus, the country is considered small in the sense that the foreign repercussions of its policy actions can be neglected.[5]

e) Monetary policy is defined as a change in the exogenous money supply by means of open market operations.[6] Constant monetary policy implies a constant money supply. This means that the effects of changes in reserves on the money supply are neutralized by open market operations and that the automatic monetary mech-

4) For the removal of this assumption see Argy and Porter (1972) and Baguley (1971).

5) Other established meanings of the small country assumption are (1) that capital mobility is perfectly interest rate elastic, and (2) that the home supply of imports and the world demand for exports are perfectly price elastic.

6) The money supply is backed by the monetary base, i.e. the central bank's domestic and foreign assets. This constitutes the sources side of the monetary base. The domestic assets consist of government securities, and the foreign assets equal the domestic currency equivalent of the foreign exchange reserves. On the uses side the monetary base consists of currency and notes in circulation and commercial bank reserves. For analytical convenience the domestic monetary system is supposed to entail hundred percent reserve requirements and no facilities for commercial banks to borrow from the central bank. Furthermore, the banking system is always fully loaned up. The money supply then equals the monetary base.

anism for balance of payments adjustment is prevented from operating. This so-called orthodox monetary policy represents in fact a combination of two policies: a money stock policy and a related neutralization flow policy. [7]

f) Fiscal policy is defined as a change in the exogenous government budget flow, brought about by a change in government expenditures with constant monetary policy. Such expenditures consist solely of public consumption, no public investments being assumed. The income tax structure remains constant. Budget deficits are continuously financed by official sales of securities to the private sector.

g) High but less than perfect capital mobility. The implications of this assumption are pointed out in the following two sections.

2. The Geometry in each Exchange Rate Regime

We shall now provide the geometry [8] by means of which we can give a graphic content to various crucial concepts like: equilibrium in the real and the money market, current and capital account balance, absorption, external and internal balance, optimal growth, and relatively high capital mobility. All this is illustrated for each exchange rate regime in the figures 1 to 4.

---

7) The term "orthodox" is from Tsiang (1961). The latter terms have been coined by Swoboda (1972b).

8) Based on Stern (1973), ch. 8.

Equilibrium in the real market. Both the desired and the actual aggregate demand equal the supply of domestic output along the IS-line which we assume to be downward sloping. In the unified floating rate system an incipient deficit on the balance of payments depreciates the exchange rate. The IS-line then shifts outwards because of the increase in aggregate demand caused by expenditure-switching. Both income and the rate of interest thus tend to increase. As the interest rate goes up the supply of foreign exchange increase. Consequently, the higher is the capital mobility the smaller the depreciation ultimately needed to equilibrate the foreign exchange market. Given the budget deficit and the capital mobility there thus corresponds one and a different IS-line to each exchange rate. This is reflected in figure 2 where the IS-line is qualified by de=o, meaning: no change in the exchange rate (e). Thus for an incipient payments deficit at a given exchange rate, the depreciation and the outward shift of the IS-line will be more pronounced, the larger the elasticities of the supply of imports and of the demand for exports (defined as positive) and the smaller the capital mobility. The IS-line in the figures 1, 3 and 4 is qualified by e_o which stands for the fixed (current account) parity.[9)]

Equilibrium in the money market. For all points on the upward sloping LM-line the desired demand equals the actual demand and the supply of money. The LM-line is assumed to be unaffected

9) A devaluation of the unified fixed rate, or of the fixed rate which applies to current account transactions in both dual rate systems, has the same effects as a depreciation of the unified floating rate. But in our analysis the (current account) parity will be kept constant.

by changes in any exchange rate.

Current account balance. For all systems the equilibrium current account line is depicted by the TT-lines. The qualifying T=o stands for the net current account surplus equals zero. TT is vertical because the current account is unaffected by the interest rate. In the unified fixed and both dual rate systems there is only one level of income compatible with current account balance. Given the parity ($\bar{e}_o$) the current account is in surplus for points to the left of the $T\bar{T}$-line. In the unified floating rate system the current account equilibrium line will have the same location as in the other exchange rate systems only if the exchange rate equals the parity ($e=\bar{e}_o$). For a depreciation of the floating exchange rate the reference TT-line ($e=\bar{e}_o$) shifts to the right, the more so the larger the elasticities of the supply of imports and the demand for exports (defined as positive) and the smaller the capital mobility. The current account balance line is thus compatible with an infinity of income levels.

Capital account balance. In all but the dual rate system with interventions the locus of points for which the net capital inflow is zero (K=o) is represented by the KK-line(s) which is horizontal because the capital account is unaffected by income change. In the case of unified fixed and floating rates there is but one interest rate level compatible with a zero net capital flow. For points above the KK-line there is a net capital inflow. For a dual rate system without interventions the capital account always balances. There thus exists a family of KK-lines each of which corresponds to a different free exchange rate. It follows that the capital account balance line is consistent with an infinity of interest rate levels. For points above the reference KK-line ($de' = o$; $e' = \bar{e}_o$) the free rate is appreciated. In the dual rate system with interventions the KK-line coincides with the external balance line. This will be explained below.

External balance. The foreign exchange reserves remain constant for all points along the CR-line(s) with an identical slope in all but the dual rate system without interventions. In the unified fixed rate system the demand and supply of foreign exchange are equal for all points along the CR-line ($B = o$; $\bar{e}_o$). $B = o$ means that the autonomous balance of payments is zero. The qualifying "autonomous" implies that the reserves, and the commercial and international financial policies, have remained constant. For points above this line there is a balance of payment surplus. In the unified floating rate system external balance ceases to be a policy target. There thus exists a series of parallel CR-lines each of which applies to a different exchange rate. For points above the reference CR-line ($de = o$; $e = \bar{e}_o$) the exchange rate is appreciated. With dual rates without interventions the locus of external balance points coincides with the TT-line. For the dual rate system with interventions, external balance is of no policy concern because reserves (R) are continuously kept constant ($dR = o$) by the authorities' interventions on the free market. There thus exists a series of parallel CR-lines each of which corresponds to a different free exchange rate. We explain. An increase in income deteriorates the current account. This results in an increased demand by the authorities for foreign exchange on the free market. The free rate then depreciates. By contrast, an increase in the rate of interest increases the net supply of foreign exchange on the free market. As a result the free rate appreciates. It follows that there exists an infinity of combinations of income and the rate of interest which let the free exchange rate unaffected. For points above these reference lines the free rate appreciates.[10)]

Internal balance. The Y_{fe}-line stands for the level of full employment output or internal balance. For points to the left of this line there is unemployment.

Optimal growth. Only for the rate of interest r′ there will be a flow of gross investments which optimizes the rate of growth of productive capacity. For interest rates higher than r′ the rate of growth will be less than optimal.

Relatively high capital mobility. Whether in the context of this model capital mobility with respect to the uncovered interest rate differential is said to be high or low depends on the relative slopes of the LM- and the CR-lines. The degree of capital mobility, so defined, crucially determines whether expansionary fiscal policy causes (1) the balance of payments to improve or to deteriorate in the case of unified fixed exchange rates, or causes (2) the floating or free rate to appreciate or to depreciate in the

10) If the other country or the rest of the world were on the same dual rate system with interventions the increased demand by the authorities due to a deteriorating current account would be matched by an increase in supply by the other country(ies) so as to leave the free rate determined only by the interest rate differential. The reference external balance line ($de'=o$; $e'=e_o$) would then coincide with the reference KK-line in figure 3.

cases of unified floating and dual rates with intervention. Capital mobility is defined as high if the LM-line is steeper than the CR-line.

3. The Effects of Fiscal and Monetary Policy

What are the final effects of an expansion in government expenditures when the monetary effects of the balance of payments are neutralized? Income and the rate of interest increase to the same extent under all but the unified floating rate system. Under this latter system the increase in income and the rate of interest is less because of the appreciation of the exchange rate which via expenditure-switching exerts a deflationary effect on aggregate demand. In the unified fixed exchange rate system the capital account improvement dominates the deterioration in the current account. The balance of payments thus improves. In the unified floating rate system the improvement in the capital account is exactly matched by the deterioration in the current account which due to the appreciation is larger than in the other systems. Absorption thus increases more in the unified floating than in the other exchange rate systems. (In both dual rate systems the current account deteriorates with the same amount as in the unified exchange rate system.) The free exchange rate in both two-tier systems appreciates, but by more in the dual rate system without interventions than in the one with interventions. Indeed, with interventions the increased supply of free foreign exchange on account of the rise in the rate of interest is somewhat - but less than totally - offset by the authorities' demand[11] for free foreign exchange to keep their foreign exchange reserves constant given the deterioration of the current account.

Next, what are the effects of an increase in the money supply? Ultimately, income increases with more, and the rate of interest decreases with less, in the unified floating rate system than under the other systems for which the income and interest rate effects are identical. The reason, again, lies in the depreciation of the unified floating rate which via expenditure-switching constitutes a reflationary factor. Now, what are the foreign sector effects? In the unified fixed exchange rate system the balance of payments worsens because both the current and the capital account deteriorate. In the unified floating rate system the exchange rate depreciates. The interest rate thus decreases by less than under the unified fixed system. Thus, finally the deterioration in the capital account will be less pronounced than in the unified fixed system. Hence, the current account must improve. So, absorption has increased less in the unified floating rate system compared to the other systems. In both two-tier systems the free exchange rate depreciates, but by more in the dual rate system with interventions than in the one without interventions. The reason is that with interventions the increased demand for free foreign exchange on account of the decrease in the rate of interest is supplemented by the authorities' demand for free foreign exchange to restock their foreign exchange reserves.

---

11) Or increased demand, or decreased supply, according to whether initially the current account was in balance, in deficit, or in surplus.

4. The Concept of Quasi-Equilibrium

With orthodox monetary policy equilibria are subject to a time constraint if they entail an imbalance in international payments.[12] Because of this constraint such situations are called quasi-equilibria in contrast to full-equilibria which imply balance in international payments. However, as will be shown in the remainder of this section, the stringency of this time constraint differs between the three considered exchange rate systems: ceteris paribus it is smallest in the dual rate system with interventions and largest in the unified fixed exchange rate systems.

When, in the case of a unified fixed and dual rate system without interventions, variations in reserves occur, the money supply is kept constant by so-called neutralizing or defensive open market operations. From the new quasi-equilibrium onwards the composition of the fixed stock of central bank assets keeps changing at the constant neutralization rate. What now determines the time constraint on quasi-equilibrium situations? In the unified fixed and dual rate system without interventions this time constraint depends on (1) the required rate of neutralization which equals the net balance of payments flow (i. e. the current account imbalance in the dual rate system without interventions), in conjunction with (2) the stock of government securities held by the central bank, (3) the private sector's portfolio of such securities, and (4) the foreign exchange reserves. In the case of a payments deficit the reserves and the private sector's stock of government securities keep decreasing if the payments deficit is larger than

12) See Swoboda (1972a).

the budget deficit which is financed by the Treasury's sale of securities to the public. On the other hand, if the payments deficit is smaller than the budget deficit, only the international reserves of the central bank decrease while the private sector's portfolio of securities increases. Thus, for a payments deficit the time span over which neutralization remains tenable will be shorter, (1) the larger the deficit, (2) the smaller the stock of reserves, (3) the smaller the private sector's initial portfolio of securities, and (4) the smaller the budget deficit.

In the dual rate system with interventions reserves always remain constant. Thus neutralization cannot be due to changes in foreign exchange reserves. Whence the need for neutralization in this case? In contrast to the case of unified fixed and dual rates without interventions there now exists no one-to-one relationship between the reserves valued in foreign exchange and their equivalent in terms of domestic currency.[13)] The link between these two reserve concepts depends on the discrepancy between the parity and the free rate at which the authorities intervene on the free market. The explanation runs as follows. In the quasi-equilibrium point a in figure 4 the loss of reserves due to the current account deficit is compensated by an official spot purchase of the same amount on the free market at a free rate depreciated with respect to the parity - that is, as it will be called, at a free rate premium. Thus, for the central bank this operation results in a

13) In the unified floating rate system the existence of reserves is assumed away. Indeed, without neutralization the stock of foreign exchange reserves in domestic currency equivalents, and hence also the money supply, would alter when the exchange rate changes.

loss of domestic currency to which there corresponds an incipient increase in the money stock. In order to then keep the money supply constant the authorities sell securities in the open market at a rate equal to the deficit on current account _times_ the free rate premium. Hence, the determinants of the time constraint on quasi-equilibrium in a dual rate system _with_ interventions are: (1) the current account imbalance, (2) the free rate premium, (3) the stock of public securities held by the central bank, and (4) the private sector's portfolio of government securities.

Conclusions can now by stated. First, the stock of foreign exchange reserves is of no consequence in the dual rate system _with_ interventions which on this account has the edge over the other two systems. Second, the only remaining determinant of the time constraint which differs between the three systems is the required rate of neutralization which is (1) largest for the unified fixed rate system, (2) smaller for dual rates _without_ interventions, and (3) smallest for dual rates _with_ interventions. The reason is straightforward. Suppose that, given an initial equilibrium with balance in international payments, e.g. _point c_ in _figure 1, 3 and 4_, the money supply is increased. In the unified fixed rate system a deficit results on both the current and the capital account. In the dual rate system _without_ interventions only the current account moves into deficit (the same as above). Finally, in the dual rate system _with_ interventions the rate of neutralization equals the current account deficit (the same as above) _times_ the _free rate premium_.[14)]

14) E.g. if in the new quasi-equilibrium the free rate premium is ten percent, the required rate of open market sales equals only one tenth of what it would be in the dual rate system _without_ interventions.

II.1. Economic Policy under each Exchange Rate System

The analysis of section I.3 will now be reversed: given the actual state of the economy, how does economic policy have to be manipulated in order to attain certain targets?

In all four figures we start in point a. The current account is in deficit while the capital account balances at a free rate equal to the parity in the two dual rate systems. Internal balance attains and the flow of gross private investments optimizes the rate of growth. It is required to get into external balance while it is desired that the other two targets continue to be attained. Given this situation, what happens when either (1) fiscal or (2) monetary policy is used? (3) Can a policy-mix attain not just external balance but also keep to one or both of the other targets? Under each of these scenarios, how are the floating rates and the current-capital account balance affected?

a) The unified fixed rate system. To keep the money supply constant in point a the monetary authorities continuously engage in open market purchases at a rate equal to the reserve losses.

(1) Expansionary fiscal policy would be called for to achieve external balance in point h in which there is, however, overfull employment, inflation, a less than optimal flow of investment, and a larger current account deficit than before.

(2) Alternatively, contractionary monetary policy would be required to reach point f. There is now unemployment, less than optimal investment, a smaller current account deficit than before, and surplus on capital account.

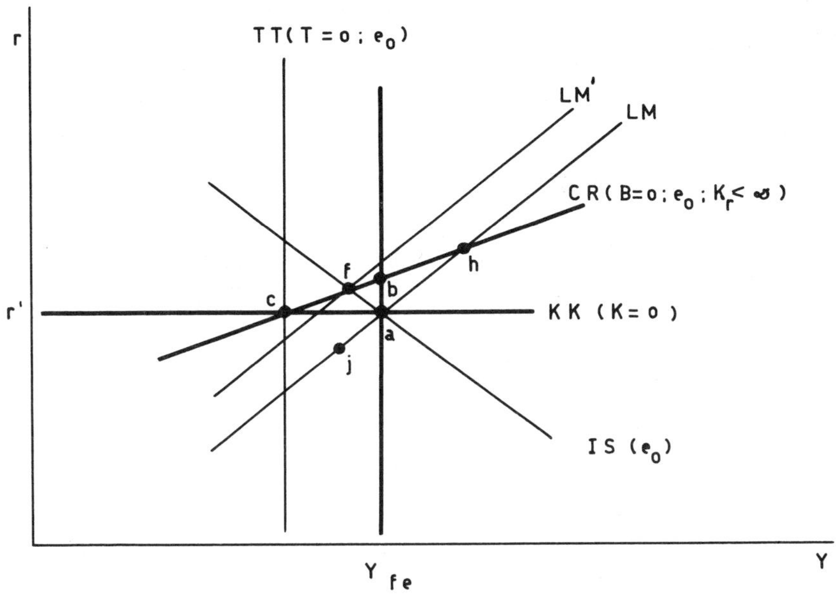

Figure 1: The unified fixed exchange rate system

In this and the following figures the fat lines represent policy targets in the case where monetary policy is orthodox.

(3) When both policy instruments are manipulated in the process of attaining external balance only one of the two other targets can remain fulfilled. Whether the one or the other is chosen, the money supply will have to be decreased while fiscal policy should be expansionary for internal balance (point b) and contractionary for optimal investments (point c). Note that in the former and the latter point absorption respectively exceeds and equals aggregate demand.

b) The unified floating rate system. Point a in figure 2 does not represent an equilibrium because the exchange rates tends to depreciate due to the payments deficit. Equilibrium would finally attain in a point like g (somewhere on the LM-line between a and h). Employment is now overfull, investments suboptimal, and the capital account in a net surplus matched by the deficit on current account. The central problem now becomes: from g onwards get into internal balance with optimal growth.

(1) Contractionary fiscal policy can make for the attainment of both internal balance and optimal growth in point a.[15] The exchange rate then depreciates.

(2) Restrictionary monetary policy can provide for internal balance but growth may then become more suboptimal than in point g. The resulting equilibrium point lies on the internal balance line between a and d, say in point b. The exchange rate will then appreciate. Depending on whether the rate of interest in b is higher or lower than in g, absorption has respectively increased

15) That one instrument can cater to two policy targets in this case is purely accidental because point a happens to be on the LM-line.

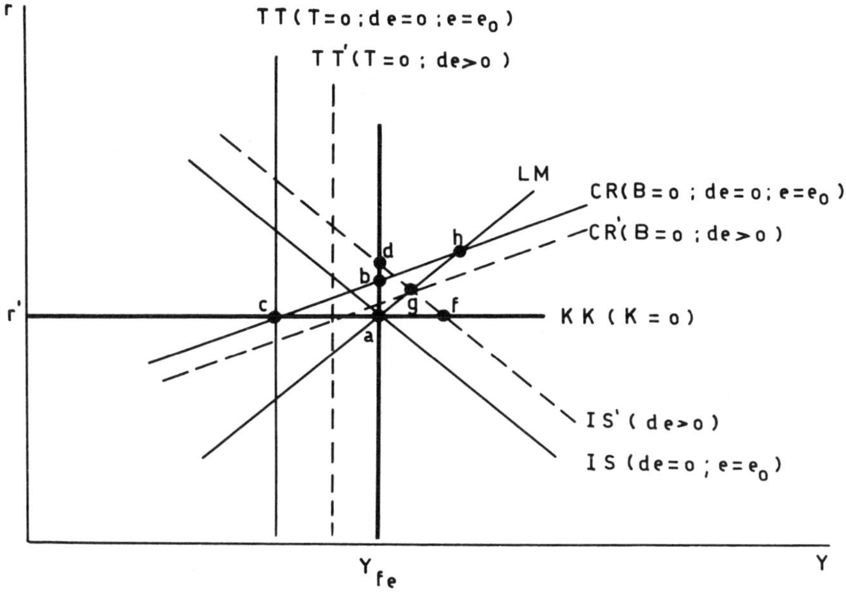

Figure 2: The unified floating exchange rate system

or decreased. Alternatively, optimal growth can be attained by increasing the money supply but at the cost of more overfull employment. The exchange rate than depreciates. The resulting equilibrium point lies somewhere on the KK-line to the right of point f. Thus the capital account balances, as does the current account.

(3) Starting from g the instrument mix to attain the two targets is a constant money supply and contractionary fiscal policy. This coincides with the policy prescription under (1) above. In general though two instruments are required to attain two policy targets.

c) The dual rate system without interventions. Point a in figure 3 stands for the initial equilibrium situation: internal balance, optimal growth, a current account deficit, and a capital account which balances at a free rate equal to the fixed one. To keep equilibrium in point a the authorities have to engage in open market purchases.

(1) External balance - that is, balance on current account - can be attained in point h by contractionary fiscal policy. The rate of interest decreases and the free rate depreciates. There is now unemployment and more than optimal growth.

(2) Contractionary monetary policy can make for current account balance in point f. The rate of interest increases. Thus, the free rate appreciates. But there is unemployment and suboptimal growth.

(3) A combination of deflationary fiscal and monetary policy yields external balance. The free rate has remained constant.

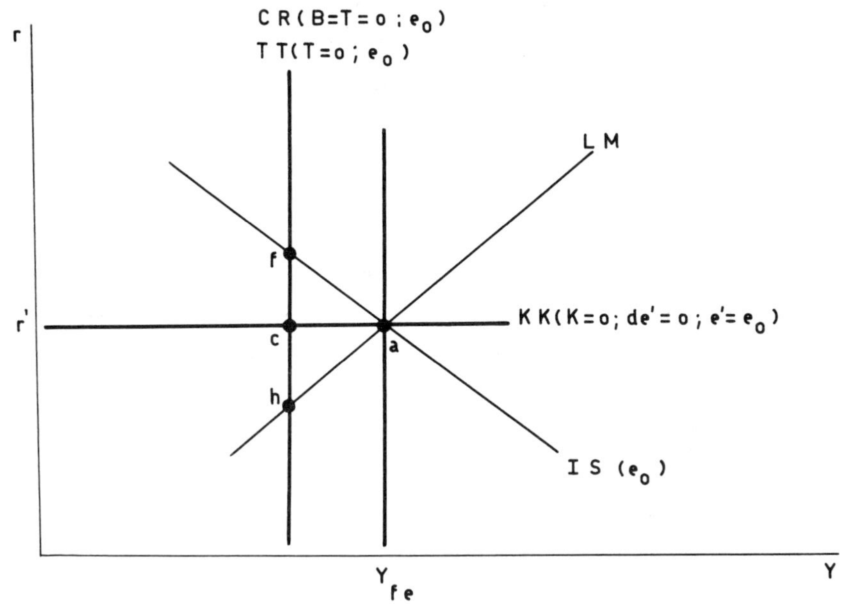

Figure 3: The two-tier system without interventions

With classical monetary policy, equilibria are confined to the reference TT-line, unless the parity is altered, because external balance ceases to be a policy concern.

While optimal growth is retained in point c, there is now unemployment.

d) The dual rate system with intervention. Again, point a in figure 4 represents the initial equilibrium, in which the current account is in deficit but with the free rate now depreciated with respect to the fixed one. By definition there occur however, like in the unified floating rate system, no changes in reserves because the foreign exchange lost, due to current account deficits, is officially repurchased on the free market. As a result the free rate depreciates. The domestic currency equivalent of these official purchases consists of borrowings by the considered country. Because the lost reserves are regained at a higher domestic price (the free rate premium) than the one at which they were lost (the parity), the authorities loose in terms of domestic currency. As a result the money supply tends to increase. This tendency, however, is counteracted by open market sales which at the same time finance the losses which the authorities incurred by operating on the free market. Since point a already implies triple goal achievement, consider as the initial equilibrium point b where there is unemployment and more than optimal growth. The current account deficit has now become smaller while the free rate premium has increased because the interest rate has been lowered.

(1) By increasing government expenditures, either internal balance (point d) or optimal growth (point j) can be attained. In both cases the current account deficit increases while the free rate premium decreases.

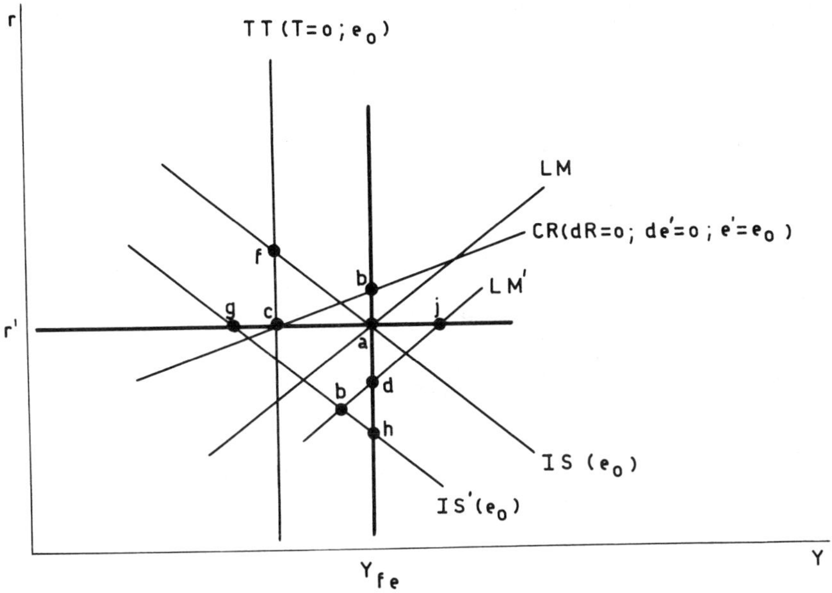

Figure 4: The two-tier system with interventions

In the absence of neutralization of the monetary effects of the balance of payments, monetary policy is inoperative because its effects are explosive, while fiscal policy cannot affect income. Thus, as with the former two-tier system, equilibria are constrained to lie on the reference TT-line.

(2) Open market sales can provide for optimal growth (point g) but open market purchases are required for internal balance (point h).

(3) A mix of deflationary monetary policy and expansionary fiscal policy can yield both internal balance and optimal growth (point a).

2. Economic Policy Compared between the Four Systems

We will now compare the feasible choices of target fulfilment between the various exchange rate systems. In the unified floating and dual rate system with interventions external balance ceases to be a policy target because the exchange rate respectively is, or is made to be, such that the foreign exchange market clears while reserves remain constant. Both internal balance and optimal growth can then always be attained by an appropriate instrument mix. However, in the unified fixed and dual rate system without interventions there are three policy targets. In a unified fixed system any two of these three can be attained by an adequate instrument mix. But, in the dual rate system without interventions, internal and external balance are incompatible[16), barring their fortuitous coincidence. In the absence of such coincidence, only two, but not any two, of the three targets can be reached by an appropriate instrument mix: optimal growth can either be combined with internal balance (point a) or with external balance (point c).

All of this follows from the economic policy rule formulated by

16) Unless the current account happens to be interest-elastic.

Meade and Tinbergen: in order to attain a number of targets (a) there have in general to be at least as many independent instruments as independent targets[17)] and (b) each of the instruments should affect at least one and a different target, in which case the instruments are said to be effective.

III.1. Monetary Policy Defined as a Change in the Domestic Assets of the Central Bank

For this classical[18)] definition of monetary policy, equilibrium will only be attained when the net balance of payments flows is zero. Indeed, as long as there are variations in reserves in

---

17) In figure 3 external and internal balance are not independent because for any change in policy the GNP and the current account change in constant proportion to each other. Internal and external balance are in fact incompatible for all instrument mixes. If alternatively the external balance line in figure 3 were to coincide with the full employment line, the two targets, while dependent, would be compatible for an infinity of instrument mixes, one of which can in addition yield optimal growth.
The "in general" means that the exceptions to the rule can be due either to the particular configuration of values for the independent targets or to the particular character of the initial equilibrium. E.g. if in figure 1 the external balance line were to intersect both the internal balance and the optimal growth line in a same point, there exists a two instrument mix to attain the three targets. On the other hand, given e.g. the initial equilibrium point j in figure 1, the manipulation of only fiscal policy would be required to reach both internal balance and optimal growth in point a.
Finally, the meaning of "at least" is that there is a choice of instrument mixes, and not just one, to attain the targets if there are more independent and effective instruments than independent targets.

18) The terms "classical" and "Keynesian" (in the next section) are taken from Tsiang (1969).

terms of domestic currency, the money supply keeps changing. The reason is that a constant monetary policy now means that the domestic assets of the central bank, and not the money supply, remain constant. Thus, an automatic mechanism for balance of payments adjustment is at work.

In the unified fixed and two-tier system without interventions monetary policy becomes powerless because it cannot affect, more than temporarily, income, the rate of interest, or the balance of payments, whatever the degree of capital mobility. Indeed, an increase in the central bank's stock of domestic assets ultimately results merely in a decrease of the same magnitude in the country's reserves such as finally to leave the money supply unaffected. Thus, classical monetary policy only alters the composition of the money base and not its aggregate.

Alternatively, under the two-tier system with interventions, monetary policy yields explosive income effects. The explanation is as follows. Assume an initial equilibrium with the free rate equal to the parity, and a current account in balance, as with point c in figure 4. The money supply is increased. So, the resulting decrease in the interest rate makes for a free rate premium. Thus, the official interventions on the free market, in order to counter the effects on reserves of a current account deficit, result in losses. As a result the money supply increases further. This then reinforces the tendency of the rate of interest to fall, and of income to increase, Consequently, the free rate depreciates further, while income keeps increasing: the system does not converge to a new equilibrium.

On the other hand, with classical monetary policy, fiscal manipulation cannot affect income under both two-tier systems, while under unified fixed rates the income effect of fiscal policy is larger than with orthodox monetary policy.

From section I.3 and from the above analysis the crucial policy implications of the two-tier systems emerge. These can best be stated with reference to the unified pegged rate system. In a fixed exchange rate system with capital mobility, monetary policy cannot affect income while fiscal policy can. This is by now an old piece of knowledge, although the latter conclusion implies an automatic adjustment mechanism for the balance of payments. By contrast, so it has been argued[19)], in a two-tier system with or without interventions both fiscal and monetary policy can effect income. Nevertheless, this conclusion is crucially dependent on the neutralization of the monetary effects of (1) the balance of payments in a dual system without interventions, and of (2) the authorities' profits or losses registered in the process of their double intervention in a dual system with interventions.[20)]

How is the formulation and the solution of our policy problem affected? External balance ceases to be a policy target and the money supply becomes an automatic or passive instrument geared to balance of payments equilibrium. We are then left with two policy targets (internal balance and optimal growth) and one

19) Barattieri and Ragazzi (1971), part III, and Decaluwe (1974), section VI.
20) Though with interventions the burden of neutralization is smaller than without interventions as has been argued in section I.4.

discretionary policy instrument (fiscal policy). The locus of full-equilibrium points which constitute the only possible equilibrium situations thus coincides with the CR-line in the unified fixed rate system, and with the reference TT-line in both dual rate systems. Note that in the dual rate system with interventions the relevant concept of external balance is now confined to situations with balance in the current account. In the figures 1, 3 and 4 the point a, which earlier characterized the initial situation, ceases to represent an equilibrium. The money supply keeps automatically decreasing, such that LM moves to LM', until point f is reached with unemployment and less than optimal growth.

Compared to orthodox monetary policy the choice of attainable targets has been narrowed. In the unified fixed rate system fiscal policy can either yield internal balance (point b) or optimal growth (point c). And, in the two dual rate systems only optimal growth can be attained by fiscal policy (point c). A second implication of classical monetary policy is that the speed of adjustment from one equilibrium point to another differs between the three exchange rate systems. With orthodox monetary policy these speeds of adjustment were identical for all three systems.

Although monetary policy is powerless in affecting the equilibrium situation, it can, in conjunction with fiscal policy, still play a role with regard to the speed of adjustment and the change in reserves during the adjustment period.

Take the case of unified fixed exchange rates. Given the equilibrium point f the attainment of c requires a decrease in the budget deficit. This causes lagged decreases in the money supply through the resulting balance of payments deficits during adjustment. (It is assumed that adjustment proceeds along a leftwards moving LM-line.) In point c the decrease in the money supply equals the accumulated balance of payments deficit flows during adjustment. Alternatively, assume that at the time deflationary fiscal policy is applied, the monetary authorities engage in open market sales. The dependence of decreases in the money supply on payments deficits would then be somewhat (totally) short-circuited because less (no) reserves would have been lost in the process. (Adjustment would then proceed along a path in r-Y space closer to (or on) the CR-line.) Also, adjustment to c would be speedier.

Both with a constant monetary policy and an active one (the same amount of open market sales as above), adjustment to a new full-equilibrium takes longer in the two dual rate systems than in the unified fixed rate system. And, again either with an active or passive attitude by the monetary authorities, it takes longer for adjustment to proceed from f to c with interventions than without interventions. Why? Deflationary fiscal policy causes the money supply to increase. But, in the former dual system, this results from the temporary surpluses in the current account valued at the discount of the free rate, while in the latter system, from current account surpluses of the same size now valued at the fixed parity. Note that this ranking of exchange rate systems with respect to the length of the adjustment period is the reverse of their ranking according to the required rate of neutralization in quasi-equilibrium.

2. Monetary Policy Defined as a Change in the Rate of Interest

This is the case of Keynesian monetary policy[21]. The money market equilibrium condition becomes a mere accounting identity because, at the ruling rate of interest, the desired demand for money is automatically and continuously accommodated by changes in the money stock. Thus, the money supply behaviour of the authorities (and the LM-line) is perfectly interest rate elastic. Unless the budget deficit happens to be compatible with external balance at the chosen level of interest, quasi-equilibria are involved. Hence, the possibility for letting the money supply vary with reserve changes does by definition not arise.

What are the effects of fiscal and monetary policy? First consider expansionary fiscal policy. Under all but the unified floating rate system the income effects are identical and larger than for both orthodox and classical monetary policy because there is no monetary feedback effect. Under unified floating rates this already larger income effect is reinforced by the depreciation. Which are the foreign sector effects when the multiplier process has come to an end? In the unified fixed exchange rate system the current account worsens while the net balance on capital account remains constant: the balance of payments thus deteriorates. In the unified floating rate system the capital account remains unaltered while the increase in income and the depreciation result in

21) This is monetary policy as defined by Meade (1951). Monetary policy would also be constrained to one interest rate level (1) if the demand for money were perfectly interest rate elastic in all exchange rate systems, or (2) if the net capital flow were infinitely interest rate elastic under unified fixed and floating rates.

equal increases in imports and exports such as to leave the net current account unaltered. In both dual rate systems the current account deteriorates with the same amount as in the unified fixed rate system. In the two-tier system *without* interventions the free exchange rate remains put. On the other hand, in the two-tier system *with* interventions the free rate depreciates due to the authorities' increased demand for free foreign exchange to re-stock their reserves.

Likewise, for deflationary Keynesian monetary policy equal to the impact effect on the rate of interest of deflationary orthodox or classical monetary policy under all but the unified floating rate system, income will ultimately decrease with more than under either orthodox or classical tighter monetary policy. Again, the reason is that by definition there is no monetary feedback effect. Under unified floating rates this income decrease is reinforced by appreciation. Finally, the foreign sector effects can be derived as above.

The generalization in *section II* of the solution to the policy problem is in no way affected.

Summary

The policy characteristics of four exchange rate systems are compared under orthodox, classical, and Keynesian monetary policy, and with capital mobility high but less than perfect. The four exchange rate regimes are: dual rates *without* and *with* official interventions on the free market (in order to keep foreign exchange reserves constant), and, unified fixed and unitary floating rates.

In the still scant literature on the two-tier system without interventions, the conclusion has been reached that both fiscal and monetary policy can affect income. This result nonetheless implies orthodox monetary policy. If on the other hand monetary policy is defined as classical, neither fiscal nor monetary policy can exert leverage on income.

Alternatively, under the two-tier system with interventions, orthodox monetary policy has the same effect on income as under unified fixed and two-tier rates without interventions, while for classical monetary policy income effects are explosive. For fiscal policy coupled with constant orthodox monetary policy the income effect is the same as under unitary fixed and two-tier rates without interventions. But, for fiscal policy with constant classical monetary policy there is, as under the two-tier system without interventions, no income effect, unlike for unified fixed rates where the effect on GNP is larger than under constant orthodox monetary policy.

The crucial implication is that, under both two-tier systems, monetary policy becomes more independent from the external constraint in the sense that for orthodox monetary policy the burden and the feasibility of neutralizing the effects of the balance of payments on the money supply, is respectively smaller and larger than under unitary fixed rates.

Like under unified floating rates, external balance in the dual rate system with interventions is automatically attained. Thus, with orthodox monetary policy, the two discretionary instruments can be reserved for the attainment of internal balance and optimal growth of productive capacity in the latter two systems, unlike under unified fixed and dual rates without interventions where external balance is a policy target.

With classical monetary policy, which by assumption applies to all but the unified floating rate system, external balance ceases to be a policy concern. Or, what amounts to the same, monetary policy becomes both powerless and passive. The possible equilibrium situations then always imply external balance in the unified fixed rate system, and an equilibrating current account in both two-tier systems. Thus, under the two-tier systems, fiscal policy can only cater to optimal growth, and not to internal balance, unless external balance coincides with full employment.

REFERENCES

Argy, V. and Porter, M. G., (1972), "The Forward Exchange Market and the Effects of Domestic and External Disturbances under Alternative Exchange Rate Systems", IMF Staff Papers, Nov.

Baguley, R. W., (1971), "The Effectiveness of Monetary and Fiscal Policies under Pegged and Floating Exchange-Rate Systems", Appendix A in: R. E. Caves and G. L. Reuber, Capital Transfers and Economic Policy - Canada 1951-1962, Harvard University Press.

Barattieri, V. and Ragazzi, G., (1971), "An Analysis of the Two-Tier Foreign Exchange Market", Banca Nazionale del Lavoro Quarterly Review, Dec.

Boll, F., (1975), "Two-Tier Exchange Markets and Other Systems: Comments", Tijdschrift voor Economie en Management, nr. 2.

Carlson, K. M., (1974), "Monetary and Fiscal Actions in Macroeconomic Models", Federal Reserve Bank of St. Louis Review, Jan.

Decaluwe, B., (1974), "Two-Tier Exchange Markets and Other Systems", Tijdschrift voor Economie, nr. 1.

Fleming, J. M., (1962), "Domestic Financial Policies under Fixed and under Floating Exchange Rates", IMF Staff Papers, Nov.

Fleming, J. M., (1968), "Dual Exchange Rates for Current and Capital Transactions: A Theoretical Examination", chapter 12 in Essays in International Economics, Allen and Unwin, 1971.

Johnson, H. G., (1966), "Some Aspects of the Theory of Economic Policy in a World of Capital Mobility", in T. Bagiotti (ed.), Essays in Honour of Marco Fanno, Cedam.

Meade, J. E., (1951), The Balance of Payments, Oxford University Press.

Mundell, R. A., (1963), "Capital Mobility and Stabilization Policy under Fixed and Flexible Exchange Rates".

Canadian Journal of Economics and Political Science, Nov.

Sohmen, E., (1969), Flexible Exchange Rates, The University of Chicago Press, ch. V.

Stern, R. M., (1973), The Balance of Payments, Aldine, ch. 8.

Swoboda, A. K., (1972a), "Equilibrium, Quasi-Equilibrium and Macroeconomic Policy under Fixed Exchange Rates", The Quarterly Journal of Economics, Feb.

Swoboda, A. K., (1972b), "On Limited Information and the Assignment Problem", in E. Claassen and P. Salin (eds.), Stabilization Policies in Interdependent Economies, North-Holland.

Swoboda, A. K, (1973), "Monetary Policy under Fixed Exchange Rates: Effectiveness, the Speed of Adjustment and Proper Use", Economica, May.

Tinbergen, J., (1952), On the Theory of Economic Policy, North-Holland.

Tsiang, S. C., (1961), "The Role of Money in Trade-Balance Stability: Synthesis of the Elasticity and Absorption Approaches", American Economic Review, Dec.

THE BELGIAN DUAL EXCHANGE MARKET SYSTEM: AN INEQUITABLE AND INEFFECTIVE SYSTEM

By Paul De Grauwe

Decaluwe and Steinherr have written an interesting paper on the workings of the dual exchange market in Belgium. In a first part they skillfully combine institutional and theoretical knowledge to give the reader important insights into the working of the system of dual exchange markets. In a second part they present a Kouri-and-Porter type model of the balance of payments applied to Belgium. The model yields reasonably good estimates.

Instead of running down a list of points this comment concentrates on the central problem associated with dual exchange markets, i.e. its usefulness, first in discouraging speculative capital movements and second in enabling the monetary authorities to control the domestic money supply more closely than in a system of a unified fixed exchange rate. Although they add strong qualifications, Decaluwe and Steinherr conclude that on both counts the dual exchange market in Belgium has been useful. In this com-

Comments on the paper by Decaluwe and Steinherr, "The Two-Tier Exchange Market in Belgium"

ment it is argued that the evidence provided by Decaluwe and Steinherr does not warrant this optimistic conclusion.

1. The Dual Exchange Market as an Inhibitor of Short-Term Capital Movements

The idea that the dual exchange market could be an instrument in controlling short-term ("disruptive") capital movements has been an important argument used by the proponents of this ystem[1]. Decaluwe and Steinherr provide evidence to completely discount this argument when applied to the period after 1971, i.e. to the period with the largest speculative capital movements. They show that when speculative movements grow large the premium (discount) of the financial rate necessary to discourage speculative capital flows would be high enough to attract widespread arbitrage between the official and financial market and to induce further speculative behavior through leads and lags in current transactions.

What about the period before 1971? Proponents of the system usually prefer to concentrate on the pre-1971 experience when justifying to two-tier exchange market. Decaluwe and Steinherr provide evidence that before 1971 the existence of the dual market in Belgium did discourage capital outflows. They interprete this "success" as being due to the relatively small scale of the capital flows and, to the fact that current account and capital account moved in opposite directions. The former was usually in

1) See Fleming for a recent statement of this view: J. Fleming, Dual Exchange Markets and Other Remedies for Disruptive Capital Flows, Staff Papers, March 1974.

surplus the latter in deficit. This situation, in effect, put minimal pressure on the system and guaranteed its "success". All this leads to the conclusion that the dual exchange market system is most effective when it is least needed. In addition, it is obvious that the pre-1971 situation (offsetting current and capital accounts) could have been dealt with as effectively in a unified exchange rate system. In fact, it can be argued (and it is argued below) that a unified exchange rate system would have been better both from the point of view of equity and from the point of view of balance of payments equilibrium.

The pre-1971 dual exchange market system was essentially a system aimed at taxing and thereby discouraging capital outflows. This leads to two important questions. First, where did the proceeds of the tax go? Second, was this tax necessary to equilibrate the balance of payments?

Although empirical evidence on the first question is difficult to arrive at it is possible to show that a substantial part of the tax proceeds went to those persons who were able to arbitrage (legally or illegally) between the official and the financial markets. From a-priori reasoning it is obvious that this had to happen. As capital outflows increase the discount of the financial rate vis-à-vis the official rate they also increase the opportunities for arbitrage between the official and financial market. A-priori, there is also no reason to believe that the size of these arbitrage funds would be any smaller than the speculative capital flows which the authorities want to discourage. After all speculators and "arbitrageurs" are usually the same people with the same profit motives and the same access to information. The paradox, of the dual exchange market system, therefore, is that the tax aimed at discouraging capital flows encourages legal and illegal arbitrage between the two exchange markets and that a large part (if not all) of the tax proceeds is channeled to the successful "arbitrageurs" in the form of windfall profits of the latter[2].

The evidence on the size of arbitrage funds between the official and financial markets tends to support these conclusions. Table 1 presents the changes in the official exchange position of the com-

TABLE 1

Order of magnitude of arbitrage and capital flows (billion francs)

Change in official exchange position of commercial banks		Net private capital flows			
1968 IV	5.9	68 IV	-1.5	71 III	0.5
1969 I	4.7	69 I	-5.1	71 IV	-7.0
1969 II	-8.2	69 II	4.8	72 I	-9.9
1969 III	-2.2	69 III	0.7	72 II	-4.8

Sources: National Bank of Belgium and Belgian-Luxembourg Institute of Exchange

2) It is often argued that it is sufficient to completely separate the two markets to eliminate this paradox. Which is true, of course. The point however is that if one can separate the two markets one can also have a complete control over capital movements. Both are as difficult (or as easy) to achieve. The dual exchange market then becomes redundant, and the same result can be achieved by the second kind of control.

mercial banks during 1968-69. (These changes largely reflected arbitrage operations of banks.) These are compared with the net capital flows during periods of strong speculative movements. The comparison reveals that the order of magnitude of arbitrage funds by banks alone in 1968-69 was not very different from the order of magnitude of the capital flows in high speculation years.[3)]

The second question raised about the pre-1971 period, i.e. whether the tax on capital outflows was necessary to equilibrate the balance of payments, leads to the following observations. In a unified exchange rate system a current account surplus leads to monetary expansion and thus, induces capital outflows. The latter have to be regarded as equilibrating. As Kouri and Porter have found for several industrialized countries this equilibrating mechanism is a significant phenomenon in fixed exchange rate regimes.[4)] In a dual exchange market system this equilibrating mechanism is aborted. The current account surplus cannot be offset by equilibrating capital outflows.

This is precisely what happened in the pre-1971 period in Belgium. Current account surpluses were left to accumulate but potentially equilibrating capital outflows were discouraged.[5)]

---

3) The loophole existing before 1969 which allowed banks to hold balances in the two exchange markets in unlimited amounts has been partly closed. However, other loopholes still exist. After 1971 the official and free rate have moved very closely together so that the scope for arbitrage was reduced correspondingly.

4) Kouri and Porter, International Capital Flows and Portfolio Equilibrium, Journal of Political Economy, May/June 1974.

As an observer of this period one is left with the definite impression that the dual exchange market system in Belgium was nothing but a mercantilistic device. Its essential purpose was the accumulation of international reserves.

2. Dual Exchange Markets and Monetary Independence

A second argument used to justify the existence of a dual exchange market in Belgium is that it has allowed the Belgian monetary authorities to follow a more independent monetary policy than in the absence of dual exchange markets. Decaluwe and Steinherr share this opinion and present some evidence to support this view. This evidence consists in estimating the "offset coefficient" for Belgium, i.e. the average leakage per unit of monetary expansion (or contraction) in Belgium. Finding a value of 0.57 for the period 1960-71, they conclude that this relatively small offset coefficient enables the "monetary authorities in Belgium . . .. to enjoy a relatively high degree of control over the domestic money supply". They then go on to say that "since estimates for other small, open economies indicate a much lower autonomy, this result could be due to the split of the exchange market into two compartments". Unfortunately they do not provide an example of such other small open economy.

In the remainder of this note the proposition that the dual ex-

5) Of course, as Decaluwe and Steinherr point out, the monetary authorities did intervene occasionally. In doing so, however, they simulated conditions that would have prevailed in a unified fixed exchange rate system. By selling in the financial market foreign exchange obtained in the official market they reduced the tax on capital outflows and thereby allowed some outflows to occur.

change market in Belgium has allowed some additional monetary independence is tested and refuted. One way to test this proposition is to compare Belgium to another country with similar characteristics such as size and openness and which has not had a dual exchange market. The first country that comes to mind is the Netherlands.[6] If one finds that monetary conditions in Belgium were typically less dependent on monetary conditions in the rest of the world than in the Netherlands there is a presumption that this lower dependence of Belgium is due to the existence of the dual exchange market.

A first test is to compare the "offset" coefficients. As mentioned before, Decaluwe and Steinherr estimate this coefficient for Belgium at 0.57 (sample period is 1960-71). On the other hand, Kouri and Porter have estimated an analogous offset coefficient for the Netherlands at 0.59 (sample period 1960-70).[7] Both use

6) The Netherlands has operated a mini-dual exchange market from Sept. 1971 to Feb. 1974. During that period nonresidents wishing to buy or sell bonds denominated in guilders had to obtain or sell guilders in the so-called O-guilder market where the rate was left free. Obviously this O-guilder market was much smaller than the Belgian financial exchange market. In addition, the Dutch system was not in use during most of the sampling period to be used in the test.

7) Kouri and Porter, <u>op. cit.</u>, p. 456. The coefficient estimated by Kouri an Porter relates to the leakage through the capital account, whereas the coefficient estimated by Decaluwe and Steinherr relates to leakages through the balance of payments. However, given the fact that quarterly data are used and that the offset coefficient measures the impact effect in the same quarter, it is unlikely that the offset coefficient measures anything but the offsets through the capital account. In order for monetary policy to affect the trade balance, prices and/or income have to be affected. This transmission mechanism certainly takes more time than one quarter.

quarterly data. The results are surprisingly similar. This indicates that if the offset coefficient is used as an indicator of the ability of national monetary authorities to control the domestic money base, one has to conclude that in Belgium and in the Netherlands the degree of domestic control was strikingly similar despite the existence of the dual exchange market in Belgium.

It can reasonably be argued, however, that estimating an offset coefficient in the fashion of Kouri and Porter (and Decaluwe and Steinherr) provides insufficient information about the potential of domestic monetary control which national authorities can attain. In particular, it can be argued that the offset coefficient overestimates the potential for domestic control of monetary aggregates, because it fails to capture the interdependence between different countries. To give an example, suppose Belgium expands its domestic base money by $ 100 million. The offset coefficient then predicts that $ 57 million will flow out of the country in the same quarter. As a result if Belgium wants to attain a target increase of the monetary base of $ 100 million it will have to increase the domestic component by $ 233 million (which also will lead to a loss of reserves of $ 133 million). This scenario, however, assumes no change in the rest of the world. Suppose now, things do not remain constant in the rest of the world and assume e. g. the rest of the world follows a contractionary monetary policy. In that case the leakage from Belgium will increase and the Belgian monetary authorities will need to expand the domestic component of the monetary base by a multiple of $ 233 million to attain the same $ 100 million target increase. (Belgium will also lose a multiple of $ 133 million in international reserves.) Of course, the opposite can happen too. If the rest of the world expands simultaneously with Belgium, the latter will experience less or even no offsetting leakage. The conclusion, however, is that the crucial variable is the rest of the world. If monetary disturbances in the rest of the world are large and frequent Belgium (and for that matter the Netherlands) will have to introduce large and frequent changes in its domestic component of the monetary base to offset those disturbances and will have to be willing (and able) to sustain these policy changes by large and frequent variations in its international reserve stock.

A second, and more fruitful, test of how Belgium and the Netherlands differ (or do not differ) with respect to the issue of national monetary independence is to compare domestic interest rates in both countries with a proxy of the world interest rate. The obvious candidate proxy is the Eurodollar interest rate. In figures 1 and 2 these interest rates are graphed on a monthly basis. For Belgium the interest rate on the 4-month Rentenfonds (Fonds des Rentes) Certificate was selected; for the Netherlands the 3-month municipal loan rate and for the Eurodollar market the prime bank's bid rate for 3-month deposits in London. It is immediately evident that the three interest rates move closely together.

In order to test for differences in the pattern of movements between the Belgian and the Dutch rate in relation to the Eurodollar rate several statistics were computed. These are presented in Table 2. The sample period 1966-75 (March) is divided into two subperiods mainly to find out whether the pre-1971 period exhibited a different pattern of behavior.

Figure 1: Short-term Interest Rates in Belgium and in the Eurodollar market

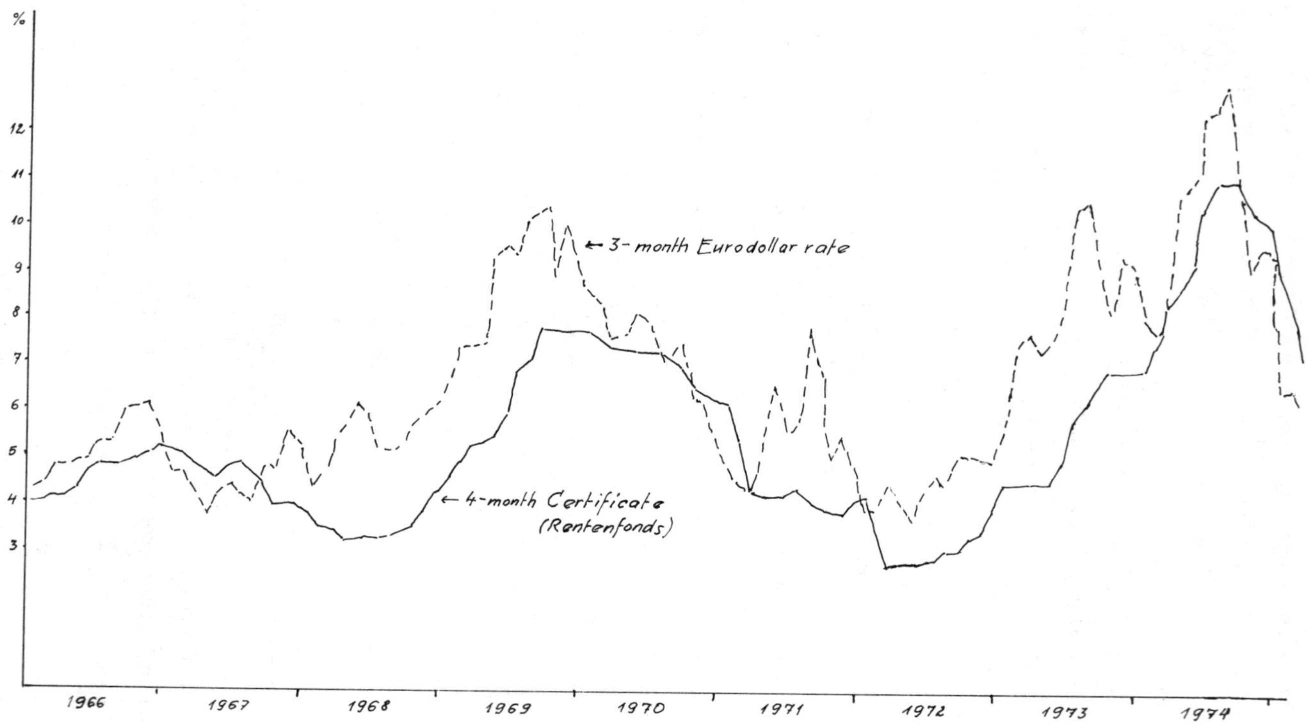

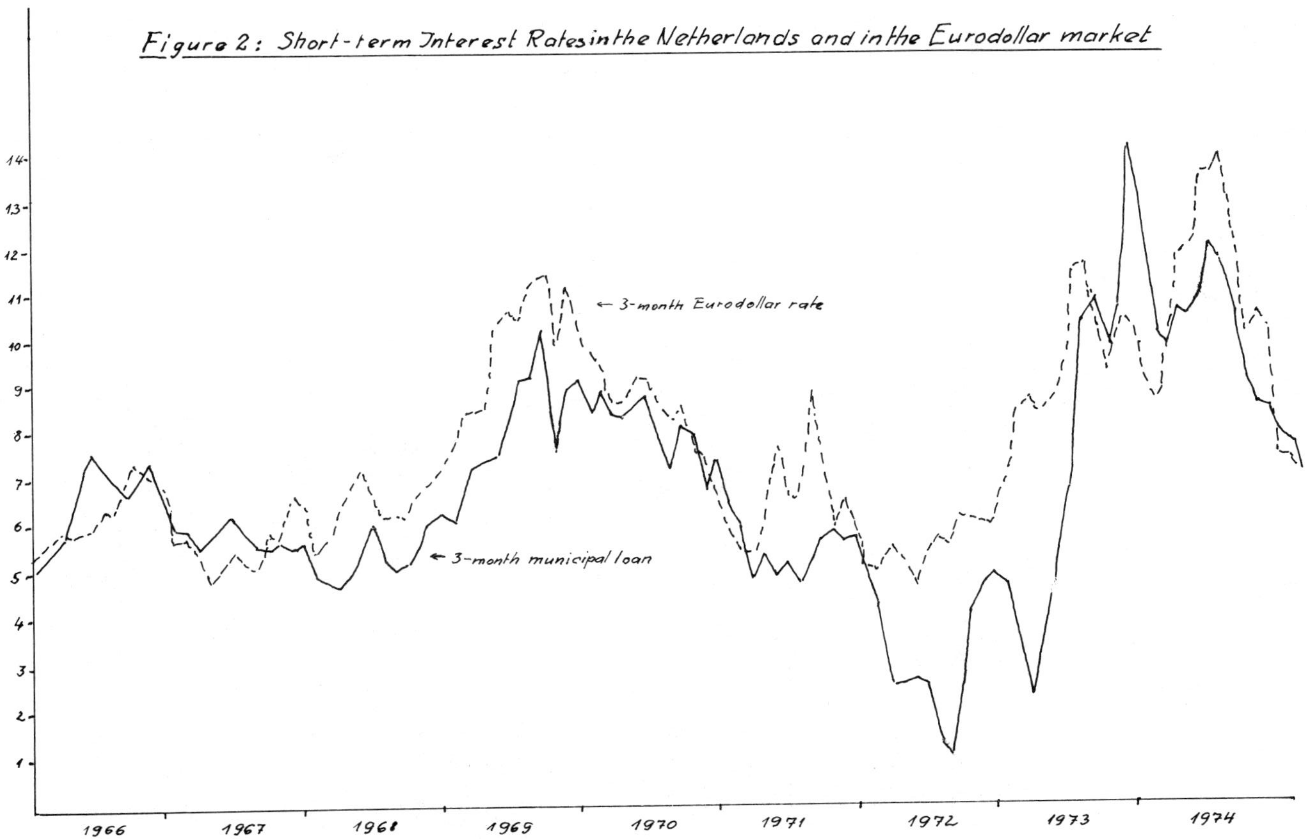

Figure 2: Short-term Interest Rates in the Netherlands and in the Eurodollar market

The correlation coefficients and Theil's inequality coefficients[8]) clearly indicate that on the average during the period from 1966 to March 1975, monthly covariations between the Belgian and the Eurodollar rate, and between the Dutch and the Eurodollar rate were not significantly different. The same conclusion holds for

TABLE 2

Correlation and Inequality Coefficients of the Belgian and Dutch short term interest rates with the Eurodollar rate. Monthly data.

Sample period	1966-75 (March)		1966-70		1971-75 (March)	
	Belgium	Neth.	Belgium	Neth.	Belgium	Neth.
Correlation coefficient	0.81	0.77	0.78	0.85	0.84	0.81
Theil's inequality coefficient	0.12	0.13	0.11	0.08	0.12	0.16
Percentage of Theil's inequality coefficient explained by						
a) difference in mean	42	29	46	28	40	36
b) difference in standard deviation	1	1	4	12	0	12
c) imperfect covariation	57	70	50	59	60	52

Source: Morgan Guarantee Trust, World Financial Statistics

---

8) See Theil, Economic Forecasts and Policy, p. 31. A low value of Theil's inequality coefficient indicates a high degree of equality. The coefficient can vary between 0 and 1.

the two subperiods 1966-70 and 1971-75 (March)[9]. Since it is reasonable to assume that the causality relation goes from the Eurodollar rate to the respective national interest rates this result supports the proposition that Belgium, despite its dual exchange market system, has not been able to maintain a higher degree of monetary independence than the Netherlands.

A further test is to decompose Theil's inequality coefficient. This decomposition allows to explain the inequality between pairs of time series in terms of differences in the mean, differences in the standard deviation, and in terms of covariation. The results of this decomposition are presented in the lower half of Table 2. These indicate that some slight differences do occur in the sources of inequality between the Eurodollar rate and the Belgian and Dutch interest rates respectively. During the period 1966-75 (March) differences in mean explain more of the total inequality in the case of Belgium than in the case of the Netherlands. On the other hand, a lower correlation explains more of the total inequality in the case of the Netherlands than in the case of Belgium. These results suggest that if there was any difference between Belgium and the Netherlands it is that the mean Belgian interest rate deviated more than the mean Dutch rate from the mean Eurodollar rate, but that the Belgian interest rate tended to move more often than the Dutch rate in the same direction as the Eurodollar rate. This suggests that the nature (not the degree) of

9) As can be seen from Table 2 some slight differences do occur. For instance for the whole period the Belgian rate correlates better with the Eurodollar rate than the Dutch rate. The opposite is true for 1966-70. The differences, however, are so low as to be insignificant.

monetary dependence of Belgium and the Netherlands vis-à-vis the rest of the world may be somewhat different. However, as the table indicates these differences are small. They almost disappear during the period 1971-75 (March). It is therefore not clear how much weight should be attached to these differences.

3. Conclusion

In concluding it is fair to say that, judging from the evidence of the last 10 years, the existence of the dual exchange market has not allowed the Belgian monetary authorities to achieve a higher degree of domestic monetary control than the Netherlands, which has lived without a dual exchange market system.

It has also been argued that the dual exchange market cannot cope with large scale speculative movements (a point which Decaluwe and Steinherr also stress). In addition, from the pre-1971 evidence, it has been deduced that the system is nothing but a mercantilist instrument aimed at accumulating international reserves. Finally, it was stressed that the system is particularly inequitable in that it channels the proceeds from the taxation of capital flows to the persons and institutions (mainly banks) who are able to arbitrage between the official and financial exchange market.

This leads us to the inevitable proposition: Since the dual exchange market has had no significant usefulness, and since the costs of its operation in terms of inefficiencies and inequities are blatant, it should be abolished and be replaced by a unified exchange rate system.

DISCRIMINATING BETWEEN ALTERNATIVE EXPLANATIONS OF INFLATION

By Malcolm Gray
Michael Parkin*

What causes inflation and how may it be cured? These are possibly the two most important questions on which economists continue to fail to reach agreement. What precisely is the disagreement about? Which disagreements are important in the sense that they lead to different policy prescriptions and which are mainly matters of scientific curiosity? What tests need to be performed in order to resolve the disagreements over policy? Which of those tests have been performed and what are their implications? Which tests remain to be carried out and what can be said about policy in the absence of results on those tests? These are the principal questions which we tackle in this paper. We have chosen to focus on disagreements which lead to different policy prescriptions for two reasons. First, they are presumably the important ones and secondly, they are disagreements which, in principle, and given enough data, can in practice be settled by normal scientific methods. We are also interested, however, in disagreements about the consequences for variables other than the rate of inflation of pursuing particular policies. Of central im-

* This paper is part of the S.S.R.C.-University of Manchester Inflation Research Programme. We are grateful to David Laidler and George Zis for helpful discussions on this topic.

portance here is the effect on the unemployment rate of alternative policies for reducing inflation.

Whilst there are many different answers on offer to the basic question "what causes inflation?" the policy prescriptions generated by those answers fall into two broad groups. First, there are those who advocate the pursuit of a monetary rule in the form of a constant rate of expansion of the stock of nominal money balances. Secondly, there are those who advocate the management of aggregate demand so as to avoid excess demand or excessive unemployment by the use of discretionary fiscal and/or monetary policy in combination with direct controls on wages and/or prices. Purely for convenience we refer to these two groups respectively as "Monetarists" and "Keynesians". The "Monetarists" may be divided into two sub-groups on the basis of their predictions about the behavior of unemployment consequent upon a rapid reduction in the rate of monetary expansion: the "adaptive expectations" sub-group would predict a temporary but perhaps large, lenghty and systematic rise in the unemployment rate while the "rational expectations" sub-group would be more optimistic and predict only random departure of unemployment from its "natural" or equilibrium rate. Monetarists are nervous of Keynesian policies because, if in the pursuit of an unemployment target, too low a level of unemployment is chosen, then, according to the monetarist's view of the world, inflation will persistently accelerate. They dismiss direct controls as being incapable of controlling inflation in the face of excess demand and are worried by their potential allocative and other disruptive consequences. Keynesians regard the pursuit of a monetary rule as likely to induce too much variability in, and raise to too high a level, the average unemployment rate and, therefore, favour discretionary policy to achieve an unemployment target with direct controls on wages and prices to moderate the inflationary consequences of the chosen unemployment rate. Some would go further and argue that the pursuit of the Monetarist rule would lead, not simply to more variable and higher, but to permanently increasing unemployment.

In view of the policy prescriptions of these two groups and their predictions of the consequences of pursuing the prescriptions of their opponents, it appears to be of considerable importance to attempt to discriminate between them. No group has a monopoly of goodwill or of scientific detatchment. "Monetarists" and "Keynesians" alike abhor both high unemployment and the inflationary prospects implied by recent trends. Both "Schools", with minor exceptions on each side, are made up of economists who regard logical consistency combined with a capacity to "fit the facts" as the appropriate test of a theory. It should be possible, therefore, without departing from the realm of normal science, both to clarify precisely the hypotheses of each School and to specify tests of each view which are acceptable to all. It is this task which we attempt here.

We have chosen to focus our attention on an economy which, in a monetary sense, is closed. We have done this for two reasons. First, in a world of rigidly fixed exchange rates, inflation, whatever its cause, will be equalized across countries by arbitrage in tradable commodities[1]. Thus, to study inflation in a single, fixed exchange rate country is to study the transmission

1) See next page.

process of inflation rather than its causes. If causes and policies for reducing inflation are the focus of interest, as they are here, then the closed, fixed exchange rate world economy is the relevant aggregate to consider. This set of considerations is especially relevant in unravelling the causes of the worldwide inflation take off in the 1960's. Secondly, an economy with a variable exchange rate is, from a nominal and monetary point of view, a closed economy. Hence, our analysis is relevant to either a fixed exchange rate world economy in aggregate or to a variable exchange rate national economy.

The paper is organised as follows. First, we specify a model of the generation of inflation which is sufficiently general to encompass the views of both "Monetarists" and "Keynesians". We then examine the predictions of that model and establish the necessary and sufficient conditions which must be satisfied for their alternative sets of predictions to be true. We then examine the empirical problem of discriminating between the alternatives and suggest a feasible discriminating test.

Our most general model contains seven "variables" and a set of inter-relationships between them. The "variables" are:

(1) The rate of change of wages (w)

(2) The rate of change of prices (p)

---

1) It has been pointed out to us by Karl Brunner that some "economists" regard market forces as being so weak that they would challenge this statement. We ignore these views as being demonstrably wrong on rather simple direct evidence concerning international and intranational price differentials.

(3) The expected rate of change of prices (p^e)

(4) Excess demand (with no distinction between goods markets and factor markets) (x)

(5) The rate of change of the nominal money supply (m)

(6) Index of the strength of fiscal policy (f)

(7) Index of push factors (z)

The first five are straightforward variables but the last two are not and need some clarifying comments. Rather than separately listing a larger number of fiscal and push variables, we seek to capture their effects through indexes of their strength. In the specific models which will be analysed, these will specialise to particular push and fiscal variables. At this stage, however, we merely seek to keep our analysis as general and eclectic as possible while at the same time maintaining a model which is simple enough to understand. The relationships are four simultaneous difference equations to determine w, p, p^e and x given the behavior of m, f and z. Thus, we are treating monetary and fiscal policy and push factors as exogenous and, in general, as the "causes" of inflation[2].

---

2) In treating m and f as exogenous we are not asserting that they are set independently of all other factors. Rather, the implication is that they are set independently of w, p, p^e and x only. We readily admit that some hypotheses about the causes of inflation cannot be fitted into this framework since it may be the case that both m and f respond mainly to w, p, p^e and x and especially the latter if it is interpreted as the unemployment rate.

Let us now examine the most general formulations needed for each of the four relations and the various particular hypotheses advanced. At this stage we do not attempt to classify alternative formulations of each relation according to whether they are "Monetarist" or "Keynesian" for this classification relates to an entire system of relations and the way in which they interact.

The most general hypothesis about wage determination which embraces all those proposed is that they respond to prices, expected prices, excess demand, taxes and a variety of push factors such as militancy, frustration, relativity maintaining leap-frogging, direct controls etc. In principle, there could be time lags in the relationship between these variables and wages. Many special cases of this have been advanced but, in terms of the level of generality at which we are working, and ruling out old hypotheses such as, for example, the Phillips curve, which no-one seriously believes, there seem to us to be three of interest. These are: (1a) the Phelps-Friedman (Phelps (1968), Friedman (1968)) hypothesis; (1b) the push augmented Phillips hypothesis regardless of the precise specification of the nature of the push (e.g. Ashenfelter, Johnson and Pencavel (1972), Bispham (1972), Schultz (1969), Jackson, Turner and Wilkinson (1971), Meade (1971), Turner and Jackson (1971)); and (1c) "pure push" hypothesis (e.g. Balogh (1970), Harrod (1972), Marris (1972), Wiles (1973), Jones (1972), Glyn and Sutcliffe (1972), Weidenbaum (1972), and Ackley (1972))

There seems to be less controversy about price determination, the primary dispute being between those who do and those who do not regard excess demand as having an independent role, (see

Nordhaus (1971) for a survey of the U.S. literature and Godley and Nordhaus (1972)). There is also a dispute as to whether "profits push" exerts an independent upward pressure, (Galbraith (1957)). All agree that other things equal, the higher is the rate of wage inflation, the higher will be the rate of price inflation. A price equation equivalent to the Phelps-Friedman hypothesis would focus only on w, p^e and x. A pure mark-up or a normal cost hypothesis would focus only on w and a profits push hypothesis would allow w and z to play a role.

In view of the agreement wages, cet.par., influence prices, it is possible to specify a quasi-reduced form relation to determine price inflation which includes all those variables presumed to influence both wages and prices but which excludes the rate of wage change. To capture these ideas in formal terms, we may write,

$$(1) \qquad p_t = \gamma(L)x_t + \delta(L)p^e_t + g(L)f_t + \ell(L)z_t$$

where $\gamma(L)$ etc. are finite polynomials in the lag operator L.

Not all models have expectations explicitly introduced and many which do regard them as a purely psychological/sociological factor which may be subsumed under z. Those which do have explicit expectations as an integral part of their economic analysis usually postulate an error-learning or adaptive expectations scheme which reduces to a distributed lag of past actual inflation (see e.g. Cagan (1956)). Others formulate a "rational expectations" process in which "expectations ... about a variable depend, in a proper way, on the same things that economic theory says actually determine that variable" (Sargent and Wallace p. 328 (1973)). In the non-stochastic model with which we are working, this implies that the expectation is always realised. In formal terms, both of these ideas are captured by,

(2) $\mu(L)p_t^e = \varepsilon(L)p_t + n(L)z_t$

where, in the adaptive expectations case, $\mu(L) = 1 - (1-\mu)L$, $\varepsilon(L) = \mu$ and $n(L) = 0$, and, in the rational expectations model, $\varepsilon(L) = 1$, $\mu(L) = L$ and $n(L) = 0$.

The determination of excess demand is a much less straightforward matter than the determination of the previous three variables. The whole of macroeconomic theory and the traditional[3] "Keynesian" versus "Monetarist" interest elasticities and transmission process debate, as well as many more subtle matters, are in principle relevant. We cut through the entire debate by postulating, as a general proposition, that excess demand responds, with distributed lags, to changes in wages, prices, expected prices, the money supply and fiscal policy.[4] A variety of alternative detailed models of the demand for and supply of goods and services and the demand for and supply of money and other assets would yield this quasi-reduced from propostion. Excess

---

3) By the traditional "Keynesian" versus "Monetarist" debate we mean the debate over the question do both monetary and fiscal policies have real effects or does only one of them. We regard this debate as over and the middle position as having won. Our "Monetarist" - "Keynesian" distinction is between a monetary rule and discretionary demand management augmented with other policies.

4) Even the St. Louis group accept a short temporary role for fiscal policy. See Anderson and Jordan (1968).

demand will, in general, respond negatively to the first two variables and positively to the others, i.e.,

$$(3) \quad x_t = \alpha(L)p_t + \beta(L)p_t^e + a(L)m_t + b(L)f_t$$

Bringing the general model of three equations together gives the system,

$$(4) \quad \begin{bmatrix} 1 & -\alpha & -\beta \\ -\gamma & 1 & -\delta \\ 0 & -\varepsilon & \mu \end{bmatrix} \begin{bmatrix} x \\ p \\ p^e \end{bmatrix} = \begin{bmatrix} a & b & 0 \\ 0 & g & \ell \\ 0 & 0 & n \end{bmatrix} \begin{bmatrix} m \\ f \\ z \end{bmatrix}$$

where, to simplify the notation, we have suppressed time subscripts and the argument in the lag polynomials. In order to see the influence of monetary, fiscal and push factors on the rate of inflation, its expectation and excess demand, it is necessary to examine the solution of this system. That solution may be written as,

$$(5) \quad [\mu(1-\alpha\gamma)-\varepsilon(\delta+\beta\gamma)] \begin{bmatrix} x \\ p \\ p^e \end{bmatrix} = \begin{bmatrix} \mu-\delta\varepsilon & \alpha\mu+\beta\varepsilon & \alpha\delta+\beta \\ \gamma\mu & \mu & \delta+\beta\gamma \\ \gamma\varepsilon & \varepsilon & 1-\alpha\gamma \end{bmatrix} \begin{bmatrix} a & b & 0 \\ 0 & g & \ell \\ 0 & 0 & n \end{bmatrix} \begin{bmatrix} m \\ f \\ z \end{bmatrix}$$

At this level of generality, little can be said which is not trivial about the impact of a given policy on the course of inflation and excess demand and without additional restrictions on the structure of the model, it is impossible to generate the strong predictions advanced by either the "Monetarist" or "Keynesian" Schools. Establishing precisely what those additional restrictions are will provide a basis on which we can answer the major questions posed at the beginning.

Let us begin by considering the propositions advanced by the "Monetarists". Although we have distinguished between two sub-schools - "adaptive" and "rational" expectations - both agree that push factors have no effects. From the structure of the solution displayed in (5) it is immediately clear that this requires that ℓ and n be zero. If either were non-zero, in order to remove the effects of z, the appropriate column of the adjoint matrix would have to consist entirely of zeros in which case the determinant itself would be zero and the model meaningless. The two "Monetarist" subschools differ only in their view of the effects of monetary policy on excess demand. Both assert that fiscal policy has short-run but no long-run effects and that in the steady state, the rate of inflation will equal the rate of monetary expansion expectations will be fulfilled and excess demand will be zero. The rational expectations view is that, in the absence of stochastic disturbances, the steady state always prevails whilst the adaptive expectations view is that a change in the rate of monetary expansion will generate transitory excess demand while ever expectations fail to be fulfilled. Further, both sub-schools agree that to pursue a "Keynesian" policy of aiming for a positive value of excess demand and passively adjusting the money supply to maintain that level of demand will lead to a persistendly accelerating rate of both inflation and monetary expansion. In order to see how these propositions are generated it will be convenient to write down the solution (5) incorporating the "Monetarist" assumptions about ℓ and n. This is,

$$(6)\qquad [\mu(1-\alpha\gamma)-\varepsilon(\delta+\beta\gamma)]\begin{bmatrix} x \\ p \\ p^e \end{bmatrix} = a\begin{bmatrix} \mu-\delta\varepsilon \\ \gamma\mu \\ \gamma\varepsilon \end{bmatrix} m + \left[b\begin{bmatrix} \mu-\delta\varepsilon \\ \gamma\mu \\ \gamma\varepsilon \end{bmatrix} + g\begin{bmatrix} \alpha\mu+\beta\varepsilon \\ \mu \\ \varepsilon \end{bmatrix} \right] f$$

Let us first establish the assumptions necessary to generate the steady state predictions. We can display the steady state properties of the system by supposing x, p, p^e, f and m to be constant through time in (6). Under these circumstances, polynomials in the lag operator are replaced by constants equal to the sum of weights of the polynomials. Denoting the sum of weights of a polynomial by a bar over the polynomial symbol, we have for p:

$$(7)\qquad [\bar{\mu}(1-\bar{\alpha}\bar{\gamma}) - \bar{\varepsilon}(\bar{\delta} + \bar{\beta}\ \bar{\gamma})]\ p = \bar{a}\ \bar{\gamma}\ \bar{\mu}m + (\bar{b}\bar{\gamma}\bar{\mu} + \bar{g}\bar{\mu})f$$

Equation (7) makes use of the fact that the sum of the weights of the sum or product of two polynomials is the sum or product of the sums of weights of the individual polynomials[5]. In order to have p equal to m and independent of f we must have,

$$(8)\qquad \bar{\mu}(1 - \bar{\alpha}\bar{\gamma}) - \bar{\varepsilon}(\bar{\delta} + \bar{\beta}\ \bar{\gamma}) = \bar{a}\bar{\gamma}\bar{\mu} \qquad \text{and}$$

$$(9)\qquad \bar{b}\ \bar{\gamma}\ \bar{\mu} + \bar{g}\bar{\mu} = 0.$$

Similar arguments indicate that zero x requires,

$$(10)\qquad \bar{a}(\bar{\mu} - \bar{\delta}\ \bar{\varepsilon}) = 0 \qquad \text{and}$$

$$(11)\qquad \bar{b}(\bar{\mu} - \bar{\delta}\ \bar{\varepsilon}) + \bar{g}(\bar{\alpha}\ \bar{\mu} + \bar{\beta}\ \bar{\varepsilon}) = 0$$

---

5) The sum proposition is obvious; the product proposition is demonstrated in Gray (1974).

and actual equals realised expectations require that:

$$(12) \quad \bar{a}\bar{\gamma}\bar{\mu} = \bar{a}\bar{\gamma}\bar{\varepsilon}$$

Since $\bar{a}\bar{\gamma}$ cannot be zero without causing the determinant of the system to be zero through (8), equations (10) and (13) imply,

$$(13) \quad \bar{\mu} = \bar{\varepsilon} \qquad \text{and}$$

$$(14) \quad \bar{\delta} = 1.$$

Substituting (13) and (14) in (8) yields,

$$(15) \quad \bar{\mu}(1 - \bar{\alpha}\bar{\gamma} - 1 - \bar{\beta}\bar{\gamma}) = \bar{a}\bar{\gamma}\bar{\mu} \quad \text{or}$$

$$(16) \quad -(\bar{\alpha} + \bar{\beta}) = \bar{a}$$

In the light of these results, (11) becomes:

$$(17) \quad -\bar{g}\bar{\mu}\bar{a} = 0$$

and a non-zero determinant for the system in (8) implies:

$$(18) \quad \bar{g} = 0.$$

These results reduce (9) to:

$$(19) \quad \bar{b} = 0.$$

Conditions (8), (9), (10), (11) and (12) are logically equivalent to (13), (14), (16), (18) and (19) and it is these last five which have the most natural economic interpretation. Equation (13) implies that expectations are unbiased; (14) is a long-run Phelps-Friedman condition, (16) is a long-run homogeneity condition and (18) and (19) are the conditions for long-run fiscal neutrality.

The rational expectations sub-school of monetarists replace (10) by,

(20) $a(\mu - \delta\varepsilon) = 0$

in order to remove the influence of money on excess demand. This condition implies (10) but is stronger and yields, in addition to the above,

(21) $\mu = \delta\varepsilon$.

The reaction of both schools to the Keynesian policy can be shown to be consistent with this view. If we assume f to be constant[6], the first two equations of (6) imply,

(22) $a(\mu - \delta\varepsilon)p = a\gamma\mu \cdot x$.

Condition (10) tells us that the weights of the left-hand side polynomial sum to zero. This implies that unity is a root of this polynomial[7]. Treating x as the forcing function in (22) and noting

6) It may be thought that this is an unduly restrictive assumption. It can be shown however that in order to generate a constant value of p with a positive value of x it is necessary for f to be linearly explosive. Although we have not defined f with complete precision, it clearly is positively related to both the sign of the government budget and the budget deficit. Neither of these variables can be placed on a linearly explosive path and so the constancy assumption seems an entirely appropriate one, especially for conducting a long-run analysis.

7) See Gray (1974).

that the weights of the right-hand side polynomial cannot sum to zero, we see that maintaining any value for x other than zero would put p on a linearly explosive path. Thus the monetarist's argument, that an attempt by the Keynesians to maintain excess demand above zero would lead to accelerating inflation can be derived from these restrictions. Given the other properties of the system already established, it is clear that an accelerating rate of monetary expansion would be necessary in order to maintain the positive excess demand.

In contrast to the monetarist view of the system the Keynesians allow both fiscal and monetary policy to affect excess demand and inflation. In addition the push factors, represented by z in our model, play a major role in determining both these variables. Indeed, it is this influence that leads the Keynesians to regard a prices and incomes policy as an indispensable part of a successful and acceptable anti-inflation policy. Their attitude to the monetarist strategy for ensuring price stability, a zero rate of monetary expansion[8)], which is based on the belief that such a policy would cause high and perhaps ever increasing unemployment by causing negative excess demand, is also traceable to the special role that z factors play in their model

Their assertions on the influences of m, f and z imply that certain right-hand side polynomials in (6) must be non-zero. In detail they assert,

---

8) Note that we are abstracting throughout from economic growth so that m = 0 is the appropriate zero inflation monetarist rule. With m = 0, a steady state requires also a balanced budget.

(23) $a(\mu - \delta\varepsilon) \neq 0$

(24) $a\gamma\mu \neq 0$

(25) $b(\mu - \delta\varepsilon) + g(\alpha\mu + \beta\varepsilon) \neq 0$

(26) $b\gamma\mu + g\mu \neq 0$

(27) $\ell(\alpha\mu + \beta\varepsilon) + n(\alpha\delta + \beta) \neq 0$

(28) $\ell\mu + n(\delta + \beta\gamma) \neq 0$

The monetarists assert precisely the reverse of the last two, so this is a major disagreement on model specification. If we were prepared to characterise the Keynesians as also believing that price expectations were also influenced by all three exogenous variables, we would sharpen the focus of the disagreement somewhat. But this hardly seems necessary. The Keynesian attitude to monetarist policy carries an implication about the influence of z on excess demand. The monetarists would have us set m and f to zero (i.e. zero monetary growth and balanced budget); in the Keynesian model this would produce:

(29) $[\mu(1 - \alpha\gamma) - \varepsilon(\delta + \gamma\beta)]\, x = [\ell(\alpha\mu + \beta\varepsilon) + n(\alpha\delta + \beta)]\, z$

The Keynesians assert that the influence of z on x through this equation is a negative one, so that a given constant z produces excess supply. Then, in order to generate the increasing unemployment/excess supply that some Keynesians assert would accompany monetarist policies, we need to postulate a continuously increasing z. We can see now that some of the Keynesian conclusions rest, not only on the structure of their model, but on hypotheses <u>about the future evolution of an exogenous variable</u>. In order to justify their case for incomes policies it is clear that they must postulate a positive association between z and the rate of inflation. They may then argue that the mix of monetary and fiscal policy capable of mitigating the effects of z on x would certainly, and especially in combination with the effect of z, lead to a positive and possibly accelerating rate of inflation. In this situation there are two alternative policies which might come under the general heading of "prices and incomes policies". In the first place we might attempt to directly influence z, or, alternatively we could attempt to ameliorate the inflationary consequences of the low unemployment policies by direct controls on prices.

Our ability to influence z hinges crucially on its precise nature. By sketching a specific route for the influence of z we can see how we might attempt to exercise this influence in a concrete way. If we suppose that the only variable that z affects is w, money wages, and further that money wages are determined exclusively by z factors, a very Keynesian postulate, then for the purposes of our model, z is replaceable by w in the equations under a suitable reinterpretation of the lag polynomials to take account of the substitution. Now we have a rather starker and clearer characterisation of the Keynesian position. Here an "incomes policy" (or more precisely, a wages policy) would, under our earlier taxonomy, be classed as an attempt to directly influence an exogenous variable. A "prices policy" in contrast, leaves exogenous influences untouched and attempts, in spite of the mechanisms present in the model, to control directly the target variable. It might appear that incomes policies are preferable since they are not in conflict with the mechanism of the model. But presumably there is an (unstated) model that explains how z factors affect wages and incomes policies conflict with this mechanism. It is this conflict with pre-existing socio-economic relations that leads monetarists to expect price and incomes policies to result in strikes and other kinds of social unrest.

We have now set out all the necessary and sufficient conditions which must be satisfied if we are to accept any of the views of the world embodied in "Monetarism" and "Keynesianism". It is worth presenting those conditions again in a more compact summary form. In terms of the general model,

$$(4)\quad \begin{bmatrix} 1 & -\alpha & -\beta \\ -\gamma & 1 & -\delta \\ 0 & -\varepsilon & \mu \end{bmatrix} \begin{bmatrix} x \\ p \\ p^e \end{bmatrix} = \begin{bmatrix} a & b & 0 \\ 0 & g & \ell \\ 0 & 0 & n \end{bmatrix} \begin{bmatrix} m \\ f \\ z \end{bmatrix}$$

they are:

(i) Adaptive Expectation Monetarist:

$\ell = n = 0$ and

(13) $\bar{\mu} = \bar{\varepsilon}$

(14) $\bar{\delta} = 1$

(16) $-(\bar{\alpha}+\bar{\beta}) = \bar{a}$

(18) $\bar{g} = 0$

(19) $\bar{b} = 0$

(ii) Rational Expectation Monetarist:

$\ell = n = 0$ and

(13) $\bar{\mu} = \bar{\varepsilon}$

(14) $\bar{\delta} = 1$

(16) $-(\bar{\alpha}+\bar{\beta}) = \bar{a}$

(18) $\bar{g} = 0$

(19) $\bar{b} = 0$

(21) $\mu = \delta\varepsilon$

(iii) Keynesian:

(23) $a(\mu - \delta\varepsilon) \neq 0$

(24) $a\gamma\mu \neq 0$

(25) $b(\mu-\delta\varepsilon) + g(\alpha\mu + \beta\varepsilon) \neq 0$

(26) $b\gamma\mu + g\mu \neq 0$

(27) $\ell(\alpha\mu+\beta\varepsilon) + n(\alpha\delta+\beta) \neq 0$

(28) $\ell\mu + n(\delta + \beta\gamma) \neq 0$

We now turn to an examination of the econometric work which is needed in order to distinguish the alternatives.

Clearly, an ideal procedure would be to estimate by full information maximum likelihood methods the eleven finite distributed lag functions α (L), ... n(L) and then test the hypotheses specified above. However, such estimates are not available for three reasons. First, data deficiences both in terms of the number of variables which are systematically recorded and their lengths of run would not permit such an exercise. Secondly, even if data were available, it is likely that multicollinearity would be such as to give rise to badly defined parameter estimates and hence make hypothesis testing imprecise. Thirdly, and this can be overcome, in many cases hypotheses are too ill specified, especially where they include z variables, to permit their explicit parameter estimation and testing.

What we have, in the absence of this ideal maximum likelihood estimation of the entire model, is partial information arising from both structural and reduced form studies which have utilised prior restrictions on the length and/or form of the lag distributions involved. To provide an extensive survey of this literature would be both laborious and unnecessary for there are already in existence several such surveys (see especially Eckstein (ed) (1972), Parkin (1974), and Laidler and Parkin (1975)). On the basis of these last two surveys of the empirical literature, we tentatively conclude that, whilst there is room for doubt, it looks increasingly probable that the data are more nearly in accord with the adaptive expectations monetarist position than with any other, and that the rational expectations monetarist position is entirely untenable. However, there is room for doubt and disagreement on the basis of this work and, given our primary objective, we must find ways of generating evidence which is less ambiguous.

A more hopeful line of enquiry involves augmenting the single equation structural studies with reduced form estimation and testing. The most commonly performed test is the regression of p (or sometimes w) on m. Let us see what the above alternative views of the world predict about the relation between p and m. From the general solution (4) together with the restrictions required by each view we have:

(i) Adaptive Expectations Monetarist:

(29) $A(L)p = B(L)m + C(L)f$ with

(30) $\bar{A} = \bar{B}$ and

(31) $\bar{C} = 0$ where

$A = \mu(1-\alpha\gamma) - \varepsilon(\delta+\beta\gamma)$, $B = a\gamma\mu$ and

$C = b\gamma\mu + g\mu$

(ii) Rational Expectations Monetarist:

(32) $p = m$

(iii) Keynesian:

(33) $A(L)p = B(L)m + C(L)f + E(L)z$

From the above, it is immediately clear what is implied by the alternative hypotheses and, <u>on the basis of p, m and f data alone,</u> it should be possible to discriminate between them. The adaptive expectations monetarist model implies a stable transfer function relation between p and m and f with the sum of weights being equal in the two p and m polynomials and zero in the f polynomial. The rational expectations monetarist model implies a perfect correlation between p and m, and is of course a special case of the adaptive expectations reduced form. The "Keynesian" reduced form is a stable transfer function involving p, m, f and z and hence implies that there will be no stable transfer function between p, m and f. Thus, estimation of the relevant transfer functions can yield substantial information even in the absence of z data and well specified models involving z variables.

Many writers have suggested that inflation has been primarily an economic phenomenon up to 1966-7, but has since then been a sociological phenomenon. The time series predictions of our analysis readily suggest tests of such an hypothesis. For the hypothesis to be true, there should be a stable transfer function between p, m and f before 1966-7 and no stable transfer function after that date. Thus, not only are we able to discriminate between hypotheses which are advanced as relevant to all time, but those somewhat "extra-special case" models which are held to apply only in a limited period.

The tests that we have just proposed have the virtue of being feasible (a) with very limited information, (b) without specifying the push hypotheses precisely or measuring the push variables, and (c) in the face of an hypothesised change in structure. It would, of course, be possible to perform more powerful tests if all the models were completely spelled out and the variables which they obtain measured. For example, if a sufficient number of observations were available it might be possible to employ spectral methods.

It is perhaps worth emphasizing that the tests which emerge from our analysis involve examining the entire time structure of the relationship between money and prices and not simple correlations, either contemporaneous or leading or lagging. Such correlations in the form of a cross correlation function can yield some limited information about the structure of the transfer function relationship but is not a substitute for that relationship. Thus, alleged tests of the "monetarist" explanation such as that found in Nordhaus (1972) are of no value at all in discriminating between "Monetarist" and "Keynesian" explanations, but are clearly interpretable as tests which convincingly reject the rational expectations monetarist position.

We simply list our major conclusions. First, the causes of inflation can only be established by analysing the entire economy. Secondly, even in the absence of well specified push models, tests are available for discriminating between "Monetarist" and "Keynesian" views of the world and between the two sub-schools of "Monetarism" but not between alternative "Keynesian" models. Thirdly, the primary feasible test concerns the existence and stability of a transfer function between monetary and fiscal variables and prices. If a stable transfer function exists with weights which have equal sums in the money and price polynomials and zero in the fiscal polynomial, then the adaptive expectations "Monetarist" model cannot be rejected but the "Keynesian" model can. If there does not exist a stable transfer function satisfying the weight sum condition, then "Monetarism" has to be rejected.

REFERENCES

Ackley, G., "An Incomes Policy for the 1970's" in the Review of Economic Statistics, 54 (2), August 1972, pp. 218-223.

Andersen, L. C. and Jordan, J. L., "Monetary and Fiscal Actions: A Test of their Relative Importances in Economic Stabilization". Fed. R. B. of St. Louis Review, 34 (4), Nov. 1968, pp. 11-24.

Ashenfelter, O. C., Johnson, G. E. and Penvavel, J. H., "Trade Unions and the Rate of Change of Money Wage Rates in United States Manufacturing Industry", the Review of Economic Studies, 39 (1) No. 117, Jan. 1972, pp. 27-54.

Balogh, T., Labour and Inflation, Fabian Tract no. 403, London 1970.

Bispham, J. A., "The Current Inflation and Short term Forecasting" Ch. 13, pp. 250-268 in Parkin J. M. and M. T. Sumner (eds.), Incomes Policy and Inflation, Manchester University Press, 1972.

Cagan, P. H., "The Monetary Dynamics of Hyperinflation", pp. 25-117 in Friedman, M. (ed.), Studies in the Quantity Theory of Money, Chicago University Press, 1956.

Friedman, M., "The Role of Monetary Policy", American Economic Review, 58 (1), March 1968, pp. 1-17.

Galbraith, J. K., "Market Structure and Stabilization Policy", Econometrica 39 (2), May 1957, pp. 124-133.

Glyn, A. and Sutcliffe, R., British Capitalism, Workers and the Profit Squeeze, Penguin Special, 1972.

Godfrey, L., "The Phillips Curve: Incomes Policy and Trade Union Effects" Ch. 6 in Johnson, H. G. and A. R. Nobay (eds.), The Current Inflation, Macmillan, 1971.

Godley, W. A. H. and Nordhaus, W. D., "Pricing in the Trade Cycle, Economic Journal, 82 (327), Sept. 1972, pp. 853-882.

Gray, M. R., "On the Identification of the Coefficient of the Expectational Variable in Price and Wage Equations", University of Manchester,(mimeo) 1974.

Harrod, R., "The Issues: Fice Views" in Hinshaw R. (ed.), Inflation as a Global Problem, London, John Hopkins Press, 1972.

Hines, A. G., "Trade Unions and Wage Inflation in the United Kingdom 1893-1961", Review of Economic Studies, 31 (4), No. 88, Oct. 1964, pp. 221-252.

Jackson, D. A. S., Turner, H. A. and Wilkinson, F., "Do Trade Unions Cause Inflation", University of Cambridge, Dept.of Applied Economics Occasional Paper no. 36, Cambridge University Press, 1972.

Jones, A., The New Inflation: The Politics of Prices and Incomes, Penguin Books and Andre Deutsch 1972.

Marris, S., "World Inflation: Panel Discussion, in Claassen, E. and P. Salin (eds.) "Stabilization Policies in Interdependant Economics, Amsterdam: North-Holland, 1972.

Meade, J. E., "Wages and Prices in a Mixed Economy", 2nd Wincott memorial Lecture delivered at L. S. E. 29.9.71 and published as I. E. A. Occasional Paper no. 35, 1971.

Nordhaus, W. D., "The Worldwide Wage Explosion" Brookings Papers on Economic Activity, 1972 (2), pp. 431-463.

Nordhaus, W. D., "Recent Developments in Price Dynamics" in Eckstein, O. (ed.), "The Econometrics of Price Determination Conference", Washington, D. C.: Board of Governors of the F. R. B. and the S. S. R. C., 1972.

O. E. C. D. Inflation - The Present Problem, Paris, 1970.

Parkin, J. M., "The Causes of Inflation, Recent Contributions and Current Controversies", University of Manchester Inflation Workshop discussion paper no. 7405, forthcoming in the proceedings of the 1975 Manchester AUTE Conference.

Phelps, E. S., "Money Wage Dynamics and Labour Market Equilibrium, Journal of Political Economy, (76) 4, pp. 678-711, July/Aug. 1968 pt. II. Amended and reprinted as pp. 124-166 in Phelps E.S. (ed.) The Microeconomic Foundations of Employment and Inflation Theory", New York W.W., Norton & Co., 1970.

Sargent, T. J., and Wallace, N., "Rational Expectations and the Dynamics of Hyperinflation", International Economic Review, 14 (2), June 1973, pp. 328-350.

Schultz, C., "Sectoral Shifts and Inflation" in Ball R. J. and P. Doyle (eds.), Inflation, Penguin, 1972.

Taylor, J., Incomes Policy, the Structure of Unemployment and the Phillips Curve: The United Kingdom Experience 1953-1970", Ch. 10, pp. 182-200 in Parkin, J. M. and M. T. Sumner (eds.), Incomes Policy and Inflation, Manchester University Press, (1972).

Turner, H. A. and Jackson, D. A. S., "On the Determination of the General Wage Level - A World Analysis or Unlimited Labour forever", Economic Journal, 80, pp. 827-849, 1970.

Wiles, P., "Cost Inflation and the State of Economic Theory", Economic Journal, no. 330, pp. 377-398, June 1973.

Weidenbaum, M. L., "New Initiatives in National Wage and Price Policy", Review of Economic Studies, (54) 3, Aug. 1972, pp. 213-217.

Comments on the paper of Gray and Parkin

By

Anton P. Barten[*]

1. The paper by Gray and Parkin provides an attractive framework to discuss some issues of the controversy about inflation between the monetarist and Keynesian schools. Three relatively simple, but dynamic, relations make up their model. The monetarist and the Keynesian view are each a special case of the more general model. As an expository device this approach has considerable advantages. The simplicity of it enables one to concentrate on the major issues. It is a quite different matter to apply such an extremely simplified representation of the real world to actual data with the intention to discriminate empirically between the two schools, i.e. to decide which of the two views explains reality better than the other.

2. To start with an example of the limitations of the approach: the authors have assumed a closed economy. They argue that un-

---

[*] These notes contain the gist of the remarks made at the conference but are based on the revised version of the paper by Gray and Parkin. I benefitted from discussions with Franz Palm (CORE) on a first draft of these comments.

der fixed exchange rates the world is a closed economy while under flexible exchange rates a single country can be considered a closed economy. Quite apart from the rather hopeless task of finding the relevant data for the whole world economy, it is also doubtful that the exchange rate regime of the 1950's and 1960's has been characterized by complete rigidity of the exchange rates. There have been many adjustments between the parity of the pound sterling and the Deutsche Mark, for example. Furthermore, in the recent system of more flexible exchange rates monetary authorities have been intervening to a considerable extent. What body of data will satisfy the basic assumption of "closed economy"? Looking at the United Kingdom one observes already a considerable divergence in growth rates in domestic and international prices, measured in local currency. In the period 1953-1972 the price index of private consumption increased annually by 3.62 percent, that of gross national product by 4.09 percent, that of the exports of commodities by 2.88 percent and that of the imports of commodities by 1.63 percent. There does not seem to be a long-run alignment of these prices. It is perhaps more suitable to define a closed economy not by an exchange rate regime but by the negligible size of the foreign sector, which might be the case for the United States. It is worthwhile to point out that the theme of the conference explicitly refers to inflation in open economies. It is not clear what the paper under discussion has to offer on this issue.

3. The basic model consists of equations (1) through (3). The introduction of expectations and lagged adjustments adds attractive and realistic features. It is not sure that all "monetarists" or

"Keynesians" will accept this model as consistent with their views. One misses, for example, the downward rigidity in prices, which certainly some Keynesians would emphasize. One might argue that this is a "sociological" factor contained in z, the push factor, but it is a dangerous proceeding to treat this variable too much as a residual. Some monetarists might not agree with equation (3). If excess demand is defined, as it seems to have be done by the authors, as the demand not satisfied at the existing prices - cfr. their equation (1) -, then it is not the rate of increase of money supply that should appear as the explanatory variable in (3) but the rate of increase of money supply in excess of that of physical production. Indeed, there are few monetarists that claim that to reduce inflation in the long run to a zero level the money supply should be kept constant. Instead, the majority would argue that the money supply should not increase faster than physical production. Furthermore, there are some possible doubts about the role played by the fiscal factor in equations (1) and (3). In (3) the fiscal factor refers exclusively to those fiscal measures that do not directly affect the money supply in order to avoid double counting. This limitation is not necessarily relevant for the fiscal factor in equation (1), except, of course, if the choice between the alternative ways of financing ex ante government deficits are again part of the push factor.

4. As far as the restrictions on the model are concerned one can also dispute the authors representation of the views of the various schools. Do monetarists really consider all push factors to be completely irrelevant even in the very short run? Why are Keynesians not allowed to assume rational or adaptive expecta-

tions and to maintain that these are unbiased, implying $\mu = \varepsilon$ or $\overline{\mu} = \overline{\varepsilon}$, respectively. Then also $\overline{\delta} = 1$. Why should a Keynesian not accept long-run homogeneity in (3), hence (16)? Even long-run fiscal neutrality may be part of a Keynesian framework, depending on the definition of the fiscal factor. Moreover, the characterisation of the Keynesian view by constraints (23) through (28) is too strong. Zero's could appear only by accident. A more adequate representation is to state that the left-hand sides of these inequalities are not necessarily zero. The Keynesian theory is simply more general than the monetarist one, as can be seen from a comparison of (29) and (33).

5. The discussion of policy issues by the authors is not very clear. Their derivation of equation (22) is puzzling. According to the "rational" monetarist there is no way to influence x by manipulating the money supply. Consequently, in mathematical terms, one cannot eliminate m from the equation for p by way of the equation for x, since the last equation does not contain m. What is presumably meant by the authors is the monetarist view that the policy makers by trying to influence x, by means of m, will not change x but only p. Observing no effect on x they will again change m and hence p but not x and so on. With respect to the "Keynesian" relation (29), it is not specified whether the negative effect is transitory or permanent. Furthermore, the authors maintain that z is an exogenous variable, which is true in their model, but the Keynesians take it to be dependent on inflation, i.e. consider it to be endogenous. Then, of course, their model is essentially incomplete, i.e. not a valid representation of the Keynesian views and cannot serve as an adequate means to dis-

criminate between the two schools. Moreover, the discussion becomes entirely confusing when money wages are considered as the z variable. Money wages are prices and, therefore, explained by equation (1), i.e. by excess demand (unemployment), price expectations, fiscal factors and perhaps an effort to affect the income distribution. Considering money wages not to be a price to be explained by (1) but part of z is conceptually possible, but then this should be done symmetrically, i.e. also for the monetarists. It requires then some fancy acrobatics to maintain the monetarist claim that money wages have no relation with the formation of prices and their expectations.

6. It is useful to consider somewhat further the monetarist view on economic policy. The already mentioned problem of aligning the rate of increase of the money supply with that of physical production, an issue overlooked by the authors, is left aside here. According to the authors, the monetarists believe that the absolute price level and the money supply are independent of the real sector, in the long-run if the monetarist is of the "adaptive" sub-school or always if he is of the "rational" species. This frees the money supply for one purpose: the control of the absolute price level. However, what is the interest in the absolute price level? If it does not affect the real sector, it is indeed completely uninteresting. Inflation is then certainly no "social evil". Of course, the "adaptive" monetarist would see some transitory effects. If increasing the money supply these transitory effects are beneficial, it might be a good thing to have a permanently accelerating money supply and inflation. Since only relative prices matter, ever increasing inflation can do no harm.

Imagine, however, that inflation has some damaging effects on the real sector and that the monetarist view of the real world, as portrayed by the authors, is incorrect, then this view is indeed misleading.

7. The theory of quantitative economic policy can be brought in to promote a deeper insight in the inflation phenomenon, even within the context of the authors' model. Given a transfer function between a set of endogenous variables and a set of controllable variables and given an objective function on the set of endogenous variables, one can, in principle, obtain a time path for the controls such that the objective function is optimized. In particular, if one has only x and p as the relevant arguments of the objective function and m and f as the controls, it is possible to find a time path for the latter two such that x and p are right on target all the time, i.e. permanent full employment without inflation. Why seems reality to be so far from this rosy state of affairs. Are public authorities too inept? It is sometimes amazing to hear certain economists assert that "the market knows best" and that by contrast the authorities are stupid. The assumption of irrational behavior by an economic agent, private or public, is foreign to the tradition of economic reasoning and will be not further discussed here. Are public authorities not well informed? It might be that the learning process is much more slowly for public authorities than for private agents, but this shifts the search for a cause to the explanation of the divergence in the speeds of the learning processes. Perhaps the answer to the question about the failure to maintain full employment without inflation, lies in the nature of the objective function of the public authority, which

might be more encompassing than employment and price levels. Next to a whole string of economic variables, a large set of non-economic variables enter the objective function. In this view inflation and lack of full employment are prices to be paid to reach other objectives better. One might argue that these prices are too high, i.e. that the marginal rates of substitution in the objective function of the government are too far off from those in the objective function the government should have in one's own view. This is a valid but subjective point of view. Anyway, to analyze the whole complex of government objectives and decisions could tell us more about the causes of inflation than a partial economic one. Still, for such an analysis one needs knowledge about the various interactions, including the economic ones. Therefore, it is useful to return to the framework proposed by the authors to discriminate between the monetarist and the Keynesian view of the real world.

8. The test proposed in the last part of the paper amounts to the test of stability of (29). The following remarks can be made:

a) One should bear in mind that (29) is based on the assumption of a closed economy. Data should be taken only for an actual closed economy. Which one?

b) What will be the variables? What money supply is used? How is the fiscal factor defined? How is one going to treat that part of fiscal policy that involves changes in the money supply? There is the danger of tautology by selecting those variables that perform best, i.e. give the desired result of a stable transfer function.

c) What is the specification of the lag structures? Searching for these on the basis of relative performance again implies the danger of tautology.

d) What is meant by "stable"? In the usual terminology of time series analysis a transfer function is stable if its roots are not outside the unit circle. Equations (29) and (33) can be both stable or unstable in this sense. Stability of the one does not exclude stability of the other.

e) Stability can also have the meaning of goodness of fit. This is a relative measure. One cannot determine this type of stability without also fitting (33).

f) Assume that one would be able to fit both (29) and (33) and compare their behavior and that (33) is not significantly better than (29), does this mean that (33) is false? Clearly not. One can only state that z has not been effective in the sample considered, not that it is potentially ineffective. (For example, it might have been hardly different from zero in the particular sample.) Only if one believes a priori that (29) describes the true state of affairs such a result can be considered as confirming one's belief. Moreover, (29) and (33) are not strictly disjoint hypotheses, i.e. they share the bound $E(L) = 0$. Even if $E(L)$ is estimated to be equal to zero one can never reject empirically the hypothesis that $E(L) \neq 0$.

g) It might also happen that (29) is incorrectly rejected in favor of (33) if the random component of (29) happens to be correlated with z, which could indeed be considered random in view of its composite nature. For the same reason, if z is generated by an ARMA model, i.e. $G(L)z = H(L)e$, with e being a random variable, (33) can be reduced to (29), i.e. the two specifications cannot be identified from an analysis of the data. For identification one needs specific assumptions, preferably based on economic considerations, for the distribution of the error terms.

h) The two preceding remarks refer to the hypothetical situation that one would actually fit (33), which is not the intention of the authors. Perhaps their concept of stability or rather instability means that in part of the period analysed the fit of (29) is poor. However, this might be due not to the omission of other variables, but to incorrect specification of the functional form of the included explanatory variables. They might then reject their approach of the monetarist view, while in fact indeed only the money supply and, transitorily, fiscal factors suffice to explain the general price level. The same is true for incorrect definitions of the variables.
Summarizing, the approach of the authors to discriminate between various explanations of inflation will only convince those that do not need to be convinced. Why then bother to try to establish an empirical transfer function like (29), which certainly will be far from easy?

9. One should not conclude from the rather sceptical nature of the preceding section that the answer to the question at its end should be negative. First of all, the money supply is undoubtedly

involved in the inflationary process. To get a better understanding of the time shape of the response will help to make predictions more accurately. Secondly, in the course of the empirical study certain assumptions might be modified and the model might become richer. Thirdly, the methodological problems involved are not trivial and their solutions might have externalities outside the original context. Hence, quite apart from the testing purpose, the estimation of (29) is worthwhile.

10. To conclude, I would like to make some personal remarks as an outsider to monetary analysis. Monetary analysis seems to stop the moment one has traced back the line of reasoning to the money supply or to the money base. As a general economist I am willing to accept monetary analysis as such, but would also like to know what determines the money supply. It might very well be that "sociological" factors exert their influence on the economic system by means of the money supply. In other words, a more fundamental explanation of inflation might use the "monetarist" channel of propagation. To understand the nature of inflation it would be of interest to study who is (or thinks he is) benefitting from inflation and who is damaged by it. It is the very nature of economic reasoning to explain the actions of agents as inspired by their desire to better reach their objectives (which too frequently happen to be rather selfish). If by theoretical reasoning and patient empirical research we are able to show those agents that their actions are not (much) in their own interest and possibly unnecessarily damaging to others so that they adjust their actions in a more socially satisfactory direction, we have contributed to a better functioning of our society. It is my conviction

that further work by Gray and Parkin and others on the relationships between inflation and monetary factors is an essential part of this, broader, approach.

THE INTERNATIONAL TRANSMISSION OF INFLATION: MECHANISMS, ISSUES AND EVIDENCE

By

R. J. Sweeney

T. D. Willett *

I. Introduction

With the acceleration of inflation on a worldwide basis, the international transmission of inflation has become a topic of major concern to both professional economists and the public. What are the various mechanisms by which inflationary pressures in one country are transmitted to another? How much of our worldwide inflation can be explained via such mechanisms? And how are these influenced by different international monetary systems? While much useful work has been done on these questions, we are still far from definitive knowledge on many crucial aspects. Our lack of knowledge includes not only empirical questions but also theoretical questions as well. The purpose of this paper is to attempt to lay out some elements of a broader framework for analysis of the many complex sub-issues involved than is presently

* Sole responsibility for the contents of this paper rests with the authors. The contents do not necessarily represent official Treasury views. The authors wish to thank Karl Brunner, Gottfried Haberler, Michele Fratianni, Edward Tower, and particularly Dennis E. Logue for comments and criticism. Ira Kaylin, Ron Meek and Charlotte Miller provided outstanding research assistance.

available in the literature (though we cannot attempt to present here a complete framework). As such, we concentrate more upon attempting to pose sub-issues in a fruitful manner and suggest lines for further theoretical and empirical work than upon presenting a comprehensive survey of the current state of knowledge.

This paper concentrates on describing the mechanisms of the transmission of international inflation and presenting some of the relevant empirical evidence. (No pretense is made of offering a comprehensive empirical survey.) A principal conclusion is that, while certainly important, these mechanisms do not seem sufficient to explain the major portion of worldwide inflation, for imported inflation could have been neutralized at least for several years by all but the smallest and most open economies. It does appear, however, that the large payments imbalances in the 1970-72 period did induce a substantial increase in the rate of monetary expansion in Europe and hence did make a significant contribution to the rapid increase in prices in recent years. Examination on a country by country basis, however, suggests that the linkage between the large U.S. payments imbalance in 1970-72 and the rapid acceleration of monetary expansion during this same period was not nearly as close as is suggested by looking at aggregate relationships alone.

We shall concentrate on three main economic mechanisms that have been recognized as crucial in the international transmission of inflation.[1)] These three mechanisms we refer to as the Keynesian direct demand pressure mechanism, the monetary expansion mechanism, and the tradeable goods price mechanism.

The Keynesian direct demand pressure mechanism operates through the balance of trade and current account in the international payments accounts. Foreign demand (perhaps induced by increased home competitiveness due to foreign inflation) adds to home demand pressure and thus tends to increase home prices. Our discussion of this mechanism emphasizes that changes in the balance of trade or current account are poor measures of the inflationary impact of foreign developments. Different items in these accounts can have different multipliers associated with them, even though this point is frequently overlooked. Analogies between government spending and tax multipliers and international accounts multipliers can be useful but must be used with care. In particular, the inflationary impact of a change in an item in these accounts will depend substantially on the financing of the change. The notion of the full employment budget can be extended to consider full employment balance of trade or current account surpluses. To the extent these measures are not consistent across countries (that is, the surpluses do not sum to zero) countries' goals are inconsistent and actions taken to achieve these goals may be at cross purposes.

The monetary mechanism has two distinct components. The first is the domestic monetary expansion mechanism, where interna-

---

1) For a list and discussion of these mechanisms and others, see the OECD Special Report on the International Transmission of Inflation, July 1973. Two other recent papers on the subject of the international transmission of inflation are Samuel I. Katz, "'Imported Inflation' and the Balance of Payments", The Bulletin, New York University, October, 1973; and Walter S. Salant, "International Transmission of Inflation", delivered at Brookings Conference on World Inflation, November, 1974 (proceedings forthcoming).

tional payments flows can tend to increase the surplus country's money supply and hence its inflation, whether through the Keynesian route of making interest rates lower and investment thus higher than otherwise or the more monetarist route of simply increasing aggregate demand at any given interest rate. (The second aspect of the monetary mechanism, the international reserve mechanism, operates by influencing policy-makers' decision. We treat this at some length elsewhere.[2]) Consideration of this mechanism requires clarification of several strands of monetarism. In particular, we distinguish sharply between strong and weak forms of monetarism, and between monetarism's implications for a country under fixed or floating exchange rates. While the influence of the Eurocurrencies markets on inflation remains subject to debate, we argue and present some evidence, based on work by Willett, that these markets' role is primarily to increase the mobility of capital and hence the influences of these markets can be neutralized by policy to the same extent as can international capital mobility. A major policy question is whether under fixed exchange rates national governments can offset reserve flows and run independent monetary policies. After reviewing some of the literature in this debate, we argue that while long-run autonomy is impossible under fixed rates, there is little evidence such autonomy is impossible in the short-run, and considerable evidence it is possible. In particular, though the issue is very difficult to untangle empirically, work by Logue and Sweeney suggests that U.S. monetary action has a substantial impact on other OECD nations, but these

2) See R. J. Sweeney and T. D. Willett, "Eurodollars, Petrodollars, and World Liquidity and Inflation", in K. Brunner and A. Meltzer (eds.), Carnegie-Rochester Conference, Series on Public Policy, Volume V, North-Holland, Amsterdam, forthcoming.

countries' own monetary initiatives have substantial independent effects. While the aggregate evidence is that the very large U.S. payments deficits of 1971-72 contributed significantly to the domestic monetary expansion of a number of OECD countries, we show that a review on an individual country basis very much weakens the argument that these countries were overwhelmed by international imbalances.

The <u>tradeable goods price</u> mechanism recognizes that inflation in trading partners' (or competitors') prices puts upward pressure on the home country's tradeables prices and through demand substitution and factor payments on its non-tradeables prices, thus shifting its short-term trade off between inflation and unemployment. The initial effects on the home economy of increases in trading partners' prices will depend on the degree of substitutability between domestic and foreign tradeables, the size of the tradeable goods sector relative to the domestic non-tradeables sector (that is, the economy's openness), the degree of interaction of these two sectors, and the flexibility of the economy. We argue that in a very flexible economy that is always at full employment, an increase in foreign tradeables prices will increase domestic tradeables prices but cause non-tradeables prices to fall to maintain employment in the short-run. However, in an economy with less flexibility, the foreign price increases lead to a less favorable short-run inflation - unemployment trade off.

We emphasize the important distinction between rates of inflation in tradeable goods price indices and in other indices such as the consumer price index (CPI). In the long run under fixed exchange rates, tradeables prices must move together and hence the various countries' tradeables inflation rates must tend to move together. However, there tends to be a higher CPI than tradeables inflation rate in each country, and over long intervals this difference varies systematically and positively across countries according to their per capita income growth. Some of our work shows that this relationship holds more or less well across countries, with the difference depending positively on industrial output and negatively on measures of balance of payments contraints. Thus, given external inflation, a country can hold down its CPI at the cost of restrictive domestic policies. Similar implications can be imputed to estimated Phillip's curves that include external inflation as an explanatory variable. These results tend to argue for exchange rate flexibility.

Using these results, Section V then discusses factors affecting the ease with which the inflationary pressures transmitted by these mechanisms can be fought under fixed rates for a given length of time. Keynesian demand pressure can be partially resisted by offsetting fiscal policy, but we show that this policy is an imperfect substitute for short-run price and wage flexibility. Countries must, of course, have appropriate institutional frameworks even to attempt to use monetary and fiscal policy to resist imported inflation. Flexible economies that are growing, have trade sectors large relative to world trade but small relative to the domestic economy, and have well integrated domestic financial markets have the best chance of resisting such inflation.

II. The Keynesian Direct Demand Pressure Mechanism

At the outset it is important to keep in mind that our discussion focuses on the mechanisms through which inflation is transmitted among countries and not on the causes of inflation. Thus, an improvement in the balance of trade can be a mechanism by which foreign demand pressure affects home prices, but such an improvement *per se* need not be inflationary -- it might have been caused by a home recession. Mechanisms are not causes and often not even proximate causes.

The first two mechanisms considered -- the Keynesian direct demand pressure and the domestic monetary expansion mechanisms -- both affect domestic prices by directly affecting aggregate demand, and both work through the international accounts.

The literature has given intense attention to the Keynesian demand pressure mechanism that operates through the international payments accounts.[3)] Nevertheless, even this well-trodden field holds some pitfalls, as can be illustrated through consideration of various national income multipliers and the "full employment balance of trade (or current account)", the analogue of the full employment budget surplus or deficit.

First, even on the highly aggregated level usually considered, there can be different multipliers associated with various items in the international accounts that are treated as if identical in much

---

3) Fritz Machlup, *International Trade and the National Income Multiplier*, Blakiston, Philadelphia, 1944, gives detailed attention to foreign influences on aggregate demand.

contemporary analysis. Apart from distributional considerations, income generated by sales of services to foreigners presumably has the same multiplier as consumption or government expenditures. However, interest income from abroad enters the current account statement in the same way as services but lacks the first round effect of such expenditures; consequently, its multiplier is presumably similar to government transfers. Thus, since the government spending and tax multipliers differ by unity, a change in the composition of a constant current account from interest to services should increase national income by the amount of the shift to services from interest.[4)]

The multiplier associated with government goods and services provided to foreign countries will depend on how these are financed. If they are paid for by an increase in domestic taxation, the balanced budget multiplier of unity results. If paid for by bond financing, the full government expenditure multiplier is relevant. This financing in turn may be reflected in the international account as either a gift to foreigners or a loan, with no differential impact on domestic national income. That is to say, the multiplier associated with an increase in military sales coupled with a grant to finance these sales is the full government expenditure multiplier, not the balanced budget multiplier, unless the grant itself is financed by current taxation.

It is possible that the composition of the current account between products and services may affect the inflationary impact of foreign

---

4) On these multipliers, see Alchian and Allen. University Economics, 3rd ed., Wadsworth; Belmont, California, 1972.

demand. In the typical Keynesian model with unemployment, the business sector operates on the labor demand curve with increases in employment associated with decreases in the real wage rate induced by price increases relative to a downwardly sticky nominal wage rate. (The real wage rate must fall because labor is operating with a fixed capital stock and hence faces declining marginal physical productivity.) Now, an increase in foreign demand for home output initially requires a movement down the labor demand curve and hence a price increase, as will subsequent rounds through the multiplier process. However, an increase in service demand that can be met more or less simply by expanding the quantity of employment rather than increasing physical output -- tourism may be an example -- requires no initial movement down the labor demand curve and hence should be less inflationary. More generally, to the extent any demand increase concentrates on sectors with plant and equipment bottlenecks, this should be more inflationary than if concentrated on sectors that can readily expand by drawing on the pool of unemployed.

It may be tempting to argue that there may be a "balanced trade account" multiplier analogous to the balanced budget multiplier. When foreigners increase their demand for home country exports, they cannot also increase home demand for imports in the same way government can simultaneously raise expenditure and taxes. But will not simultaneous equal autonomous increases in export and import demands give the balanced budget multiplier?

In general, no. The multiplier may plausibly range from zero up to the government expenditure multiplier. For consider that the increase in import demand must be financed by either a decrease in consumption or in savings, or some combination. At one extreme, a drop in the savings function by the amount of the increase in import demand leaves the consumption function unchanged so the increase in exports has the full multiplier effect of a change in government spending. At the other extreme, the increase in import demand is accompanied by an equal decrease in consumption demand, so the increase in exports just offsets this decrease in consumption leaving income unchanged -- the multiplier is zero.

The "full employment budget" -- what government expenditures less taxation would be if the economy were at full employment -- has become part of popular discussions. Two of its roles are (a) to serve as a goal, in place of the measured deficit, and (b) to indicate the general tenor of policy.[5)] Under (a), one might argue that "proper" fiscal conservatism requires a balanced budget when the economy is at full employment, not that the budget be continuously balanced. Under (b), one might argue during recession that government moves to make the full employment budget show a deficit are expansionary, and therefore working in the correct directions. In a related way, one might point out that a given full employment surplus is so large that either it will make attainment of full employment very difficult, or it will have side effects that are unacceptable.

Keeping in mind all the caveats necessary in considering the full

---

5) See Daryl Dixon, "The Full Employment Budget Surplus Concept as a Tool of Fiscal Analysis in the U.S.", IMF Staff Papers, March 1973.

employment budget, an analogous full employment balance of trade (or current account) could be constructed. Indeed, this is exactly what is done in exercises to estimate cyclically adjusted current account balances. Given estimates of propensities to import, one can calulate what a country's deficit would be if it and its trading partners were at full employment. The extent to which countries "should" have balance of trade (or current account) goals is certaintly questionable, but it is possible such goals might be couched in terms of the full employment concept rather than in terms of actual figures. It might then be argued that policies based on current actual figures may prove to be inappropriate when economies are near to full employment. Further, a country that is adopting policies to improve its full employment balance may perhaps argue that its policies should be judged on this measure rather than on actual figures. Similarly, the size of the full employment balance might be held to be inconsistent with other goals, thereby making an exchange rate change, for example, seem required.

Now, beyond the usual warnings about using the full employment budget -- (i) it uses one figure to measure the impact of two instruments, spending and taxation, which have different impacts, (ii) by varying marginal and average tax rates, the same expansionary pressure today can produce radically different full employment budgets, or the same full employment budget can be made consistent with radically different expansionary pressures currently -- it is important to note that two trading partners may have very different notions regarding the same balance. Suppose that instead of resting the analysis on propensities to import, the government uses the Keynesian equation for the IS-curve,

$$(X-M) = S-I + (T-G),$$

where X is exports, M imports, S savings, I investment, T taxation and G is government expenditure. Given T and full employment income, S is determined. But that still leaves I and G to influence X-M -- presumably I can be influenced by monetary policy. Now, the full employment surplus of this country is the rest of the world's deficit, but the rest of the world may have in mind values of its own G and I that give very different results. Not only will this give conflicting policies, it will lead policy makers in different countries to take opposite views of the macroeconomic desirability of particular trade or current account positions.

Despite all the caveats that must be entered about using the trade balance or current account as a measure of demand pressure, the temptation to do so apparently is frequently overpowering. Even on this rough basis, the Keynesian mechanism hardly seems irresistable, even in the case of the large deterioration in the U.S. current account during the 1960's. Looking at several major industrial countries' real budget surpluses and deficits over the course of the 1960's and 1970's, it would not have been implausible for most of these countries (and for the group as a whole) to have run a government budget surplus that offset their trade and current account surpluses. Given the institutional capability of using fiscal policy and the will to do so, even the large imbalances of those years could have been neutralized.

Instead of offsetting the expansionary effects of trade surpluses, however, in a number of countries government deficits were expanded at the same time as trade or current account surpluses increased. For example, consider the data for the Group of Ten (less Canada) in Tables 1 and 2 and in Figure 1. These do not include Canadian data since trade balance figures are not presently available for Canada for 1971-1973. Figure 1 plots the totals for the Group of Ten less both Canada and the U.S.

III. The Domestic Monetary Expansion Mechanism

A second mechanism that works through the international payments accounts to expand aggregate demand and hence influence prices is the domestic monetary expansion mechanism. However, this mechanism is somewhat more complicated than the Keynesian mechanism since the reserve inflow *per se* does not affect aggregate demand but works to expand the domestic money supply and thus affects prices *provided* the monetary authorities cannot sterilize or are persuaded by inflows to allow the money supply to expand. Discussion of the liquidity mechanism often runs together questions about the nature or meaning of the Quantity Theory of money with questions about the possibility of sterilization of reserve flows and also questions about optimum stabilization policy. We think it is worthwhile here to separate some of these questions and their component parts and then reassemble them in a hopefully more coherent analysis.

1. Closed Economy Versions of the Quantity Theory of Money

In order to discuss the quantity theory of money, we find it useful to make several distinctions which by no means exhaust all of the distinctions to be made about this theory.[6)] One is between loose and strong quantity theories. Now a strong quantity theory might say that if the money supply doubles then the price level will

TABLE 1

Government Deficit Totals: 9 Countries and 9 Countries minus the U.S.

	10 Countries minus Canada	10 Countries minus (Canada + US)
1950	- 3,229.082	- 1,019.082
1951	5,107.904	- 2,482.096
1952	- 4,628.871	- 4,678.871
1953	- 9,094.577	- 3,824.577
1954	- 4,208.858	- 3,978.858
1955	- 7,131.596	- 4,431.596
1956	+ 978.592	- 3,491.408
1957	- 2,826.403	- 4,006.403
1958	-10,474.309	- 3,234.309
1959	-12,304.956	- 4,444.956
1960	- 2,592.350	- 2,842.350
1961	- 5,294.295	- 1,884.295
1962	- 9,647.244	- 2,497.244
1963	- 9,711.411	- 4,951.411
1964	-10,199.955	- 4,279.955
1965	- 8,132.439	- 6,532.439
1966	-12,264.081	- 8,474.081
1967	-19,899.876	-11,199.876
1968	-36,328.258	-11,168.258
1969	- 77.244	- 3,307.244
1970	- 8,254.317	- 5,404.317
1971	-35,307.472	-12,267.472
1972	-43,291.146	-20,061.146
1973	-39,095.827	-24,685.827

TABLE 2

Trade Balance Totals:

9 Countries and 9 Countries minus the U.S.

Date	10 Countries minus Canada	10 Countries minus (Canada + U.S.)
1950	-2466.17	-3117.17
1951	-2324.81	-5443.81
1952	-920.406	-4419.41
1953	-16.3370	-3952.34
1954	434.595	-3489.41
1955	-1922.88	-4091.88
1956	241.631	-4873.37
1957	506.557	-5746.44
1958	1311.07	-1992.93
1959	-285.609	-922.606
1960	1166.17	-3067.83
1961	1811.62	-3286.38
1962	26.7599	-3909.24
1963	-1237.87	-6008.87
1964	-540.656	-6886.66
1965	682.008	-3662.91
1966	-238.084	-2924.08
1967	-325.924	-3203.92
1968	-2113.49	-1430.49
1969	-1276.18	-968.175
1970	-1238.15	-2033.15
1971	934.732	5196.73
1972	-1854.01	7729.99
1973	-3725.39	-1840.30

Figure 1

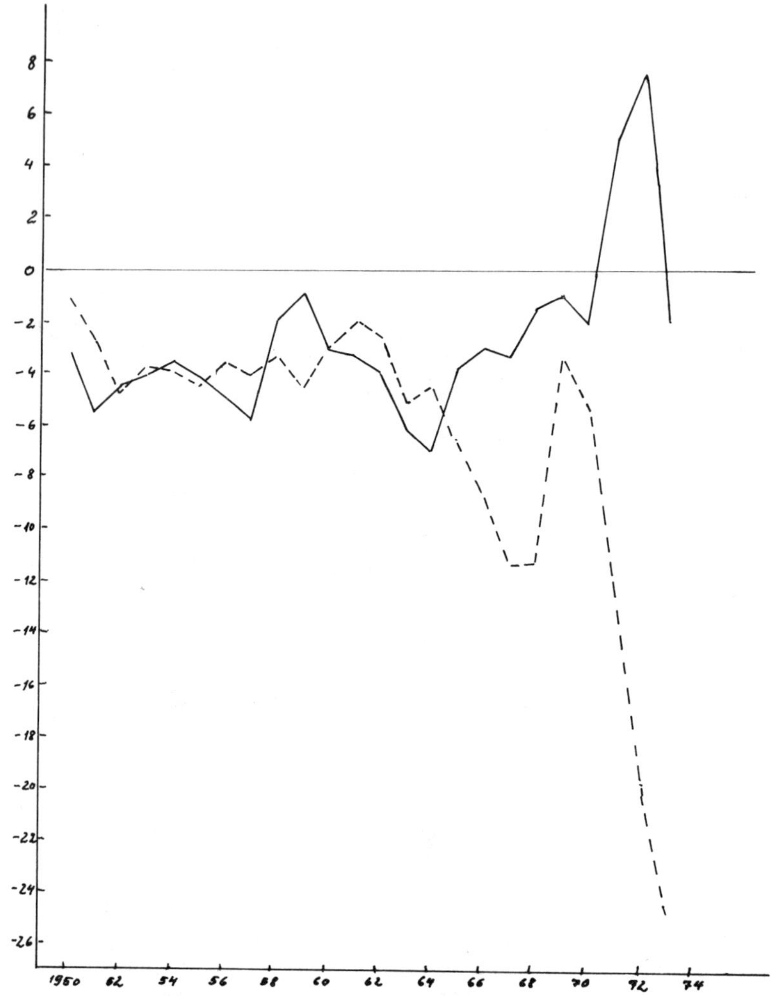

Trade Balance (C.I.F.): ————
Gov't Deficit: – – – – – – – –

Totals for: U.K., Japan, Germany, France, Sweden, Belgium, Italy, Netherlands in Billions of U.S. Dollars

double. A looser theory which is widely accepted now -- for example, see the more recent versions of Samuelson's principles text[7] -- would say that large money supplies are associated with high price levels and that persistent and large price inflation requires persistent and significant increase in the money supply (relative to the rate of real economic growth).

Many discussions of open economies view the primary connection between the international and domestic economies as through international influences on the domestic money supply. Thus, in such theories, the home economy behaves essentially as a closed economy once the money supply is given.

Again using a loose-strong dichotomy to discuss monetarism in open economies we can talk about a loose form of <u>international monetarism</u> which merely would say that high money supplies in Europe are associated with the high European price level. There are, however, two stronger versions of international monetarism which sometimes pop up in the literature. The more plausible and frequently encountered argument runs that the U.S. balance of payments deficit causes a higher money supply in OECD countries and these higher money supplies cause higher prices in Europe.[8]

6) For several more distinctions about quantity theories, see R. J. Sweeney and T. D. Willett, "The Inflationary Impact of Exchange Rate Changes: Some Theoretical Considerations", in P. B. Clark, D. E. Logue and R. J. Sweeney (eds.), <u>The Effects of Exchange Rate Adjustments,</u> forthcoming.

7) Paul A. Samuelson, <u>Economics,</u> 9th ed., McGraw-Hill Publishers, New York, 1973.

8) See the OECD <u>Special Report</u>, <u>op. cit.</u> p. 90, which finds this version "rather difficult to reconcile with a year by year examination of the facts...."

An even stronger version of international monetarism might say that excessive growth in the U.S. money supply causes the U.S. payments deficit which in turn causes European reserve gains, thus causing high money supplies in Europe and high prices in Europe. Now the loose form of international monetarism is not inconsistent with the data; that is to say, it does not appear to be any weaker than the U.S. in the same sort of single-equation test that we are familiar with on the U.S. economy, for an example by the St. Louis Fed.[9)] The degree of operation of the stronger versions is a good deal more controversial.

In a recent study, David Meiselman found an inverse relation between changes in the U.S. money supply (M1) and the U.S. payments deficits (official settlements) contrary to the positive relationship implied by simple versions of the strong monetarist hypothesis.[10)] Laffer, on the other hand, reports a strong, positive relationship between his estimates of U.S. excess demand for money and the ratio of the U.S. balance of payments to GNP.[11)] Likewise, there is some disagreement over the strength of the link between reserve accumulations and domestic monetary expansion.

---

9) Leonall Anderson and Jerry Jordan, "Monetary and Fiscal Actions: A Test of their Relative Importance in Economic Stabilization", St. Louis Fed Review, November 1968; and Michael Keran, "Monetary and Fiscal Influences on Economic Activity: The Foreign Experience", St. Louis Fed Review, February 1970.
10) David I. Meiselman, "World Inflation: A Monetarist View", in D. I. Meiselman and A. B. Laffer, The Phenomenon of World Wide Inflation, American Enterprise Institute, Washington, 1975.
11) Arthur B. Laffer, "Monetary Policy and the Balance of Payments", Journal of Money, Credit, and Banking, February 1972.

The OECD Special Report argues that the strong monetary mechanism has not been of major importance. Meiselman, on the other hand, argues that this was a major factor in the early 1970's, but had not been during the 1960's. Henry Goldstein concludes from his investigations that during the 1960's payments imbalances and reserve accumulations were not signifcant determinants of the rate of European monetary growth but that the huge payments imbalances of the early 1970's did help to generate a concomitant rapid expansion of European money supplies.[12)]

If we consider a particular economy for a period of several months or even for a few years, it would seem that sterilization policy can generally work except perhaps for sharp, short, massive flows that countries may not be institutionally equipped to handle. (See below for some empirical work on this question.)

We would, however, note three points about this even in the short run. First, international mobility in capital makes it harder to sterilize these reserve flows. That is to say, the more sensitive are capital inflows to a country's interest rate, the larger must be its open market operations for it to set and maintain its interest rate. This does not say the country cannot sterilize; it just says that if, for example, it desires a lower money supply, then this will tend to increase its interest rate which will tend to cause funds to flow in, which will mean it will have to do more ster-

---

12) Henry N. Goldstein, presentations at U.S. Treasury seminars and "Monetary Policy Under Fixed and Floating Exchange Rates: Some Lessons from Recent Experience in the Leading Industrial Countries", National Westminster Bank Quarterly Review, November 1974.

ilization than it would have, had there been less capital sensitivity.

We would note, however, that we do not want to go as far as some authors and argue that in the face of high capital mobility the money supply of (say) Belgium may be an insignificant economic variable. For, if Belgian shopkeepers prefer to take their payment in Belgian francs rather than French francs, there is every reason to think that the Belgian money supply is important, just as there is reason to think that the U.S. money supply is important even though in some ways it is a very close substitute for U.S. Treasury bonds. The same sort of transactions costs that make U.S. residents want to hold U.S. dollars for day-to-day activities will make people in Belgium want to hold Belgian francs.

Some of this dispute is easily resolved by putting it in the familiar Mundell framework.[13)] Here, perfect capital mobility implies monetary policy is ineffectual, and attempts to change the money supply will generate international flows that very quickly offset the attempt. That is, sterilization will not work with perfect capital mobility. But, of course, under less-than-perfect capital mobility, short-run monetary policy <u>can</u> be effective in the Mundell framework; for expansionary moves, it has the long-run defect of causing reserve outflows, but for a country attempting deflationary policy, the reserve inflows generated can merely be sterilized (though the higher the interest rate aimed for, the

13) See Robert Mundell, "Capital Mobility and Stabilization Policy Under Fixed and Flexible Exchange Rates", Canadian Journal of Economics and Political Science, XXIX, No. 4 (Nov. 1973), pp. 475-85.

greater are the reserve flows as capital mobility increases) and the reserve pressure is on the outside world, much as Keynesians would view the distribution of adjustment pressure.

As a second point, the distribution effects of sterilization policy may make policy-makers unhappy. Policy-makers who decide to reduce the rate of growth of the money supply because of anti-inflation goals will find the interest rate rising above the level it would be with no sterilization. They may be quite unhappy that, for example, the housing sector is severely effected by this, as in the U.S. This is, of course, a way of saying that policy-makers may well have goals beyond price stability and full employment.

Third, we would like to take note of an interesting point that combines portfolio theory with an empirical fact. If you have fairly stable relationships among interest rates, the proportion of national money supplies in the international portfolio that financial investors consider optimal will be itself fairly stable. Now if a country places any reserves it gains through its official settlements balance into U.S. securities, then it automatically tends to sterilize any U.S. reserve outflows for the U.S.[14)] In fact, this automatic sterilization was the usual policy at least through the mid-1960's. Even before the U.S. closed the gold window, U.S. reserves could not easily be claimed by foreign holders of dollars and hence foreign official accumulations of dollar assets constituted reserve

14) This tendency for automatic sterilization has been emphasized by R. I. McKinnon in "Sterilization in Three Dimensions", Stanford (mimeo), 1972. See also Thomas D. Willett, "Discussion", Issues in Federal Debt Management, Federal Reserve Bank of Boston, 1973.

accumulation which would not usually affect the U.S. money supply -- though the holders were now foreigners rather than U.S. residents. Indeed, only by holding assets at the Fed or in Treasury special bonds could foreign official reserve holders affect the U.S. money supply. Any relative constancy of national moneys in portfolios then make it necessary for European money supplies to fall into line. Thus, this early practice of sterilizing for the U.S. payments outflows, and the later lack of connection between the U.S. money supply and foreign reserve gains, made it harder for other countries to control their own money supplies. We must say, however, that even without this assistance the U.S. would have found it little problem to sterilize payments outflows by discretionary actions.

2. The Role of the Eurocurrency Markets

It is worthwile to insert here a brief aside on the Eurocurrency markets before going on with the discussion of monetarism. One can validly compare the Euro markets to the U.S. overall balance of payments deficit only in that both are uncontrolled by a country such as Germany. Capital inflows from the Euro market are just as uncontrolled as the U.S. payments deficit. However, these flows from the Euro market can be offset just as U.S. deficits can be offset. Thus, it seems to us that the expansion of the Euro markets in many respects may be treated analytically as higher international capital mobility (or an increase in the international mobility of capital).[15)] (There is of course an interesting question as to what extent the expansion of the Eurodollar market is a

15) For this view, see R. J. Sweeney and T. D. Willett, "Eurodollars", op. cit.

cause versus a reflection of higher capital mobility.) Where countries place official deposits in the Eurocurrency markets, this may also induce expansion of the foreign exchange component of international liquidity. It has been argued that such "creation" of international reserves has been significant.[16)]

In the view of a number of writers the Eurocurrency market has been a major contributor to the acceleration of worldwide inflation, not only by its effects on increased capital mobility which has made it more difficult for individual countries to pursue tight money policies under fixed exchange rates, but also because of its direct effects in creating private and official international liquidity outside of the control of national or international authorities.[17)]

As a source of private liquidity, the Bank for International Settlements' measure of the net size of the Eurocurrency markets shows them to have grown to a sizeable proportion of the industrial countries' combined money supplies, as shown in Tables 3 and 4. As is indicated in Table 3, by 1970 the BIS net Eurocurrency market had grown to more than 10 percent of the combined money sup-

16) See H. M. Mayer, "Some Theoretical Problems Relating to the Euro-Dollar Market", Princeton Essays in International Finance, No. 79, 1970. For a different view and approach, see M. Fratianni and P. Savona, "International Liquidity: an Analytic and Empirical Reinterpretation", in G. Carlie et al., A Debate on the Eurodollar Market, Rome, 1973. D. E. Logue, M. Salant and R. J. Sweeney, "International Financial Integration: Survey, Synthesis and Results", in D. E. Logue, J. Makin and C. Stem, Eurocurrency Markets and the International Monetary System, American Enterprise Institute, 1976, argue that the placement of such funds should not affect international interest rates.
17) For a critical discussion, see Sweeney and Willett, "Eurodollars", op. cit.

TABLE 3

Aggregate Indices of Money Supply--M1

M1TOT, EUROMKT, M1TOTE, PROP

M1TOT	Levels of World Money Supply (M1), in billions of U.S. Dollars
EUROMKT	Size of Eurodollar Market, in U.S. Dollars
M1TOTE	World Money Supply (M1) Plus Eurodollar Market
PROP	Eurodollar Market as % of World Money Supply + Eurodollar Market

DATE	M1TOT	EUROMKT	M1TOTE	PROP
1/48	-		-	-
1/49	-		-	-
1/50	-		-	-
1/51	-		-	-
1/52	-		-	-
1/53	189.04		-	-
1/54	197.70		-	-
1/55	205.32		-	-
1/56	211.02		-	-
1/57	210.32		-	-
1/58	219.47		-	-
1/59	227.43		-	-
1/60	234.77		-	-
1/61	250.49		-	-
1/62	263.90		-	-
1/63	285.35		-	-
1/64	303.65	9.00	312.65	2.88
1/65	326.31	11.50	337.81	3.40
1/66	311.44	14.50	355.94	4.07
1/67	368.42	17.50	385.92	4.53
1/68	400.62	25.00	425.62	5.87
1/69	420.19	44.00	464.19	9.48
1/70	464.61	57.00	521.61	10.98
1/71	548.19	71.00	619.12	11.47
1/72	632.10	92.00	724.10	12.71
1/73	717.99	144.00	861.99	16.71

TABLE 4

Aggregate Indices of Money Supply--M2

Money Plus Quasi Money

M2TOT	Level of World Money Supply (M2), in billions of U.S. Dollars
EUROMKT	Size of Eurodollar Market, in U.S. Dollars
M2TOTE	World Money Supply (M2) + Eurodollar Market
PROP2	Eurodollar Mkt as a % of World Money Supply (M2) + Euro Market

DATE	M2TOT	EUROMKT	M2TOTE	PROP2
1/48	-		-	-
1/49	-		-	-
1/50	-		-	-
1/51	-		-	-
1/52	-		-	-
1/53	230.93		-	-
1/54	277.07		-	-
1/55	289.04		-	-
1/56	300.95		-	-
1/57	314.00		-	-
1/58	336.97		-	-
1/59	3 6.86		-	-
1/60	372.15		-	-
1/61	406.08		-	-
1/62	445.47		-	-
1/63	492.96		-	-
1/64	539.81	9.00	547.81	1.64
1/65	597.67	11.50	609.17	1.89
1/66	644.41	14.50	658.91	2.20
1/67	718.37	17.50	735.87	2.38
1/68	800.82	25.00	825.82	3.00
1/69	942.95	44.00	886.95	4.96
1/70	957.20	57.00	1014.20	5.62
1/71	1156.77	71.00	1227.77	5.78
1/72	1362.95	92.00	1454.95	6.32
1/73	1630.14	144.00	1774.14	8.12

Notes to Tables 3 and 4

1. The world money supply aggregate (M1) consists of the total of the year-end money supply levels (M1) of ten industrial nations, converted to dollars at exchange rates prevailing at the end of each calendar year. The ten nations include the United States, the United Kingdom, Germany, Japan, France, Canada, Italy, Belgium, the Netherlands, and Sweden.

2. The money supply aggregate labeled M2 consists of the sum of the series called "money" and "quasi money" in the IMF's International Financial Statistics. National currencies are converted to dollars in the manner described above.

3. The levels of the Eurodollar market come from the 40th Annual Report (1970, p. 158) and the 44th Annual Report (1974, p. 175) of the Bank for International Settlements, Basle, Switzerland.

M2 is a broadly defined monetary aggregate, consisting of the sum of the "money" and "quasi money" series of the IMF's International Financial Statistics. M2 is generally equivalent to the conventional M2, although for some countries it is closer to M3. The following defines "quasi money" for ten industrial countries:

Belgium	time and foreign currency deposits
Canada	time and foreign currency deposits
France	time deposits
Germany	time deposits
Italy	savings deposits
Japan	time deposits
Netherlands	time, savings & foreign currency deposits
Sweden	time deposits
United Kingdom	time deposits in banks and discount houses, plus overseas sector sterling deposits with banking sector
United States	time deposits

plies (M1) of ten major industrial countries. By 1973 this proportion had risen above 15 percent. However, Sweeney and Willett argue that much of this BIS net size is simply interbank deposits whose influence is already reflected in national money supply figures, much like the U.S. federal funds market. They argue that an appropriate measure for December 1974 is more the $ 31 billion liabilities of Eurobanks to non-resident non-banks, rather than the BIS figure of $ 180 billion (inclusion of deposits outside the BIS reporting area raises the $ 31 billion to approximately $ 44 billion). They also argue that even this figure should appropriately be included only in analyses using M3-M5, rather than M1.[18)]

There is also a considerable divergence of opinion, however, concerning to what extent this unregulated expansion of credit has undermined national financial policies and generated more expansionary financial pressures than were anticipated by national authorities. Warren McClam[19)] has recently argued quite strongly that the credit expansion in the Eurocurrency market has primarily been a substitute for, rather than an addition to, other forms of credit expansion.

There are two major aspects to the substitution question. One is the ability of national authorities to offset the domestic effects of international lending and borrowing by their residents. This is the question of how much autonomy for domestic monetary policy can national authorities obtain. The second is to what extent may na-

---

18) Sweeney and Willett, "Eurodollars", op. cit.
19) Warren McClam, "Credit Substitution and the Eurocurrency Market", Banca Nazionale del Lavoro Quarterly Review, 1973.

tional authorities be mislead in their policy actions by lack of knowledge of the effects of growth in the Eurocurrency market. For instance, by concentrating on national monetary and credit aggregates, do policy-makers miss some of the expansionary effects of Eurocurrency market growth so that they are mislead into following more expansionary domestic policies than if they had a full picture of total credit expansion? In other words, how does the existence of the Eurocurrency markets and international capital mobility influence the way in which domestic monetary aggregates should be measured and interpreted?[20)]

The existence of international capital mobility is likely in and of itself also to influence velocity, at least as related to the narrower monetary aggregates. Capital mobility may be viewed as increasing the ease with which funds may be borrowed. This in turn may be expected to reduce the demand for owned balances -- i.e., increase velocity. This effect should be related primarily to changed options for borrowing, and its strength need not be closely related to the rate of growth of the Eurocurrency markets.

The appropriate response to these possible problems for monetary management would be at least in part to obtain better statistical measures of the growth of monetary aggregates and to obtain any desired degree of financial tightness to adjust down the rate of growth of domestic monetary expansion to compensate for growth in international components and changes in velocity induced by international developments.

---

20) Such issues are discussed at length in Sweeney and Willett, "Eurodollars", op. cit.

We might expect that if capital mobility and credit expansion in the Eurocurrency market have had a major impact in undermining monetary policies through these mechanisms then the income velocities of the national monetary aggregates should have risen. As is shown in a recent study by Willett, however, this has not been the case (with respect to the broader monetary aggregates such as M2 in the U.S.)[21] (Of course, the anticipated increase in velocity is a *ceteris paribus* proposition; and we should attempt to control for the major factors which may have influenced velocity.) The absence of an observed increase in velocity does, however, cast doubt on the proposition that the expansion of the Eurocurrency markets has had a major impact on world economic activity over and above any influence which it may have had on the growth of national monetary aggregates and foreign exchange reserves.

3. The Quantity Theory in Open Economies under Fixed Exchange Rates

We have so far made several distinctions about various kinds of monetarism. However, the most important distinction to be made is between monetarism under fixed exchange rates and monetarism under flexible exchange rates. In fact, previously we have been more or less discussing monetarism for a closed economy or monetarism for a country under flexible exchange rates, where

---

21) See Thomas D. Willett, "The Eurocurrency Market, Exchange Rate Systems, and National Financial Policies", D. E. Logue, J. Makin and C. Stem (eds.), *Eurocurrency Markets and the International Monetary System*, American Enterprise Institute, 1976.

Sweeney and Willett, "Eurodollars", *op. cit.*, argue that Euro market assets are more comparable to assets included in the M3-M5 aggregates rather than the more narrowly defined M1 and M2.

monetary authorities can arbitrarily set the money supply. Now it seems plausible that a country that is not too dependent on trade can in the short-run control its money supply much like an economy that is closed. However, in considering the longer-run, it is apparent that this cannot be so under fixed exchange rates. Indeed, in the longer-run maintenance of a system of fixed exchange rates implies that if one money supply is given, all other money supplies and foreign prices must fall into line with that money supply. As discussed by Sweeney and Willett, this is merely an implication of a world where in the long run the world excess demand functions are homogeneous of degree zero in all prices and all money supplies.[22)]

Harry G. Johnson's influential exposition of a monetarist theory of the balance of payments[23)] can be fruitfully discussed in the context of this long-run scenario. But it is profitable first to consider the implications of a more naive sort of monetarism for the short run in an economy sufficiently closed to allow for an independent monetary policy. Supposing that velocity is constant, the short-run inflation vs. unemployment consequences of an increase in the rate of foreign inflation will depend on the price and wage flexibility in the home goods sector.[24)]

The increase in foreign prices, domestic and tradeable, will drag

---

22) For elaboration, of this distinction, see Sweeney and Willett, "The Inflationary Impact of Exchange Rate Changes", op. cit.
23) See Harry G. Johnson, "The Monetary Theory of the Balance of Payments", Journal of Financial and Quantitative Analysis, 1972.
24) See Sweeney and Willett, "The Inflationary Impact of Exchange Rate Changes", op. cit.

up the home country's tradeables prices by almost the same amount as abroad, any difference depending principally on the degree of substitutability of the home country's tradeables for foreign tradeables and the home country's market share. Given the money supply and a constant velocity, if nontradeables prices are downwardly rigid, the equation of exchange implies that real output must simply decline to offset the increase in the average price level due to the increase in tradeables prices. In particular, if wages are downwardly rigid and make up a large percentage of variable costs (broadly defined to include shut-down and start-up costs), then home goods prices cannot fall very far and the rise in prices is accompanied by an increase in unemployment.

However, if prices and wages are downwardly flexible and adjust to clear markets in the short-run, then the increase in tradeables prices should be roughly met by a fall in nontradeables prices (and a decline in factor rewards in the nontradeables sector relative to the tradeables sector) that suffices to keep real output and employment constant. (These broad outlines may be partially obscured by second-order wealth and substitution effects.)[25] It is true that the initial pressure on prices and wages will come from excess supplies, so the requirement for short-run equilibrium in the flexible economy is that price variables change rapidly enough to eliminate excess demands in the short-run.

Monetarism in the longer-run under fixed exchange rates would work something like the following scenario adapted from Harry G.

25) Sweeney and Willett, op. cit.

Johnson.[26] Prices in the international economy grow at a given rate, and international interest rates are also given. Assume a small country's price level equals the international level and its interest rates are governed by international rates, and it enjoys full employment; then assuming the demand for real balances depends on real income and the interest rate, the demand for nominal balances is determined. Now, the only way to supply the demand for real balances under fixed exchange rates is by increasing the quantity of money when the rising price level is given externally. If the government does not wish to increase the quantity of money, then it will face reserve inflows from the international economy which will sooner or later force it either to increase the quantity of money or to appreciate in order to stop the reserves flows, or the same flows will force other countries to devalue relative to the country we are discussing.

This monetarist model leaves relatively little scope for discretionary policy. As with most monetarist models, fiscal policy is given short shrift; however, the country is not even capable of an independent monetary policy to the extent that monetary policy does not affect the economy but only reserve flows. Consequently, under fixed exchange rates, a country had better fall into line with what is going on in the rest of the world or it will be forced to adjust its exchange rate.

Clearly, a major question for the domestic monetary expansion mechanism is the ability and desire of countries to sterilize re-

---

26) Johnson, op. cit.

serve flows and run an independent monetary policy.[27] Manfred Willms,[28] examined the German economy using quarterly data and concluded that Germany could indeed run an independent monetary policy. Michael Porter,[29] using monthly data examined the German economy and concluded that any move Germany made to change its money supply was at least 80 percent offset by capital inflows within one month. Kouri and Porter[30] studied the capital reflow problem, finding it a significant problem for Germany, Australia and other countries. A major and quite damaging flaw in these studies is their failure to specify both a capital flow equation and a government reaction function. Herring and Marston[31] esti-

27) That is, we distinguish between countries' ability to run independent monetary policies and governments' reaction functions -- their desire to sterilize reserve flows. See also the Summary of the Conference on Monetarist Models of National Economic Activity and the International Payments Accounts, Research Office, U.S. Treasury, 1975, and the relevant papers cited there, for further discussion of the interaction of these two considerations.
28) See M. Willms, "Controlling Money in an Open Economy: The German Case", St. Louis Fed Review, April 1971.
29) See M. Porter, "Capital Flows as an Offset to Monetary Policy: The German Experience", IMF Staff Papers, July 1972.
30) See P. Kouri and M. Porter, "International Capital Flows and Portfolio Equilibrium", Journal of Political Economy, May 1974. Note that earlier, much cited, versions of the Kouri and Porter work found the offset coefficients for Australia and Germany not to be statistically significantly different from unity, that is, that there was complete offsetting, while the published version shows less than complete offsetting. Thus, some economists devote energy to showing how theoretically implausible the former results are, while others cite the published version to show that complete offsetting is empirically not a problem.
31) See R. J. Herring and R. C. Marston, forthcoming volume, North-Holland, Amsterdam, 1976; and also J. Artus, "Exchange Rate Stability and Managed Floating: The German Experience", IMF Staff Papers, 1976. Note that the capital flow equation approach used in these studies is not necessarily the best approach, but when used must be accompanied by a reaction function.

mate both functions and argue that, for example, Germany could and did sterilize massive flows, as large as twenty-five percent of its money supply.

Recent work on international monetary interrelationships by Logue and Sweeney[32] tends to support the position that the U.S. money supply is a significant determinant of international economic behavior but that each individual country seems to have some scope, perhaps only transitory and in the short run, for significant monetary policy of its own, even under fixed exchange rates.

Logue and Sweeney tested three monetarist hypotheses regarding the determination of nominal economic activity in each of sixteen OECD countries. Using polynominal distributed lag techniques with a fourth degree polynominal and a sixteen quarter lag (to allow for the possibility of the relatively long lags found in U.S. experience), they regressed each country's nominal industrial production (a proxy for nominal economic activity) on its money supply. Second, they regressed each country's nominal industrial production on the U.S. money supply, with the same lag structure and degree polynomial. Thirdly, each country's nominal industrial production was regressed on the country's own money supply and the U.S. money supply. The first two experiments gave sums of lagged coefficients that were always positive and significant; the third showed severe multicollinearity problems, so attention was focussed on the $\bar{R}^2$'s which are not biased by multicollinearity. The Durbin-Watson statistics for all of the original experiments

---

32) See D. E. Logue and R. J. Sweeney, "Aspects of International Monetary Influences", OASIA/Research Discussion Paper, 1975.

seemed to indicate high first degree serial correlation: when Cochran-Orcutt techniques were applied to remedy this (the D.W.s were all finally between 1.5 and 2.5), the country's own money supply yielded $\bar{R}^2$'s of approximately .7, the U.S. money supply $\bar{R}^2$'s of approximately .8[33] and the two together average $\bar{R}^2$'s of over .9.[34] Using both money supplies always produced results significantly better than using only the country's own, and well over half the time was superior to using just the U.S.'s -- see Table 5. Thus the conclusions reached by Logue and Sweeney are somewhat more optimistic than the conclusions of Porter and of Kouri-Porter, although they follow very much in the spirit of a monetarist model. It is interesting to note that the Logue and Sweeney work finds that Germany among all countries had the most ability to offset the influence of the U.S. money supply on their own domestic activity.

A good bit of the empirical monetarist work that deals with countries other than the U.S. treats these economies in exactly the same way as the U.S. is often treated. For example, work by M. Keran[35] takes the St. Louis Fed single equation approach used for the U.S. and applies it indifferently to Belgium, the United Kingdom, Canada, and Germany without taking account of the variety of monetarism described by Johnson for a system of fixed exchange rates.

---

33) Eliminating a few countries with poor results improves the average $\bar{R}^2$'s to .9.
34) Again, eliminating a few countries improves results significantly.
35) Keran, op. cit.

TABLE 5*

$\bar{R}^2$ for Nominal Output = f(·)

Period: 57:1-71:1 except as indicated

COUNTRY	MS own	MS US	MS own, MS US
(equation)	1	2	3
NORWAY (61:1-71:1)	.9732	.9931	.9968
SWEDEN	.1420	.7894	.9981
UNITED STATES	.7218	.7218	--
CANADA	.8126	.9435	.9956
FINLAND	.4072	.6083	.5095
GERMANY	.9238	.4974	.9518
JAPAN	.5432	.8197	.9622
NETHERLANDS	.9546	.9358	.9890
UNITED KINGDOM	.9110	.8798	.9761
SWITZERLAND (59:1-71:1)	.9446	.9558	.9933
PORTUGAL	.7577	.9675	.9662
FRANCE	.4706	.8418	.7469
ITALY (61:1-71:1)	.9718	.9661	.9878
BELGIUM	.1595	.4442	.7030
SPAIN (61:1-71:1)	.9077	.9685	.9943
IRELAND	.8883	.9861	.9871

* Reproduced, in part, from Table 1 in D. E. Logue and R. J. Sweeney, "Aspects of International Monetary Influences," OASIA/ Research Discussion Paper, U.S. Treasury, 1975.

4. Some Empirical Evidence on the Effects of Reserve Flows on Domestic Money Supplies

Henry Goldstein[36] has regressed quarterly changes in money supplies as the dependent variable against changes in reserves and has found no significant relationship for the period 1959 through 1971 (our Table 6 reproduces his Table 1), from which he concluded that countries were able to sterilize thoroughly, if they wished, over this period. However, in light of longer-run monetarist theory, such as that expounded by Johnson or considered by Sweeney and Willett, Goldstein's data would also be consistent with the interpretation that countries basically desire to ratify international inflation rather than suffer unemployment but that relative to trend, sometimes countries want to expand their money supplies too much and sometimes they want to expand them too little. Though the trend rate of growth of the money supplies is not changed, there will be reserve fluctuations up and down as countries are too conservative or too expansionary, in turn.

It should be noted that over the period 1970-1973, Goldstein argues that the massive payments imbalances and reserve accumulations of the major industrial countries (other than the U.S.) were a major cause of the speed-up in monetary growth rates in all major countries during that period. Goldstein notes that with the exception of Canada the speed-up in monetary growth in his group of industrial countries was associated with a substantial increase in reserve inflows. However, even in this later period, it is not clear how dominant a role international developments played in domestic monetary expansion.

36) See Henry Goldstein, op. cit.

TABLE 6

Correlation between quarterly changes in external reserves and quarterly changes in money supply for six different countries (value of R^2 for four alternative equation forms)

Equation form	Belgium	Netherlands	Germany	France	Italy	Japan
(1) $\Delta M_t = a + b \Delta R_t$	.02	.13* (N)	.02	.00(N)	.05	.11*
(2) $\Delta M_t = a + b \Delta R_{t-1}$	.00	.05	.01(N)	.04	.00	.09*
(3) $\Delta \log M_t = a + b \Delta \log R_t$	.03	.08* (N)	.02	.00(N)	.12	.02
(4) $\Delta \log M_t = a + b \Delta \log R_{t-1}$	.01	.01	.02(N)	.04	.02(N)	.01

Notes: (N) denotes a negative value of b; * denotes an F statistic significant at the .05 level.
All data from IMF, International Financial Statistics.

A brief rundown of individual country experiences gives some flavor of the difficulty in accepting the view that countries have been severely constrained by international considerations in pursuing different rates of monetary expansion. Goldstein's tables indicate that for Belgium from 1967-68 to '69-70, the two year average reserve change position improved by over $ 800 million, from -$ 163 million to +$ 660 million but money supply growth remained unchanged. The inflow grew to slightly over $ 1 billion in 1971-72, and the monetary growth rate doubled from 5.3 to 10.9 %.

Canada's monetary growth rate fell from 12.9 % in '66-68 to 3.5 % in '68-70 despite an increase in reserve inflows from $ 342 million to $ 1.6 billion. Then the rate of reserve inflow declined somewhat in '71-72 to 1.37 billion, but the monetary expansion shot up to 23.2 %.

France also does not fit the strong monetarist pattern well. Her international position strengthened from a $ 2-1/2 billion reserve loss in 1967-68 to a $ 759 million gain in '69-70, but her rate of monetary expansion fell from 5.6 to 3.1 %. Her accumulation of $ 5 billion in 1971-72 was, however, associated with substantial acceleration of monetary growth to 12.5 %.

Italy displayed an acceleration of monetary expansion from '66-68 through '70-72, but without huge changes in reserve flows. Reserve accumulations dropped from $ 429 million in '67-68 to $ 11 million in '69-70 without reducing monetary expansion. Nor did the more rapid rate of reserve accumulation in '71-72

($ 727 million) lead to an increase in the rate at which monetary expansion was accelerating. The rate of monetary expansion did increase, but by less than 2 percentage points, from 18.8 to 20.4, compared with the increase from 13.0 to 18.8 in the preceeding bienniums.

Neither does Japan's experience fit a strong monetarist model very well. Her rate of acceleration of monetary expansion was only slightly more rapid in '70-72 than in '68-70 from 14.0 to 18.4 percent between 1966-68 and '68-70, and from 18.4 to 23.7 percent, 5.3 points, between '68-70 and '70-72, than in '68-70 despite the fact that reserve accumulations during the biennium had grown from $ 1.9 billion to $ 13.5 billion, as compared with a growth of only $ 0.9 billion to $ 1.9 billion in the preceeding biennium.

The U.K.'s rate of monetary expansion slowed between '66-68 and '68-70 despite the improvement of her international position from a reserve loss of $ 677 million to a gain of $ 405 million. Her accumulations of $ 2.8 billion in 1970-72 were associated with a tripling of the rate of monetary expansion, however.

Germany, the Netherlands, and Switzerland all three did display behavior consistent with the strong monetarist model. In each of the three bienniums, they displayed increases both in the rate of domestic monetary expansion and in the rate of reserve accumulation.

As is indicated in Tables 7 and 8, for the group as a whole, there

TABLE 7

	(A) Changes in International Reserves, 1971-72		(B) Rate of Monetary Expansion, 1970-72		(C) Absolute Increase in Rate of Monetary Expansion From 1968-70 to 1970-72	
	$ Million	Country Rank	% Increase	Country Rank	% Increase	Country Rank
Belgium	+ 1,023	8	10.9	9	5.6	9
Canada	+ 1,371	7	23.2	2	10.3	1
France	+ 5,055	3	12.5	8	6.9	8
Germany	+10,175	2	13.1	7	7.6	6
Italy	+ 727	9	20.4	3	7.4	7
Japan	+13,525	1	23.7	1	9.7	2
Netherlands	+ 1,551	6	17.2	4	9.5	3
Switzerland	+ 2,356	5	15.9	5	7.5	5
U.K.	+ 2,820	4	14.6	6	8.8	4

	Spearman's Coefficient of Rank Correlation	Coefficient Needed for 5 % Significance Level
Between (A) and (B)	-.150	.683
Between (A) and (C)	-.058	.683

TABLE 8

	(A) Changes in International Reserves, 1971-72		(B) Rate of Monetary Expansion, 1970-72		(C) Absolute Increase in Rate of Monetary Expansion From 1968-70 to 1970-72	
	% Increase	Country Rank	% Increase	Country Rank	% Increase	Country Rank
Belgium	35.9	7	10.9	9	5.6	9
Canada	29.3	8	23.2	2	10.3	1
France	113.5	2	12.5	8	6.9	8
Germany	74.8	4	13.1	7	7.6	6
Italy	13.6	9	20.4	3	7.4	7
Japan	279.4	1	23.7	1	9.7	2
Netherlands	47.9	5	17.2	4	9.5	3
Switzerland	45.9	6	15.9	5	7.5	5
U.K.	99.0	3	14.6	6	8.8	4

	Spearman's Coefficient of Rank Correlation	Coefficient Needed for 5 % Significance Level
Between (A) and (B)	-.10	.683
Between (A) and (C)	+.13	.683

is a negative though quite insignificant, correlation between the amount of reserve accumulation over the 1970-72 period and either the rate of monetary expansion or the absolute or percentage increases in the rate of monetary expansion.

We should also note once again a very important difficulty in interpreting such empirical tests. When Goldstein finds there is no relationship between reserve changes and money supply changes, he views this as evidence of complete ability to sterilize. However, these results imply that on average the international component of the country's monetary base moves in a manner offsetting any change in the base's domestic component. Depending on causal interpretation, this can be taken as showing either that any increase in the domestic component is offset by induced capital outflows (à la Kouri and Porter's reasoning) or any increase in the international component of the base is offset by successful sterilization policies that reduce the domestic component.[37)]

IV. The Tradeable Goods Price Mechanism

The direct price transmission mechanism works through the competition of tradeable goods in domestic and world markets. Its main impact is to present policy-makers with a progressively worsened inflation-unemployment trade off, rather than working through aggregate demand pressures as do the Keynesian demand pressure and the domestic monetary expansion mechanisms. Note,

---

37) On this point, see M. Fratianni, this volume, and M. Neuman who adopts an interpretation exactly contrary to Kouri and Porter in "A Theoretical and Empirical Analysis of the German Money Supply Process, 1958-1972", draft dated May 1974.

however, that both the Keynesian and direct price mechanism are merely analytically separable aspects of the same phenomenon, demand for goods.[38)]

When trading partners' and competitors' prices rise, domestic tradeables prices (export and import) must also tend to rise. If the country's tradeables are perfect substitutes with foreign goods, their prices must rise by the full extent of world prices; and, to the degree they are imperfect substitutes, the rise in price can be mitigated by increased output to feed the increasing foreign demand due to the relative price change resulting from lower inflation at home. This increase in foreign demand is, of course, the Keynesian transmission mechanism and can be neutralized by fiscal and monetary policy to hold aggregate demand constant. A reduction, say, in government expenditures is not likely to fall on exactly the goods where foreign demand has risen and hence is likely to induce some unemployment. To the extent that the reductions in government spending do not induce compensating price reductions, the increase in tradeables prices makes a net contribution to inflation -- the Phillips curve unemployment-inflation trade off has worsened.

1. The Total Inflationary Impact of Tradeable Goods Price Increases

The extent to which total domestic prices rise, given constant aggregate demand, will depend on the degree of substitutability the country's tradeables with world commodities and also the share

38) The importance of emphasizing this point was stressed to us by Karl Brunner.

that tradeables represent in the country's production. On this point, it is necessary to distinguish between the amount of goods actually traded and the larger amount of goods that is potentially tradeable. These include not only domestic consumption of goods that are identical with those actually traded but also goods and services that are close substitutes and complements of directly traded goods. Even services can sometimes be exported -- for example, the use of Mexican dentists by U.S. citizens residing near the border. However, for a moderately large and diversified economy, it is not meaningful to talk of all its goods being tradeables.[39)]

The initial impact, then, of foreign price increases depends on openness and substitutability. For instance, if the tradeables are perfect substitutes and comprise 20 percent of the economy, a 10 percent rise in world prices tends to raise the country's price level by 2 percent -- the short-run Phillips curve tends to shift up by 2 percentage points. This is exactly analogous to a worsening of the Phillips curve due to cost-push pressures. Repercussions beyond this direct impact will depend on the reactions of both the government and private sectors, with possible short-run results ranging from virtually no change in the overall internal price level to a massive inflationary spiral.[40)]

---

39) This is not at all to say that a given dividing line between the two categories of goods is a fundamental datum -- rather it is itself endogenous. However, the distinction is an analytically useful device, exploited often below.
40) See Sweeney and Willett, "The Inflationary Impact of Exchange Rate Adjustments", op. cit.

At the one extreme, suppose velocity and the money supply are constant. If the economy is very flexible, prices and wages in the home goods sector will fall to preserve real output and employment there and the overall price level will show only minor change. At the other extreme, workers and their representatives may be unwilling to take even a transitory cut in their real wages. The 2 percent rise in average prices is then put forward as a 2 percent wage increase demand which if granted is likely to be followed by price increases, and the spiral begins. Wage escalator clauses that work quickly may well facilitate this process and may thus be a detrimental institutional arrangement when trying to resist international inflation. The process would presumably die out if government held nominal aggregate demand constant, for unemployment would likely moderate wage demands. But if government will not tolerate increased unemployment, it must ratify the inflation through expansionary policies; and the possibility arises that the impact effect of higher tradeable goods prices will set in motion a continuing and perhaps even accelerating inflation.

Beyond the initial impact effects, succeeding periods will see an ever worsening Phillips curve as foreign and domestic prices diverge even more. Long-run trade equilibrium requires that foreign and domestic tradeable goods prices return to their previous equilibrium relationship and under fixed rates this requires that the foreign country devalue or the home country fall into line with world inflation. How long such inflation can be resisted depends on how stringent is the tendency of the economy to move quickly to balance of payments equilibrium. The price rises from abroad will put into force the Keynesian demand pressure mechanism, as noted previously, and will also be likely to lead to reserve inflows that will tend to increase the money supply. If left unneutralized, these forces will bring a return to equilibrium more or less quickly, depending on the home country's size and openness. These same two factors are important both in determining the ease of neutralizing these mechanisms and in the decision to abandon neutralization attempts.

At the present time our empirical knowledge concerning these various aspects of the inflationary mechanism is quite deficient. We know that the size of tradeable goods sectors is considerably larger than actually traded goods, so that export and import shares in GNP will understate the impact effect of a change in tradeable goods prices. We do not, however, have a good deal of empirical evidence on how much larger tradeable goods sectors tend to be. Indeed, when we recognize that what is at issue is a wide gray area of varying degrees of imperfect substitutability rather than the relevant size of a sector of perfect substitutability (pure traded goods) and a sector of zero substitutability (pure non-traded goods) the difficulty of making such estimates may be more fully appreciated. We may reasonably despair of reaching definitive empirical results on such a question, but we may hope that future research will reduce some of the range of uncertainties here. Work is underway on these questions using both input-output analysis and regression analysis of the behavior of prices and some interesting preliminary results have been found. For example, using quite different methods Kwack and Nordhaus have made quite similar estimates of the impact effect of a percentage point change in U.S. import prices of 0.12 and 0.14, respectively.

This would suggest that the effective size of the U.S. traded goods sector was perhaps 2-1/2 to 3 times the size of actual imports.[41)]

More work has been done on the reactions to impact effects, but again our knowledge is sketchy. Kwack (op. cit.) estimates a total impact for the U.S. of roughly 2-1/2 times the impact effect, but this depends crucially upon his formulation of the Phillips curve relationship. A recent review and extension of three major studies which attempted to model the inflationary process in the U.S. indicated little similarity in their conclusions as to the profile of inflation-unemployment dynamics in the United States.[42)] (None of the three studies found a normal shaped Phillips relationship. One implied a horizontal relationship, one a positively sloped (explosive) relationship, and one gave a normally sloped relationship up to a threshold rate of inflation, and a positive (explosive) slope above this rate.) We also do not have sufficient knowledge of government reaction functions to the private market behavior which generates inflation-unemployment trade offs.[43)] Thus, at this point we must remain relatively humble concerning our knowledge of the dynamics of current inflationary processes. Indeed, given the crucial role which non-observable variables play in the process, it should not be surprising that it has proven so difficult to

---

41) See Sung Kwack, "The Effects of Foreign Inflation on Domestic Prices and the Relative Price Advantage of Exchange Rate Changes" in P.B. Clark, D.E. Logue and R.J. Sweeney (eds.), The Effects of Exchange Rate Adjustments (forthcoming). Nordhaus' work was presented to a Federal Reserve seminar and is cited in Kwack.

42) A. Bradley Askin and John Kraft, "Similarities and Differences Among Three Models of Inflation", Southern Economic Journal, July 1974, pp. 62-77.

43) See the references in footnote 31.

find stable relationships among the observed variables. This, of course, does not imply that we cannot learn a great deal from trying. For instance, as is discussed in the following subsection, the impact of an increase in tradeable goods prices may be expected to vary from country to country depending not only on differences in the inflationary dynamics discussed above but also because of differences in real factors such as productivity growth.

2. Real Relationships between Tradeable and Domestic Price Movements

Even when home prices fall into line with international price developments and the home country adopts the world rate of inflation, it is important to realize that these equal inflation rates refer only to tradeables prices.[44] Consumer price indices may still move at different rates in different countries. As emphasized by Haberler,[45] this is an important point, for its moral is that in a world where different countries have different relationships between consumer price inflation and tradeables price inflation, fixed exchange rates are simply inconsistent with equal consumer price inflation rates in all countries, and it is only by the merest chance of matching preferences with possibilities that the rate of consumer price inflation one country prefers implies exactly the (usually different)

---

44) In fact, these "equal" inflation rates in tradeable goods are only an abstraction, since trade patterns are constantly shifting and biases in index-construction are present. See below for remarks on the construction of the U.S. wholesale price index. We might note that we have found significant time trends in the ratios of U.S. export price indices relative to the dollar value of various other countries export prices indices.

45) Gottfried Haberler, "International Aspects of U.S. Inflation", P. Cagan, et al, A New Look at Inflation, American Enterprise Institute, Washington, D.C., 1973.

rate another finds optimal. To see this, consider the empirical results of Balassa and McKinnon,[46)] who found across countries that there is a stable relationship between the rate of inflation in a country's consumer price index and the rate in its tradeable goods price index: The higher is the country's rate of growth in productivity, the larger is the gap between these two rates of price inflation, with the CPI always the larger rate on average. One way of looking at this is to view each country as having a "stick". At the top of the stick is the rate of change of the CPI and at the bottom of the stick is the rate of change of the tradeable goods price index. The length of the stick will vary positively over countries depending on the rate of growth of per capita income. We might note that the U.S. and the United Kingdom in the post-war period were relatively low growth countries compared, for example, to Germany and Japan.

46) See Bela Balassa, "The Purchasing Power Parity Doctrine: A Reappraisal", Journal of Political Economy, 1974; and Ronald I. McKinnon, Monetary Theory and Controlled Flexibility in the Foreign Exchanges, International Financial Section, Princeton University, 1971. Note that these articles of course did not consider the last few years of serious commodity price rises -- McKinnon covered 1953-70. As is discussed below, biases in the construction of, for example, the wholesale price index can cause serious problems in comparing indices for the same country and across countries. Balassa considered a sample of countries for a given single year, and argued that each country's deviation from purchasing power parity with the U.S. was positively and significantly related to per capita GNP. L. H. Officer, "The Productivity Bias in Purchasing Power Parity: An Econometric Investigation", IMF, mimeo, argues that Balassa erred by including the U.S. itself in the regression sample, and that the results do not hold for his large sample of industrialized countries for the more than twenty years he examined. Note that McKinnon compared how various prices had changed between 1953 and 1970; that is, he examined intertemporal price changes. This seems to us more in line with what we expect of the purchasing power parity doctrine.

Let us turn now to the economic causes for the existence of a stick. In an intuitive explanation, it is simply that as the country grows rapidly it tends to have relatively more weight thrown on its low productivity domestic sector. The faster the country grows, the larger is the growth in demand for the domestic output relative to tradeable goods output; and, since domestic goods contain a large service component in which productivity grows slowly relative to manufactured goods, we tend to find a higher rate of price inflation here than in the tradeable goods sector.

There are, however, two more rigorous ways of explaining the stick relationship. One, discussed below, is to derive the relationship on the basis of the usual trade theory assumptions -- for example, constant returns to scale and full employment of all factors. The assumptions give a stick for each country which depends positively on the rate of growth of technological progress in each country's tradeable goods sector relative to the rate of growth in its non-tradeable sector.[47)]

The other way of approaching the topic is to use the so-called Nordic model of administered prices, where government, business, and labor agree on prices and wages but with an eye towards international competitiveness. This model was developed by various Scandinavian economists to explain what seemed to them to be the salient features of Scandinavian economies.[48)] Suppose we consider a country that is small and relatively open. If it is not to ex-

---

47) See R. J. Sweeney, "The Relationship Between the Rates of Consumer and Tradeable Goods Price Inflation and the Rate of Economic Growth", OASIA Research Discussion Paper, 1975.

perience severe balance of payments problems, its tradeable goods prices must remain relatively close to foreign tradeable goods prices. Now suppose that prices in the tradeable goods sector are determined on a cost-plus basis in comparison with domestic wage rates. Since tradeable good prices have to equal foreign tradeable goods prices, we can use this mark-up from wages to prices to determine what wages must be if external balance is to be maintained. That is, given foreign price developments, and productivity growth in the tradeable goods sector, we can determine the equilibrium wage rate. It is quite likely that wages in the tradeable goods sector will have to equal wages in the home goods sector. However, it is very likely that productivity in the home goods sector will grow at a lower rate than it does in the tradeable goods sector. Consequently, when the same mark-up is applied to wages, prices in the home goods sector grow at a faster rate than prices in the tradeable goods sector. (As an aside it is interesting to note that "the Nordic economy", though it is supposed to be based on administered pricing, runs very much like the competitive economy. In fact this may be another example of the general point that people do not have to know about the forces of competition in order to be subject to them. It would be interesting to see if the mark-up factor applied to administered wages varies with economic conditions in a way compatible with competitive theory.)[49]

---

48) See Odd Aukrust, Wage and Price Interdependence in Competitive and Sheltered Sectors, mimeo paper for OECD Regional Trade Union Seminar on Price Policy, OECD, 1972; and "Inflation in the Open Economy: The Norwegian Model", paper presented at the Brookings Conference on World-Wide Inflation, November, 1974 (proceedings forthcoming). See also G. Edgren, K. O. Foxen, C. E. Odner, "Wages, Growth and the Distribution of Income", Swedish Economic Journal, 1969.

A number of empirical studies are of interest. In Balassa and McKinnon's articles[50] on the relationship between rates of tradeables and home goods inflation there are reported empirical results on the tradeable goods price mechanism. As noted above, comparing countries cross sectionally showed a positive relationship between the difference of each country's rate of consumer price inflation and tradeables price inflation versus the country's rate of growth in per capita income. Note, however, that this is an average relationship; from quarter to quarter, the difference between CPI inflation and inflation in the export price index (or the import price index) can be very volatile and even negative.

Secondly, and in somewhat the same spirit, the OECD in a Special Report in June 1973 regressed countries' export price levels on their contemporaneous internal price levels and their trading goods partners' export price levels. The statistical results were quite good as measured by the many high $\bar{R}^2$'s; and the finding that for smaller, more open economies, domestic prices are a less important determinant of export prices conforms with our theoretical expectations. However, the Report's ommission of the Durbin-Watson statistic allowed no inference as to the influence of serial correlation which we found to be a serious problem in somewhat similar tests. Another problem we found was that the tendency of international price indices to move roughly together allowed no causal inferences to be drawn. For example, using polynominal distributed lag techniques to see if U.S. export prices explained

---

49) See Aukrust (1974), op. cit., for evidence that the mark-up factor in the "exposed" sector is by no means constant.
50) Balassa, op. cit., and McKinnon, op. cit.

other countries' tradeables prices, yielded $\bar{R}^2$'s above .9, and when combined with some plausible trade balance variables, D.W.'s around 1.3. However, running these countries' prices on Germany's export prices and trade balance variables yielded even better results. In fact, German variables can better explain the U.S. export price index than can U.S. variables explain the German index. But attempts to infer any causality of any sort should be considerably subdued by the fact that, for example, the U.S. export price index can be very well "explained" by a combination of the contemporaneous German trade balance and distributed lags on Swedish import prices and Italian export prices. The fact that the ratio of the dollar value of export prices of any non-U.S. Group of Ten member to the dollar value of U.S. export prices has a significant time trend further predisposed us to accept the probability that there might be massive spurious correlation and great difficulty in inferring causality.

Third, consider some of the results obtained by Scandinavian economists who have estimated the so-called Nordic model mentioned above.[51)] In some tests, this model seems to work rather well for the Scandinavian economies but not so well for other economies. William Nordhaus, in his discussion of the world-wide wage inflation,[52)] compared several naive models that might be used to explain wage behavior. For example, he compared the monetarist model (at least his version of the monetarist model), the Phillips curve model with expectations of inflation, and his model of im-

---

51) See Aukrust et al., op. cit.
52) William D. Nordhaus, "The World-Wide Wage Explosion", Brookings Papers on Economic Activity, 1972.

ported inflation based on the Nordic model. He found that the Phillips curve model worked the best for the U.S. and Canada. Nothing seemed to work very well for Germany and France, and the Nordic imported inflation model worked best for Sweden, Japan and the U.K. We are not surprised, of course, that it worked well for Sweden -- it was in the context of Scandinavian economies that the model was developed -- but it does strike us that to imply the U.K. and Japan are small, open economies is perhaps a bit questionable.

Nordhaus tested an extremely strong version of the quantity theory. He assumed that the real wage rate was equal to a constant plus a trend and that the money supply affects the price level and not real output. Most monetarists would be very surprised at this, for they would tend to argue that in the short run monetary policy does have significant effects on real factors such as the real wage rate and real output. (Indeed, Gordon[53)] pointed out in a comment on Nordhaus' work that it is quite consistent for quantity theorists to use a price change equation that is identical to the Phillips curve equation that Nordhaus uses, and thus Nordhaus' test does not discriminate between fiscalism and monetarism since they can both use the Phillips curve. In fact, the St. Louis Fed model[54)] incorporates a price change equation with much the same underlying rationale of the Phillips curve.)

---

53) See Robert Gordon's comment on Nordhaus in Brookings Papers on Economic Activity, 1972.
54) See L. Anderson and K. Carlson, "A Monetarist Model for Economic Stabilization", St. Louis Fed Review, 1970.

Eric Spitaller,[55] found that in some OECD countries the import goods' price inflation did have a significant effect on domestic price inflation -- for example, it was the only significant variable in Austria's equation. But Spitaller's use of a lagged endogenous variable -- last period's price inflation -- and the well-known tendency of this technique to bias the $\bar{R}^2$ upward and the D. W. towards 2, makes us consider his results to be at best somewhat tentative, especially since many $\bar{R}^2$'s are unimpressive. As previously mentioned, work by Sung Kwack[56] on the Phillips curve for the U.S. showed that price inflation in foreign tradeable goods is likely to have a significant effect on the U.S.'s level of price inflation -- a 10 percent increase in foreign tradeables prices would cause approximately a 3 percent increase in U.S. prices over the long run.

It is also of interest to compare empirical work on the "stick" relationship. The observed stick relationship for any one country is not stable over time empirically, in the sense that the gap between the two rates is very erratic from quarter to quarter for many countries, with tradeables price frequently showing a higher inflation rate than consumer prices. Sweeney[57] has shown under the assumptions of full employment, constant returns to scale, a constant real rate of interest and Harrod neutral technological progress that the length of the stick should equal the rate of prog-

---

55) Eric Spitaller, "Prices and Unemployment in Selected Industrial Countries", IMF Staff Papers, Nov., 1971.
56) See Sung Kwack, "The Effects of Foreign Inflation on Domestic Prices and the Relative Price Advantage of Exchange Rate Changes", The Effects of Exchange Rate Adjustments, op. cit.
57) Sweeney, op. cit.

ress times labor's share in the income of the non-tradeable goods sector. The relationship was estimated for the Group of Ten countries using polynomial distributed lag techniques on the log-level form

$$\ln CPI - \ln XPI = f(\ln IP, \ln TB)$$

which gives the time derivative form of the theory

$$\frac{\dot{CPI}}{CPI} - \frac{\dot{XPI}}{XPI} = f_{IP}\frac{\dot{IP}}{IP} + f_{TB}\frac{\dot{TB}}{TB}$$

where CPI and XPI are the consumer and export price indices, respectively, IP is the industrial production index and TB is some measure related to the trade balance and its components. Industrial production was used to proxy the effects of both technological progress and factor market slack, while the trade balance represented an international constraint on private pricing and public fiscal and monetary policies. Table 9 presents a variety of results for the ten countries -- it is important to note that little "data-mining" occurred. Generally, the $\bar{R}^2$'s exceed .9, at least in some version (the poor results for the U.S. may be due in part to the well-known deficiencies in its export price index). For almost every country, some version has a D.W. in the acceptable range of 1.5 to 2.5, and for several countries, for example, Germany and Japan, the $\bar{R}^2$, D.W. and size and sign of the coefficients on industrial production are very robust across specifications. The inclusion of trade balance variables often very much improves those equations with poor D.W.'s, indicating the problem is a missing variable rather than serial correlation. However, the harm such inclusion does to the sign of Belgium's coefficients and the sign and significance of Canada's coefficients on industrial production is perhaps disturbing, though it is often the case that including a distributed lag on another variable will improve the sign or significance of the first coefficients, as is the case with France and the U.S. Finally, note that given tradeables prices determined by the international economy we would expect domestic policy to be more expansive, and hence the stick longer, the better is the trade balance. This implies the coefficients on exports should be positive and those on imports negative. Only in three cases -- twice for the Netherlands, once for Sweden -- is the sum of coefficients on the trade balance variable significant but with the wrong sign. (It is interesting to note that the results for Norway, also reported in Table 9, show this country as roughly average among the others considered.)

Though the empirical evidence is not conclusive and further work is necessary -- for example, experiments using the imports price index were tried, with comparable results -- it was felt that the major explanatory power was with industrial production. In consequence, the empirical instability of the stick is explained as due to variations in industrial growth. Note that this argues that an increase in tradeables price inflation can be prevented from increasing consumer price inflation only at the cost of reducing growth and thus increasing unemployment. Further it implies that an increase in tradeables price inflation, given constant rates of growth in industrial production and the trade balance, will lead to an equal increase in CPI inflation. (These results thus further strengthen the case for a considerable degree of exchange rate

TABLE 9 *

	ln (Ind. Prod.)	ln(Trade Balance)	Other	$\bar{R}^2$	D.W.
Belgium	-0.663657 / .187544 (2, 16, None)	lnX-1nIM 6.17978 / .896863 (2, 16, None)	Germany's lnX- nIM -3.35087	.9595	1.8045
	-1.43126 / .344655 (2, 16,None)	lnIM .755529 / .131528 (2, 16, None)	Germany's lnX- lnIM -2.81239	.9544	1.6837
	-1.44000 / .389073 (2, 16, None)	lnIM .698652 / .146072 (2, 16, None)	lnX .943519	.9447	1.1826
	.534315 / .116035 (2, 16, None)	–	lnX -.0589 lnIM .2031	.8953	.7360
Canada	0.215315 / .072487 (2, 16, None)	--	lnX -1.95265 lnIM -0.280850	.8725	.9019
	-.0347154 / .0963030 (2, 16, None)	lnX- lnIM .132152 / .157218 (2, 16, None)	U.S.'s lnInd. Prod. .474609	.9586	1.5298
	.247573 / .144900 (2, 16, None)	lnX -.9023 / .07077 (2, 16, None)	lnIM -2.449	.9465	1.2324

TABLE 9 (Continued)

	ln(Ind. Prod.)	ln(Trade Balance)	Other	$\bar{R}^2$	D.W.
Canada (Cont'd)	.009589 .023396 (2, 16, None)	lnX- lnIM .068515 .0811215 (2, 16, None)	–	.9595	1.5463
	.00291159 .0247871 (2, 16, None)	lnX- lnIM .0800193 .0826007 (2, 16, None)	U.S.'s nX- nIM -.8459	.9592	1.4771
	-.0232329 .422093 (2, 16, None)	lnIM .0154692 .23291 (2, 16, None)	U.S.'s lnX- lnIM -1.71268	.9298	1.1696
France	3.20186 .802779 (2, 16, None)	lnIM -1.29029 .347046 (2, 16, None)	–	.7216	1.0897
	1.52223 .802779 (2, 16, None)	lnIM -1.686078 .271546 (2, 16, None)	German lnInd. Prod. 3.70733	.8238	1.4801
	.0752045 .0449752 (2, 16, None)	–	lnX .198066 lnIM 1.77282	.7145	1.1881
Germany	.573421 .0996609 (2, 16, None)	lnIM .0538336 .0696359 (2, 16, None)	lnX -.165146	.9833	1.5215

TABLE 9 (Continued)

	ln(Ind. Prod.)	ln(Trade Balance)	Other	$\bar{R}^2$	D.W.
Germany (Cont'd)	.540078 / .0224530 (2, 16, None)	lnX- lnIM -.189070 / .14997 (2, 16, None)	–	.9849	1.7536
	.530810 / .0221006 (2, 16, None)	–	lnX .209293 lnIM -1.24959	.9842	1.6964
Italy	.459189 / .0907149 (2, 16, None)	–	lnX -.701809 lnIM -1.21061	.8573	1.3660
	.668751 / .0928276 (2, 16, None)	lnIM -.128804 / .0665888 (2, 16, None)	lnX -.924221	.8903	2.0824
	.171902 / .0401907 (2, 16, None)	lnX- lnIM .171902 / .0401907 (2, 16, None)	–	.9061	1.2341
Japan	.675749 / .0841371 (2, 16, None)	–	lnX -.842474 lnIM -2.83151	.9513	9.524
	.221501 / .0486417 (2, 16, None)	lnX-lnIM .766587 / .162867 (2, 16, None)	–	.9707	1.4974

TABLE 9 (Continued)

	ln(Ind. Prod.)	ln(Trade Balance)	Other	$\bar{R}^2$	D. W.
Nether-lands	.433763 / .0890404 (2, 16, None)	–	lnX .778974 lnIM -.159282	.9653	.9198
	1.04635 / .109715 (2, 16, None)	lnX- lnIM -3.00607 / .596505 (2, 16, None)	–	.9823	1.0700
	.965475 / .106772 (2, 16, None)	lnX- lnIM -2.72913 / .564390 (2, 16, None)	Germany's lnX- lnIM 2.51436	.9848	1.5372
	-2.84473 / .566465 (2, 16, None)	lnX 2.24727 / .377779 (2, 16, None)	Germany's lnX- lnIM .684192	.9881	1.6253
Sweden	.233374 / .0392469 (2, 16, None)		lnX- lnIM -1.81106	.7787	.7299
	.384378 / .0272210 (2, 16, None)	lnX- lnIM -1.03848 / .152097 (2, 16, None)	–	.9361	1.4239
U.K.	.489238 / .13177 (2, 16, None)	lnIM -.108257 / .0408803 (2, 16, None)	lnX 2.67861	.8308	1.6744

TABLE 9 (Continued)

	ln(Ind. Prod.)	ln(Trade Balance)	Other	$\overline{R}^2$	D.W.
U.K. (Cont'd)	.269283 / .162033 (2, 16, None)	lnX .0851199 / .037656 (2, 16, None)	lnIM -3.14807	.7269	2.1783
U.S.	-.107084 / .0425897 (2, 16, None)		lnX- lnIM -2.38269	.6986	.6639
	0.387817 / .166195 (2, 16, None)	lnX- lnIM 1.04729 / .336427 (2, 16, None)		.8414	1.0245
Norway	.690805 / .1222071 (2, 16, None)		lnX 3.09931 nIM -2.91330	.9351	.8351

*Notes to Table 9:

All data are from International Financial Statistics, from first quarter 1960 through fourth quarter 1973.
CPI is the consumer price index, XPI is the export price index, IP is the industrial production index, X is the nominal value of exports, and IM is the nominal value of imports.
The first column shows the sum of the lagged coefficients on the natural log of IP, over the standard error of the estimate of this sum, the sum being significantly different from zero at the 95 % confidence level if this ratio is approximately 2 or larger; the notation (2, 16, None), for example, means the data were fitted with a second degree polynominal, with 16 lags, and no constraints. The second column's entries represent various trade balance influences, and are interpreted as with the first column. The third column presents the t-statistics of various contemporaneous variables, either the country's own or some other country's, that were conjectured as possibly significant. The $\overline{R}^2$ column gives the R^2 adjusted for degrees of freedom, and the D.W. is the Durbin-Watson statistic.

flexibility so as to reduce the importation of inflation from abroad via the behavior of tradeable goods prices as expressed in domestic currency.)

Comparing this last result to Phillips curve work, a majority of the twelve OECD countries Spitaller considered had import price inflation as a significant variable in their Phillips curves, at least over some time period he considered -- indeed, this was the only significant variable for Austria. In all cases the coefficient was positive and less than unity, which is not necessarily consistent with the stick relationship discussed above, for from the equation $\frac{\dot{CPI}}{CPI} - \frac{\dot{XPI}}{XPI} = f_{IP} \frac{\dot{IP}}{IP} + f_{TB} \frac{\dot{TB}}{TB}$, it would seem that a percentage point increase in tradeables price inflation should be accompanied on average by a percentage point increase in consumer price inflation over the long run when $\frac{\dot{IP}}{IP}$ and $\frac{\dot{TB}}{TB}$ return to the initial values. However, these conflicting results may be due to the need to use a lag structure on import prices longer than the one period lag Spitaller used, particularly in light of the Phillips curve debate over whether the size of the lag coefficients on past inflation does or should equal unity.[58)]

Phrased alternatively, as Haberler has stressed, for a given rate of inflation of world tradeable goods prices, faster growing countries would be forced to endure higher rates of domestic price inflation and slow growing countries lower rates of inflation as

58) See, for example, E. Phelps, "Money Wage Dynamics and Labor Market Equilibrium", in E. Phelps et al., Microeconomic Foundation of Employment and Inflation Theory, New York: W. W. Norton and Co., 1970; and T. Sargent, "A Note on the Accelerationist Controversy", Journal of Money, Credit and Banking, August, 1974.

measured by the CPI. It should be emphasized that this relationship is a property of full equilibrium under fixed exchange rates. In other words, this is a relationship brought about by the restoration of balance of payments equilibrium. As balance of payments equilibrium is only a long-run requirement under fixed exchange rates, and can be quite loose in the short run if there is ample international liquidity, this set of price relationships would be expected to be only a loose, long-run one. In the short term, where payments imbalances are feasible, the direct impact of changes in tradeable goods prices on CPI's is much more a function of the openness of the economy in question. For a given amount of allowed cumulative payments imbalance, the degree of openness of the economy would then influence the speed of adjustment of domestic to international prices -- i.e., the length of time domestic neutralization policies could be maintained -- but openness would not affect the amount of inflation required to restore full equilibrium.[59] These will be a function of the type of growth and productivity factors discussed above. Given these different types of linkages between tradeable goods prices and CPI's, it is obviously a quite delicate matter to interpret the results of regressions which include tradeable goods prices in Phillips curve relationships.

Before turning in the next section to explicit consideration of the possibility of a country neutralizing external inflationary pressures, it is worthwhile to draw an implication for the recent oil price in-

59) See Richard Caves, "Inflation in an Open Economy", Harvard Institute of Economic Research Discussion Paper, and Alexander Swoboda, "Monetary Policy Under Fixed Exchange Rates: Effectiveness, the Speed of Adjustment and Proper Use", Economica, May 1973.

creases. From our discussion of the short run of a strong quantity theory world where the country has great price and wage flexibility, it is clear such an economy's reaction would be a decline in other prices in order to preserve production and output at full employment levels. There would be little overall impact on the price level. In the somewhat less flexible world we live in, the autonomous increase in oil prices causes an outward shift in the short-run inflation-unemployment trade off. In response, countries may well resort to expansionary monetary policy to prevent unemployment; and there may well be more domestic inflation due to worsened cost-push pressures as firms find increased prices of oil-based inputs and workers increase their demands to recoup their losses due to oil price increases and further induced inflation.

Deficiencies in the construction of price indices make it difficult to determine the extent of the shift in the short-run trade off, and to compare such shifts across countries. For example, recent work by Nordhaus and Shoven[60)] indicates that the official wholesale price index calculated for the U.S. double-counts commodities and commodity-based products by including them at several stages in the total production process. For the period November 1972 to August 1973 they estimate that "approximately one-sixth of the announced wholesale inflation was due to the flaw of double counting in the weighting system used." Applying their work to oil, they conclude that a 55 percent rise in the wellhead price of crude oil causes a 3.1 % increase in the official WPI and a 1.7 % increase in their preferred version. Clearly, such discrepancies

---

60) William Nordhaus and John Shoven, "Inflation 1973: The Year of Infamy", Challenge, May-June 1974.

make empirical work very difficult, for example, in investigating the relationships among the consumer, wholesale and export price indices,[61] where a stick-like relationship normally exists between the consumer and wholesale price indices. Further, the unknown biases among indices in a given country and across countries make comparisons dubious.

3. Other Direct Transmission Mechanisms

We want briefly to note three other transmission mechanisms. The first is international expectations of inflation,[62] where the rise of foreign prices creates the domestic expectation of inflation. This tends to generate inflation both from cost-push labor demands and from an increase in current aggregate demand due to the relative decrease in current prices compared to expected future prices. Such expectations may be perfectly rational among countries whose prices do tend on average to move together. Another mechanism is international labor mobility,[63] which under fixed rates tends to make wages in the home country rise when foreign inflation drives up foreign wages (or wage-push drives up foreign prices) and attracts home country workers. With labor unions present, this mechanism may be coupled with union demands that tend to cause home wages to rise without the necessity of actual labor migration

---

61) Balassa, op. cit., and McKinnon, op. cit., both find a uniform ranking of these indices, in the order listed, across countries. In times of commodity-induced inflation, this relationship may well be different. Use of the WPI in place of a suspect export price index, a common practice, is likely quite inappropriate in such a case.

62) OECD Special Report, op. cit.

63) See R. Caves and G. Reuber, Capital Transfers and Economic Policy: Canada, 1951-1962, Chapter 5.

(which may be only day labor, for example, along the U.S. - Mexican border). Thus, it can be somewhat difficult to disentangle the effect of this mechanism from the third mechanism, international labor unions[64] that make uniform -- or constant (percentage) differential -- wage bargains across borders.

V. Neutralization of External Inflationary Pressures

In an inflationary world a country on fixed rates must eventually fall into line with inflation or revalue. All of the mechanisms contribute to this conclusion. It does not depend on one's brand of Keynesianism or monetarism. But it is worthwhile to consider the conditions that would aid a country under fixed rates in neutralizing external inflationary pressure for the short to medium run of several months to several years.

We might first note that it is perfectly consistent for monetarists to insist that all three mechanisms play crucial role in their theory. In Harry G. Johnson's exposition of a monetarist theory of the balance of payments described above, the tradeable goods price mechanism transmits price increases from abroad. If the home country does not expand its nominal money supply in step with this inflation, it experiences reserve inflows which will tend to, eventually, force it into line.[65] The ultimate cause of the domestic in-

64) OECD Special Report, op. cit.

65) In the strongest version of this theory, domestic prices always equal foreign prices, and foreign interest rates determine the domestic rate. Hence, income is always at full employment levels since output can always be sold abroad. Thus, the nominal demand for money is completely determined, and the continuous equality of demand and supply of money means massive short run capital flows will force the domestic money supply into line.

flation is excessive monetary expansion abroad. The Keynesian demand pressure mechanism is also consistent with this monetarist scenario since it can come into play to cause prices to begin their rise.[66)]

The Keynesian demand pressure mechanism has received the greatest emphasis in the literature, but such pressures are really the easiest to counter on the basis of our current understanding of macro theory. Excessive spot demand can be offset by government expenditure cuts or tax increases. Of course, this neutralization is by no means costless. Clearly, foreigners end up with more goods and home residents with fewer. In addition, there are likely costs involved in shifting factors from one sector to another, since deflationary fiscal policy is unlikely to fall on exactly and only those sectors subject to foreign demand. In the perfectly flexible quantity theory economy we previously discussed, an increase in export demand would induce an increase in the interest rate and thus a cutback in home investment demand. Increases in export prices would be offset by decreases in investment goods prices. On average the price level would remain constant but goods would be diverted to exports. In actual economies the use of fiscal policy will not exactly correspond to this process; that is, fiscal policy is an imperfect substitute for price and wage flexibility.

---

66) Once inflation is underway and continues to be fed by monetary expansion, the excess demand pressure may disappear, replaced by inflationary expectations pressure. For consideration of growth models which rely on continued excess demand pressure, and those which do not, see Jerome L. Stein, "Monetary Growth Theory in Perspective", American Economic Review, 1972.

Given the size of the disturbance, relative to the size of the trade sector, it clearly follows that the smaller is the trade sector relative to government policy economy, the better is the chance that government policy will not prove excessively expensive. For example, if it is desired to divert goods from the investment to the trade sector, then given the size of the trade sector and also the interest elasticity of investment, the larger is the investment sector the smaller is the increase in the interest rate that is needed to divert an amount equal to say 10 % of the trade sector.

Institutionally, most countries may simply be unable to use fiscal policy with any great flexibility. And the political costs to decision-makers in using fiscal policy may be so high as to make it unattractive. It has been argued that fiscal policy cannot be optimally used in the U.S. until the President has discretionary power to change taxes, a policy strongly resisted in Congress.

The problem of neutralizing the domestic monetary expansion mechanism has also received much attention. The first necessity for such neutralization is to have an institutional arrangement that allows sterilization. Once this exists, the discretionary use of sterilization seems to encounter far fewer political difficulties than use of fiscal policy.[67)]

The appropriate criterion for sterilization policy is not obvious. Even in a simple quantity theory world, the distribution of money

---

67) See J. R. Hicks' comments on discretionary monetary policy in his "Monetary Theory and History -- An Attempt at Perspective", Critical Essays in Monetary Theory, Oxford, 1967.

balances between domestic holders and foreign holders will affect nominal activity (and with elements of price and wage inflexibility, real activity) if these holders have different transactions velocity, or to put it in older terminology, if one group or the other holds a larger proportion of its balances as inactive balances. If, for example, all foreign balances are inactive, held only for portfolio reasons, foreign acquisition of 10 % of the money supply can be successfully sterilized, but there will be deflationary pressures to reduce prices by 10 %. On the other hand if most foreign balances are held to facilitate transactions, they may have a higher velocity than domestically held balances, and thus an increase in the foreign held component of a constant money supply will induce inflationary pressures. Clearly, the magnitude of this problem is smaller the smaller are foreign accumulations relative to the money supply and (given velocity) home nominal economic activity.

Such disturbances are also likely to be less serious the larger is the national capital market and the better integrated is the market both regionally and among instruments, for the additional flexibility of integration will tend to spread the impact. To the extent that monetary policy has severe effects on one or a few particular sectors -- for example, housing in the U.S. -- the better integrated are capital markets and the more free they are from segmenting and distorting regulations, the less damaging will be the microeconomic effects of monetary policy.

It would also seem that the more flexible is the economy the less serious are all these problems on the grounds that price and wage flexibility is a good substitute for appropriate monetary policy, but this issue needs a good deal more attention.

While highly integrated domestic capital markets facilitate monetary neutralization, a high degree of international integration makes it more difficult to sterilize. As integration becomes perfect, sterilization becomes impossible even over a moderately short period. This, however, is merely Mundell's point that with perfect integration monetary policy is ineffective. The appropriate tool for neutralization is then fiscal policy, which can now be used without the necessity of worrying about its coordination with monetary policy.[68)]

---

68) For a discussion of international integration from a finance theory perspective, see D. Logue, M. Salant and R. J. Sweeney, "International Financial Integration: Survey, Synthesis and Results", op. cit. They agree with M. Fratianni, in his paper in this volume,

> "Empirical tests (e.g., Kouri-Porter) which have shown that for some countries the endogenous foreign component of the (monetary) base offsets dollar for dollar changes in the domestic and policy controlled base corroborate only one of the two conditions which must be satisfied to completely disable policy in a regime of fixed exchange rates. The other condition is that, as capital flows in and out of the home country, the foreign demand for domestic security is not affected. But once domestic securities are traded, a capital flow, "offsetting" an autonomous injection of base money, implies a reduction in the foreign holdings of domestic securities and thus a downward shift in the aggregate demand for domestic securities. The rate of interest is altered even though the total amount of base money has not." (p. 3)

Logue, Salant and Sweeney argue that complete capital reflow generally requires that the initiating country not sterilizes reserve flows but that other countries sterilize completely, and that countries' bonds be perfect substitutes. Fratianni's point is then taken to be a conceptual experiment showing that the initial price (cont'd)

With all mechanisms it would seem that the more rapid is a country's real growth the greater scope is there for low cost neutralization. It may be far easier to cut back a sector's growth than its level. To the extent that new factors are entering the market, they can with much less cost be directed among sectors than factors can be shifted when once in place.

In contrast to the Keynesian demand pressure and domestic monetary expansion mechanisms, the tradeable goods price mechanism does not work through aggregate demand but directly on goods prices. In considering the country that has the best chance to resist these forces, at least in the short run, it seems apparent that such a country would have a trade sector that is large relative to the entire amount of international trade. This is no more than saying that the country will then have some pricing power in international trade and when it tries to resist, for example, price increases generated through the tradeable goods sector, it has sufficient weight to resist these forces to some extent.

Secondly, however, the tradeable goods sector of this economy ought to be small relative to the entire economy. Thus, suppose for example the economy is inflating at a somewhat faster rate than

---

(footnote 68) cont'd) vector no longer gives equilibrium, since the relative stocks of imperfectly substitutable bonds have changed.

Brunner's point, in his essay in this volume, is also well-taken. He argues that in a model with a range of financial assets, monetary policy can be effective by altering some asset prices even if other asset prices are tied to foreign, constant prices. Logue, Salant and Sweeney argue that monetary changes are not completely offset by reflows, except under the very stringent assumptions noted above, and in general act by affecting all asset prices.

the rest of the world and this is causing the tradeable goods prices to go up faster than the rest of the world. The burden of unemployment on the entire economy is smaller than it would be if tradeables were a more important part of the economy. Alternatively, if the country is trying to resist imported inflation, it may not allow its domestic prices to rise as fast as tradeables prices are trying to push them up. This tends also to keep tradeables prices somewhat below the international level of price inflation, causing reserve inflows, perhaps, and excess demand in the tradeable goods sector. Again this excess demand is less severe the smaller the tradeable goods sector is relative to the economy. Finally, we might note that the country is in a better position to control its domestic price level the more its tradeable goods are composed of items that are imperfect substitutes for other tradeable goods. It seems the U.S. is a country that meets these specifications better than other countries -- even those such as Germany and Japan.

An important question is how the factors which influence the cost or ease of neutralization under fixed rates affect the costs of exchange rate adjustments as the major policy alternative for neutralization. The necessary theoretical underpinnings for such comparisons are given in the theory of optimum currency areas.[69] One point from this literature is particularly worth making. A standard result in the optimum currency area literature is that

---

69) See E. Tower and T. D. Willett, The Theory of Optimum Currency Area and Exchange Rate Flexibility, International Financial Section, Princeton, Special Papers in International Finance, 1976.

the effectiveness of exchange rate adjustments varies inversely with the openness of the economy. This relationship holds, however, only when the purpose of the exchange rate change is to alter relative prices.

As we have argued elsewhere, where the purpose of the exchange rate change is to maintain a previously existing equilibrium, this relationship between effectiveness and openness does not hold.[70] If the exchange rate moves immediately to offset a general increase in the prices of internationally traded goods, then this can be done equally well whether the tradeable goods sector represents five or forty percent of the economy. In either case the exchange rate change serves to maintain rather than change the domestic currency price of tradeable goods. Even a small open economy can insultate itself from general changes in world tradeable goods prices by appropriate exchange rate policy.

Of course, to the extent there are transactions whose real value is not influenced proportionately by the increase in traded goods prices, there will be some adjustment costs imposed by exchange rate changes; but by and large we would not expect the openness of an economy to be a major determinant of the effectiveness with which it can use exchange rate adjustments to insulate itself from the inflation of world tradeable goods prices.

The discussion has concentrated on "smooth" phenomena -- for example, neutralizing an inflow of $ 1 billion per year for three

---

70) Sweeney and Willett, "The Inflationary Impact of Exchange Rate Changes", op. cit.

years -- with no emphasis on whether these inflows are bunched at particular times. Rather clearly, though, such bunching can be serious. Institutions may not have sufficient flexibility to deal with short bursts, and the lags in policy-making become more serious. Thus, one would expect relatively poorer results for neutralization policy the more variance there is in the phenomena being offset. However, it is not at all clear that the relatively lesser success of neutralization would not be accompanied by poorer results for revaluation also.

VI. Concluding Remarks

Our paper has concentrated on the operation of direct economic mechanisms. While definite evidence can be found of international transmissions of inflationary pressures, it is questionable whether these can provide the major explanation of the acceleration of world inflation over the past decade. Yet acceleration of inflation rates was so widespread across individual countries that the odds of this occuring by chance are miniscule. While domestic factors (monetary and fiscal policies and developments shifting short-run inflation-unemployment trade offs) seem to present the major portion of explanation for inflation in most countries, causal observation suggests a good deal of similarity in the behavior of these domestic factors.

Indeed one of the most powerful international transmission mechanisms may have been that of ideas, beliefs, and attitudes. The Keynesian revolution and beliefs in fairly stable Phillips curves may have raised economists' and governments' expectations of how much the operation of the macroeconomy could be improved by more than was in fact possible. Combined with increasing demands by citizens for both greater personal income and public service and redistribution policies, expectations in one country after another may have been raised more rapidly than the capacity of the economic systems to meet them. Under such circumstances political pressures for excessively expansionary monetary and fiscal policies are difficult to resist. On top of this, the general decline in money illusion has greatly reduced the capacity of inflationary policies to bring consistency to demand for income shares. While over the long run one might hope this would reduce the incentives for inflationary policies, in the first instance, such diminished "effectiveness" of inflationary policies to satisfy income claimants may accelerate rather than reduce the strength with which they are applied. This is the classic prescription for accelerating inflation and the prevalence may well stem more from the similarity of social pressures and government mechanisms in different countries than from direct economic transmissions of inflationary pressures from one country to another.

Systematic investigation of this indirect transmission of inflation, however, goes well beyond the scope of this study and indeed beyond the science of economics alone. At a minimum knowledge and insight from economics, sociology, and political science would be required for a satisfactory analysis of the recent phenomena of worldwide inflation.[71)]

71) The November 1974 Brookings Conference on Worldwide Inflation touched on these issues as part of an ongoing study which will in part focus on them. They were the subject of the March 1976 International Institute for Economic Research-Treasury Workshop on the Political, Social and Economic Causes and Consequences of Worldwide Inflation, which was part of a series of conferences, workshops and studies on these matters.

Comments on the paper
of R. J. Sweeney and T. D. Willett

By
Marcello de Cecco

I shall restrict my comments to two aspects of the Sweeney and Willett paper: what they call the Keynesian mechanism, and the Eurodollar market.

Although it has been often said before, it must be reiterated that there is a marked difference between Keynes himself and those who call themselves Keynesians. Keynes, in the "General Theory", was really only interested in quantities, not in prices. This is, of course, a matter of emphasis. There is plenty, in Keynes' writings, about prices, but if a transmission mechanism exists in Keynes' analysis, it certainly deals with the transmission of impulses, and their multiplication, from certain quantity aggregates to certain others, for instance from investment to output and employment. Keynesian analysis, as developed in Keynes' own writings, is an attempt to bring into relief, from the cobweb of economic relations, some "privileged" communication subsystems. It is a masterpiece of "partial" analysis which has, as a counterpart, a price to pay, and that is its olympic disregard for other "unprivileged" sub-systems. Of these, one of the most disregarded is the classical transmission mechanism, which is expressed in prices. Keynes tried to show how it was possible to by-pass effectively a good seventy-five per cent of the total economic network, by insisting on sending impulses, signals, through his "privileged" quantity sub-system. This he thought to be essential, as the rest of the economic control network was in disarray. Impulses, generated by a traditional economic policy through traditional channels, would only be transformed, through the working of the "unprivileged" part of the system, into incoherent "noise". An economic policy message, therefore, sent out in classical fashion, would only very inefficiently and haphazardly be transmitted to the relevant macroeconomic aggregates.

Much more relevant to an analysis of the mechanism of inflation is Keynes' expectation theory. And equally relevant to it, as it is to an analysis of the generation and transmission of depression, is Keynes' study of how entrepreneurs and savers choose between industrial and financial assets, depending on what the outlook is, at any time, for profits, interest rates, and industrial activity. More generally, a reading of Keynes enlightens our view of the inflationary process especially because of what he has to say about speculation, expectations, and cumulative phenomena.

What, on the other hand, goes under the name of Keynesianism, has certainly very little to do with Keynes, in the analysis of inflation as well as in related fields.

As I said earlier, it is extremely difficult to extend a partial analysis, conducted in quantities, within a closed model, such as that of the "General Theory", to a general equilibrium analysis, conducted in prices, as is that of a world inflationary process.

There is only one chance of, at least partially, resolving this contradiction. Namely of considering the Western world as one economic centre, with the United States which really dominates the rest of the system in sheer weight, determining, by itself, the course of Western economic cycles.

If this model of asymmetrical international economic relations is a realistic picture of the actual world, things become much easier analytically, but no less difficult to appraise from a Keynesian standpoint.

This outlook seems to me to be the basis of the new approach to balance of payments theory sponsored by H. G. Johnson, R. A. Mundell and others. Their view of the international transmission of inflation would have little bearing on reality if it did not, as it does, assume that there has come to exist since 1958 a more direct link between the American and the other Western financial systems, such that it has been and is still possible for the U.S. monetary authorities to determine, by omission or commission, the rate of inflation of the world economy.

Again, the new approach highlights a sub-system within the world economic system, that of international financial relations: messages, emanating from the American monetary system, reach the Western countries' monetary systems without much loss of efficiency. The impact is direct and powerful. That it is so is essentially a result of the particular type of financial integration that has been gradually achieved, in the West, since 1958; the monetarist approach to balance of payments theory owes its undoubted realism and poignancy to the actual mode of integration of world financial markets as much as to anything else.

This takes me to my second comment. I beg to differ from Messrs. Willett and Sweeney for what concerns the Eurodollar market. In their paper, they deal with this phenomenon in a short aside, while I am of the opinion that, in a survey of the "International transmission of inflation: mechanisms and issues" the Eurodollar market deserves first-priority treatment as a basic mechanism for the international transmission of inflation.

The Eurodollar market is a fundamental feature of the mode in which international financial integration has taken place in the last fifteen years: it is indeed impossible to understand the monetary approach to balance of payments theory without introducing it as a basic element. What the Eurodollar market does, in a nutshell, is to multiply any new unit of international currency reserves by a rather large factor, or, if we want to paraphrase the expression coined by Milton Friedman, it raises the power of a unit of international high-powered money. The Eurodollar market's main function is to increase the velocity of circulation of international reserves. Moreover, since the Eurodollar market deposits are not subject to reserve limits, every increase in them means, other things remaining the same, an increase in the profits of the banking sector of the international economy. It is this microeconomic stimulus, coupled with the already mentioned macroeconomic one, that has induced the unceasing growth of the Eurodollar market, in the last 15 years. And this market, whose gross size has grown from one hundred to three hundred billions of dollars in the last five years, works as a highly sensitive transmission mechanism between the U.S. monetary system and those of the rest of the world.

Moreover, the transfer of deposits that has taken place from the national markets to the Eurodollar market has permitted the working of a much larger multiplier on any given international monetary base, with the result that world total credit supply has been much larger than what it would have been had no Eurodollar market existed.

In general, it can be said that the huge privatization of monetary functions that the growth of the Eurodollar market has meant in the last decade has permitted through the effective lowering of reserve ratios and the international circulation of reserves, a dramatic increase in the velocity of circulation of money and, by this means, an equivalent increase in the world money supply.

No study of the contemporary inflationary process makes sense if it does not go deeply and exhaustively into the political economy of the Eurodollar market.

INTERNATIONAL INFLATIONARY LINKAGES
AND THE RECENT EXPERIENCE
IN INDIVIDUAL COUNTRIES

By
John C. Pattison*

I. Introduction

The analysis of economic events is fraught with difficulties. With hindsight it is possible to attribute causes to the great depression of the 1930's, the post-war inflation and similar events, but at the time interpretation is difficult because of short-run preoccupations, unreliable statistics and a body of popular economic and political thought that almost always relates to past situations. The present world inflation is another example. Academic economists had become aware of the international aspects of inflation under a fixed exchange rate system, but this knowledge was only assimilated and passed on to policy makers after exchange rate movements had become commonplace. Policy makers themselves have contributed to our current difficulties by failing to discriminate between real and nominal magnitudes. Many econometric models used for policy simulations also failed to make such a distinction particularly for interest rates. As well, most of our statistics were constructed during periods of relative price stability and many of these can be

* The comments of the discussants and participants at the Conference were appreciated. Michele Fratianni and Grant Reuber also gave helpful advice. The statistics were prepared by A. Angeloupos and L. Hui. The final product is the author's responsability.

misleading when applied in inflationary situations.

The purpose of this paper is limited to providing a statistical background to enable events and theories concerning inflation as an international phenomenon to be placed in their proper perspective. All too often widely held views or theories are incompatible with actual economic developments or the timing of the acceleration of inflation itself. By following such an approach, the range of possible explanations can be narrowed. Since politicians are fond of saying that inflation is caused abroad by events outside their control it is hoped that this exercise will prove useful. The format is as follows. The first section discusses the dispersion of inflation rates while the second examines recent exchange rate developments to determine the applicability of alternative theories. This is followed by an analysis of monetary developments, trade prices, demand, exchange rate regimes and the relevance of the boom in commodity prices.

II. Some Arithmetic

One of the interesting aspects of inflation on a world scale is the difference among countries. In a previous paper I examined the standard deviation as a measure of dispersion.[1] Alternatively the coefficient of variation could be used. Since the coefficient of variation is the ratio of the standard deviation to the mean, the implicit idea behind its use would be that a given distribution of inflation rates represents less of a dispersion at higher average rates. If complete arbitrage among national prices via the mechanism of

1) See [16].

international trade flows is possible, the standard deviation would be the more appropriate statistic. Since the measure or meaning of the dispersion of inflation rates is not obvious, more detail will be given here. Table 1A contains the relevant data by year, while Table 1B points out the highest and lowest movements in GNP deflators and the countries involved as well as the mean and the range between the highest and lowest figures.

Clearly the coefficient of variation shows a decline in the dispersion while the standard deviation shows only a very slight decline which is not statistically significant.[2)] Most of the fall in the coefficient of variation is attributable to the recent higher mean rate of inflation. Some economists have noted that the standard deviation of inflation rates has not declined lately and have suggested that a sharp decline probably occurred with the postwar return to currency convertibility in 1958. Aside from the aberrant year of 1958 itself the data do not support this view. Perhaps the most interesting aspect of these statistics is the wide range of inflation rates that existed under the fixed exchange rate system. Various countries were often several standard deviations from the mean, and the average range of inflation rates in the 1960's was six percent. Of the 18 years shown, Ireland and Finland had the highest rates of inflation on four occasions. On the low side, the United States had the best performance for 5 of the 18 years. If one wanted to divide the countries into big and small with Canada as the dividing line in

2) For example, the mean standard deviation for the most recent 5 years is 1.69 against 1.86 for the first five years. Assar Lindbeck has argued that even this decline disappears if extreme values are removed. In my own view that would remove what one is trying to look for in these statistics.

TABLE 1A

Mean and Dispersion of GNP Deflator
in 17 OECD Countries(1)

	Mean	Standard deviation	Coefficient of variation
1956	4.5	1.7	0.4
1957	4.0	1.5	0.4
1958	2.8	3.2	1.1
1959	2.0	1.5	0.7
1960	2.6	1.3	0.5
1961	3.0	1.6	0.5
1962	3.6	1.6	0.5
1963	4.0	1.8	0.5
1964	4.6	2.1	0.4
1965	4.4	1.3	0.3
1966	4.2	1.2	0.3
1967	3.7	1.1	0.3
1968	3.8	2.0	0.5
1969	4.5	1.5	0.3
1970	6.1	2.0	0.3
1971	6.7	1.7	0.3
1972	6.5	1.7	0.3
1973	6.4	1.5	0.2

(1) Canada, United States, Japan, Australia, Austria, Belgium, Denmark, Finland, France, Germany, Ireland, Italy, Netherlands, Norway, Sweden, Switzerland, United Kingdom.

TABLE 1B

Highest, Lowest and Mean Rates of Inflation in OECD Countries

	Highest		Mean	Lowest		Range High-Low
1956	9.1	Finland	4.6	1.3	Switzerland	7.8
1957	7.4	Finland	4.0	1.2	Denmark	6.2
1958	12.0	France	2.8	-1.6	Norway	13.6
1959	6.2	France	2.0	-0.3	Italy	6.5
1960	5.0	Sweden/Japan	2.6	0.5	Ireland	4.5
1961	6.8	Japan	3.0	0.7	Canada	6.1
1962	6.7	Denmark	3.6	1.2	Belgium/ United States	5.5
1963	8.6	Italy	4.0	1.3	United States	7.3
1964	9.4	Ireland	4.6	2.6	Australia/Canada	6.8
1965	5.9	Netherlands	4.4	1.9	United States	4.0
1966	7.1	Denmark	4.3	2.1	Italy	5.0
1967	5.6	Finland	3.7	1.2	Germany	4.4
1968	10.7	Finland	3.8	1.5	Italy	9.2
1969	8.4	Ireland	4.5	2.9	Sweden/ Switzerland	5.5
1970	11.5	Norway	6.1	3.2	Finland	8.3
1971	10.7	Ireland	6.7	3.2	Canada	7.5
1972	11.0	Ireland	6.5	3.2	United States	7.8
1973	12.5	Australia	6.4	5.3	United States	7.2

terms of GNP, one of the biggest seven countries (U.S., Japan, Canada, France, Germany, Italy and the United Kingdom which have almost 90 per cent of the combined GNP) would have had the highest rate of inflation in only 5 out of the 18 years, whereas they would have had the lowest rate in 11 out of 18 years. In this vein, it is often suggested that price stability in a few major countries is a requirement for world price stability.

One final point on the dispersion issue. The fact that inflation rates should be similar across countries under a fixed exchange rate system is often compared with the situation in an individual country (which has to have fixed exchange rates among regions). It is asserted that within a country prices must be equalized. To test this latter theory, inflation rates for ten cities in Canada were subjected to the same analysis as for countries. The resulting data are given in Tables 2A and 2B. Although the coefficient of variation does decline in a similar manner, it is less than the same statistic for the industrialized countries. As well, the average standard deviations for the first and last five-year periods for the Canadian cities are virtually identical. The spread between high and low rates is quite small in absolute terms, when compared with the earlier statistics and this explains to some extent how some cities switch frequently from having the highest to the lowest rates and vice versa.[3)]

---

3) Genburg [6] has shown that on average inflation rates have not differed more between countries than between U.S. Cities.

TABLE 2A

Mean and Dispersion of Regional
Inflation Rates in Canada

	Mean rate(1)	Standard deviation	Coefficient of variation
1950	3.3	0.7	0.2
1951	10.5	1.0	0.1
1952	1.7	0.8	0.4
1953	-1.1	0.6	0.5
1954	0.9	0.3	0.3
1955	0.5	0.4	0.8
1956	1.4	0.5	0.3
1957	2.9	0.4	0.2
1958	2.5	0.3	0.1
1959	1.3	0.7	0.5
1960	1.1	0.2	0.2
1961	0.9	0.3	0.4
1962	1.1	0.4	0.3
1963	1.4	0.4	0.3
1964	1.1	0.5	0.4
1965	1.8	0.3	0.2
1966	3.1	0.6	0.2
1967	3.2	0.6	0.2
1968	4.0	0.4	0.1
1969	3.8	0.5	0.1
1970	2.9	0.7	0.2
1971	1.9	0.7	0.4
1972	4.1	0.4	0.1
1973	6.9	0.6	0.1

(1) St. John's (Nfld), Halifax, St. John, Montreal, Ottawa, Toronto, Winnipeg, Saskatoon, Edmonton, Vancouver.

TABLE 2B

High and Low Rates in Canada
with their Location

	Highest rate		Mean	Lowest rate		Range High-Low
1950	4.1	Toronto	3.3	2.2	Halifax	1.9
1951	12.0	Montreal	10.5	9.3	Saskatoon/ Edmonton	2.7
1952	3.0	St. John	1.7	1.0	Saskatoon	2.0
1953	0.2	Saskatoon	-1.1	-1.8	Halifax/St.John	2.0
1954	1.3	Toronto	0.9	0.4	Montreal	0.9
1955	1.4	St. John's	0.5	-0.2	Edmonton	1.6
1956	2.5	St. John's	1.4	0.9	St. John	1.6
1957	3.8	Toronto	2.9	2.4	St.John's/ Winnipeg	1.4
1958	3.1	Montreal	2.5	1.9	Ottawa	1.2
1959	2.5	Halifax	1.3	0.2	Toronto	2.3
1960	1.5	Winnipeg	1.1	0.8	Montreal	0.7
1961	1.5	Winnipeg	0.9	0.3	Vancouver	1.2
1962	1.7	Saskatoon	1.1	0.3	Vancouver	1.4
1963	2.0	St. John's	1.4	0.8	Saskatoon	1.2
1964	1.7	Toronto	1.1	0.4	Halifax	1.3
1965	2.5	Toronto	1.8	1.5	St.John's/St. John/Edmonton	1.0
1966	4.4	Toronto	3.1	2.4	St. John's/ Vancouver	2.0
1967	4.0	Edmonton	3.2	2.3	Halifax	1.7
1968	4.5	St. John's	4.0	3.4	Montreal	1.1
1969	4.6	Halifax	3.8	2.9	St. John's	1.7
1970	4.1	Halifax	2.9	1.9	St. John's	2.2
1971	2.6	Ottawa	1.9	1.0	Saskatoon	1.6
1972	4.1	Ottawa/ Toronto	4.1	3.7	Halifax	0.4
1973	8.2	St. John's	6.9	5.8	Saskatoon	2.4

III. Alternative Theories of International Inflation

There are many aspects and theories of the international transmission of inflation although they are often specific to one exchange rate regime. Consequently knowledge of the prevailing exchange rate system is a precondition for any proper analytic discussion. Although it is obvious that exchange rates presently vary substantially, it is less obvious when the fixed rate regime ceased. Formally, a generalized period of floating began in February 1973 after the second dollar devaluation, however, considerable flexibility existed from the time of the U.S. decision to make the dollar inconvertible on 15th August, 1971. Going further back in time, the number and frequency of exchange rate changes seemed to increase after the devaluation of the pound sterling in late 1967. Table 3 contains indices of effective exchange rates, where the weights have been calculated using the multilateral trade model of the IMF.[4)] It can be seen that substantial flexibility did exist from 1967 but that movements in the 1970's were much more dramatic. Surprisingly, there was a substantial amount of variability shown in the first few years of the table (1959 to 1961).[5)] This was the period just after the return to currency convertibility in Europe.[6)]

The most widely discussed monetary theory of the international

4) Source: O.E.C.D.

5) In 1960 only one of the countries shown had a negative change in the effective exchange rate. This strange pattern can be attributed to the large devaluations of Iceland, Spain and Turkey which are not shown.

6) It is worth noting that the average rate of inflation was higher over the three years preceding this period. The average change in the consumer price index for the OECD area was 1.9 per cent from 1959 to 1961 whereas it was 3.3 per cent from 1956 to 1958.

TABLE 3

Percentage Changes in Effective Exchange Rates from 1970 First Quarter 1)

	1958	1959	1960	1961	1962	1963	1964	1965	1966	1967	1968	1969	1970	1971	1972	1973
Canada	7.6	9.7	9.2	4.4	-1.0	-2.0	-2.0	-1.9	-1.8	-1.8	-0.2	-0.1	2.7	5.2	3.8	-1.3
United States	-9.4	-7.7	-5.4	-3.7	-2.5	-2.2	-2.1	-2.1	-2.0	-1.7	0.3	0.4	-0.7	-3.3	-9.3	-16.1
Japan	-6.4	-5.1	-3.7	-3.2	-2.8	-2.8	-2.9	-2.8	-3.0	-2.7	-0.6	0.2	-0.4	1.5	12.2	18.6
Austria	-4.9	-2.9	-1.8	-1.8	-1.5	-1.5	-1.5	-1.4	-1.3	-1.0	1.2	1.2	-0.2	0.7	1.9	8.3
Belgium	-6.7	-3.0	-1.6	-2.4	-2.5	-2.7	-2.5	-2.1	-2.3	-2.0	-0.9	-0.7	-0.4	-0.5	2.2	2.8
France	27.2	10.9	13.1	12.8	12.8	12.8	12.8	12.9	12.7	12.7	14.2	9.1	0.1	-2.1	-0.1	2.0
Germany	-20.9	-17.9	-16.1	-12.4	-11.9	-11.5	-11.2	-11.7	-11.7	-11.1	-9.3	-7.1	1.0	4.0	6.6	17.0
Italy	-7.1	-2.9	-0.8	-0.5	-0.6	-0.7	-1.2	-1.2	-1.0	-0.8	1.0	0.9	0.1	-0.7	-1.8	-12.1
Nether-lands	-8.6	-5.7	-4.3	-1.3	-0.5	-0.5	-0.7	-0.4	-0.8	-0.2	1.4	1.6	0.1	1.1	2.4	5.0
Switzer-land	-7.5	-5.5	-3.3	-3.0	-3.2	-3.1	-3.0	-3.1	-3.0	-2.7	-0.1	0.3	-0.4	2.3	3.5	13.8
United Kingdom	7.7	10.3	13.1	13.7	14.1	13.9	13.6	13.8	13.8	12.0	-0.5	-0.3	-0.5	-0.5	-4.2	-14.1

1) Note that the data are all deviations from the 1970 level and are not yearly changes.

transmission of inflation assumes that under a fixed exchange rate system the balance of payments deficits of the United States, as a key currency country, spill over into the reserve bases and ultimately the money supplies of the surplus countries. In this framework the issuance of SDR's provides an increase in international money which promotes inflation. Under flexible exchange rates countries are free to determine independent monetary policies. If countries' policy makers abuse this freedom the world money supply could grow excessively. The pressure of demand can also transmit inflation under a fixed exchange rate either directly or via the monetary implications of changes in trade balances.

The role of the prices of internationally traded goods in transmitting inflation seems clear. Domestic price effects can come from the prices of imported goods which are not produced domestically and from changes in the prices of goods which compete with domestic goods which may not be traded. Scandinavian theorists have developed a model of external inflationary linkages by dividing economies into "exposed" and "sheltered" sectors. A sector is exposed if it sells its production abroad or if it competes domestically against foreign firms. The sheltered sector is assumed to have little competition and would include the public sector and the service sector. The local currency prices of the exposed sector are determined by world market prices and the exchange rate, while prices in the sheltered sector depend upon costs and a desire to maintain some given level of profits. Consequently, if world prices or the exchange rate alter, wages in the exposed sector will be altered in the short to medium term. These wage changes will spread to the sheltered sector and, given the lower level of productivity growth, will lead to price increases in this sector. This theoretical framework can adapt to either exchange rate regime.

Finally, there are a number of theories which relate world inflation to sociological factors concerning income distribution or extravagant expectations. These do not consider the relevance of alternative exchange rate regimes. Since such theories seem ill-suited to the simultaneous worldwide nature of inflation they will not be pursued here.

1. Monetary Aspects

The simplest monetary theory of world inflation relates the acceleration of prices to United States balance of payments deficits and the fact that under a fixed exchange rate system these would cause increases in the money supplies of surplus countries. It is easy to discount this theory by noting that 1968 and 1969 were years of United States surpluses on the balance on official reserve transactions. This is not an adequate refutation of the theory for two reasons. First, neither the balance on official reserve transactions nor the net liquidity version is appropriate for a key currency country. The gross liquidity balance is preferable since liquid claims and liabilities of a non-key and a key currency country do not have symmetrical monetary effects.[7] The following table shows both the official reserve transactions balance and the gross liquidity balance. Clearly the theory cannot be refuted on the grounds of the existence of a surplus if a more appropriate measure of the monetary impact of the balance of payments is used. As well, the existence

7) For a thorough discussion of balance of payments accounting and the monetary base see Fratianni and Savona [5].

of lags in the mechanisms whereby payments imbalances affect the money supply and money affects prices imply that simple correlations with price behavior are unlikely to yield strong results. Although there is some superficial relationship between the gross liquidity deficit of the United States and world inflation these two magnitudes did not move consistently on a year-by-year basis.

TABLE 4

Alternative Definitions of the United States Balance of Payments (millions of dollars)

Year	Official Reserve Transactions	Gross Liquidity Balance (Excluding SDR Allocations)
1965	- 1290	- 1421
1966	+ 219	- 2165
1967	- 3418	- 4890
1968	+ 1641	- 2169
1969	+ 2739	- 5919
1970	- 9839	- 4466
1971	-29753	-23779
1972	-10354	-15813
1973	- 5304	- 9740

Source: Survey of Current Business, U.S. Department of Commerce, June 1974, p. 30.

Given that the basic requirement exists for this theory it is largely an empirical matter to examine the portfolio behavior of national monetary authorities. In a study of the period from 1950 to 1966

Michaely has shown that deficit countries generally embarked upon a policy of tight money while surplus countries eased monetary conditions although the evidence was not uniform [11]. In the years since that study it would appear that countries have been less willing to allow their monetary policy to be decided abroad. In the face of sustained balance of payments disequilibrium the sterilization of large surpluses would be difficult in many countries because of the thinness of domestic money markets. Nonetheless the growth in the money supply of non-U.S. OECD countries did not accelerate until 1971. From 1965 to 1970 for example the average annual rate of increase was about 12 per cent, whereas in 1971 it jumped to 17 per cent.[8)] As can be seen from Table 4, 1971 was the year of peak U.S. deficits but by this time exchange rates were beginning to perform some of the adjustments.

Portfolio decisions of central bankers are now much more complicated than simply buying or selling gold and dollars. Deposits are held with other central banks, in Eurodollars and in United States Treasury bills. Shifts in a portfolio with an unchanged balance of payments can produce quite different monetary impacts. One of the most dramatic was the pyramiding of intitial surpluses when redeposited by central banks in the Eurodollar market by the BIS. Pyramiding in the Eurodollar market will only end when leakages occur from Eurodollars into the official reserves of a central bank that would acquire direct claims on the United States. The following table gives some indication of the size of the Eurocurrency

---

8) The statistics were taken from [16]. The difficulties in interpreting domestic monetary statistics in light of balance of payments changes should be noted. See Argy and Kouri [1].

market since 1964. In 1968 the 27 billion dollar size of the Eurocurrency market compares with the money supply of Germany which was 22 billion dollars, or France at 44 billion or the United Kingdom at 37 billion.[9)] This was a major increase in liquidity to supplement the domestic money supplies, and the timing would not be inconsistent with the rise in the world rate of inflation. Unfortunately there is virtually no empirical work linking the growth of the Eurodollar market to domestic non-financial variables.

TABLE 5

Size and Growth of the Eurocurrency Market
(billion U.S. dollars)

Year	Size	Growth Rate (per cent)
1964	9	--
1965	12	33
1966	15	25
1967	18	20
1968	27	50
1969	44	63
1970	57	30
1971	70	23
1972	92	31
1973[e]	130	41

e: estimated

9) Converted to U.S. dollars at 1968 exchange rates, Source: OECD, Main Economic Indicators.

A related monetary issue concerns the role of special drawing rights. These have been issued three times: on 1st January, 1970, 3,414.3 million, on 1st January, 1971, 2,949.2 million, and finally on 1st January, 1972, for 2,951.5 million, for a total of 9,315 million. The current value of an SDR is approximately 1.2 U.S. dollars. Compared with domestic money creation and the growth of the Eurodollar market, there does not appear to have been a great inflationary stimulus in the amounts issued, although it is true that they added to world money at a time when this was not desirable. Using a very simple model, Neumann has recently shown that changing SDR's for dollars at a fixed price does not alter domestic money supplies whereas the financing of deficits with SDR's would allow the rate of inflation to rise, but would not have caused the inflation [12]. Given the awareness of the misguided rate of money creation in recent years, it seems unlikely that more SDR's will be issued in the near to medium term, thereby defusing this topic.

One direct test of the simple global monetary thesis is possible. A world price equation is derived in the monetary approach to the balance of payments which assumes that inflation is generated by the creation of domestic and international money; here, current income is the principal argument in the demand for money equation.[10] If the income elasticity of demand for real cash balances is unity, the theory would suggest that the world rate of inflation should be given by the following equation:

---

10) See H. G. Johnson [8] for details.

$$(1) \quad \dot{p} = \sum_i w_i r_i G_{R_i} + \sum_i w_i (1-r_i) G_{D_i} - \sum_i w_i G_{y_i},$$

where:

$\dot{p}$ is the predicted world rate of inflation,

w_i is country i's share in the world money stock,

r_i is the ratio of country i's official reserves to the domestic money supply,

G refers to the growth rate, while

R_i is the official reserves of country i,

D_i domestic credit in country i, and

y_i is real income in country i.

This is, of course, a long-run model and no allowance is made for sterilization or other such short-run phenonema which would cause the true rate to diverge from the predicted rate. This model was used to generate a predicted rate of inflation for the seven largest OECD countries which was then compared to the actual rate as in the following table.

The predicted values are always much higher than the actual, although the signs of the changes are similar until 1967. Both progressed upwards from 1961 to 1963 but the decline in the predicted value for 1964 was only matched by a constant actual level.[11] Both moved sharply ahead in 1965 and declined in 1966. After 1970 the assumption of a fixed exchange rate is not valid so that consistent results would not be expected. In general this test refutes the very simple monetarist model upon which it is based. If the demand for

11) This could be explained by inflationary expectations.

TABLE 6

Actual and Predicted Rates of Inflation
from the monetarist model

Year	Actual[1)]	Predicted
1961	2.4	4.6
1962	2.5	7.7
1963	2.6	8.0
1964	2.6	6.3
1965	3.1	9.5
1966	3.0	5.7
1967	3.0	9.6
1968	3.4	9.5
1969	4.9	5.6
1970	5.9	8.6
1971	5.4	17.7
1972	4.5	12.9

1) U.S., Japan, Canada, France, Germany, Italy and the United Kingdom, weighted by countries shares in the world money supply.

money function had included interest rates the results would have been worse. The lack of expectations, financial markets and lags in adjustment would bias such a simple approach yet such an approach to world inflation has often been advanced.

Under fixed exchange rates, interest sensitive capital flows undermine the effectiveness of monetary policy. With a flexible exchange rate an easy monetary policy affects demand by reducing interest rates and increasing the availability of funds as well as by reducing capital inflows or encouraging an outflow and depreciating the exchange rate. The latter effect depends of course on relative monetary conditions. The greater the interest elasticity of capital flows the greater the extent to which monetary policy works on prices via capital flows, the exchange rate and, with some lag, the trade balance. The inelasticity of expectations of exchange rate changes is also of importance in determining the result of a given change in monetary policy. As the sensitivity of capital flows to movements in the exchange rate approaches infinity the aggregate demand effects of monetary and fiscal policy approach the fixed exchange rate situation as speculators are simply replacing the exchange stabilization authorities. Consequently endogenous capital flows can be incorporated into the analysis of the inflationary process via the effects of changes in aggregate demand.

Under floating exchange rates, greater national autonomy in monetary policy is possible. It is therefore possible for rates of money creation to exist which would otherwise have produced a balance of payments crisis and domestic deflation. Table 7 contains growth rates of the monetary base and its domestic and foreign components for a number of countries. The domestic component consists of central bank advances to commercial banks, government securities and other government assets net of deposits with the central bank, and other non-government sector sources of base money. The foreign component is essentially the international reserves of the consolidated government sector and monetary authority. The monetary base times the money multiplier identically equal the money supply.[12] The

12) See page 545

TABLE 7

Percentage Changes in the Monetary Base and its Components

		1970/1960 [1]	1971/1970	1972/1971	1973/1972	1974 III/1973 III
Canada	Total	6.7	15.1	15.6	16.1	13.0
	Foreign	9.4	20.7	5.4	-4.7	-0.4
	Domestic	-3.8	-32.7	173.0	140.0	55.6
United States	Total	4.7	9.4	3.8	8.0	8.9
	Foreign	-3.8	-10.3	4.9	10.2	9.4
	Domestic	8.6	13.3	3.7	7.7	8.8
Japan [2]	Total	18.8	14.6	29.0	34.3	22.0
	Foreign	16.1	171.5	19.6	-33.3	-11.0
	Domestic	19.9	-46.9	48.0	143.7	51.1
France	Total	7.9	10.6	31.6	7.5	0.7
	Foreign	9.8	78.1	17.4	-14.9	-9.2
	Domestic	7.6	-15.3	43.1	22.1	4.7
Germany	Total	7.5	15.0	26.3	7.4	-6.5
	Foreign	5.7	18.2	26.1	17.7	-10.6
	Domestic	19.1	4.5	27.2	-31.6	79.2
Italy [2]	Total	22.9	17.0	14.0	17.1	16.0
	Foreign	8.4	16.7	-10.4	-1.3	-61.5
	Domestic	40.4	17.2	25.7	23.3	40.8
Switzerland	Total	9.4	20.3	8.9	4.7	-1.7
	Foreign	9.4	19.7	7.6	1.8	-3.6
	Domestic	13.2	113.3	115.6	121.7	100.0
United Kingdom	Total	7.3	-5.1	21.2	31.5	10.7
	Foreign	9.2	82.9	-182.7	18.5	-23.6
	Domestic	5.1	-40.7	42.5	18.4	13.5

Source: International Financial Statistics, International Monetary Fund, various issues.

1) Compound Average annual percentage change.

2) 1964 data are the earliest used.

monetary base is necessary to discuss the impact of international monetary flows on the monetary systems of individual countries as well as to analyze the operations of the monetary authorities and government sector. The foreign component is clearly endogenous to the system under fixed exchange rates as are some of domestic source components of the base. However, endogeneity ultimately depends upon the policies of the authorities. For example, monetary authorities often use the exchange rate or interest rates as targets which render the base endogenous. While the authorities are bound to accept a change in the foreign source component from balance of payments changes they have some scope for offsetting this amount over a given period of time by acting on the domestic base components that are exogenous. Michaely [11] considered that the authorities are motivated to react to movements in the foreign component by altering the domestic component although his evidence was not uniform. In a Humean sense if a country is small and there is a high degree of substitutability between domestic and foreign output the country is bound to have the world rate of inflation in the long run. Consequently there is an incentive for an increase in the domestic base given the presence of world inflation rather than to wait for its reflection in the balance of payments and the foreign component of the base. The policy choice also reflects the willingness of governments to exchange goods for international reserves thereby subsidizing foreign countries. The exchange rate

---

12) This is obviously too short an explanation both of the concept of the base and of the determination of the supply of money although it will suffice for the purposes of this discussion. The definition of the base is general to accommodate the standard statistical source used although this does not reflect the institutional arrangements in individual countries.

may also be allowed to vary as a policy response and this has been the case for most of the time period covered in Table 7.

As indicated above these statistics reflect a large number of endogenous factors as well as policy decisions. First consider the period of essentially fixed exchange rates. In 1971 the growth of the foreign component was a major factor in the growth of the total base in many countries such as France, Germany, Japan and Canada (although the Canadian dollar began to float in June 1970). If we assume that the domestic component is exogenous and can be used as a policy instrument, it would appear that the authorities restricted the domestic component in order to partly affect the foreign influence. The net effect reflects the inflationary impact of payments imbalances under the fixed, but crumbling exchange rate regime. Under floating rates movements in the foreign source of the base decelerated for many countries, as reflected in the 1972 statistics, while the domestic base grew at a much greater rate. Because of the large foreign swings the net effects were mixed across countries. In Japan, France, Germany and the United Kingdom sharp upward movements in the domestic base were responsible to a significant but variable extent for the growth in the total monetary base. The rate of inflation began to rise sharply in 1973 in Japan, France and the United Kingdom in response to the monetary events of 1972. However some declines in the high growth rates of the monetary base were noted in most countries as the industrial countries moved into a period of stagnation and a reduction in the momentum of price rises.

Two other points should be noted. First, the volatility of the base and its components in the 1970's is much greater than earlier, and second the monetary base is growing much faster than in the 1960's. The exceptions are Switzerland and Germany where the deceleration of recent years has been reflected in an appreciation of these currencies and a lower rate of inflation.[13)]

2. Trade Prices

A number of writers have accented the role of traded goods prices in the acceleration of world inflation. For example, after surveying a large number of theories Nordhaus concluded:

> The wage inflation in the United States and Canada can be attributed to the tightness of labour markets. Outside of North America the rise in wages can be more tenably ascribed to the permissive economic climate generated by a rise in import prices.[14)]

It should be noted that the fact that trade prices are discussed does not mean that it is an entirely separate process from the monetary mechanism as, in both the Hume price-specie flow mechanism and its modern monetary variants, trade prices are an integral part of the adjustment mechanism under a fixed exchange rate regime.

Table 8 contains percentage changes in import and export average values in local currencies as well as in the gross barter terms of trade from 1967 to 1973. This is supplemented by an index of trade

13) Two caveats are in order: first, these statistics are standardized and are not totally appropriate for all countries, and second, the statistics for countries with negative international reserves are not easily interpreted consistently with the same figures for other countries.
14) See W. D. Nordhaus [13] p. 459.

TABLE 8

Percentage Changes in Export and Import Average Values and Terms of Trade[1)]
(in local currencies)

		1967	1968	1969	1970	1971	1972	1973
Canada	Imports	0.1	2.4	2.3	2.0	1.6	3.1	6.8
	Exports	3.0	2.5	2.5	2.5	-0.1	2.9	10.8
	T. of trade	3.0	0.1	0.2	0.6	-1.7	-0.2	3.8
United States	Imports	0.9	1.2	3.5	6.6	5.2	7.4	18.8
	Exports	1.6	1.3	3.8	5.3	3.3	2.8	16.7
	T. of trade	0.7	0.1	0.3	-1.2	-1.8	-4.3	-1.8
Japan	Imports	-0.3	-1.4	0.0	4.2	1.8	-7.5	12.4
	Exports	3.1	0.1	4.5	5.6	0.4	-1.8	8.4
	T. of trade	3.4	1.5	4.5	1.3	-1.4	6.1	-3.6
Austria	Imports	-1.7	-4.1	1.2	10.2	4.2	-0.5	3.3
	Exports	-0.1	-4.0	0.7	7.0	0.4	-0.9	3.0
	T. of trade	1.6	0.1	-0.5	-2.9	-3.7	-0.4	-0.3
Belgium	Imports	-2.0	0.3	3.1	3.8	1.6	-0.9	..
	Exports	-0.4	-1.2	4.7	4.7	-2.8	1.5	..
	T. of trade	1.6	-1.4	1.5	0.9	-4.3	2.5	..
France	Imports	-0.5	-2.2	6.5	10.8	3.5	0.9	7.8
	Exports	-0.7	-0.7	7.3	10.4	5.7	1.1	10.0
	T. of trade	-0.3	1.6	0.8	-0.4	2.2	0.1	2.0
Germany	Imports	-1.2	-2.3	2.3	-2.0	-1.1	-1.9	4.9
	Exports	-0.9	-1.5	1.8	1.8	1.6	0.9	1.6
	T. of trade	0.3	0.8	-0.5	3.8	2.8	2.9	-3.2
Italy	Imports	1.0	0.7	0.9	4.2	7.7	1.4	21.0(a)
	Exports	0.4	-0.2	3.3	5.1	6.4	1.6	11.3(a)
	T. of trade	-0.5	-0.9	2.4	0.9	-1.1	0.2	-7.7(a)
Netherlands	Imports	-1.0	-2.9	3.0	6.8	4.7	-0.9	6.6(a)
	Exports	0.0	-1.9	2.0	3.8	1.9	0.9	5.6(a)
	T. of trade	1.0	1.0	-1.0	-2.8	-2.7	1.9	-0.8(a)
United Kingdom	Imports	0.1	11.2	4.1	4.7	4.6	3.9	28.4
	Exports	1.4	8.0	3.4	6.9	5.6	5.2	12.5
	T. of trade	1.3	-2.9	-0.7	2.1	1.0	1.2	-12.4

Source: Main Economic Indicators, OECD

1) The terms of trade is the growth rate in export average values divided by the growth rate of import average values.

(a) First three quarters

weighted foreign trade prices for OECD countries from 1965 in Table 9 which also includes the non-U.S. OECD GNP deflator, weighted by GNP weights.[15)]

TABLE 9

Percentage Changes in OECD Foreign Trade Prices[1)]
and non-U.S. GNP Deflators in Local Currency

	1965	1966	1967	1968	1969	1970	1971	1972	1973
Foreign Trade Prices	1.1	1.6	0.2	1.1	3.2	4.0	2.9	1.0	10.0
GNP deflator	4.4	4.2	3.3	3.3	4.7	6.3	6.6	6.6	9.6

1) Average of export and import prices.

Source: OECD

As can be seen the acceleration in foreign trade prices began in 1969 or perhaps in 1968 while the acceleration in GNP deflators began in 1969. In 1968 the countries which devalued late in 1967 began to experience sharp increases in both export and import prices.[16)] The remaining countries generally experienced lower export prices perhaps because of competition with countries which devalued. Many of the remaining countries also experienced a drop in import prices because of their effective revaluations. This was a period of substantial demand pressure with most OECD countries

15) The U.S. is excluded since its weight is dominant.
16) This is also true of Spain, which devalued, but which is not included in these statistics.

operating at a high level of demand. In 1969 substantial trade price increases followed the revaluation of the DM as Germany was operating above the potential rate of GNP growth and export prices in DM continued to rise. In 1967 and 1968 German export average values had declined in local currency. Since Germany had been a restraining force in terms of price on world markets, and in many respects a price leader, when other countries priced up to the much higher German export prices in foreign currencies, still further increases in traded goods prices resulted. Although further exchange rate changes occurred in 1971 and 1972 foreign trade price increases decelerated in aggregate even though the rate of (non-U.S.) world inflation moved up. In 1973 the prices of traded goods accelerated, led by the very sharp increases in commodity prices as well as export prices in many OECD countries. Even for countries with effective revaluations increases in import prices were substantial. (The oil price increases of late 1973 would not be reflected to any great extent in the average value statistics for 1973.)

There are a number of ways of analyzing the impact of foreign trade prices on domestic prices. The most obvious impact occurs via the direct effect on import prices. This is often (incorrectly) assumed to be the totality of imported inflation. The potential mechanical impact of import price changes, that is excluding input-output effects, can be measured with varying degrees of accuracy. Table 10 provides a rough measure for a selected group of industrial countries. This has been calculated by measuring the ratio of the change in import average values in local currency weighted by the share of imports in GNP to the percentage change in the consumer price index.[17] This statistic is therefore a percentage of the rise in consumer prices that actually occurred and obviously abstracts from exogenous influences and, for example, the effects of demand or varying profit margins. The magnitude of the imported inflation element in 1973 is immediately apparent, although the extent varies with the effective exchange rate change and the product composition of imports. The table also shows that the effect was significant in earlier years even when raw material prices were declining. This was the case in 1970 and 1971.

TABLE 10

Potential "Mechanical" Contributions of Import Average Value Changes[1)] to the Rise in Consumer Prices[2)]

	1967	1968	1969	1970	1971	1972	1973
Canada	+ 1	+12	+11	+13	+11	+14	+13
United States	+ 2	+ 2	+ 4	+ 6	+ 7	+13	+17
Japan	- 1	- 3	0	+ 5	+ 3	-16	+10
Austria	-13	-45	+12	+72	+28	- 2	+13
Belgium	-29	+ 5	+34	+40	+15	- 7	+47
France	- 3	- 8	+16	+33	+10	+ 2	+17
Germany	-17	-31	+17	-11	- 4	- 7	+14
Italy	+ 6	+ 9	+ 7	+16	+30	+ 5	+46
Netherlands	-15	-38	+19	+75	+30	- 6	-49
United Kingdom	+ 1	+52	+17	+16	+11	+12	+67

1) In local currencies
2) A positive (negative) sign indicates a price increasing (decreasing) effect of an increase (decrease) in import average values.

17) Since GNP does not include imports the national accounting basis for this approximation is not exactly correct, but any error is likely to be less than ten per cent.

A question of more importance is the extent to which exchange rate changes could have influenced domestic price performance. Therefore the above exercise was recalculated replacing the change in the import average value with the change in the effective exchange rate.

The results of this exercise are given in Table 11. In the case of revaluing countries the indicated mechanical contribution would assume that prices are not sticky downwards. What is surprising is that this mechanical effect in most countries in most periods could hardly account for much of a change in consumer prices. Various devaluations such as the U.K. and France have provided exceptions in particular years as has the continued strength of the DM. Still the exchange rate effects would average much less than one percentage point of the annual increase in the CPI and even the sharp exchange rate changes would rarely amount to much more than two percentage points. Consequently as the average rate of world inflation moves higher the mechanical impact of exchange rate changes (particularly revaluations) becomes less.

The above statistics have been concerned with the potential mechanical impact of import price or exchange rate changes. In reality several further effects can be noted. One positive effect of revaluation is to cut into the profits of exporting firms, thereby reducing their ability to grant large wage increases. Any direct impact of a revaluation on consumer prices would also reduce wage demands. Furthermore the cheapening of imports and potential imports in local currency after a revaluation will tend to keep down prices for import substitutes. On the other hand the greater the instability of trade prices the less incentive there is for importers to pass on declines in their costs since this situation could be reversed at their expense, particularly where a price control regime is in operation.

TABLE 11

Potential "Mechanical" Contributions of Exchange Rate Changes to the Rise in Consumer Prices[1)]

	1967	1968	1969	1970	1971	1972	1973
Canada	0	- 8	0	-18	-17	+ 6	+13
United States	- 1	- 3	0	+11	+ 3	+11	+ 7
Japan	0	- 4	- 1	+ 1	- 3	-23	- 5
Austria	- 2	-24	0	+10	- 7	- 6	-26
Belgium	- 6	-15	- 2	- 4	+ 1	-21	- 4
France	0	- 5	+11	+25	+ 6	- 5	- 5
Germany	- 9	-27	-19	-46	-12	- 9	-28
Italy	- 1	-25	+ 1	+ 3	+ 3	+ 4	+ 1
Netherlands	-11	-21	- 1	+16	- 6	- 8	-15
United Kingdom	+14	+52	- 1	+ 1	0	+12	+24

1) A positive (negative) sign indicates a price increasing (decreasing) effect of a depreciation (appreciation).

One theory that has been in vogue in recent years, particularly in some small European countries, has evolved from Scandinavian experience and relates to the role of export prices. In this model the economy is broken down into "sheltered" and "exposed" sectors where the exposed sectors have their prices determined on world markets.[18)] The sheltered sector is assumed to be largely the service sector and the government sector, both of which are

18) For some references to this literature see Pattison [15] or Edgren, Faxen and Odhner [3] .

assumed to operate with less competition and with a lower trend growth rate of productivity than the exposed sector. Wage changes are assumed to be equalized throughout the economy. Increases in export prices will increase wages generally and cause an increase in the rate of inflation since the rate of productivity growth is lower in the sheltered sector. Devaluations will be inflationary in this model since they increase profits in exposed sectors, but so will inflation abroad or a fluctuating level of world trade prices. One of the difficulties with this model is that it contains only a price-wage sector without consideration of aggregate demand or monetary relationships. A further difficulty is that all causes of inflation are exogenous and all the model does is transfer the price rises. In empirical terms the movement of trade prices in the context of this model is not enough to account for the recent levels and acceleration of inflation.

A number of writers have accented the central role of the United States in the development of rising world trade prices, since this country alone did not have to worry about the effect of its prices on the balance of payments. Even the sheer size of the economy is of considerable importance in terms of the volume of world transactions. In terms of GNP the United States would consist of about 45 per centof the OECD total (at 1970 exchange rates), whereas in terms of trade the U.S. weight is about 25 per cent. The timing of U.S. trade price changes is consistent with the rise in the non-U.S. OECD GNP deflator in 1969 but this was also a time when European economies were running at capacity or above potential output so that it would be difficult to blame U.S. prices without more information. As I pointed out in an earlier paper the United States weight in many European countries imports and exports is relatively small. Furthermore the rise in German export prices played a key role in European inflation. Still the weight of the U.S. is important in aggregate and the timing is consistent so that some influence must be accorded to this explanation.

3. Demand Pressures

The mechanism of the transmission of inflation via the pressures of demand is quite straightforward and overlaps with the monetary mechanism as trade surpluses or deficits alter the domestic monetary base. On a bi-country basis this mechanism would generally seem insufficient to explain the synchronous rapid acceleration of world prices. On the other hand the influence of a rapidly growing world money supply could encourage such a development. Indeed the world business cycle expansion from 1972 through mid-1973 was one of the few occasions when all major countries were expanding together and mutually reinforcing the pressure of demand. One important study investigating inflation at the world level found precisely that "the world inflation take off in the late 1960's was caused (in proximate terms) by the excess demand pressures in the aggregate world economy."[19] Not only is excess demand necessary but there is a feedback from prices to demand. Laidler has shown that the initial effect of a rise in the world rate of inflation could be contractionary since the resulting increase in the demand for cash balances would go ahead of the supply.[20] However in the longer run, excess demand must exist to bring domestic prices up to the world level via the process of balance of payments imbalances.

---

19) See Duck, Parkin, Rose and Zis [2] .
20) See Laidler [9] .

In the mid-1960's the industrialized countries began to operate their economies at close to potential output. In 1967-1968 these countries were operating at or even above their potential. This was when world inflation began to accelerate. A number of European countries, notably France and Germany, maintained this level of output, although the rate of capacity utilization declined in the United States, Japan and Italy. Through this period of cooling off the rate of inflation climbed well above that of 1969 in 1970 and did not decelerate much in 1971. The world boom in 1972 and 1973 led to a rapid increase in the rate of inflation. If account is taken of the development of inflationary expectations the failure of the rate of inflation to decline in 1970 is not surprising and the pressure of demand hypothesis stands up well to recent history.

4. The International Monetary System

The reform of the international monetary system is of fundamental importance to world economic stability and welfare. Curiously, both fixed and flexible exchange rates are considered to be inflationary by various groups. Dr. Emminger of the German Bundesbank is a leading exponent of the view that the fixed exchange rate system was inflationary. He has stated that the Bretton Woods system broke down "because the *limit of tolerance for the inflationary effect* of currency inflows had been reached."[21] Others would argue that exchange rate changes are irrelevant because of the domestic adjustments which occur to produce the appropriate real rather than nominal prices, wages, etc., which offset the effect of the exchange rate system. Prices rise in the devaluing country be-

---

21) See his Per Jacobsson lecture [4], p. 2 (Emminger's italics).

cause of the higher cost of imports in local currency, but if prices are not flexible downwards the revaluing country does not get an equivalent improvement in its rate of inflation. Consequently, any exchange rate change is inflationary on balance. Given the fact that world inflation began to accelerate in the late 1960's, after the pound sterling and a number of other currencies were devalued, increased even further at the time of the Smithsonian adjustments and soared after the move to a system of floating exchange rates in February 1973, the timing at least accords with the theory. The theory also accents the fact that with floating exchange rates, the monetary authorities are able to follow an independent monetary policy which, in the case of excessive money creation, allows the higher average price level resulting from exchange rate changes to be financed as well as promoting inflation directly. The statistics presented above indicate that the rate of money creation began to accelerate in 1971.

One aspect of floating exchange rates that has not attracted much attention is that without the need to intervene in foreign exchange markets the demand for international liquidity must fall drastically. Given that the supply has been increasing, these funds will likely find their way into other uses. This further suggests the need for a proper portfolio choice model of the international financial system.

Furthermore, the way exchange rates are changed can have an important effect upon the rate of inflation in the world. This is partly a question of the burden of adjustment, whether surplus or deficit nations should undertake exchange rate changes. The problem is that the continuation of adjustments in one direction increases the number of exchange rate changes ultimately needed since this places more pressure on countries that were initially in a balanced position.[22)] If prices are inflexible in a downwards direction minimizing the number of exchange rate changes would minimize the inflationary impact. The effect of delaying a required revaluation can also be inflationary. Willett has pointed out how a consequent reduction in demand with sticky wages and prices may cause governments to expand which would increase the prevailing rate of inflation.[23)] This then is an argument for more flexibility and against an adjustable peg mechanism.

Superficially, it is tempting to agree with the theory of the inflationary bias of flexible exchange rates. We do have many prices which are inflexible downwards and inflation did accelerate when exchange rate changes became more frequent. On the other hand, the period since 1967 has been one of higher than average capacity utilization and demand pressures, and it is difficult to separate these factors from the exchange rate and inflation story. Furthermore, any inflationary bias in exchange rate flexibility must be traded off against the liqudity influences on domestic money supplies under a fixed system. As well, it is an open point whether the balance of payments should itself be a constraint on domestic policy making, that is, exchange rate adjustments should be the mechanism used to restore equilibrium. In any event it would not be the system which is responsible but the use that is made of it.

---

22) E. S. Howle [7] .
23) T. D. Willett [18] .

Some small amounts of evidence do exist. For raw materials, where the large number of producers and consumers guarantee the existence of competition there has been a clear indication of the inverse relationship between changes in raw material import prices and exchange rate changes. However, for imports as a whole the inverse relationship only holds for periods of low demand pressure.[24)] In periods such as June 1972 to June 1973 with a high level of demand pressure asymmetrical behavior did exist, that is devaluing countries experienced a notable increase in import prices, whereas there was no comparable favorable impact on import prices in revaluing countries. On the question of the optimum number and direction of exchange rate changes, the pivoting of parity changes around the dollar would have resulted in the minimum or near minimum adjustment from 1961 to 1971.[25)]

5. Commodity Prices, Gold and Inflation[26)]

The sharp increase in commodity prices during the current inflation was a symptom rather than a cause of inflation. The world business cycle and long lags in the supply of new output in response to higher prices explain only some of the increase in commodity prices. Historically commodity prices and industrial output have moved closely together, yet spot commodity prices rose by 12 per cent from August 1973 to March 1974 although there was no difference in the index of industrial production for OECD countries. While inflation accelerated gold and commodity prices rose togeth-

24) Some evidence is given in [14], pp. 25-29. This result has been further substantiated in cross-section studies with a larger number of countries.
25) Howle, [7], p. 928.
26) See also Pattison [17].

er. Not only can this be seen from a cursory examination of the aggregate data, but it prevailed in individual commodity markets. For example, a recent report stated that "cocoa followed gold up and down on the London market every trading day of the month except two."[27] It appeared that commodities generally as well as gold were purchased as a hedge against currency uncertainties in terms of both inflation and exchange rate changes.

The reason why commodity price movements should be treated largely as a symptom rather than a cause of inflation is easy to see. Gold has traditionally been acquired when confidence has been lost in paper currencies. An investment in gold must be made on the basis of the risk and return on alternative assets including currency. As the price of gold rises, the risk attached to buying more gold increases as does that attached to the existing stock. As the gold price increased the acquisition of commodities provided diversification. Diversification reduces risk if the prospects for alternative assets do not depend upon the same events. Commodity prices have historically been affected by the pace of real economic activity and would seem to provide a degree of covariance with the gold price at the same time as both commodities generally and gold are real assets and hence a hedge against inflation. Consequently as the price of gold rose speculation and hedging spilled over into commodity markets. This would require movements in gold prices to occur before those in commodity market prices. This pattern held well into 1974 with a noticeable but variable lag of commodity prices after gold price movements. After mid-1974 the lack of industrial demand for commodities resulted in a sharp decline in their prices.

The factors behind this behavior are easy to see. The lack of confidence in the international monetary arrangements was an important factor. Gold prices began to increase from roughly 40 dollars an ounce after the Smithsonian Agreement of December 1971 and continued to rise slowly through 1972. Although commodity prices were also increasing the movements were not dramatic. The coordinated upward movements of gold and commodity prices began in January 1973 and coincided with the currency turmoil. In January 1973 the Swiss franc was floated, the dollar was devalued in February when the yen and the lira were also floated. From January to February the gold price rose by almost 30 per cent while commodity prices increased by 9 per cent. In March currency markets were closed, the Deutsche Markwas revalued and a number of European countries began to try and align themselves in a joint float. The Guilder and Deutsche Mark were revalued later in the year. Exchange rates moved erratically later when the war in the middle east errupted and energy costs were seen to cause sharp movements in the current account balances of the industrial countries. In this situation the movement into gold and commodities and out of financial assets should not have been surprising.

As suggested earlier domestic inflation rates also played a major role as commodities and gold provided a real store of value in contrast to depreciating paper currencies. To test this relationship an equation was estimated relating the spot prices of commodities (P_{COMM}) to the gold price (P_{GOLD}), the rate of inflation and the Eurodollar rate, with all variables in natural logarithms:[28)]

---

27) G. McNair [10].

$$\ln P_{COMM} = \underset{(19.3)}{2.0} + \underset{(17.3)}{0.56} \ln P_{GOLD} \quad (2)$$

$$\underset{(0.5)}{-0.02} \ln EURO\$ + \underset{(6.0)}{0.34} \ln \dot{P}, \bar{R}^2 = 0.95$$

where EURO$ is the three-month Eurodollar interest rate and $\dot{P}$ is the weighted OECD consumer price index. Given the functional form the relationship of the rate of inflation to the spot price of commodities is quite strong. The relationship has held over shorter periods. For example, as the "world" rate of inflation went from less than 1 per cent per month late in 1973 to 1.5 per cent in February both the price of gold and the prices of commodities continued to rise. When the rate declined to a monthly rate of just over 1 per cent, both gold and commodity prices also declined.

Although the rationale for the commodity price boom seems reasonable, the exchange rate movements and rates of price rises had to be caused by underlying economic forces and had to be financed. In both respects, recent monetary policies seem to have fed the "inflation" as discussed earlier. Monetary policy also had an undesirable effect on interest rates. Although nominal interest rates rose rapidly, real rates adjusted only partially because of the interest rate induced wealth effect, lags in the adjustment of price

---

28) The data used in this section comes from the following sources: Commodity prices are taken from the Economist dollar index. The gold price in U.S. dollars is taken for the end of each month from the Bank of England Quarterly Bulletin. The three-month Eurodollar rate is for Eurodollar deposits and is taken from the end of each month. The source is Morgan Guaranty Trust, World Financial Markets. Consumer price indices are from the OECD. The monthly observations run from January 1968 to April 1974.

expectations, and policy actions in many countries to keep down nominal rates. In this situation of disequilibrium it was profitable to borrow in order to purchase gold, commodities and other real assets. Rapid money creation kept down nominal rates, hence real rates were negative in many countries. It is more than a coincidence that the decline in the prices of commodities as well as gold began early in 1974 only after Eurodollar interest rates had risen substantially. In equation (2) the sign on the interest rate term is correct but the coefficient is not statistically significant. This is not discouraging because the equation itself is a simple one and there would have been an *a priori* presumption that the correlation of interest rates with inflation and commodity prices would have led to a positive rather than the required negative sign.

Clearly, commodity prices and gold prices moved closely together over a period characterized by monetary uncertainty and hence this link contributed to domestic rates of inflation. Although special circumstances helped to encourage inflation and exchange rate hedging as well as speculation, domestic and international monetary developments were primarily responsible.

IV. Final Comments

Although some monetarists have laid claim to the acceleration of world inflation in the late 1960's under the operative mechanism of balance of payments surpluses accumulating under a fixed exchange rate system, greater importance could probably be attached to the role of money creation after 1970 (or perhaps 1967) as central bankers felt less constrained by the balance of payments in managing their domestic economies. Although the early 1970's was a period of record U.S. deficits, the fixed exchange rate system had begun to break down. The growth rate of monetary aggregates in many industrialized countries was at an extremely high rate in the 1970-1973 period. Increased flexibility would seem to give finance ministers and central bankers more wild oats to sow, yet restricting flexibility would act against balance of payments adjustment and the achievement of the proper policy mix. There exists some optimum pattern of exchange rate changes that would minimize the world amount of necessary adjustment, yet given different national preferences for inflation and exchange rate variations the optimum is unlikely to be reached.

Trade prices decelerated sharply in 1971 and 1972 even though there was only a levelling off at best in the world rate of inflation. Although expectations could play a role in this development the differences between domestic and international trade prices suggests that some further consideration should be given to the microeconomics of inflationary processes. The economics of information and search costs suggest that those holding stocks of goods in short supply acquire monopoly privileges to set prices since further searching will reduce the probability of stocks being left. Yet during the 1971 and early 1972 period there were no major shortages or bottlenecks. Demand pressure alone was clearly not <u>sufficient</u> to produce the recent development in inflation, although the recognition of inflationary expectations makes the role of demand quite significant in a number of studies. The overheating of almost all industrial countries from mid-1972 to 1973 suggests that the simultaneously reinforcing feedbacks among countries were not fully appreciated in formulating national macroeconomic policies. Although this gave a stimulus to commodity prices, their sharp rise was more a symptom than a cause of inflation, contrary to popular political opinion.

REFERENCES

1. Argy, V. and Kouri, P., "Sterilization Policies and the Volatility in International Reserves", forthcoming in R. Aliber (Ed.), National Policies and the International Monetary System.

2. Duck, N., Parkin, M., Rose, D. and Zis, G., "The Determination of the Rate of Change of Wages and Prices in the Fixed Exchange Rate World Economy" in M. Parkin and G. Zis [15].

3. Edgren, S., Faxen, K.-O. and Odhner, C.-E., "Wages, Growth and the Distribtuion of Income", Swedish Journal of Economics, 1969.

4. Emminger, O., Inflation and the International Monetary System, Per Jacobson Lecture given at Basle 16 June 1973 (mimeo).

5. Fratianni, M. and Savona, P., "International Liquidity: an Analytic and Empirical Reinterpretation", in G. Carli et al., A Debate on the Eurodollar Market, Rome 1973.

6. Genburg, H., "A Note on Inflation Rates under Fixed Exchange Rates", Graduate Institute of International Studies, Geneva (mimeo), 1974.

7. Howle, E. S., "On Devaluations versus Revaluations", American Economic Review, 1973.

8. Johnson, H. G., "The Monetary Approach to Balance of Payments Theory", in Further Essays in Monetary Economics, London, 1973.

9. Laidler, D., "Price and Output Fluctuations in an Open Economy" in D. Laidler, (Editor), Essays on Money and Inflation, Manchester, 1975.

10. McNair, G., "Gold Appears Hinge for Commodity Swings", Report on Business, Toronto, June 1, 1974, p. B2.

11. Michaely, M., The Responsiveness of Demand Policies to the Balance of Payments: Postwar Patterns, National Bureau of Economic Research, New York, 1971.

12. Neumann, M., "Special Drawing Rights and Inflation", Weltwirtschaftliches Archiv, 1973.

13. Nordhaus, W., "The Worldwide Wage Explosion", Brookings Papers on Economic Activity, 1972.

14. O.E.C.D., Economic Surveys, Switzerland, March 1974.

15. Parkin, M. and Zis, G., Inflation in the World Economy, Manchester, 1975.

16. Pattison, J. C., "The International Transmission of Inflation" in M. Parkin and G. Zis [15].

17. Pattison, J. C., "Commodity Prices and the Price of Gold", Journal of World Trade Law, 1975.

18. Willett, T. D., "Secular Inflation and the International Monetary System: A Comment", Journal of Money, Credit and Banking, 1973.

Comments on the J. C. Pattison's paper

By

Karel Tavernier

The stimulating paper of J. Pattison suggests that our understanding of present international inflation is not very high because very often irrelevant theories are applied to imaginary situations which do not exist any longer. Therefore, a thorough empirical analysis of statistical facts and circumstances must first be made in order to learn in what direction to look for a suitable explanation. This broad inductive approach is a most interesting strategy. It has however its drawbacks. It is always difficult to arrange data a priori in such a way that they are able to really test in sufficient detail what competing theories are claiming. The danger exists - and, in our opinion, Pattison does not escape from it - that one has to be satisfied with a broad statistical description of the inflationary processes, on one side, and with a loose and approximative content of what different theories have to say in different situations, on the other side. More focus on the specific content of alternative explanations might have been desirable. From the data presented, is it possible to say much more than that money is important? Is it possible to learn anything about the lag structure and the acceptability of the transmission mechanism postulated in different explanations? In one sentence, is this kind of statistical analysis able to discriminate sufficiently between alternative inflation models?

It might be of interest to dig somewhat deeper in the dispersion of inflation rates among countries and cities, on which the author presents interesting material. A first conclusion is that differences in inflation rates are significant even in a system of fixed exchange rates. To a large extent, this can be due to the fact that year to year data are used. Rough calculations suggest that the dispersion is smaller when longer periods are taken. The standard deviation for the period 1965-1968 falls to 1.4 for 1968-1971 to 1.3 and 1971-1974 to 1.4. This is a normal result as soon as one accepts that the international transmission of inflation takes time and that one country follows the other with a lag. As to the proper measure of dispersion rates, an argument against the preference of the author for the coefficient of variation over the standard deviation rests on the puzzling observation (due to higher average inflation rates) that a smaller dispersion of inflation rates is obtained for periods with larger exchange rate flexibility. According to theory we would have expected the contrary.

A second more tentative conclusion drawn by the author is that large countries seem to perform better than smaller ones. It is possible that anti-inflation policy is indeed less efficient in small countries, still there might be a measurement problem involved. From a regional point of view cycles and inflation rates are not homogeneous: a remarkable difference between New York and California can exist between peak and trough. The national price index is the result of averaging different elements which might follow the same pattern but with a different lag. For that reason we also would expect that the year to year fluctuations of inflation rates of small countries to be higher than for larger ones. Still it is puzzling to see how fast small or medium sized countries are able to reduce their inflation rates. I refer to Italy in 1963-1966 when the rates go from 8.6 to 2.1 percent; in Finland in 1968-1970 from 10.7 to 3.2; in Ireland in 1960-1964 from 0.5 to 9.4. Does this suggests that individual and also small and open economies have more manoeuvre room to reduce their inflation rates in the short run than is generally recognized?

A second set of remarks is directed at the monetary impulses as a source of inflation. First, the author states that the simple theory which asserts that the U.S. deficits are at the origin of the acceleration of prices in 1968 is not denied by the statistics. This statement is not very convincing, at least on the basis of the figures given. Even if one takes the balance on monetary transaction, there has hardly been any acceleration before 1971, when because of floating and devaluations countries could in principle better isolate themselves from the United States. Secondly, the tests on the global monetary thesis of inflation appear to be very damaging for this theory. The predicted inflation rate behaves very erratically and, for most years, exceeds the actual inflation rate by a factor of two and even three. One reason for the poor showing is suggested by Pattison himself: the Eurocurrency market is not incorporated in the model. The omission of this market might have handicapped the outcome of the tests much more seriously than Pattison seems to give credit to. From a pure statistical point there seems to be a perfect correlation between the year to year dollar increases in Eurodollar currencies and the world inflation rate. (The simple correlation coefficient is 0.98.) In addition, the world inflation rate follows the increase in Eurocurrency, with a lag of one year.

Although this observation is based on first differences rather than percentage growth rates of the international money market, the close connection with the world inflation rate is so powerful as to suggest that a better understanding of the Eurocurrency market and its links with domestic money supplies might prove very useful in explaining the international transmission of inflation.

Comments on the Pattison's paper

By
Carlo A. Mortara

I think Mr Pattison has done a useful job of summarizing the main issues and giving some of the statistical evidence on the subject of world inflation.

I will immediately state my main objection to his approach which is that giving a number of causes for the acceleration of inflation does not constitute a theory. It is not true that he who believes in two gods is more religious than he who believes in only one god. To have one theory is to have one theory, to have two theories is really just to hold an opinion. This doesn't mean I am personally inclined to a monistic explanation of world inflation, but I think a dominant factor should be singled out.

On the first part of the paper which is on the coefficient of variation of individual countries' inflation rates, the author himself says that the meaning of the measure "is not obvious" and I must add that it remains so also after reading his paper.

The selection of the coefficient of variation rather than the standard deviation must be explained perhaps through a cost of adjustment model of price changes.

In any case both measures are not directly relevant to the issue of the international transmission of inflation. Inflation propagates directly only through the tradeable goods, be they exports or import substitutes. The impact on nontradeable goods must be slower and work through a reallocation of resources from one sector to the other. As is well known, at least in the case of Japan, the indexes of import-export prices and GNP deflators don't necessarily move together. In Japan export prices remained stable while the rate of inflation was rapidly increasing (the reason given was the reduced cost of foreign imports because of yen revaluations). As it stands, the index doesn't seem to me much more than an indication that the world economy is getting more integrated: which we know already in many other ways.

The second part of the paper surveys the theories of international inflation. On the monetary aspects clearly we must all agree that without the huge increase in international liquidity caused by American deficits over the years such an increase in inflation would not have been possible. But to go from here to a world price equation is a very big step. The equation tested is of the crudest quantity theory of money type and I have even more objections to this when it is applied to the world than when it is applied to a single country. All the problems of identification are there and it is obvious that the increase in world prices has itself produced an increase in domestic money supplies and in international reserves.

The results of the regression are in any case not good. Actual and predicted values are entirely different, and significant variations are predicted where in fact there was stability, and this crude monetarist approach entirely misses the '71-'72 values, expecting very large inflation rates which did not take place.

I would also like to object to a statement that comes again among the conclusions to the effect that the balance of payments is not a constraint under flexible exchange rates. This is true only in theory. The experience of my own country with flexible exchange rates and big balance of payments problems offer an observation to the contrary.

Many bad things may be said about monetary authorities: often they look like people who play the violin solo in public and learn the instrument as they go on. But one shouldn't fault Central Banks and governments for trying to limit the range of fluctuations of the exchange rate rather than let it go up and down with all sorts of speculative movements as if it were a stock market index.

The Mundellian models, yielding internal and external equilibrium with, under flexible exchange rates, fiscal policy taking care of the domestic side and monetary policy setting whatever exchange rate is consistent with that equilibrium, are possible because they don't consider the impact of prices on internal equilibrium. The equilibrium exchange rate might be such as to cause so great a rate of inflation that it is bound to disturb internal stability.

If price instability is what we have to pay for b. of p. equilibrium, I say that all our faults (in this case b. of p. difficulties) are more pardonable than some of the methods we resort to in order to hide them.

The governments must have a third objective, the target rate of inflation; so we are left with 3 objectives and only 2 tools at our disposal.

On the real explanations of inflation I think it is important to note also some long-run causes rather than just the timing of world economic cycles. One such long-run factor is the change that has occurred in labour markets in Europe and Japan in the sixties, with the previous situation of an excess supply of labour vanishing away.

On the fixed versus flexible exchange rates debate I think it's paradoxical that just as the Academic community had almost agreed that the villain was the fixed exchange rate system, the change to the new system coincided with a significant worsening of world inflation rates. Of course for Americans to say that the fault lay with the Bretton Woods system rather than with American deficits reminded me of a yiddish proverb that the girl who can't dance says that the band can't play! Well, you know, countries cannot blush! In any case the change to flexible rates showed again that experience is really only half of experience! We landed on our back and we bruised our nose to quote another yiddish proverb.

I only hope that after we have decided that with downward price inflexibility and larger autonomy of monetary policy flexible rates have an even larger inflationary bias than fixed rates, it won't be shown that present price increases are in fact simply the lagged effects of the old system.

On commodity prices and the price of gold I will only note that the prices of raw materials had gone constantly down from the early sixties. And that their increase started long before the oil crisis and applied to practically all raw materials, both agricultural and nonagricultural. Such a general increase can be explained only by demand factors. But the problem of explaining these factors remains. Why did it happen in 1967? In what way did our fellow men change in that eventful year: I think economists must have at least some conception of how men who are not economists behave!

So I have come back to what I said at the beginning: what is it that caused the acceleration of the inflation, once of course you introduce also central banks among the endogenous variables?

The last few words of Mr. Pattison strike a note of optimism. A brighter future is based on indexation. I think that in this case, to repeat a famous sentence of Oscar Wilde, the basis of optimism is sheer terror!

THE MONETARY APPROACH TO INFLATION AND THE BALANCE OF PAYMENTS: THEORETICAL AND EMPIRICAL CONTRIBUTIONS AT THE LEUVEN CONFERENCE

By

Allan H. Meltzer *

The problem of world inflation and the desire to compare our theories of inflation in open economies with the accumulating evidence prompted the sponsors to organize a conference on Bank Credit, Money and Inflation at the Katholieke Universiteit Leuven in September 1974. The papers and comments in this volume are the contributions of the conference and its principal work.

Most of the papers fall within the very broad framework known as the monetary approach to the balance of payments and inflation. The distinguishing characteristic of this approach is not a particular analytical structure or model but a set of general principles guiding research. Two principles appear to be generally and perhaps universally accepted by those who use the framework. Both are long-run propositions.

*) I owe more than my usual debt to Karl Brunner. The paper benefited from many helpful discussions with Michele Fratianni, Michael Hamburger, Hai Hong, Pieter Korteweg and Johan Myhrman and the financial support of the National Science Foundation.

In a long-run, steady state, all goods must trade at the same price, and all assets must have the same return. These propositions about prices and interest rates, properly understood, are the standard fare of monetary economics. Their truth values are neither greater nor less than the proposition that tastes, productivity, opportunities, endowments and given distribution of wealth determine relative prices, and the quantity of money determines the absolute price level. The novelty, if the novelty has not worn off in two hundred years, of the monetary approach to the balance of payments lies in the concept of a world level of absolute prices and the application of relative price theory to explain the price levels of individual countries and equilibrium exchange rates.

The monetary approach to the balance of payments and inflation is more explicit about the long-run consequences of policies or decisions than about the mechanisms of short-run adjustment or the adjustments themselves. Alternative theories of short-run adjustment are consistent with the long-run proposition that the quantity of world money determines the world price level. Dornbusch (1973), Johnson (1972), Mussa (1974), Swoboda (1974).

Many attempts to contrast the monetary approach to the Keynesian emphasis on foreign trade multipliers fail to distinguish the two theories sufficiently. The usual statement of the monetary approach says nothing about the trade balance or about changes in the terms of trade. Keynesian multiplier theory is best understood as an explanation of the short-run response of the trade balance to autonomous spending. The price level in each country is fixed. It is difficult, therefore, to treat the multiplier theory as a theory of the balance of payments or as a theory of inflation, and the pristine form is no longer advanced for either purpose. The international version of the Keynesian model, like the domestic counterpart, has survived, however, by adding some "cost-push" elements to make prices rise and a Phillips curve to keep them rising. Inflation is transmitted by the balance of payments mainly through the price of imports used to produce exports or as substitutes for consumption of domestically produced goods and services.

The appeal of this version of the Keynesian theory to politicians and central bankers should be obvious. In an extreme, but common, version, all inflation is imported from abroad, and none is the result of domestic policies. The appeal to the economists at the conference was much less. None of the authors attempted to explain world inflation in this way. T. Willett and R. Sweeney raise and comment on some of these issues in their lengthy survey, and M. Parkin and M. Gray attempt to develop a model that is capable of discriminating among rival explanations.

There are three principal explanations of inflation in open economies, Keynesian or neo-Keynesian, institutionalist and monetarist. Each is incomplete.

The neo-Keynesian theory explains inflation in each country by referring to events in other countries. The inflationary impulse comes from abroad. Propagation occurs through some built-in mechanism that is best described as a general cost-push or Phillips-type relation. The so-called Nordic model is an example. Everyone imports inflation, and possibly everyone exports inflation to a lesser extent. Why does world inflation start or end? Why does the rate of inflation increase or decrease? The neo-Keynesians have not produced an answer and generally do not ask such questions.

The institutionalist approach is more in the nature of a description than of a set of testable propositions. Confusion between particular prices and the general price level is one of the few unifying characteristics. The third approach is the monetary approach. Much credit is due to Harry G. Johnson (1958) and Robert Mundell (1968) for reaffirming the monetary approach and stimulating interest in the analysis of inflation in open economies. Wide acceptance is now given to the proposition that the world economy is a closed economy, a proposition that Johnson and later Mundell advanced with much vigor. There is also renewed, widespread acceptance of the ancient proposition that, with fixed exchange rates, countries cannot continually inflate at different rates.

It is both a useful analytical device and, I believe, a reliable basis for policy to assert that in the long-run prices of all goods and assets, financial and real, are equalized. Evidence to support the proposition for short periods is lacking and seems unlikely to be found in observations for prices of assets and output drawn monthly, quarterly and even annually. Moreover, it is difficult to reconcile the existence of non-traded goods -- the device commonly used to explain observed differences in output prices -- with the neglect of "non-traded assets". Why are all rates of interest everywhere equal when prices of goods are not? What mechanism assures that deviations from the single, world rate of interest are always negligible and that domestic bonds are perfect substitutes not only for domestic capital but for foreign bonds and foreign capital? These questions merit attention and seem particularly relevant to a world with multiple currencies and independent, autonomous budget policies.

Insistence on the high degree of truth in the monetary theory of the balance of payments must not be confused with the particular forms in which the analysis has been cast, for example by Mundell (1968). Most papers at the conference did not make this error. Some compared the predictions of the Mundell versions of the monetary approach with the accumulating evidence on world inflation or the evidence from the Belgian experience with a two-tier market in foreign exchange. Others extended the monetary analysis of inflation in open economies to a world with multiple assets by developing the relation between money, bank credit or earning assets and the markets for debt at home and abroad. Still others tested open economy models on new sets of data.

In the remainder of the paper, I use Mundell's general approach as an organizing device. The following sections present the theory, discuss some shortcomings and offer an extension to permit analysis of a world with multiple currencies. A principal difference between a multi-currency world and a world with a single international money is that individuals adjust portfolios by selling one currency for another. A principal difference between the world of Bretton Woods and the world of the classical gold standard is that countries pursue independent fiscal policies.

Below, I analyze fiscal policy in a model that retains as much of the structure of the Mundell model as is possible. Fiscal policy is destabilizing in this simple model. There appears to be an inconsistency between fixed exchange rates and independent fiscal policies.[1a] Either countries adjust their fiscal policies, or fixed exchange rates are unstable. Moreover, I am able to give an interpretation of the "small country" assumption commonly made in analyses of this kind.

The Leuven Conference gave considerably more attention to empirical findings than is customary at meetings of this kind. My summary discusses extensions of the theory and some of the evidence presented at the Conference, and offers some interpretations of the relation of the evidence to the theory.

1. The Mundellian Theory

Mundell's analysis of the balance of payments is not a single, uniform theory of the relation between money, output, prices, exchange rates, interest rates and the balance of payments. There are a number of models containing changing subsets of the variables mentioned. McKinnon and Oates (1966) add wealth to the list without altering the basic procedures.[1)]

1a) This conclusion is reinforced by two recent papers. Fratianni (1976) explores the relation between fiscal policy and external forces. Alphandery (1975) reconsiders the relation between fiscal policy and the balance of payments in the context of the assignment problem.
1) See the survey by Willett and Sweeney in this volume and the more direct comparison of various models in the survey by Mahrman (1974). Brunner and Meltzer (1974) develop a model that includes stocks, flows, prices and interest rates. See also Fratianni (1976).

A common feature of most of the analysis is the "small" country assumption: the home country must sell or buy at world market prices and borrow or lend at world market interest rates. In some versions, fixed prices and interest rates are postulates. Prices or interest rates are invariant, and quantities adjust. Other versions assume ever-full employment. Output is fixed, but prices adjust to maintain world equilibrium. I have chosen to work with a version in which prices and interest rates are variable, and output is fixed. This version seems more useful than others for discussing the roles of money and credit markets in inflation that was the theme of the conference.[2)]

There are four markets. The assumption of full use of resources and fixed real output means that the labor market is always in equilibrium. Walras' law is invoked to eliminate analysis of the securities market. If the remaining markets for output and money are in equilibrium, the securities market and the economy are in full equilibrium.

Three equilibrium conditions summarize the balance of payments, the output and money markets and their interrelations. I have written the equilibrium conditions as three excess supply or excess

2) The model in Mundell (1968, Chapter 11) is my starting point. This choice was criticized by some participants who suggested that the model in Mundell (1968), Chapter 18, was more appropriate. The latter permits real output to change, but prices are fixed because the problem considered is the effects of monetary and fiscal policies on employment in open economies operating with idle resources. The model seems wholly inadequate for an analysis of inflation. Since a choice must be made in the Mundell analysis, fixed output seems least undesirable. Below, I adjust the model of Chapter 11 to eliminate some of the more peculiar features.

demand equations.

(1) $X = E + B - Y = 0$ for the output market;

(2) $F = B - T = 0$ for the foreign exchange market;

(3) $M = M^s - M^d = 0$ for the money market;

(4) $M^s = R + D$ is the stock of money.

Variables are defined as follows:

B = the balance of trade

D = the stock of domestic debt at the central bank, a policy variable

E = expenditure

F = the excess supply of foreign exchange

M = the excess supply of money

M^d = the demand for money

M^s = the stock of money

R = the stock of foreign reserves at the central bank

T = the net flow of securities to and from the rest of the world

X = the excess demand for goods

Y = current output

Three equations describe the adjustment of the economy under fixed exchange rates.

(5) $X = X(r, p; e)$ $X_1, X_2 < 0$

(6) $F = F(r, p; e)$ $F_2 < 0 < F_1$

(7) $M^d = L(r, p; e)$ $L_1 < 0 < L_2$

where p is the domestic price level, proximately determined on the output market;

r is the market rate of interest, proximately determined on the foreign exchange market; and

e is the exchange rate assumed to be fixed.

In a regime of fixed exchange rates, eqs. (5) and (6) determine p and r. Eq. (7) then has no independent role. Once p and r are determined, the demand for money is determined. Substituting eqs. (4) and (7) into eq. (3) brings out a main implication of the monetary approach to the balance of payments.

(8) $R + D = L(r, p; e)$

Any change in D necessarily results in an equal and opposite change in R. The central bank or government has only one degree of freedom. Within the limits imposed by existing stocks and a rigid commitment to fixed exchange rates, the government can determine the composition of the monetary base. I call this proposition Ricardo's law.

A simple adjustment yields a common interpretation. If interest rates are determined in the world market, r is a given to which the home country must adjust. One equation must be eliminated. Equation (6) is usually choosen, and if this is done, $F = \frac{dR}{dt}$, and p is determined, as before, in the output market. Equilibrium in the money market, $M^d = M^s$, now implies that $\frac{dR}{dt} = -\frac{dD}{dt}$. This is a strong implication that is unlikely to hold in many economies and fortunately so. The central bank continuously offsets changes in D and R without any feedback.

Johnson (1972) has a similar interpretation. He chooses to retain the demand for money (as a function of income). If we make explicit that, in equilibrium with fixed exchange rates,

$$p = p^{\star}e$$

where $p^{\star}$ is the price level in the rest of the world and real income is determined by productivity and real resources, all that remains is Ricardo's law.[3] All price changes and inflation are imported.[4]

---

3) We can write Johnson's (1972) system as

$$E(r, y) - y = -B(y, y^{\star})$$
$$B = F$$
$$F = \frac{dR}{dt}$$

with $y^{\star}$ the real income in the rest of the world. Ricardo's law is unaffected. In this version, the model is similar to Mundell's Chapter 18, and the frequent objection that Johnson's version is more "monetarist" than Mundellian vanishes. Adding, $L(r, y) = \frac{M^D}{p}$ does not change any result but is necessary to assure that the money stock is constant at full employment.

4) Analysis of stability conditions is unnecessary to show the conditions under which Mundell's fixed exchange rate system is stable. There are always policies at home and abroad that maintain fixed exchange rates. If all countries maintain the domestic source component unchanged -- accept the gold or single currency standard -- exchange rates are stable. If any country changes the domestic source component, it loses reserves to the others. Sufficiently large changes in either direction either force devaluation or revaluation somewhere in the world or require offsetting changes in the domestic source components of other countries. If all countries are "small", all adjustments are made at "home" if this model is correct.

2. Some Extensions of the Theory

Ricardo's law is an important long-run implication, and insistence on the proposition is a contribution to policy discussions because the proposition was overlooked for a long time. The main shortcomings of Mundell's approach, however, are the neglect of short-run positions and his neglect of stock-flow interaction. In this section, I retain his "small country" assumption, add some content, and expand the analysis to permit changes in the demand for money.

In Mundell's system, the demand function for money has no independent role. Stocks are adjusted by flows, and all flows are willingly accumulated. A decision by the citizens of a country or the central bank to shift from one reserve money to another can be implemented only, if at all, by allowing balance of payments flows to adjust the stock of reserves. An essential difference between the multi-currency world, that emerged under the Bretton Woods agreement, and the gold standard is overlooked or neglected.

A second problem is Mundell's postulated adjustment process. The adjustment of interest rates depends on the flow excess supply of foreign exchange and generally is independent of the existing stock of reserves and assets. This peculiar feature has been noted by others. McKinnon and Oates (1966), Branson (1968), Myhrman (1974). Mundell writes (1968, p. 171)

$$\frac{dp}{dt} = k_1 X(p, r)$$

$$\frac{dr}{dt} = -k_2 F(p, r)$$

where the k's are speeds of adjustment.[5)]

To partly correct for the neglect of asset positions, let the stock of reserves, R, enter the excess demand functions. The system now determines R, r, and p for given value of D and e. The total stock of assets includes money, domestic securities owned by domestic residents and foreign securities owned by domestic residents. Bonds and capital are perfect substitutes, as in Keynes-Metzler models, and the flow supply of foreign bonds is perfectly elastic at the world rate of interest, r^*. Individuals may reduce money holdings to purchase foreign securities. Let $\frac{dL}{dt}$ be the change in the demand for money per unit time. The accumulation or loss of reserves is

$$\frac{dR}{dt} = F(R, r, p) - \frac{dL}{dt}(R, r, p).$$

These definitions and postulates, the assumption of full employment, and Walras' law permit us to write adjustment equations for a modified version of the Mundellian theory. With obvious changes to incorporate the stock of reserves in eqs. (1) to (8) as required, the motion of the system is determined by eqs. (9) to (11). Domestic debt held by the central bank, and actual and anticipated exchange rates remain fixed by assumption. The constants, k_i, are speeds of adjustment.

---

5) I am not clear how one reconciles $k_i \neq 0$ with the other features of the model, notably the absence of wealth transfers and the assumption that prices and interest rates are the same everywhere. With prices and interest rates everywhere "the same", why is adjustment slower than instantaneous?

(9) $\frac{dR}{dt} = -k_1 M(R, r, p) \quad M_R, M_r > 0 > M_p$

(10) $\frac{dr}{dt} = -k_2 F(R, r, p) \quad F_r > 0 > F_R, F_p$

(11) $\frac{dp}{dt} = k_3 X(R, r, p) \quad X_R > 0 > X_r, X_p$

Holders of money are permitted to shift from domestic to foreign assets by exchanging existing stocks. An excess supply of money lowers the change in foreign reserves. Although interest rates are as before proximately determined in a flow dominated market, changes in the demand to hold money, $\frac{dL}{dt}$, change R and F.

Using standard techniques to analyze dynamic stability shows that the fixed exchange rate system is stable unless M_p is large and the excess demand for goods is much more responsive to R than the excess supply of foreign exchange. This seems unlikely. It follows that the modified Mundellian system attributes the numerous devaluations and revaluations and the instability of the Bretton Woods system mainly to government policies, for example changes in D that induce losses or gains in reserves.[6] The incorporation of stocks of reserves and changes in the demand for money does not change the main implications of Mundell´s theory.

---

6) In Brunner and Meltzer (1974), we have shown that in a model that permits changes in interest rates, asset prices, output and output prices, the fixed exchange rate system is likely to be unstable. The instability of the Bretton Woods exchange rates is attributed to independent domestic fiscal policies.

3. The Role of Fiscal Policy

The importance of D as a policy variable suggests that we should look in greater detail at the fiscal policy required to maintain fixed exchange rates. In this section, I incorporate fiscal policy and the financing of budget deficits. I show that the model requires domestic and foreign bonds and capital to be perfect substitutes and that a small country can be defined in terms of the slope of the excess demand for goods. Unless a country is very small, fiscal policy is destabilizing in a fixed exchange rate regime.

The current value of D is a record of current and past government borrowing from the central bank and shows the cumulated effect of the budget on the monetary base or the money stock. Debt retirement and new borrowing at the central bank is direct in some countries; in others, the government buys or sells securities on the open market, and the central bank finances some portion of the fiscal deficit or surplus by open market operations. The result of either procedure is the same.

The government's budget equation can be written

$$\frac{dD}{dt} = G - T - \frac{dS}{dt}$$

where G and T are government expenditures (including transfers) and tax collections, and $\frac{dS}{dt}$ is the change in the stock of government securities held outside the central bank. In models of this kind, it is easiest to let interest payments be a perfect substitute for other components of G. If the government finances all deficits at the central bank, $\frac{dS}{dt}$ and the current fiscal surplus or deficit is equal to the value of $\frac{dD}{dt}$ implied by the choice of D. Or, more accurately, the current value of D is the result of a policy of financing a surplus or deficit equal to $\frac{dD}{dt}$ at the central bank.

Suppose, however, that the government finances fiscal surpluses by retiring debt held by the public and finances fiscal deficits by selling new issues of debt to the public. Three interpretations are possible. Two are unlikely, so I discuss them briefly. The third focuses attention on some principal features of the model and provides the definition of a "small country".

First, government bonds and money are perfect substitutes in portfolios. If we treat M as the excess supply of financial assets, not the excess supply of money, we remove any special problem when bonds are issued or withdrawn instead of money. However, the conflict with the theory of prices and with empirical evidence limits interest in this interpretation.

Second, fiscal policy contracts abroad whenever the home country expands, so that world interest rates are equilibrated by world fiscal policy. This interpretation seems inconsistent with the small country assumption and, more importantly, is inconsistent with the facts.

Third, foreigners purchase or sell an appropriate amount of domestic securities to keep world interest rates in equilibrium. This solution is compatible with the Metzler interpretation of Keynes. Domestic bonds are perfect substitutes for private capital and for foreign bonds. The stock of bonds rises or falls in all countries as the home country stock rises or falls.

In a multiple currency world, the unit in which the bonds are denominated matters. If all bonds do not have a gold, or commodity unit, guarantee, the postulate that foreign and domestic bonds are perfect substitutes at a common world rate of interest is not tenable. Differences in degree of risk become an important missing element. Further, if countries at times revalue or devalue, there are wealth transfers that are not considered in the model. And, if countries pursue independent fiscal policies, even Ricardo's law does not prevent default on gold guarantees.

I will disregard some of the problems of fully incorporating fiscal policy into the Mundell model. The model does not lend itself to a full treatment of the effects of fiscal (or monetary) policy. Either there are no markets for debt, distinct from markets for private capital, or there is no debt. Either output or the price level is fixed. These and other properties restrict the analysis to a very limited range of cases.[7)]

The extension presented here is the simplest extension I can find that retains features of Mundell's model but includes fiscal policy and asset stocks. Interest rates are determined in world markets and treated as a given by citizens of the home country. Debt issued

---

7) These arguments are developed in greater detail in several recent papers with Karl Brunner. The open economy analysis is in Brunner and Meltzer (1974). Myhrman (1975) also analyzes an economy with asset stocks and fiscal policy and finds cases of instability in the fixed rate system. See also Alphandery (1975) and Fratianni (1976).

to finance fiscal policy is sold to foreign and domestic purchasers at the interest rate determined on world markets. The stock of bonds in home country portfolios is the amount remaining after purchase by foreigners.

There are many currencies, but exchange rates are fixed. Citizens of the home country can hold deposits abroad (Eurocurrency). The interest rate on these deposits is determined abroad. The capital stock is fixed, and the price of a unit of capital is always equal to the current reproduction cost; the latter is, p, the price of current output.

Domestic wealth consists of money, Eurocurrency, bonds and capital. Domestic output is constant, at full employment, but prices can change. Fiscal policy must be set to balance the government budget, and this involves a choice of tax rates or expenditure. I choose to keep tax rates as a policy variable, but tax collections change as p changes. The requirements of a balanced budget force the government to set expenditure (including interest payments) at the proper level. Let G be nominal expenditure and T be tax collections. Real government expenditure and nominal expenditure are determined by the system, not by the government.

Four equilibrium conditions summarize behavior of the government and on the markets for money, debt and output. The excess supply of money (M), the excess supply of debt net of foreign purchases (S) and the excess demand for goods (X) must be zero in equilibrium. The government budget must be balanced. The signs above the variables denote partial derivatives. R is the volume of international reserves, as above. The negative sign of S_R indicates that increases in international reserves lower the excess stock-supply of domestic bonds.

$$(12) \qquad M(\overset{+}{R}, \overset{-}{p}; D) = 0$$

$$(13) \qquad X(\overset{+}{R}, \overset{-}{p}, \overset{+}{G}, \overset{-}{T}) = 0$$

$$(14) \qquad S(\overset{-}{R}, \overset{-}{p}, \overset{+}{G-T}) = 0$$

$$(15) \qquad G = T$$

Equations (12) and (14) jointly determine R and p. Equation (13) determines either G or T, and eq. (15) determines the other. The presence of G and T in the S function as G-T is not an entirely satisfactory way of incorporating debt issues and the government budget equation. The procedure implies that, given D, tax reduction requires a sale of bonds. Interest rates rise on the world markets. Debt retirement lowers world rates. Foreigners purchase a portion of the issue that finances the deficit and sell when there is a surplus. Domestic demand rises by less than the amount of bonds issued and falls by less than the amount withdrawn. The excess stock-supply increases with a deficit and falls with a surplus. On the output market, the response to budget deficits or surpluses is restricted by the usual assumption that $X_G > - X_T > 0$.

$$1 > X_G + X_T > 0.$$

The requirement that the budget is balanced at every equilibrium and the equilibrium condition for the output market imply that net foreign investment is zero. This follows from $G-T = S-I = 0$. The balance of payments is in balance. Moreover, with K fixed and the budget balanced, all stocks are unchanging and willingly held. The four equations, (12) to (15), therefore, imply that any equilibrium in this model is a full stock-flow equilibrium at fixed exchange rates.

Analysis of dynamic adjustment shows whether the stock-flow equilibrium of the augmented model is stable. By assumption tax rates are fixed and real output is given, so real tax revenue depends on the price level,

$$t = T(p)$$

Real government spending, g, must be chosen to balance the budget at the prevailing price level. Solving

$$G = G(p, g)$$

for the appropriate value of g, balances the budget. Equation (18) specifies the adjustment of g that satisfies the tax and expenditure equations.

The system given by (16) to (18) describes the adjustment of p, R and g that maintain equilibrium with a balanced budget and a fixed exchange rate.

(16) $$\frac{dR}{dt} = - h_1 M(R, p)$$

(17) $$\frac{dp}{dt} = h_2 X(R, p, g)$$

(18) $$\frac{dg}{dt} = - h_3 S(R, p, g)$$

Stability of the system depends on the roots of the characteristic equation obtained from the following matrix.

$$\begin{bmatrix} \lambda + h_1 M_R & h_1 M_p & 0 \\ - h_2 X_R & \lambda - h_2 X_p & - h_2 X_g \\ h_3 S_R & h_3 S_p & \lambda + h_3 S_g \end{bmatrix}$$

Stability of the system requires a positive determinant of the matrix. Let a_o denote the determinant. We can write a_o as:

$$a_o = [X_g (S_p M_R - S_R M_p) + S_g (X_R M_p - X_p M_R)]$$

The sign of a_o is most likely negative. The only positive term in the equation is $- X_p M_R S_g$. This term must be very large (in absolute value) relative to other terms to assure stability. A sufficiently small absolute value of X_p is a sufficient condition for instability. A sufficiently small value of S_g is also a sufficient condition for instability. In this case, most of the deficit or surplus is financed abroad. Foreigners absorb the home country bonds and sell goods.

The dependence of stability on X_p and S_g gives content to "the small country" assumption used in the Mundellian analysis. In a "small country" the excess demand function must be very responsive to the price of domestic output. Small increases in domestic prices induce relatively large reductions in the demand for output, and small reductions in price stimulate demand. "Small countries" must finance much of their deficit or surplus by security sales or purchases to foreigners (or changes in net foreign liabilities).

Interpretation of the stability condition helps to clarify the problems raised by fiscal policy and debt finance in open economies with fixed exchange rates. We can treat X_g as the multiplier of a change in government expenditure. Any change in government expenditure, with tax rates fixed, changes total expenditure and excess demand. With domestic output given, an increase in excess demand raises domestic prices and tax collections, and a reduction in excess demand lowers prices and tax collections. The size of the price change determines the size of the government budget deficit or surplus and the amount of debt issued or withdrawn.

Any change in domestic prices reduces private expenditure following fiscal expansion and increases private expenditure following fiscal contraction. A relatively large value of X_p implies that prices transfer spending from the private sector to the government. Price increases, following fiscal expansion, are the mechanism of "crowding out" in this model. Fiscal contraction "crowds in" private spending. Import substitution reinforces the effects of "crowding in" and "crowding out".

A small X_g and large (negative) X_p contribute to stability by limiting the change in prices induced by fiscal policy. Without some limitation on fiscal policy or its effect on the price level, the fixed exchange rate system is unstable in the modified Mundell model.

There is some evidence of the effects of fiscal policy on the stability of fixed exchange rate system. The United States and the United Kingdom pursued relatively expansive fiscal and monetary policies, relative to the policies of other open economies in the fixed rate system, during the 1960's and early 1970's. Neither country operated according to gold standard rules, so countries and individuals that accumulated U.S. and U.K. securities gradually came to believe that the securities they had accumulated were not close substitutes for domestic securities. Prices rose in the U.S. and the U.K. relative to prices in other countries. The fixed rate system came to an end.

The Mundell model has a deficiency shared by all Keynesian models. The stock-flow analysis is incomplete. The deficiency is particularly important in a multiple currency world. The deficiency is less important, but remains, if countries do not engage in independent fiscal policies and do not finance deficits (or surpluses) at a rate inconsistent with world equilibrium. The deficiency can be reduced by defining a "small country" as a country that does not finance fiscal policy by issuing debt or money. The last solution limits the general applicability of the model.

A related problem arises if there is a change in taste or monopoly power that alters the terms of trade. The assumption that domestic and foreign securities are perfect substitutes implies that securities sold abroad must be denominated in foreign currency to avoid gains or losses for the rest of the world when the country revalues or devalues.[8)] Again, we are driven back to the gold standard or a gold guarantee to rationalize features of the model. Or, we can recognize the long-run truth implied by Ricardo's law while at the same time recognizing the inadequacy of the model for discussion of current policy or interpreting current events in countries conducting most of the world trade.[9)]

4. The Conference Papers

The inadequacies of the stock-flow analysis in the Mundell model are recognized implicitly in many of the papers. The adjustment of asset stocks, or portfolio adjustment, is one of the main problems addressed at the conference and is treated in both empirical and theoretical papers. A related issue that some papers addressed is the extent to which central banks and the governments in open economies can choose fiscal or monetary policies to offset inflationary or deflationary impulses from abroad. A broader aspect of the same issue is the extent to which Ricardo's law holds for annual observations in major trading countries. In this section, I summarize some of the contributions the conference papers made to the resolution of these issues.

---

8) Contrast this conclusion to Mundell's analysis (1968, Chapter 8). Devaluation and revaluation do not change wealth, so if there are securities outstanding they must be claims to real income -- perfect substitutes for real capital. Johan Myhrman has pointed out that Johnson (1972a) recognizes this problem in an appendix to his paper.

9) It is not a full solution, but a stopgap, to argue that the problem is resolved by making some commodities nontradeable. The tradition of economic theory is to decide what is traded by looking at relative prices, not to impose the choice as a constraint or fixed coefficient. Moreover, the distinction between tradeable and nontradeable goods is not only inconsistent with the long-run model to which it is joined but difficult to reconcile with the assumption that all assets in the world are perfect substitutes.

a) Theoretical Papers

Attempts to complete the analysis of asset stocks in open economies produced a number of recent papers. Three papers at the Conference are, at least partly, in this tradition. In this section, I discuss the papers by Girton and Henderson and by Brunner. Fratianni's paper deals with many of the same issues but includes some empirical work, so I discuss his paper with other empirical papers.

Lance Girton and Dale Henderson develop a short-run, partial equilibrium model of securities markets in two countries under fixed, managed floating and fully floating exchange rates. Income and prices are fixed in both countries, but interest rates are variable. Both countries issue money and securities, and in the short-run neither country is bound by Ricardo's law. Both choose policies. World reserves are fixed, as under a gold standard with no new mining.

The principal propositions obtained by the authors concern the effects of country size and exchange rate or reserve on interest rates and asset stocks in the two countries. With the dollar as a reserve currency, an open market purchase by the Federal Reserve produces a capital outflow from the U.S. that lowers interest rates in both countries. If the Bank of England (rest of the world) passively accepts the capital inflow, the U.K. money stock increases. When the monetary standard is gold or SDR's, the U.K. has the choice of acquiring these assets, and if the Bank of England so elects, there is a smaller demand for U.S. securities.

Under a gold or SDR standard, Girton and Henderson show that the size of the change in interest rates and domestic money following an open market operation depends on the demand for money and the policy of the Bank of England. If the Bank stabilizes domestic interest rates, the change in rates is smaller than if the Bank stabilizes its holding of reserves. The latter policy requires the Bank to adopt the same policies as the Federal Reserve. The Bank must buy or sell in the open market whenever the Federal Reserve buys or sells. Under dollar standard, the reserve losses to the U.S. following an open market purchase are larger than under a gold standard. Foreigners sell U.S. securities, not gold, under a dollar standard.

The point to be emphasized is that the analysis has moved beyond the rigid small country case to consider countries that choose policies. Girton and Henderson show that the small country case is a limiting case of their analysis of asset adjustment. Small and large are measured by national wealth, and small implies that world securities are perfect substitutes for domestic securities. But small countries can conduct monetary policy if securities are not perfect substitutes. There is, in short, some opportunity for all but the smallest countries to control money in the short-run.

Karl Brunner takes up a related but not identical issue. In earlier work on open, interdependent economies, Brunner and Meltzer (1974) permitted wealth holders to own money, domestic bonds, foreign bonds and real capital and to purchase current output at home or abroad. Brunner's paper disaggregates the bond (or credit) market into loans and securities. He shows that, for a broad range of problems, the addition of the loan market, does not change the principal results or conclusions of a model with money, bonds and capital. This result is distinctly anti-Radcliffe and anti-banking school. The details of financial allocation have little importance for aggregates. If Brunner is correct, additional disaggregation yields few benefits once we have included three distinct assets in our analysis of stocks.

Why is there a gain from the introduction of a third asset but not a fourth? Broadly speaking, a two asset model permits analysis of substitution between nominal and real assets and thereby introduces a principal difference between a monetary and a non-monetary economy. Wealth owners have the opportunity to substitute assets that have fixed nominal values for assets that do not. Introduction of a credit market adds some additional options, the opportunity to hold government securities and time deposits. The difference between credit (bank earning assets) and money (currency and demand deposits) is approximately equal to the differences between time deposits and central bank money or the monetary base. Hence, the introduction of a third asset, bonds, and a market for bank credit allows intermediation and disintermediation to affect real and nominal rates in the short-run and in this way to affect expenditure and prices.

The approach taken in the papers by Girton and Henderson and by Brunner differs from other recent attempts to extend the analysis of asset stocks in open economies. Several papers distinguish tradeable and nontradeable assets. This distinction is not the same as the distinction between bonds and real capital once there are differences in countries' rates of inflation.

b) Empirical Papers

I treat as empirical all papers that estimate equations or test hypotheses, even if the papers contain lengthy analytical sections. This section discusses some of the main findings and their relation to the discussion of stocks and flows above. Generally, the empirical papers support the view that there is more to international economics than has been captured in the Mundell approach or, for that matter, in its principal alternatives.

No one can read the data in John Pattison's paper without recognizing some of the difficulty of explaining inflation under the fixed and floating system. A major difficulty is separation of once and for all changes in prices and terms of trade from maintained changes in the rate of price change. Whether the price change occurs at a unique point in time or is distributed over several months, the measured rate of price change that includes the period will be affected. The measured rate of price change will differ from the maintained rate of inflation. This problem arises in other economic time series, notably in separating real growth and recovery from recession. Another difficulty arises from the use of fixed weight price indexes.

Nevertheless, two of Pattison's findings are striking. First, he finds that the standard deviation of the inflation rate for major industrial countries (world inflation) has remained approximately the same despite a doubling in the mean rate of inflation. Second, the standard deviation of the world inflation rate is about three times the standard deviation of inflation rates in leading Canadian cities.[10)]

Suppose we accept the basic truth emphasized by adherents of the monetary approach to the balance of payments. Prices in trading countries are pushed toward equality by profitable opportunities offered to traders, speculators and producers when the same commodity sells at a price differential greater than the cost of transport. The computed standard deviations of the rates of price change in major trading countries are a crude, but useful, measure of the degree to which rates of price change are equalized across countries. The approximate constancy of the standard deviation for each of the five year periods following the restoration of convertibility in 1958 suggests that there were differences in country rates of change each year, but the deviations from the mean remained about the same during the sample period. Pattison's data suggest that the standard deviation generally was between 1.5 and 1.75, so

---

10) The results differ from the findings reported by Hans Genberg (1975). Genberg used analysis of variance to test whether rates of inflation for individual countries differed from the average rate of inflation in sixteen countries. Call the latter the world rate. The world rate is defined as a band or range of two percentage points. Genberg's data show at most that under fixed rates, countries that deviate from the band persistently must revalue or devalue. This is a relatively weak test of the proposition sometimes called the "law of one price". The data do not reject the hypothesis that the rates of inflation differed in one of the three periods used. Genberg then performs a similar test for U.S. cities, obtains a similar result and concludes that if the U.S. is a single market, then the "world" is a single market. If we accept Genberg's result without qualification, we would conclude that resources do not move quickly enough to equalize prices in the U.S. at every point in time and also that countries can have different rates of inflation and fixed exchange rates for a time, but not permanently.

two standard deviations on each side of the mean include differences in rates of price change of 6 % to 7 %. For any pair of countries, the deviation may be less, and of course with fixed rates, countries cannot maintain fixed exchange rates if they are persistently at the same end of the distribution.[11)]

A difference of six to seven per cent between countries with high and low annual rates of price change leaves room for countries to pursue independent monetary policy under fixed exchange rates, even if Ricardo's law is a fully correct long-run proposition. The difference between rates of price change in Canadian cities is considerably smaller than for the world. This suggests that there is potential for equalizing rates of inflation in the major trading countries; the differences are not at a minimum.[12)]

The conference heard other evidence difficult to reconcile with Mundell's theory. Cross and Laidler show that their measures of past world rates of inflation affect the domestic rates of price change in many countries for given values of output and past rates of price change in the home country.[13)] The Mundell theory implies that rates of inflation are equalized by changes in the growth of money, a type of price-specie flow theory. Countries that inflate

---

11) If the increase in the rate of inflation is a result of increased monopoly power or trade unions as is suggested by some, it seems strange that monopoly pricing has not changed the standard deviation of inflation rates in the seventeen countries or in Canadian cities where the power of local unions is very different.

12) The standard deviations for the seventeen countries do not appear to have increased under floating rates. The range between the highest and lowest rate increased, however, when autonomy increased.

13) See next page.

fastest lose foreign reserves to countries that deflate or inflate more slowly.

Cross and Laidler compare two hypotheses. In one, each country's rate of price change depends on output and its own past rate of price change. In the other, the world rate of inflation affects each country by changing anticipations in a manner that cannot be deduced from the past home country rate of price change.

The evidence discriminates between the two and supports the hypothesis that world and past domestic rates of price change have separate effects in many countries. Cross and Laidler test this proposition in several ways. One of their tests shows that differences between domestic and world rates of price change affect the acceleration or deceleration of prices in several countries. One may question, as always, the model or its interpretation. Their equation does not adequately summarize the effects of foreign demand and domestic financial policies. In an area in which there has been little information, however, their evidence retains importance.

There is an obvious problem with the Mundell hypothesis. Countries' rates of inflation differ under fixed exchange rates. The usual attempt to rescue the hypothesis invokes the distinction between tradeable and nontradeable goods. The distinction seems at best a peculiar description of short- and long-run adjustment,

---

13) The paper, "Inflation, Excess Demand and Expectations in Fixed Exchange Rate Open Economies: Some Preliminary Empirical Results", was presented and discussed at the conference but is published in the Proceedings of the University of Manchester Conference on Inflation, July 1974.

since in the long-run relative prices determine what is traded. Moreover, the distinction is usually invoked without specifying a definition of tradeable, so content is removed. Cross and Laidler offer a definition and test the hypothesis that differences in rates of inflation can be explained by the hypothesis. They conclude that the distinction is not useful.

In a paper crammed with fascinating problems seeking solutions, Decaluwe and Steinherr analyze the distinctively Belgian contribution to recent policy -- the two-tier exchange market. Belgium would appear to be an example of a small open economy, yet the data show that Belgium was able to maintain separate exchange rates for the commercial and financial franc for many years.

I interpret the data and the authors' results as showing that the Belgian franc did not have a fixed exchange rate as that term is understood in current literature or is used in references to the gold standard. The reason is that the financial franc could float outside a fixed band. The average spread between the commercial and financial franc is a measure of the increased risk borne by holders of financial francs, the average price of risk. Decaluwe and Steinherr interpret the difference as a measure of anticipations. Differences between anticipated and actual exchange rates are to a considerable extent the result of perceived exchange risks, so our terms may differ more than our interpretation.

For monetary theory and policy, changes in the spread between the two rates are more interesting than the mean difference. Belgium was able to let the band between the intervention price and the official price widen by allowing the financial franc to float beyond the intervention point. If the financial franc remains outside the intervention point, the profit from disguising financial francs as commercial francs increases, so the commercial franc moves toward the intervention point.

If my interpretation of the data is correct, the Banque Nationale had greater opportunity to conduct monetary policy than the monetary theory of the balance of payments grants to small open economies. The central rate for the commercial franc remained unchanged throughout the decade. The monetary base was determined, in the longer-run, by the balance of payments. However, the Banque Nationale could widen or narrow the spread between commercial and financial francs by buying or selling foreign exchange. By engaging in these market operations, the Banque Nationale was able to control or offset short-term changes in the monetary base and the money stock.

The papers by Heremans, Sommariva and Verheirstraeten on the Belgian monetary and credit process and by Fratianni on the Italian monetary process dig deeply into the relations between the central bank and the markets for money and credit. These authors analyze the markets for debt and money, or bank credit and money, in a regime where debt, money and real capital are substitutes -- but not perfect substitutes -- in the portfolios of wealth owners.

The paper by Heremans, Sommariva and Verheirstraeten is part of an ambitious program of monetary theory and empirical science being carried out at the Center for Economic Studies at the

Katholieke Universiteit at Leuven. The authors develop a series for the monetary base and make preliminary tests of the relationships between the base and financial variables. The tests show that, in Belgium, foreign securities are very close substitutes for domestic securities on the bank credit market, suggesting that Ricardo's law is a good approximation in the short-run for an open economy like Belgium.

However, the authors' model implies that the two-tier system increases the power of the central bank to control the base. The degree of control had not been estimated in the work completed at the time of the conference.

The Belgian experience shows that the central bank financed a large part of the government's budget deficit. Ceilings were placed on bank credit expansion, so the banks and the public borrowed abroad. This point is recognized in Governor Vandeputte's informative discussion of central bank instruments of policy. By allowing the financial franc to float, the Banque Nationale lowered the degree to which foreign and domestic securities are substitutes in private portfolios and raised the cost of foreign borrowing.

Michele Fratianni recognizes that the usual statement of Ricardo's law presumes that all securities are perfect substitutes. If foreign and domestic securities are imperfect substitutes, monetary policy changes relative interest rates even if changes in the domestic source component of the base produces an equal but opposite short-run change in international reserves. As in his previous work, Fratianni shows that in Italy domestic and foreign securities are not perfect substitutes in portfolios. With a fixed and relatively stable exchange rate, the Banca d'Italia was able to control the base and the money stock to an extent sufficient to influence economic activity in the short-run.

Discussion of the degree to which the base is controlled or to which monetary policy is effective in the short-run is often clouded by a side issue, the extent to which the instrument of monetary policy is a change in the base or a change in the discount rate. The issue becomes more confused when the subject of endogeneity or exogeneity comes under discussion.

Consider a system with discounting but without open market operations. The central bank sets the discount rate to control the quantity of discounts, and the banks adjust the quantity of discounts by comparing the rates at the bank and in the market. Now, consider a system with open market operations and no discounting. The central bank chooses the quantity to purchase and the market determines the price. I do not deny that institutional arrangements are important for understanding how monetary processes work to shape the outcome of the process, but it is difficult to find any difference of fundamental importance in this difference in arrangements.

5. Conclusion

Most of the papers at the Leuven Conference on Bank Credit, Money and Inflation in Open Economies can be described as extensions of the framework known as the monetary approach to the balance. There are two exceptions. Michael Parkin and Malcolm

Gray attempt to develop an hypothesis capable of discriminating between alternative explanations of inflation. Richard Sweeney and Thomas Willett survey theoretical and empirical work and point out some shortcomings in current theories of inflation in open economies.

The principal work of the conference and its principal contribution, however, lies in the attempts to extend and test current theories. These extensions take the form of new analyses, detailed consideration of the Belgian contribution to recent policy tools -- the two-tier market for foreign exchange -- and examination of some empirical evidence on current theories. I believe the papers bring out the deficiencies of several current versions of the so-called monetary approach. By doing so, they focus our attention on the strengths and weaknesses of our current theory of inflation in open economies.

A main difference between the monetary theory of the balance of payments and its immediate predecessors is the attention given to the balance of payments as a whole, as opposed to a particular component, usually the trade account. The monetary approach brought back to international monetary theory the proposition that relative prices -- including exchange rates -- are, in the long-run, determined by real factors. In full, long-run adjustment of real balances and commodity prices to a change in domestic money, exchange rates are unchanged.

The problem is that conditions under which the proposition holds are often neglected, and the adjustment process is ignored entirely.

There is not a single international reserve currency; there are currencies and alternative reserves. A multi-currency reserve with a variable mix of currencies differs from a gold standard. In a multi-currency world, changes in preferences for a particular reserve asset shift the demand to hold a stock of "money" and change relative prices. Current versions of the monetary approach do not consider asset adjustments of this kind.

Recognition of asset adjustment in a multi-currency world is a first step toward a more complete analysis of stock-flow interaction. The absence of asset markets in the monetary approach neglects some principal developments in monetary theory.

A main theme of early postwar monetary theory is the importance of the real balance effect -- the response to changes in the real values of financial assets induced by changes in prices. The real balance effect is ignored in most discussions of currency devaluations or revaluations and in discussions of the monetary theory of the balance of payments. The omission has little empirical significance as long as money is a single, composite good that is only a small fraction of total world wealth, and there is a single price level for the world.

"Real balances" are a place holder in the two asset model for the broader effects of wealth in a more fully developed stock-flow analysis. All assets do not sell always and everywhere at a price equal to minimum reproduction cost in the country with lowest cost of production. Changes in the relative prices of assets and output become a relevant "wealth effect" once we separate money, bonds and real capital in our analyses. Attempts to explain why price levels differ and change cannot neglect these effects of price level changes on wealth and of changes in asset stocks on exchange rates. Attempts to explain why the fixed exchange rate system broke down cannot ignore differences in fiscal policies and the financing of these policies.

In the monetary analysis of closed economies, recent work has emphasized the role of the government budget and the stocks of debt, money and real capital. The analysis of fiscal policy and monetary policy now recognizes the dependence of financial asset stocks on the budget position. The presence of three (or more) assets in portfolios permits substitution between types of assets that change relative rates of return independently of flow adjustment processes. Such adjustments are often described as intermediation or disintermediation. Correct interpretation of the role of Eurocurrency markets cannot begin until asset adjustment of this kind becomes a relevant part of the monetary theory of an open economy.

My attempt to incorporate asset stocks and fiscal variables in a Mundellian model raises serious doubts about the stability of the expanded model and the relevance of the simpler model. Severe restrictions on fiscal policy would appear to be necessary to maintain stability of the fixed rate system. The papers and discussion at the Leuven Conference show that research on stock-flow interaction is actively underway. The analysis of inflation and our understanding of the interaction of money, debt, real capital and real output in open economies will increase as a result of these efforts and of the empirical work that will show how much or how little the implications of our analyses change.

REFERENCES

Alphandery, E., (1975), "The Alternative Use of Monetary Policy and Exchange Rate Change for Internal and External Stability", Paris (multilithed).

Branson, W. H., (1968), Financial Capital Flows in the U.S. Balance of Payments, Amsterdam: North Holland.

Brunner, Karl and Meltzer, Allan H., (1974), "Monetary and Fiscal Policy in Open, Interdependent Economies with Fixed Exchange Rates", E. Claassen and P. Salin, eds., Third Paris-Dauphine Conference on Money, (forthcoming).

Dornbusch, R., (1973), "Money, Devaluation and Non-traded Goods", American Economic Review, December.

Fratianni, M., (1976), "On the Effectiveness of Monetary Policy Under Fixed Rates of Exchange", Journal of Monetary Economics, January.

Genberg, Hans A., (1975), "Aspects of the Monetary Approach to Balance of Payments Theory: An Empirical Study of Sweden", in J. Frenkel and H. G. Johnson, eds., The Monetary Approach to the Balance of Payments, London: Allen and Unwin.

Johnson, Harry G., (1958), "The Balance of Payments", Pakistan Economic Journal, reprinted in Johnson, ed., Money, Trade and Economic Growth, London: Allen and Unwin, 1962.

Johnson, Harry G., (1972), Inflation and the Monetarist Controversy, The Professor F. DeVries Lectures, Amsterdam: North-Holland Publishing.

Johnson, Harry G., (1972a), "The Monetary Approach to Balance of Payments Theory" in Further Essays in Monetary Economics, London: Allen and Unwin.

McKinnon, Ronald and Oates, W. E., (1966), The Implications of International Economic Integration for Monetary, Fiscal, and Exchange Rate Policy, Princeton: Princeton Studies in International Finance.

Mundell, Robert, (1968), International Economics, New York: Macmillan

Mussa, Michael, (1974), "A Monetary Approach to Balance of Payments Analysis", Journal of Money, Credit and Banking, 6 pp. 333-52.

Myhrman, Johan, (1974), "Balance of Payments Adjustment and Portfolio Theory: A Survey" in E. Claassen and P. Salin, eds. Third Paris-Dauphine Conference on Money, (forthcoming).

Myhrman, Johan, (1975), "A Macroeconomic Model with Asset Equilibrium for an Open Economy", (multilithed).

Swoboda, Alexander, (1974), "Monetary Approaches to Balance of Payments Theory: Framework for a Survey" in E. Claassen and P. Salin, eds. Third Paris-Dauphine Conference on Money, (forthcoming).

LIST OF PARTICIPANTS

J. P. ABRAHAM, Faculté des Sciences Economiques et Sociales Namur

L. AERTS, Algemene Spaar en Lijfrentekas, Brussels

L. BAECK, Katholieke Universiteit Leuven (Louvain, Belgium)

BARROUX, Banque de France

A. P. BARTEN, Katholieke Universiteit Leuven

T. BELIEN, Katholieke Universiteit Leuven

J. BLOMME, Katholieke Universiteit Leuven

R. BOELAERT, Katholieke Universiteit Leuven

F. BOLL, Katholieke Universiteit Leuven

K. BRUNNER, University of Rochester and Universität Bern

G. CARRIN, Katholieke Universiteit Leuven

M. CHATTERJI, State University of New York and Katholieke Universiteit Leuven

G. CLEMER, Katholieke Universiteit Leuven

M. COCKAERTS, Kredietbank, Belgium

A. COPPE, Katholieke Universiteit Leuven

DARDEL, Banque de France

B. DECALUWE, Université Catholique de Louvain

M. DE CECCO, Royal Institute of International Affairs and University of Siena

L. DECKX, Katholieke Universiteit Leuven

S. DE KOCK, Katholieke Universiteit Leuven

M. DE SAMBLANX, Katholieke Universiteit Leuven

E. DEWEIRDT, Bank Brussel Lambert, Brussels

P. D'HAVE, Katholieke Universiteit Leuven

M. DOMBRECHT, Katholieke Universiteit Leuven

A. M. DONGELMANS, De Nederlandsche Bank, Amsterdam

L. DUPRIEZ, Université Catholique de Louvain

M. EYSKENS, Katholieke Universiteit Leuven

M. M. G. FASE, De Nederlandsche Bank, Amsterdam

A. FOURÇANS, Ecole Supérieure des Sciences Economiques et Commerciales, Paris

M. FRATIANNI, Indiana University and Katholieke Universiteit Leuven

A. GALLI, Banque Nationale de Suisse

J. GAZON, Université de Liège

H. GENBERG, Graduate Institute of International Studies, Geneva

L. GIRTON, Board of Governors of the Federal Reserve System, Washington

M. GRAY, University of Manchester

D. HENDERSON, Board of Governors of the Federal Reserve System

D. HEREMANS, Katholieke Universiteit Leuven

J. KESENNE, Katholieke Universiteit Leuven

D. A. LAIDLER, University of Manchester

A. LAMBERT, National Bank of Belgium

J. LOEYS, Katholieke Universiteit Leuven

M. LOEYS, Katholieke Universiteit Leuven

M. LOWENTHAL, Université Catholique de Louvain

S. LUCAS, Katholieke Universiteit Leuven

E. MANGELEER, Katholieke Universiteit Leuven

B. MARTENS, Katholieke Universiteit Leuven

MARTIN, Belgische Vereniging der Banken, Brussels

R. MASERA, Bank for International Settlements, Geneva

J. MELITZ, Institut National de la Statistique et des Etudes Economiques, Paris

A. H. MELTZER, Carnegie-Mellon University

J. MERTENS de WILMARS, National Bank of Belgium

M. MILLER, London School of Economics and Political Science

W. MOESEN, U.F.S.I.A., Antwerp

K. MORDHORST, National Bank of Danmark

C. MORTARA, Banca d'Italia

F. NARMON, Gemeentekrediet van België, Brussels

M. NEUMANN, Freie Universität Berlin

A. R. NOBAY, University of Southampton

J. O' LEARY, Central Bank of Ireland

R. ORSI, Université Catholique de Louvain

F. PALM, Université Catholique de Louvain

M. PARKIN, University of Manchester

J. C. PATTISON, Economic Council of Ontario

Th. PEETERS, Katholieke Universiteit Leuven

L. PENNINCKX, Katholieke Universiteit Leuven

S. PLASSCHAERT, U.F.S.I.A., Antwerp

E. POLLEFLIET, Planbureau, Brussels

T. POPPE, Katholieke Universiteit Leuven

L. D. D. PRICE, Bank of England

P. RANUZZI, E.E.C., Brussels

P. REDING, Faculté des Sciences Economiques et Sociales, Namur

REUSS, Bank Brussel Lambert, Brussels

R. ROLL, European Institute for Advanced Studies in Management, Brussels

L. ROTAECHE

A. N. R. SCHWARTZ, Centraal Planbureau, Den Haag

E. SCHENK, Katholieke Universiteit Leuven

P. SERCU, Katholieke Universiteit Leuven

A. SOMMARIVA, Katholieke Universiteit Leuven

F. SPINNEWIJN, Katholieke Universiteit Leuven

A. STEINHERR, Université Catholique de Louvain

J. STOCKX, Kredietbank, Brussels

W. SUETENS, Generale Bankmaatschappij, Brussels

A. SÜMER, Katholieke Universiteit Leuven

R. SWEENEY, U.S. Treasury

A. SWOBODA, Graduate Institute of International Studies, Geneva

K. TAVERNIER, Katholieke Universiteit Leuven

E. VAN BROECKHOVEN, U.F.S.I.A., Antwerp

R. VANDEPUTTE, National Bank of Belgium

M. VAN EECKHOUDT, Katholieke Universiteit Leuven

E. VAN LOON, Katholieke Universiteit Leuven

E. VAN ROMPUY, Katholieke Universiteit Leuven

P. VAN ROMPUY, Katholieke Universiteit Leuven

V. VAN ROMPUY, Katholieke Universiteit Leuven

R. VAN STRAELEN, U.F.S.I.A., Antwerp

J. VAN 'T DACK, Katholieke Universiteit Leuven

J. VERHAEGHE, Kredietbank, Brussels

J. VERHEIRSTRAETEN, Katholieke Universiteit Leuven

LIST OF AUTHORS

Fratianni, Michele, Indiana University and Katholieke Universiteit te Leuven

Tavernier, Karel, Katholieke Universiteit te Leuven

Brunner, Karl, University of Rochester and University of Bern

Melitz, Jacques, I.N.S.E.E., Paris

Heremans, Dirk, Katholieke Universiteit te Leuven

Sommariva, Andrea, International Monetary Fund, Washington, D.C.

Verheirstraeten, Albert, Katholieke Universiteit te Leuven

Vandeputte, Robert, Governor, National Bank of Belgium

Fourçans, André, E.S.S.E.C., Cergy, France

Plasschaert, Sylvain, U.F.S.I.A., Antwerp

Girton, Lance, Board of Governors, Federal Reserve System, Washington, D.C.

Henderson, Dale, Board of Governors, Federal Reserve System, Washington, D.C.

Decaluwe, Bernard, Université Catholique de Louvain

Steinherr, Alfred, Université Catholique de Louvain

Boll, Frank, Katholieke Universiteit te Leuven

De Grauwe, Paul, Katholieke Universiteit te Leuven

Gray, Malcolm, University of Manchester

Parkin, Michael, University of Western Ontario and University of Manchester

Barten, Anton P., Katholieke Universiteit te Leuven

De Cecco, Marcello, Università degli Studi di Siena

Mortara, Carlo A., Banca d'Italia

Meltzer, Allan H., Carnegie-Mellon University

Willett, Thomas, U.S. Treasury, Washington, D.C.

Sweeney, Richard, U.S. Treasury, Washington, D.C.

Untersuchungen über das Spar,- Giro- und Kreditwesen

Abteilung A: Wirtschaftswissenschaft.

Herausgegeben von Fritz Voigt

Seit Frühjahr 1973 sind erschienen:

69. **Die Zinspolitik der Sparkassen in der Bundesrepublik Deutschland unter wirtschaftspolitischen Gesichtspunkte.** Von B. Last. 135 S. 1973. DM 38,60.

70. **Probleme der Sparförderung in der OECD.** Von H. Albach, W. Krelle, J. Siebke, W. Wittmann. 192 S. 1973. DM 59,60.

71. **Der Einfluß von Geldwertrisiko und Wertsicherungsklauseln auf die Vermögensdisposition.** Von N. Euba. 162 S. 1973. DM 42,60.

72. **Zur Theorie und Empirie der Fristigkeitsstruktur der Zinssätze.** Von H. Faßbender. 231 S. 1973. DM 78,60.

73. **Die Auswirkungen der Liquidität auf die Firmenentscheidungen.** Von H. Pehle. 139 S. 1974. DM 56,—.

74. **Theorie der Devisenspekulation.** Von H. Hochgesand. 167 S. 1974. DM 68,60.

75. **Marktstrategien im Hypothekarkreditgeschäft.** Von H. Kittel. 354 S. 1974. DM 78,60.

76. **Lenkungsmöglichkeiten von Geldangebots- und Kreditmarktprozessen in einer extrem auslandsabhängigen Volkswirtschaft.** Von H. Rosteck. 106 S. 1975. DM 48,60.

77. **Wirkung und Wirkungsprozeß der Geldpolitik.** Von G. Dieckheuer. 304 S. 1975. DM 88,60.

78. **Bankenliquidität und Zins als Orientierungsvariable der Geldpolitik.** Von H.-H. Francke. 222 S. 1975. DM 66,60.

79. **Geldtheoretische und geldpolitische Probleme der potentialorientierten Kreditpolitik.** Von L. Stirnberg. 183 S. 1975. DM 58,60.

80. **Beiträge zur Geldtheorie und Währungspolitik.** Von H. G. Johnson. 353 S. 1976. DM 68,—.

81. **Langfristige Personalplanung im Kreditinstitut.** Von H. Benölken. 438 S. 1976. DM 78,—.

82. **Kleine deutsche Geldgeschichte des 19. und 20. Jahrhunderts.** Von B. Schultz. 294 S. 1976. DM 68,—.

83. **Finanzmärkte in der Bundesrepublik Deutschland.** Von G. Schwanewede. 264 S. 1976. DM 74,60.

DUNCKER & HUMBLOT / BERLIN

KATHOLIEKE UNIVERSITEIT TE LEUVEN

TIJDSCHRIFT VOOR ECONOMIE EN MANAGEMENT

Nr. 2 · 1976

Veröffentlichungen des Instituts für Empirische Wirtschaftsforschung

Herausgegeben von Prof. Dr. Cl. Köhler und Prof. Dr. A. Kruse-Rodenacker

---

1. **Orientierungshilfen für die Kreditpolitik.** Von Claus Köhler. 97 S. 1968. Lw. DM 24,60
2. **Bankenliquidität und Kapitalmarktzins.** Von Lothar Hübl. 155 S. mit 17 Tab. und 23 Abb. 1969. Lw. DM 38,60
3. **Die kontinuierliche Liquiditätsversorgung des Bankensystems.** Von Jürgen Becker. 145 S. 1969. Lw. DM 37,60
4. **Die Liquiditätsversorgung des schweizerischen Bankensystems.** Von Heide Wolff. 133 S. 1969. Lw. DM 36,60
5. **Kapitalhilfe.** Untersuchungen zur bilateralen Kapitalhilfe im Rahmen öffentlicher Leistungen. Von Albrecht Kruse-Rodenacker und Horst Dumke unter Mitarbeit von Niklas von Götz. 208 S. 1969. Lw. DM 48,60
6. **Regionale Leistungsbilanzsalden in integrierten Wirtschaftsräumen.** Von Rüdiger Pohl. 191 S. mit 18 Taf. 1971. Lw. DM 49,80
7. **Erfahrungen mit der Kreditplafondierung.** Von Sonning Bredemeier. 191 S. 1972. Lw. DM 49,60
8. **Die Auswirkungen der Zinsliberalisierung in Deutschland.** Von Rüdiger Looff. 148 S. 1973. Lw. DM 48,—
9. **Der administrative Aufwand der Entwicklungshilfe.** Von Karl Kirchhof und Ulrich Popp. 198 S. 1973. Lw. DM 56,—
10. **Bestimmungsgründe der nominalen Zinsentwicklung in der Bundesrepublik Deutschland.** Von Lothar Hübl. 127 S. 1973. Lw. DM 49,80
11. **Direktinvestitionen und die Politik der Entwicklungsländer.** Von Winfried Schneider. 198 S. 1974. Lw. DM 58,60
12. **Zinsarbitrage und Währungsspekulation.** Von Wolfgang Filc. 220 S. 1975. Lw. DM 68,—
13. **Probleme der Neo-Quantitätstheorie und der Geldmengenpolitik.** Von Karl-Heinz Ketterer. 121 S. 1975. Lw. DM 48,60
14. **Friedman-Plan und potentialorientierte Kreditpolitik.** Von Gerhard Honeck. 295 S. 1975. Lw. DM 88,60
15. **Kritische Betrachtungen zur nationalen und internationalen Geldordnung.** Von Rolf Gocht. 143 S. 1975. Lw. DM 48,60

DUNCKER & HUMBLOT / BERLIN